Noise Uprising

MICHAEL DENNING is the William R. Kenan, Jr., Professor of American Studies at Yale University, and the co-director of Yale's Initiative on Labor and Culture. He is the author of *Culture in the Age of Three Worlds*; *The Cultural Front: The Laboring of American Culture in the Twentieth Century*; *Mechanic Accents: Dime Novels and Working-Class Culture in America*; and *Cover Stories: Narrative and Ideology in the British Spy Thriller*. He coordinates the Working Group on Globalization and Culture, whose collective work includes "Going into Debt," published online in *Social Text's* Periscope, and "Spaces and Times of Occupation," published in *Transforming Anthropology*. In 2014, he received the Bode-Pearson lifetime achievement award from the American Studies Association.

Noise Uprising

The Audiopolitics of a World Musical Revolution

Michael Denning

VERSO
London • New York

First published by Verso 2015
© Michael Denning

1 3 5 7 9 10 8 6 4 2

Verso
UK: 6 Meard Street, London W1F 0EG
US: 20 Jay Street, Suite 1010, Brooklyn, NY 11201
www.versobooks.com

Verso is the imprint of New Left Books

ISBN-13: 978-1-78168-856-4 (PB)
ISBN-13: 978-1-78168-855-7 (HC)
eISBN-13: 978-1-78168-858-8 (US)
eISBN-13: 978-1-78168-857-1 (UK)

British Library Cataloguing in Publication Data
A catalogue record for this book is available from the British Library

Library of Congress Cataloging-in-Publication Data

Denning, Michael.
 Noise uprising : the audiopolitics of a world musical
revolution / Michael Denning.
    pages cm
 Includes index.
 ISBN 978-1-78168-856-4 (alk. paper)—ISBN 978-1-
78168-855-7 (alk. paper)—ISBN 978-1-78168-858-8
(alk. paper)—ISBN 978-1-78168-857-1 (alk. paper)
 1. Phonograph—Social aspects—History—20th
century. 2. Sound recordings—Social aspects—
History—20th century. 3. Popular music—1921–
1930—History and criticism. I. Title.
 ML3916.D48 2015
 781.6309'042—dc23
                              2015005266

Typeset in Adobe Caslon Pro by MJ & N Gavan, Truro, Cornwall
Printed in the US by Maple Press

words,
for Fred Jameson

music,
for Tony Lombardozzi

Insurgency was a massive and systematic violation of those words, gestures, and symbols which had the relations of power in colonial society as their significata. This was perceived as such both by its protagonists and their foes. The latter were often quick to register their premonition of an uprising as a noise in the transmission of some of the more familiar signals of deference.

Ranajit Guha, *Elementary Aspects of Peasant Insurgency in Colonial India*

We would also uncover the same transformations, the same progress and the same eagerness if we enquired into the fields of dance, song, rituals, and traditional ceremonies. Well before the political or armed struggle, a careful observer could sense and feel in these arts the pulse of a fresh stimulus and the coming combat.

Frantz Fanon, *The Wretched of the Earth*

Contents

List of Figures and Illustrations

Introduction

In the early twenty-first century, the world of music is in constant crisis and flux, but its overall lineaments are relatively clear and appear natural. The internet has emerged as a global jukebox of digital sound files that are uploaded, downloaded, streamed and shared, accumulated as collections, shuffled into playlists, and sampled as raw materials for new mixes. The vehicles of circulation may change—iTunes, Spotify, and YouTube loom large as I complete this book—but it seems self-evident that the wealth of music in a world where capitalist modes of production prevail appears as "an immense accumulation of commodities." These sound recordings exist in an intricate economy of genres, styles, and brands, linked to imagined communities of race and nation, and are adopted by consumers to manage their personal and collective soundscape—the ambience or atmosphere of daily life—whether through the privacy of earbuds and headphones or the publicity of DJs with sound systems.

At the same time, writing about music takes place on two radically different scales: grand generalizations about the meaning of music in the evolution of the species (its relation to language, to the order and disorders of the brain, to the sounds and songs of other species); and "rough guides" to the musical marketplace, micro-histories of specific genres and artists. The traditional sense that music is a fine art lives on in the residual culture of "classical music," which has lost much of its former glory and occupies a small market niche, while retaining some degree of cultural capital. And the older sense that music-making is a political act—which led Plato to assert that "any alteration in the modes of music is always followed by alteration in the most fundamental laws of the state"[1]—has also receded to the fringes of the musical marketplace, where the germ of an alternative culture lies in songs of protest affiliated with social movements. It is not that the contemporary world of music lacks an audiopolitics, but rather that it is coded as the politics of the market: who owns and controls the sound files. The politics of intellectual property and piracy have eclipsed the politics of musical form or content.

This musical economy that incorporates arcane sounds and sublime frequencies from every corner of the planet seems new, the product of an era of globalization—the sound equivalent of the World Wide Web itself—but when it is given a history and a context, it usually appears to radiate out from the United States, from the post–World War II explosion of "American" musics from rock to rap. Elvis Presley, the Beatles, and Bob Dylan are the Mozart, Haydn, and Beethoven of a second classical period, and the furious late twentieth-century battles over the hip-hop of Public Enemy and N.W.A. echo the late nineteenth-century furor over the operatic spectacles of Richard Wagner.

In this book, I want to offer an alternative account of the origins of our musical world: not in the rock and pop of the American century, but in a world musical revolution that took place almost a century ago. In a few short years between the introduction of electrical recording in 1925 and the onset of the worldwide depression in the 1930s, a noise uprising occurred in a series of relatively unnoticed recording sessions. In port cities from Havana to Honolulu, Cairo to Jakarta, New Orleans to Rio de Janeiro, commercial recording companies brought hundreds of unknown musicians into makeshift studios to record local musics. Thousands of inexpensive discs made from shellac (a resin secreted by the female lac bug, a colonial product harvested in the forests of South Asia) were released, disseminating musical idioms which have since reverberated around the globe under a riot of new names: son, rumba, samba, tango, jazz, calypso, beguine, fado, flamenco, tzigane, rebetika, ṭarab, marabi, kroncong, hula.

These recording sessions of vernacular musicians in the late 1920s stand out in the history of music like a range of volcanic peaks, the dormant but not extinct remains of a series of eruptions caused by the shifting of the tectonic plates of the world's musical continents. For five years, more or less, these eruptions took place as gramophone and phonograph companies fought with each other to capture the world's vernacular musics through the new electrical microphones and to play them back through the new electrical loudspeakers.[2] It was one of those speculative manias that recur in capitalist booms, not unlike the tulip mania of the 1630s or the dot.com bubble of the 1990s. The recording boom took off around 1925, as the new technology of electrical recording enabled not only an extraordinary leap in audio fidelity but also a dramatic reduction in the cost of phonographs. It is hard to overestimate the sonic transformation; to this day, we listen with pleasure to reissues of the earliest electrical recordings, whereas the slightly older acoustic recordings are a dead language, a kind of sonic Middle English, the preserve of archivists whose ear training allows them to revisit the archaic soundscape of the Edison cylinders and the hill-and-dale discs.

In less than a decade, an unprecedented range of musical voices, instruments, and ensembles were placed in front of microphones. The producers and engineers knew little about the musics they were recording; they often regarded it as noise. Like the early radio broadcasters, they were simply trying to produce software—recorded sounds—that would encourage the purchase of the hardware, the phonograph. If new listeners could be lured by these noises—whether because they evoked novelty, nostalgia, or the neighborhood—then they would be recorded and marketed.

Like other technology booms, the recording boom burned itself out in a few years. By the early 1930s, the manufacturers of phonographs and phonograph records were sitting on masses of unsold inventory, as sales of hardware and software alike plummeted in the midst of a worldwide depression. Many small companies folded; the larger ones were taken over by amalgamated radio broadcasting and electrical equipment corporations, like RCA, EMI, and Telefunken. The vast majority of the musicians who had made their way to a recording studio in the late 1920s returned to the world of dance halls and shebeens, never to be recorded again.

But those five years changed the sound and the space of the world's music; they stand as the central musical revolution of the twentieth century, a musical "turnaround" with more profound consequences than that of the "modern" musics of the European avant-garde. The celebrated shock of the 1913 premiere of Igor Stravinsky's *The Rite of Spring* has long stood as the emblem of modern music; it was a mere tremor compared to the reverberations of the still largely unrecognized recordings that created the vernacular idioms that continue to shape playlists: the Cuban son of the Trio Matamoros's "El Manisero" (The Peanut Vendor) and the New Orleans hot jazz of Louis Armstrong's "Heebie Jeebies," the gypsy jazz of Django Reinhardt's "Dinah" and the Brazilian samba of Ismael Silva's "Me faz carinhos," the Andalusian "deep song" of Pastora Pavón's "Había preguntado en una ocasión" and the Egyptian ṭarab of Umm Kulthūm's "In Kunt Asaamih" (If I Were to Forgive), the Hawaiian hula ku'i of the Kalama Quartette's "Nā Moku 'Ehā" (The Four Islands) and the Ghanaian highlife of the Kumasi Trio's "Yaa Amponsah," the Buenos Aires tango of Rosita Quiroga's "La Musa Mistonga" (The Muse of the Poor) and the Indonesian kroncong of Miss Riboet's "Krontjong Moeritskoe" (Moorish kroncong).

Noise Uprising is the story of the audiopolitics of this musical revolution. The struggle over these idioms was the central cultural struggle of what was called "modern times." Unlike modern novels, paintings, theater, or even film, which "represented" the modern "masses," these discs circulated the voices of those masses. And unlike our postmodern moment when high and low, experimental and pop, mix indiscriminately on the same playlist, modernism was a time of discrimination, when deference and defiance met. What musical languages and idioms were worthy of representing the nation and its people? The battle fought over jazz—the first great conflict over popular music— was a civil war between the ethos of the "philharmonic" (the love of harmony, an eighteenth-century coinage that captured both the symbolic centrality of the symphony orchestra and the tradition of accenting harmonic complexity over other musical dimensions), and the noise of outcast and oppressed peoples: gypsies, blacks, kanakas.

The reverberations of this musical revolution have been felt throughout the century that followed. After the apparent eclipse, even disappearance, of these musics during the worldwide depression and global war, they were rediscovered in the uncannily parallel "folk" revivals that punctuated the second half of the twentieth century. Revived as "roots" musics, part of the national heritage in a host of postcolonial societies, they became a fundamental stake in political struggles over nationalism and populism. These musics, remastered in digital form, are the forebears of twenty-first-century "world music," the raw material for postmodern remixes. These musicians were truly, as one journalist wrote as the new music dawned, "prophets of a noisy heaven and a syncopated earth."[3]

In the United States this moment is part of the history of popular music, particularly the explosion of jazz and blues on the "race records" marketed to African-American workers, and the emergence of modern country music in the "old-time" records made and distributed in the mill towns of the Appalachian Piedmont. It also included the recording of European-language "foreign" records in the Great Lakes industrial cities, which begat the hybrid music known as "polka," the border recordings of Mexican norteño sounds, and the recording of Cajun musics in Louisiana.

However, this US history is only one part of a worldwide musical explosion that included the recording of tango in Buenos Aires, son in Havana, and samba in Rio; of hula in Honolulu, huangse yinyue in Shanghai, and kroncong in Jakarta; of ṭarab in Cairo, palm-wine in Accra, and marabi in Johannesburg; of flamenco in Seville, tzigane in Belgrade, and rebetika in Athens. This book will juxtapose these musics whose histories have been told in militantly national terms—US jazz, Argentine tango, Brazilian samba—and see what happens if we map them on the globe, interweaving their histories, following the movements of the 78 rpm discs as Cuban son records echoed on the banks of the Congo and the sound of Hawaiian steel guitars was heard from Shanghai to Johannesburg, Calcutta to Buenos Aires.

In doing so, *Noise Uprising* recasts the histories and geographies of vernacular phonograph music. Rather than follow the long twentieth century of sound recording from wax cylinders to mp3s, it will focus on the sudden turnaround between 1925 and 1930; rather than concentrate on the global export of metropolitan popular music, it will chart the unexpected consequences of the recording industry's ambition to phonograph the vernacular, the global circulation of local musics across three arcs that connect port cities: the black Atlantic, the gypsy Mediterranean, and the Polynesian Pacific.

What were the audiopolitics of this musical revolution? Where did these musics come from? Why did the gramophone companies record them and what did the musical guild make of them? What was the shape of this new phonograph culture? What was its relation to what Fanon called the "coming combat" of decolonization? How did these vernacular phonograph records change the sound of modern music? These questions are the heart of this book. In answering them, I will make four central arguments: first, that these 78 rpm shellac discs emerged out of the polyphony of subaltern musical cultures in an archipelago of colonial ports; second, that they constituted a musical revolution, at once technological and cultural, that transformed the music industry as well as the musical guild; third, that they were fundamental to the extraordinary social, political, and cultural revolution that was decolonization; and finally, that they remade our musical ear.

These very different musics each had its own history and aesthetic; however, when they were recorded simultaneously in the late 1920s and early 1930s, they became part of a common historical soundscape, which I outline in Chapter 1, "Turnarounds." To many at the time, the worldwide craze for tango, jazz, rumba, and hula was merely the commercial packaging of exotic sounds for metropolitan audiences, "a resonance ... that could be imported at will from Montevideo, Waikiki, and Shanghai."[4] Well-heeled audiences drank and romanced amid visual and aural "clubscapes," like the Hawaiian Room of New York's Lexington Hotel, the imperial fantasy of Paris's Bal Nègre, or the plantation stage set in Harlem's Cotton Club, or in tropical beach resorts like Havana and Honolulu. These musics were often heard as the global echo of American popular music, homogenizing and flattening local musicking.

The real story, however, lies neither in the metropolitan crazes for exotic musics, nor in the global spread of US popular music; rather, in Chapter 2, "The Polyphony of Colonial Ports," I argue that the vernacular music revolution emerged from the soundscape of working-class daily life in an archipelago of colonial ports. Over two decades and in the midst of urban riots and upheavals, these port cities had attracted millions of migrants, some from rural hinterlands, others from across oceans, most bringing songs, instruments, rhythms, and dances to play in the city's streets, taverns, and dance halls. The recording boom amplified this musical revolution: for the first time, the musics of these working-class neighborhoods were recorded and circulated by the commercial record industry. The gramophone became, as Theodor Adorno recognized in 1928, a "proletarian loudspeaker."[5]

Second, this musical revolution inaugurated the world musical space of the century to follow. A musical world that had been dominated by printed music—ranging from the notated compositions for the symphony orchestra to the sheet music of songs for the parlor piano—quickly gave way to a world musical industry dominated by sound recordings. The electrical reproduction of sound transformed the work of music by initiating a remarkable dialectic between musicking and recording, between the everyday practices of music culture and the schizophonic circulation of musical performances on shellac discs. As I argue in Chapter 3, "Phonographing the Vernacular," this was both a technical revolution—the remaking of music by sound recording—and a cultural revolution—the inscription on discs of everyday vernacular musics. These phonograph records were thus a technical uprising of noise because they carried in them the interference of the new means of reproduction. "When you place the needle upon the revolving phonograph record," Theodor Adorno observed, "first a noise appears. As soon as the music begins, this noise recedes to the background. But it constantly accompanies the musical event ... The slight, continual noise is a sort of acoustic stripe."[6] But they were also a popular uprising of noise because the musics they disseminated were heard as noise by the established and cultivated elites of the time; they were unrespectable and unrespected. Both aspects of this musical revolution were registered in the debate over these recorded vernacular musics and their relation to classical and folk traditions, which engaged a generation of artists, social theorists, and cultural critics from the German philosopher Theodor Adorno to the Martiniquan psychiatrist Frantz Fanon, from the Argentine writer Jorge Luis Borges to the Cuban novelist Alejo Carpentier, from the Hungarian composer Béla Bartók to the Hawaiian ethnographer Mary Kawena Pukui, from the South African music critic Mark Radebe to the Spanish poet Federico García Lorca, from the African-American cultural critic Alain Locke to the pioneering ethnomusicologist Erich von Hornbostel.

I will call this the vernacular music revolution, because it is analogous to the tectonic shift from Latin to the European vernacular languages in the fifteenth and sixteenth centuries. Just as Gutenberg's movable-type printing press made possible the flowering of vernacular language publishing, and eventually marginalized the learned *lingua franca* of medieval Latin (embodied ironically in Gutenberg's own Latin Bible), so the electrical gramophone quickly enfranchised the musical vernaculars of the world, and turned the notation-based European concert music of 1600 to 1900 into a new Latin, a henceforth "classical" music (embodied in sound recording's equivalent to the Gutenberg Bible, the Victor discs of the opera arias sung by Enrico Caruso).

This vernacularization of music—through which we are still living—is not the same as the commercialization of music; a commercial music industry of concert promoters, music publishers and instrument manufacturers dates back to the earliest moments of capitalism, and the recorded music industry simply amplified its forms. Nor should it be understood—as it often is—as the degeneration from serious to trivial music, from art to pop. There is serious and trivial music, art and pop, on both sides of the divide between classical and vernacular. Learned traditions developed in the vernacular musics, as they did in the vernacular languages; each of the musical vernaculars—samba, tango, jazz—spawned its own "grammars" and "dictionaries." Just as there were early modern writers who wrote in both Latin and the vernacular, so we have postmodern musicians who compose and improvise in both classical and vernacular traditions. Rather, if "classical music" has become a modern Latin, the international language of a musical clerisy, the vernacular musics have emerged as distinct but interrelated "national" idioms.

To speak of this musical revolution as the rise of vernacular musics also reminds us that, though these musics often share forms, histories, and inheritances, they are *not* the *same* musical language. It is a mistake to lump these musical idioms together as "modern popular music." Rather, just as English and Spanish emerged as distinct if related languages, so these musical vernaculars develop as voices in counterpoint, in similar, parallel, oblique, and contrary motion. Each of these vernaculars was a particular intonation and articulation of the musics of New Worlds and Old, Easts and Wests, neither the simple adoption of exotic sounds and rhythms (as in European philharmonic Orientalism) nor the unbroken continuation of the learned or folk traditions of Africa, Asia, and the Americas. And each of these new vernaculars counterpointed idioms of lyric song, often rooted in rural traditions of agrarian music-making, with the new "rhythm sections" of instrumental dance music.

The combination of these urban vernaculars and the new technologies of sound recording created a musical culture based increasingly on records, the subject of Chapter 4, "Phonograph Culture." To many, the records were just a mechanical music, repackaging the popular song of printed sheet music—with its traditional combination of lyric and music—and the conventional rhythms and steps of fashionable dances. The music industry's marketing of song and dance is so familiar that it may seem odd to try and defamiliarize it. Though song and dance seem to be transhistorical concepts, pertaining to every time and place, modern song and dance has, in fact, dramatically cut itself off from the social functions of music. If "autonomous" music was once a minor part of musical life, far outweighed by "functional" music, capitalist modernity has reversed that: the continued social functions of music—in dance halls and discos, at weddings and funerals, graduations and sporting events—are only a shadow of the omnipresence of "autonomous" recorded music, recorded music as the background, the soundtrack, the very medium of daily life. Indeed, I will suggest that the song and dance of the record evaded the terms of musicology's classic dichotomy of autonomous and functional music. The songs and dances of vernacular phonograph music, musics for distraction, were the first great medium that articulated and constituted "everyday life," the world of "consumption" beyond the workplace.

What is the connection between such apparently apolitical sonic innovations and the complex political struggles of decolonization of the subsequent half century? In Chapter 5, "Decolonizing the Ear," I will argue that there was a political unconscious to the recorded vernacular musics. However, it was not simply one of "colonization," as Jacques Attali memorably argued, whereby "a music of revolt [was] transformed into a repetitive commodity."[7] Rather, this unexpected musical revolution, registered and amplified by the recording boom, emerged within the culture of empire and colonialism, and became the soundtrack to one of the central dramas of the twentieth century, the decolonization of the globe: the revolutionary overthrow of the European colonial empires that had dominated the world at the turn of the twentieth century, and the independence of more than 100 new nation-states in the generation after World War II.

Indeed, this noise uprising was prophetic: it not only preceded but prepared the way for the decolonization of legislatures and literatures. These vernacular phonograph musics reverberated across the colonial world, a cultural revolution in sound. Inheriting the harmonies and instruments of colonial musics, they embodied the contradictions of the anticolonial struggles: as "modern dance musics"—a common phrase of the time—they were scarred with the hierarchies of class and spectrums of color that shaped the dance halls and nightclubs, shebeens and streets, they inhabited. But if they prefigured what Fanon called "the trials and tribulations of national consciousness," they also, with their traveling if untranslatable names—son and samba, tarab and marabi, kroncong and jazz, rumba and hula—prefigured a new world, a "third" world, culturally as well as politically independent. Music did not simply sustain the soul in the struggle; the decolonization of the territory was made possible by the decolonization of the ear.

But what does it mean to decolonize the ear? If, as the young Marx famously suggested, "the *forming* of the five senses is a labour of the entire history of the world," then the reforming of the five senses is the fundamental labor of any cultural revolution. Marx's example of the history of the senses was music: "only music awakens in man the sense of music ... the most beautiful music has *no* sense for the unmusical ear."[8] And new musics awaken new senses of music, remaking the musical ear. In Chapter 6, "A Noisy Heaven and a Syncopated Earth," I argue that the vernacular phonograph musics with their noisy timbres, syncopated rhythms, weird harmonies, and forms of improvised virtuosity, transformed the very sense and sound of music. It was a sonic revolution that remade the modern musical ear.

Thus, the audiopolitics of this noise uprising can be registered on three distinct scales, three different time frames. In the narrowest historical frame—a decade of economic acceleration and crash spanning the late 1920s and the early 1930s—this is the story of "syncopated" musics and 78 rpm shellac discs, a political economy of the electrical recording boom, the history of a brief economic and cultural renaissance that coincided with the emergence of anticolonial militancy in the years after the imperial crisis of World War I. In this frame, these musics represented the refusal of deference, the assertion of noise for noise's sake, the singing of the subaltern, "a premonition of an uprising as a noise in the transmission of some of the more familiar signals of deference."[9] In a somewhat wider frame—the generational cohort of "modern times" who lived roughly from the late nineteenth to the late twentieth century—this is the story of the modern musics that were part of the cultural conflicts of modernism and decolonization, a struggle for musical justice—for a recognition of the dignity of the vernacular, the common, the everyday, a turning of the musical world upside down. In the widest frame—the *longue durée* of epochs and modes of production—this is the story of a cultural revolution enabled by a new mode of musical production—sound recording— that changed forever our relation to music-making, a revolution in the wake of which we continue to live.

Noise Uprising is not simply a history of music; rather, in the spirit of a tradition that extends from Theodor Adorno and Ernst Bloch to Jacques Attali and Paul Gilroy, it suggests that music and sound are fundamental to social and political analysis. For music is an inherently social and political art. Like the other performance arts (for example, theater and dance), music-making is a social activity, banding and bonding ensembles (to use Mark Slobin's terms). And like the other landscape arts (for example, architecture, urban planning, and landscape design), music organizes space and time. Music creates territorial markers, what Josh Kun has called "audiotopias," and temporal markers, keeping time through the rhythmic reordering of daily life.[10]

Thus the making of music—organized sound—is fundamental to the organization of social order, to creating social space and social solidarity. Sound constitutes subjects as social subjects, creating and sustaining social groups. The work of music is not only a performance of a social order; its very forms present an abstract model of the social order. It is not surprising that music is central to conserving and reproducing established social orders: the fundamental rites and spectacles of any social order are "accompanied" by music—from weddings and funerals to street festivals, military parades, and political rallies. Indeed, "accompanied" is too weak a word; it is more accurate to say that most of these rituals would seem hollow, empty, without their music, not unlike the rough cut of a film before the soundtrack has been added. For even the words spoken at these events—the ritualized speeches at rallies and prayers at weddings—take on the character of music: an organized sound that constitutes the social gathering in a specific time and place.

A recognition of music's role in establishing social order enabled the powerful critiques of the social forms of music under capitalism, of the ways a capitalist culture industry turned music—performed, printed, or recorded—into a commodity, an analysis associated first and foremost with the figure of Theodor Adorno. Adorno will be a constant presence in this book, not least because he was an ear-witness to this musical revolution. But I am less interested in attacking or defending Adorno than calling on three different Adornos to testify: first, the Adorno who analyzed the phonograph and the radio as forms of mechanized musical production, "music pouring out of the loudspeaker"; second, the Adorno who listened to the sounds of the modern dance musics, including "jazz" and "light music," and to the timbres of their guitars, saxophones, 'ukuleles, and accordions; and third, the Adorno who argued that music figures the contradictions of a society, that music is not a sign of community but of the desire for community: "the social alienation of music … cannot be corrected within music, but only within society: through the change of society."[11]

However, if music's role in binding social order together is well known—getting everyone to sing or play in harmony, to dance in time, to feel the groove—an alternative tradition has insisted that music is fundamental to social change, to the reordering, the revolution, of societies: it stretches from Ernst Bloch's account of the utopian nature of music to Jacques Attali's exploration of the prophetic nature of noise. For Bloch, music is a fundamental part of the principle of hope, the anticipatory consciousness that guides freedom movements: "music as a whole stands at the frontiers of mankind ... the order in musical expression intends a house ... from future freedom ... a new earth."[12] For Attali, music not only makes social orders: disruptive music—noise—can break them. The history of music is, he suggested in a powerful philosophical history of European music, "a succession of orders ... done violence by noises ... that are prophetic because they create new orders, unstable and changing." If noise is unwanted sound, interference, sound out of place, it is also a powerful human weapon, a violent breaking of the sonic order. Noise challenges the established musical codes, which had themselves constituted the social order by domesticating and ritualizing the energy and violence of an earlier noise. Indeed, Attali argues that traditional musicology implicitly recognizes this dialectic of noise and music when it analyzes musical works as "the organization of controlled panic, the movement from anxiety to joy, from dissonance to harmony."[13]

The dialectic of noise and music is not, for Attali, simply the static, repetitive battle of carnival and lent. Rather, new noises—often associated with the disruptive sound of new instruments—herald social change and prophesy new social orders because "change is inscribed in noise faster than it transforms society."[14] Moreover, since music is a tool for creating community, and a great musical work is always "a model of amorous relations, a model of relations with the other," new noises— new musics—are a "rough sketch of the society under construction."[15] In their distinct idioms, Bloch and Attali insist on the anticipatory, prophetic, utopian capacity of music; it transports its participants to another place and another time, an elsewhere and a not-yet. To make another sound is to project another world. If each epoch dreams the next, as Walter Benjamin suggested, it does so in music.

Unfortunately, even this tradition often conceived of "music" in the abstract, reminding one of the comment the young Karl Marx—in the midst of the "polkamania" of the 1840s—made about a Hegelian critic who spoke "neither of the cancan nor of the polka, but of dancing in general, of the category Dancing, which is not performed anywhere except in his Critical cranium. Let him see a dance at the Chaumière in Paris, and his Christian-German soul would be outraged by the boldness, the frankness, the graceful petulance, and the music of that most sensual movement."[16] In contrast to Marx's vivid appreciation of the vernacular dances of his day—the Grande Chaumière lay on the working-class outskirts of Paris and the polka was often associated with sympathy for the defeated Polish uprising of 1831—too often those who insisted on the utopian elements of European philharmonic musics have been outraged by "the boldness, the frankness, the graceful petulance and the music of" rumba and kroncong, hula and samba, jazz and marabi. "Nothing coarser, nastier, more stupid has ever been seen than the jazz-dances since 1930," Ernst Bloch wrote. "Jitterbug, Boogie-Woogie, this is imbecility gone wild, with a corresponding howling which provides the so to speak musical accompaniment."[17] And Attali saw twentieth-century musics, both "theoretical music" and "mass music," under the sign of repetition: "it serves to silence, by mass-producing a deafening syncretic kind of music, and censoring all other human noises."[18]

For decades, the Marxist critical theory of music has been dominated by these powerful interpretative models of Adorno, Bloch, and Attali, which have accented the subjection of vernacular music to the commodity form. Without abandoning their insights, I take inspiration from the young Marx's homage to the polka and the cancan and hope to outline an alternative way of understanding vernacular music, one that draws on a somewhat unrecognized tradition in Marxist reflections on music stemming from figures whose work also emerged out the debates triggered by the vernacular phonograph records, among them Wilfrid Mellers, Alejo Carpentier, Charles Seeger, János Maróthy, and Amiri Baraka.

Noise Uprising hopes to suggest that this "howling" (Bloch), this mass-produced "deafening syncretic kind of music" (Attali), this noise, had a "boldness … frankness … [and] graceful petulance." It embodied a prophetic unconscious in its very form, not only disrupting the present order but figuring new orders, new rhythms, and new harmonies. The musics of this noise uprising became the fundamental and inescapable basis for the rich and contradictory developments in music around the world over the next century, as the circulation of recordings broke down the barriers between vernacular musicking, art musics, and the vast industry of commercial musics. Just as the early films of the generation from Sergei Eisenstein and Charlie Chaplin to Orson Welles and Satyajit Ray created the vocabulary of modern cinema, so these recordings created the musical idioms with which we continue to live. This turnaround began with a series of almost accidental recording sessions, the subject of the first chapter.

1

Turnarounds: The Soundscape of Vernacular Phonograph Music, 1925–1930

In many modern vernacular phonograph musics, "turnarounds" are moments of transition, the place where the relentless rhythm section rests, "stops time," and, in the "break," a soloist improvises, leading back to the top of the tune (and then either hands off to another soloist or returns to the main theme). One might think of the apparently unrelated recording sessions between 1925 (when electrical recording was introduced) and 1930 as "turnarounds," repeating—with a difference—the same theme, remaking the soundscape of the world's music. Before looking in detail at the musical world of the port cities where these sessions took place (Chapter 2), or at the recording industry that organized the sessions (Chapter 3), I will outline the chronology and geography of these sessions. (For a playlist and discography of the tracks marked with an asterisk in this and subsequent chapters, see the Appendix.)

October 1925, Havana: In late October of 1925, in the Caribbean port city of Havana, the Victor Talking Machine Company used the new electrical process to record the Afro-Cuban son of the Sexteto Habanero, with its three string players—tres (the Cuban treble guitar), guitar, and bass—and three percussionists—bongó, clave, and maracas.[1] Their first track, "Maldita timidez,"* was, the novelist Alejo Carpentier later wrote, a "cornerstone of that repertoire, representative of that great era of the *son*, the decade of 1920–1930."[2] The following fall—September 1926—Sexteto Habanero traveled to New York to record another dozen tracks for Victor; about a month later, Columbia responded by recording the hastily assembled Sexteto Occidente, led by the popular Cuban singer María Teresa Vera and the composer and bassist Ignacio Piñeiro, who went on to lead the Sexteto Nacional.[3] Within the next five years, hundreds of recordings of son sextetos and septetos appeared (the septeto added a trumpet, most famously Félix Chappottín of Septeto Habanero), as Afro-Cuban music remade the soundscape of Cuba in the midst of labor and student struggles against Machado's dictatorship that led to the uprising of 1933. "Thanks to the *son*," Alejo Carpentier wrote in his pioneering *Music in Cuba*, "Afro-Cuban percussion, confined to the slave barracks and the dilapidated rooming houses of the slums, revealed its marvelous expressive resources, achieving universal status."[4] Moreover, Afro-Cuban music echoed around the world under the name "rumba," particularly with the huge success of "El Manisero" (The Peanut Vendor), recorded in 1927 and 1928; as Carpentier noted, "all of the dances introduced in recent years in Europe, the Americas, and Asia, under the euphonic rubric of *rumbas*, were really *sones* that were long known in Cuba."[5]

November 1925, New Orleans–Chicago: About two weeks after the Havana recordings of the Sexteto Habanero, OKeh Records—a US affiliate of the German recording multinational Carl Lindström—began recording, in Chicago, Louis Armstrong, a twenty-four-year-old trumpet player who had moved north from the Mississippi Delta city of New Orleans, together with his Hot Five, a jazz quintet of trumpet, trombone, clarinet, piano, and banjo. There had been a slightly earlier boom in recording by African-American musicians triggered by the 1920 OKeh recording of Mamie Smith's "Crazy Blues": Armstrong himself had cut tracks in 1923 and 1924 with King Oliver's Creole Jazz Band, with New Orleans reed player Sidney Bechet, and as an anonymous side man on Bessie Smith's classic recording of "St. Louis Blues." However, Armstrong's "Heebie Jeebies,"* recorded in February 1926, and the rest of the ninety or so "race records" made by Armstrong with his Hot Five and Hot Seven (which added tuba and drums) between 1925 and 1929 became, along with the September 1926 Victor recordings of Jelly Roll Morton's Red Hot Peppers, the embodiment of "hot jazz."[6] "Last spring, in the OKeh record laboratories," *Talking Machine World* reported, "a record was made under the title 'Heebie Jeebies,' with a 'skat' [*sic*] chorus." Though the report did not mention Armstrong by name—nor that "Heebie Jeebies" was a "race record"—it noted that "the recording proved to be a popular one, and was sold to dance lovers throughout the country," triggering a dance craze.[7] A young New Orleans musician, Danny Barker, later recalled that his "greatest inspiration was the regular flow of Armstrong records on OKeh … all the alert jazz musicians and local music lovers waited anxiously for each of Louis Armstrong's latest releases."[8]

Over the next four years, a second, larger, wave of "race records" boomed as recording engineers traveled across the US South recording the new "blues" and "gospel" music of songsters and street evangelists from Atlanta to Dallas, among them Blind Lemon Jefferson, Rabbit Brown, and Blind Willie Johnson. "Blues that are of the deepest indigo, jazz that stresses rhythm to an extraordinary degree, congregational singing that preserves all the atmosphere and sincerity out of which the spirituals were born, are to be found in some of the more recent recordings by nationally famous Race musicians," Dave Peyton wrote in his music column in Chicago's African-American newspaper.[9] These "race records" were central to the emerging popular culture of African-American migrants who had left the Jim Crow sharecropping South for new urban black communities like Chicago's Bronzeville and New York's Harlem.[10]

March 1926, Buenos Aires: At the beginning of March 1926, Victor made the first electrical recordings in Argentina, recording the young tango singer Rosita Quiroga, accompanied by two guitarists, singing "La Musa Mistonga"* (The Muse of the Poor) by the Afro-Argentine tango lyricist Celedonio Flores. Quiroga was the first of the great women tango singers, having been signed by Victor in 1923, and she became the voice of the working-class *arrabales* of Buenos Aires where she had been raised by her seamstress mother.[11] Tango—which had been an international dance craze on the eve of World War I—had a somewhat different recording history, thanks to the pioneering work of Max Glücksmann's Discos Nacional in Argentina: the landmark recordings are usually taken to be Roberto Firpo's 1916 recording of "La Cumparsita" and Carlos Gardel's 1917 recording of the tango song, "Mi noche triste."[12] However, tango—which accounted for 90 percent of the records sold in Argentina in 1925[13]—boomed in the electric era: in November 1926, Odeon made its first electrical recordings of Gardel, recently returned from Paris,[14] and of Firpo's pioneering *orquesta típica* (two bandoneons, two violins, piano, and bass).[15] By the time Gardel died in a plane crash during a 1935 tour of the Caribbean and Latin America, the tango had gone, as the actor and playwright Florencio Chiarello put it in 1929, "from slum to skyscraper … from tenement to palace."[16]

May 1926, Cairo: That spring, a young ṭarab singer from another cotton-growing Delta, that of the Nile, Umm Kulthūm recorded ten double-sided 78s for the Gramophone Company's traveling engineer, S. H. Sheard, in Cairo.[17] Though she may have recorded a few tracks for Odeon earlier, the Gramophone recordings of 1926 accompanied a key turning point in her career, marked by her new *takht*, an ensemble of qānūn (a plucked zither), violin, 'ūd (a plucked lute), and riqq (a small tambourine), and her new repertoire based on the colloquial poetry of Ahmad Rāmī (including her enduringly popular "Akhadt Sootak min Ruuhi").[18] "Now every home and every family listens to Umm Kulthūm's magic voice," the Cairo theater review *al-Masrah* wrote in 1926.[19] Born about 1904, Kulthūm had grown up in a poor family in a small rural village; her father was an imam in a mosque; after earning a reputation singing at weddings and religious festivals, she moved to Cairo at the time of the 1919 Wafd uprising against British rule.[20] Over the next decade, Kulthūm's recordings made her the most popular singer in the Arabic world—"In Kunt Asaamih"* (If I Were to Forgive), probably released in 1928, "sold unprecedented numbers of copies"—and her monthly live broadcast concerts on Egyptian Radio, which began in May 1934, made her a voice of Egyptian nationalism and became a central part of the popular culture of the Middle East and North Africa.[21]

1926, Istanbul: At the same time, in Ataturk's new republic of Turkey, two companies—Odeon's local agent Blumenthal Frères, and Gramophone's label Sahabinin Sesi—began to record the *fasil* ensembles of ud, kanun, and kemence (the Turkish violin), which combined Ottoman court music, Anatolian folk songs (*türkü*), and urban secular music in the nightclubs—the *gazino*—of Istanbul.[22] The Blumenthal brothers focused on more traditional music, like the *gazels* of the celebrated "hafiz," singers trained in Qur'anic recitation: among their earliest recordings were Hafiz Sadettin Kaynak's gazel "Nâr-i Hicrane Düşüp"* and Hafiz Burhan Bey's "Nitschun Guerdum"* (Why Did I Set Eyes Upon You).[23] Gramophone's Sahabinin Sesi, directed by the Armenian kanun player and composer, Kanuni Artaki, recorded more modern singers, including the renowned classical singer, Münir Nurettin Selçuk, the earliest women singers like Safiye Ayla (who, according to legend, stood behind a curtain when she first sang for Ataturk[24]), and the instrumentalists who pioneered modern virtuosic playing techniques, like the blind Armenian ud player Udi Hrant and the gypsy kanun virtuoso Ahmet Yatman.[25] "What today has become a main stream in Turkish music, *Arabesque*," record producer Harold Hagopian argues, "was born in this era."[26]

1926, Athens: Across the Aegean, in Athens, the violinist and recording director Dimítrios Sémsis, known as Salonikiós, recorded ten 78 rpm discs of the Anatolian singer Dalgás (Andónios Dhiamandídhis), one of the 1922 refugees from Smyrna (Izmir) following the war between Greece and Turkey. Accompanied by violin, santouri (a dulcimer), and laouto (the Greek long-necked lute), Dalgás's songs—like "Melemenio,"* a folk dance, the zeïbekika, sung in Greek and Turkish—were included in a Gramophone series that featured "Manedes, Rebetika, Mangika, Hasiklidika [hashish songs], Zeïbekika."[27] "The lowest class of the population," a Gramophone agent wrote in 1930, "are interested in all Greek records, but popular titles, traditional or otherwise, are in greatest favour. Rebetika appeal to everybody; Kleftika, folk songs, and folk dances, mostly to country people; Manedes to northeastern people, to the refugees and generally to those who used to live in Turkish territory."[28] Dalgás would go on to record hundreds of songs between 1926 and 1934, and become one of the major voices of the emerging Greek popular music that came to be known as rebetika, described by the Gramophone agent as "light songs of the low class people, introduced in 1923 by the refugees from Asia Minor."[29]

If Dalgás represented one half of the fusion that created Greek rebetika—he was trained in the Ottoman café music, *café aman*, that was brought by the refugees from Smyrna to the post-1922 settlements of New Smyrna and New Ionia outside Athens—the other half was represented by the young slaughterhouse worker and self-taught bouzouki player, Márkos Vamvakáris, who recorded his first song, "Karadouzéni"* (the name of a tuning on the bouzouki), with Parlophon in 1932.[30] Vamvakáris began playing in the hashish *tekédhes* of the port of Piraeus, a masculine urban underworld: "I wasn't only initiated into the hard life of a worker in Piraeus," he later recalled, "but I married for the first time, became hooked on hashish, and most important of all, I was seduced by that instrument—the bouzouki … No one had given me lessons. My only school was the *teké*. I listened to the old timers and I played."[31]

1926, Tunis: In 1926 in Tunis, the French recording company Pathé brought together a number of the major figures of the Arab-Andalusian music of the North African Maghreb for a historic session, including the celebrated singer and actress Habiba Messika, the singer and 'ūd player Khemais Tarnan, and the singer Fritna Darmon, who recorded a two-part *rast maqam*, "Aroubi Rasd Eddil."*[32] It was also the first recording of the young singer Cheikh El-Afrit (born Issim Israël Rozio) who, by the early 1930s, had become a major voice in Tunisian music, traveling to Paris, appearing on the radio, and recording dozens of discs with Gramophone.[33] Moreover, the Pathé sessions of 1926 triggered a recording boom throughout the cities of France's North African colonies in the wake of the Rif War of 1925 in Morocco: in early 1928, the Gramophone engineer Marcus Alexander made a recording trip from Casablanca to Algiers to Tunis.[34] These sessions also led to the early recordings of *chaâbi* in Algiers, pioneered by El Hadj Mohamed El-Anka who first recorded in the late 1920s;[35] as well as of the musics of Oran that were the roots of Algerian raï: the itinerant singers from the countryside known as *cheikhs* or *cheikhas*, accompanied by ensembles of bendir (large tambourines), gasbas (flutes), and guellals (drums), including Cheikh Hamada, whose "Adjouadi hadi ouadjba"* was recorded in 1929.[36]

August 1926, Lisbon: When the popular theater actress Adelina Fernandes recorded twenty-five songs for Columbia in August 1926 in the earliest electrical recordings in Portugal, her renditions of the fado of Lisbon made her the first star of the electric era.[37] She later moved to Gramophone, recording songs like "Fado Penim,"* accompanied by Portuguese guitarra (a round, double-course stringed instrument) and Spanish guitar (known in Portugal as the viola da França).[38] Lisbon's fado had emerged from the popular cafés of the working-class quarters, a "left-wing ... socialist-oriented type of song": as a 1931 reviewer noted, "in its first days [it] was the peculiar property of the lowest and most depraved classes of society."[39] The fado of Coimbra, on the other hand, was a more refined and stylized version, associated with the students of the university; in 1927 one of its founders, Antonio Menano, went to Paris to record for Odeon.[40]

After the 1926 military coup, the new regime distrusted fado: "It was originally sung by people of ill-repute—prostitutes, thieves, and marginals—and that did not carry great prestige for a song of national identity," fado historian Rui Vieira Nery noted. "In 1927, laws were introduced subjecting all lyrics to censorship. Songs that had not been approved could not be sung in public."[41] Despite the hostility of the regime, by the early 1930s fado was the sound of urban Portugal, sung in cafés and circulated on disc. "This is a living folk music, for the *fado* singers make up their own songs and adapt the airs, and they vary from the poetic and sentimental to the topical and satirical," an English traveller to Lisbon in 1931 wrote. "It is beginning to pay them to do so now for they record for the gramophone companies and they are murmuring about their fees."[42]

1926, Bombay: In 1926 in Bombay, Gramophone recorded the young Marathi theater star Hirabai Barodekar singing several songs from the play *Patwardhan*.[43] The daughter of a distinguished court musician, Abdul Karim Khan, Barodekar had first recorded devotional songs in classical ragas for Gramophone in 1923; however, to her father's dismay, she began singing in the popular theaters. "Abdul Karim reviled music theater," historian Janaki Bakhle writes, while "Hirabai was one of the first women to pick it up with tremendous enthusiasm and to great acclaim. For the former, music *natak* [drama] represented the betrayal of serious music; for the latter, it offered opportunities for respectable women."[44] The recordings of Barodekar were part of the "music boom" across India, as the price of gramophones, now assembled in India from imported Japanese parts, dropped by half. Singers of the popular urban vernacular theatre—the Marathi, Gujarati, and Parsi theater of Bombay (present-day Mumbai), the Bengali theater of Calcutta (present-day Kolkata), and the Tamil theater of Madras (present-day Chennai)—reprised their stage songs in recording studios, usually accompanied by harmonium and tabla, and became gramophone stars in port cities across the subcontinent: not only Hirabai Barodekar in western India, but Miss Indubala and the blind Bengali singer K. C. Bey, who recorded for Gramophone in Calcutta in eastern India,[45] and the theatrical duo of S. G. Kittappa and K. B. Sundarambal, who recorded for Columbia in Madras in southern India.[46]

November 1926, Mexico City: In the fall of 1926 in Mexico City, Victor made the first electrical recordings of the pioneering Mariachi Coculense Rodríguez of Cirilo Marmolejo; the mariachi music of the rural towns of Jalisco, played by string bands with one or more violins taking the melodic lead, and several guitars, vihuelas (a five-string high-pitched guitar), and guitarrón (a five-string bass guitar) playing the rhythm, had become popular in Mexico City in the years after the Mexican Revolution.[47] In the wake of Victor's trip, many Mexican artists traveled to the US to record popular *corridos*—topical ballads, often of revolutionary heroes and battles, sung as duets accompanied by guitar—among them Luis Hernández and Leonardo Sifuentes for Victor in El Paso, Los Hermanos Bañuelos for Brunswick in Los Angeles, and Pedro Rocha and Lupe Martínez for Columbia in

Chicago. "This period from 1928 to the mid-1930s" is, record producer Chris Strachwitz notes, "the 'Golden Era' for the commercially recorded *corrido*."[48] Alongside these recordings of musics that had developed in rural Mexico came the earliest recordings of the urban boleros of Veracruz and Mexico City: in May 1928, Guty Cárdenas, the young troubadour from Yucatán who had stolen the show at the 1927 Concurso de Canciones Mexicanas in August 1927 with his boleros, went to New York to make the first of dozens of records for Columbia, including "Flor" and "Rayito de Sol."*[49] He returned to Mexico City in 1930 where he had his own show on the new RCA Victor–funded station, XEW, before his untimely death in 1932. "Unfortunately," a reviewer later wrote, "the best songs by Guty Cárdenas have never been recorded or even printed as sheet music. This young man from Yucatán was killed in a tavern brawl two or three years ago and left a number of songs which show a real gift for melody ... Of his recorded songs, 'Un Rayito de Sol' is undoubtedly the best."[50]

November 1926, Jakarta/Batavia: In late 1926, Max Birckhahn of the German label Beka recorded the young Eurasian singer and dancer of Batavia's stambul theater, Miss Riboet singing the popular kroncong tune "Krongtjong Moeritskoe," accompanied by violin, flute, and piano.[51] She became the "first major recording star" of the Dutch East Indies, two decades before the independence of the new nation of Indonesia.[52] She was so successful that Beka issued a special series of Miss Riboet records featuring tunes like "Krontjong Dardanella," probably recorded during Beka's return trip in August 1928.[53] "Her acting and singing are of a very high order and have made her name a household one in all Malay-speaking countries," a reporter for *The Lloyd Mail* noted in 1933. "She has made a fortune from the royalties paid to her by Gramophone companies for her *Krontjong* and other song records," he wrote: "every Gramophone dealer in the Netherlands East Indies ... stock[s] *Krontjong* records ... this bewitching song of Western and Eastern mixture."[54]

Miss Riboet's records were a common enough part of urban daily life to be noted in a 1930 novel by the Indonesian-Chinese novelist Liem Liang Hoo: "Every afternoon without stopping I will play records, His Master's Voice, Miss Riboet, and Odeon while my wife sits in the corner sewing or reading the paper."[55] But the anthropologist D. J. H. Nyèssen also described the reception given to Miss Riboet's records in an isolated part of South Priangan where he was working in 1928: "As many people had to wait a long time before being examined, the time was filled in by them listening to native songs on our portable gramophone. Especially the vocal successes of Miss Riboet were much liked. As the majority had never before seen a gramophone, this already drew big audiences."[56]

By the 1930s, radio broadcasts of kroncong music made it an emblem of Indonesian nationalism, particularly in the large cities of Batavia and Surabaya.[57] Indeed, a kroncong tribute to the Solo River, "Bengawan Solo," written in 1940 by the Javanese singer and composer Gesang Martohartono in the new national language, Bahasa Indonesia, became the national song. "The first widely popular song by an Indonesian composer," ethnomusicologist Margaret Kartomi noted, it "assumed legendary status, conjuring up images of Indonesian revolutionary fighters to whom homage must be given."[58]

August 1927, Port of Spain–New York: In the middle of the summer of 1927, the Trinidadian calypsonian Wilmoth Houdini recorded three paseos with a New York–based Trinidadian creole string band—guitar, piano, violin, and cuatro—for Victor, including "Caroline."* Houdini was a seaman who had played in Port of Spain's calypso tents in the years after World War I before migrating to New York in the mid-1920s.[59] He was the first of the postwar calypsonians to record, and would eventually become the "most recorded calypsonian of his generation."[60] One of his first Victor recordings—"Day by Day"—was a version of the popular "Young Girls Break Away" by Atilla the Hun (Raymond Quevedo), the leading figure of the calypso tents of the 1920s and 1930s.[61] By 1934, a Port of Spain merchant, Eduardo Sa Gomes, would sense a local market for calypso recordings and send Atilla the Hun to New York to record, thereby inaugurating large-scale calypso recording.[62]

August 1927, Bristol, Tennessee: In the first week of August 1927, the Victor recording scout Ralph Peer set up a temporary recording studio in the Piedmont mill town of Bristol, Tennessee to record local singers of "old-time" music (Peer had named it "hillbilly" music in 1925), which had enjoyed unexpected success after the 1923 New York recording of the Atlanta fiddle-contest champion, Fiddlin' John Carson.[63] In what has been called the "big bang of country music,"[64] Peer made the earliest recordings of the first great stars of US country music: the Carter Family and Jimmie Rodgers. The Carter Family featured Sara Doughtery Carter, the daughter of a sawmill worker in a Virginia coalmining camp, singing and playing the autoharp, and her cousin Maybelle, whose famous "Carter lick"—playing the melody on bass strings with her thumb while brushing the chords on the treble strings—was a simple but revolutionary part of the transformation of the guitar from a rhythm to a lead instrument. They recorded only a half-dozen numbers those first two days, but one of them, a brief but eloquent narrative of the economy of gender, took off when it was released in 1928 and made their initial reputation: "Single Girl, Married Girl."*[65]

If the Carter Family captured one half of the ideological double-ness of country music—a vision of rural family music-making, closely tied to hymns and religious music—Jimmie Rodgers, the Singing Brakeman, captured the other half: country music as a road music of lone male singers on the rails. The son of a Mississippi railroad worker, he had toiled for years as a brakeman and flagman, before joining medicine shows as a blackface entertainer.[66] After the Bristol session, Rodgers was brought to Victor's Camden, New Jersey, studio in November 1927 where he recorded "his engaging, melodious and bloodthirsty 'Blue Yodel,'"* a "white man singing black songs," as a 1928 reviewer described him.[67] The success of the records of the Carter Family and Jimmie Rodgers not only established a regional "country music" industry in Atlanta and Nashville, but circulated its sound to Africa, India, and Australia.[68]

1927, Barcelona: In August 1927, Regal, the Spanish label owned by the British company Columbia recorded the greatest flamenco singer of the era, Pastora Pavón, known as "La Niña de los Peines" (The Girl of the Combs), with the young flamenco guitarist Niño Ricardo.[69] In contrast to many of the other musics recorded in these years, the fla-menco of Andalusia had been recorded on acoustic discs and cylinders since the early years of the century; Pavón herself had had a half-dozen recording sessions between 1909 and 1917. However, though she had taken part in the legendary Concurso de Cante Jondo, the 1922 attempt by the poet Federico García Lorca and the composer Manuel de Falla to revive the "authentic" cante jondo, she had not recorded commercially for a decade before the 1927 Regal session.[70] The Concurso proved less successful in reviving the classic cante jondo, "deep song," than the new electrical recording. "Perhaps the present revival of interest in *cante flamenco* is due in part to the *phonograph*," the British aficionado Irving Brown suggested in 1929, in the midst of an explosion of classic recordings: in 1928, the great singer Antonio Chacón, who had not recorded since 1913, was recorded electrically by both Gramófono and Odeon; and in 1929, the German Polydor company brought together a number of major voices—Pavón, Aurelio de Cádiz, Niño de Cabra—all accompanied by the guitarist Ramón Montoya in what has been called "the Bristol Sessions of flamenco."[71] Though Pavón had been celebrated in print by poets like Lorca and Langston Hughes, the recordings distributed the sound of flamenco around the world.[72] "This music is perhaps rather an acquired taste," the British record reviewer Rodney Gallop wrote of several 1928 Gramófono records on which Montoya accompanied singers. "The effect of the somewhat nasal voices and infectious dance rhythms is predominantly oriental, and the music is said to be a blend of three influences, the modes of the Byzantine liturgy, Arab and Berber rhythms from North Africa, and gypsy tricks of singing."[73]

September 1927, Hanoi: In the fall of 1927, Victor made more than 100 recordings in French Indochina, traveling from Hanoi to Hue to Saigon with electrical equipment, capturing among other artists the popular Vietnamese actress Dào Nha singing "Tà cảnh cô đầu thua bạc"* (The Scene of a Songstress Losing at Gambling).[74] Over the next several years, a variety of Vietnamese musics were released on discs, but "the dominant genre of the 78 rpm format" was the modern "reformed" musical theater, cai luong, songs like Van Thanh Ban's "Khổng Minh—Mẫu Tầm Tử"* (Kong Minh—Mother Searches for her Child) played by an ensemble of two-stringed lute, two-stringed fiddle, bamboo flute, and bell, recorded by the German label Beka in 1929.[75] Cai luong became a "popular fixture" on Vietnamese radio; indeed, as one historian notes, "radio, along with the gramophone, played no small part in the popularization of cai luong during the 1930s in the south."[76] In 1931, one of the first cai luong actresses to record, Nam Phi, performed outside Paris at the Colonial Exposition; moreover, cai luong's setting of Vietnamese words to Western melodies, such as the French national anthem "La Marseillaise" or popular songs of the Great War like "La Madelon," provoked controversy among Vietnamese writers: "How can I defend this ... Saigon piece called 'La Marseillaise' that our two-stringed fiddle renders so heroically," Ung Qua asked in the constitutionalist newspaper *La Tribune Indochinoise* in 1932.[77]

December 1927, Honolulu–New York: In the fall of 1927 in New York, OKeh recorded Kalama's Quartet, a vocal quartet accompanying themselves on 'ukulele, guitar, steel guitar, and harp-guitar from the US's Pacific colony of Hawaii. They sang a series of Hawaiian-language *hula ku'i,* the modern hula songs that had taken shape in the wake of the nationalist revival of hula in the late nineteenth century, including "Inikiniki Malie" (Gentle Pinches of the Wind) and "He Manao Healoha"* (Thoughts of Love).[78] "Crave you Hawaiian singing, try 'He Manao Healoha,' or words to that effect by Kalama's Quartet," the young record reviewer Abbe Niles wrote in *The Bookman*.[79] Though the international popularity of Hawaiian music had been triggered a decade earlier by worldwide touring of musicians like George E. K. Awai's Royal Hawaiian Quartet at the Panama-Pacific International Exposition in San Francisco in 1915, much of what was heard as "Hawaiian" music was simply Tin Pan Alley tunes with mock Hawaiian lyrics. The New York recordings of Kalama's Quartet, featuring steel guitarist and falsetto singer Mike Hanapi, together with Columbia's recordings of Hawaiian songs by steel guitar virtuoso Sol Ho'opi'i in Los Angeles in October, led to the international circulation of recordings by Hawaiian artists, as each recording company marketed a Hawaiian quartet.[80]

A few months later, in the spring of 1928, recording companies arrived in Honolulu. "It was the first time in the history of the territory," the *Honolulu Advertiser* announced, "that an electrical recording apparatus has come to Hawaii to make phonograph records ... [and] the first time that any apparatus of any kind has been here within the last eighteen years."[81] Brunswick's sessions in March were arranged by the well-known bandleader Johnny Noble, and included the first recordings by steel guitarists David Napihi Burrows and M. K. Moke as well as by Lena Machado and Ray Kinney, who were to emerge as the leading Hawaiian singers of the 1930s.[82] The joint Columbia–OKeh sessions in May marked the only studio appearance for many of the musicians—like slack key guitarist William Ewaliko—but they also featured the first recording of John K. Almeida, who was to become the major twentieth-century composer of hulas.[83] The same year, the 'ukulele virtuoso Ernest Kaai, who had toured Malaysia, Sumatra, Borneo, Java, Burma, and India from 1919 to 1923, went from Hawaii to Tokyo to record;[84] by 1929, Hawaiian steel guitarist Joe Kaipo was backing hillbilly star Jimmie Rodgers.[85]

December 1927, Belgrade: In December 1927, Gramophone's veteran engineer George Dillnutt recorded the Roma tzigane violinist Steva Nikolić and his Gypsy Orchestra in Belgrade;[86] at the same sessions or shortly thereafter, the celebrated Roma café singer Sofka Nikolić recorded several songs, including "Ali Pašina pesma" and "Tri put ti čuknal."[87] "The tzigane singer Sofka ... is magnificent," Rodney Gallop wrote in his 1931 review of these recordings. "She vividly expresses the pent-up feelings of the Serbs through five centuries of foreign domination … There is an inevitability about the steady beat of *Ali Pašina pesma* and *Tri put ti čuknal* which is intensely impressive." "Besides the singing," he continues, "there is on the majority of these records that wonderful gypsy fiddling which is such a feature of folk-music from Vienna to Constantinople … It is the exclusive property of the gypsy of the Balkans, and since in these parts the gypsies constitute nine-tenths of the professional musicians it has become universal."[88]

Indeed, across Europe, the music known in the 1920s as tzigane— the "verbunkos idiom" as Shay Loya calls it, "a highly hybrid and multicultural mix of Roma musical traditions, Magyar, Rumanian, and other folk musics, as well as Viennese urban music"[89]—was played by Roma musicians in "gypsy orchestras," featuring violins and the cimbalom, a concert hammered dulcimer that was played across Central Europe in the late nineteenth century. The most celebrated orchestras—those led by the Bulgarian Roma violinist Jean Gulesco, by the Romanian Georges Boulanger (born Ghita Bulencea), and by the Hungarians Magyari Imre and Bela Berkes (whose orchestra toured the US between 1927 and 1929)[90]—played in the cabarets in Paris, Vienna, and Berlin, mixing classical music, popular dances like fox-trots and tangos, and Russian and Eastern European folk musics; "the famous bands of Budapest," *The Times* of London reported in 1933, "are known to English listeners through wireless and the gramophone."[91]

Out of this world of the tzigane orchestras in Paris music halls came the young Gypsy virtuoso Django Reinhardt, who was first recorded in June 1928 by the Compagnie Française du Gramophone in Paris's Pigalle, playing banjo-guitar for Jean Vaissade's accordion-fronted musette band. But Django had discovered jazz in 1926, when he heard the African-American musicians in Billy Arnold's Novelty Jazz Band at a Pigalle restaurant, and the 1934 release of "Dinah"* (by a small German label known for its tzigane discs) marked a powerful fusion of tzigane and jazz.[92]

January 1928, Accra: The first major commercial series of West African records—the Zonophone EZ series—were released in the British colonial ports of the Gold Coast in early 1928. "We all know how many splendid West African records have been issued by Zonophone," a correspondent for the London-based weekly *West Africa* wrote in 1929. "The number has become so great that the company has printed a catalogue which gives the fullest details of dialects, artistes, and types of music."[93] The series began with a London recording session in December 1927 and lasted until 1930, eventually including songs in more than a dozen West African languages, ranging from the Twi songs of Harry Eben Quashie to the Fante songs of guitarist George W. Aingo, who became the musical arranger for many of the sessions.[94]

Though most of the early Zonophone recordings were of West Africans living in England, in June 1928 they recorded a palm-wine guitar band, the Kumasi Trio, who, as *West Africa* reported, "came specially to London to record 36 double-sided records, mostly in Fanti, for Tarquah," the largest department store in British West Africa.[95] The Kumasi Trio was made up of a group of "young Fanti cocoa brokers working for a British trading firm that stationed them in the small inland Akan farming-town of Apedwua."[96] Their leader was the pioneering palm-wine guitar player, Kwame Asare, known also as Jacob Sam, the son of a Cape Coast storekeeper, who learned his trademark two-finger guitar style from a Kru sailor.[97]

The first record issued by the Kumasi Trio, the double-sided "Amponsah,"*[98] was a version of "the best-known tune in the Gold Coast," which had been collected and transcribed by William Ward, a British music teacher, in the *Gold Coast Review* a year earlier. "Originally Fanti, it has spread all over the country, being translated into various languages in the process."[99] Although it was considered "a vulgar street-song usually sung by drunkards, labourers, lorry drivers, and low-class people: a song never to be sung by a Christian or educated person" (in part because its lyrics—"Yaa Amponsah let's be lovers/It is more romantic that way"—were considered indecent by respectable society),[100] the Kumasi Trio's 1928 recording was "an enormous hit in Ghana, especially with the rural communities and urban poor."[101] The song circulated throughout West Africa—Harry Quashie recorded a version in Twi[102] and the Jolly Orchestra of Lagos in Yoruba[103]—and reverberated across the black Atlantic: the Kumasi Trio's records were noted by the African-American music critic Maude Cuney-Hare.[104]

Though few of the artists Zonophone recorded in the late 1920s ever recorded again—it seems that only Kwame Asare of the Kumasi Trio and Harry Quashie recorded in the late 1930s and early 1940s— "Yaa Amponsah" became a standard of Ghanaian highlife in the late twentieth century, one of a pool of common palm-wine harmonic and rhythmic patterns named for the song they originally accompanied.[105] In the 1990s, the song's history and authorship was investigated by the

Ghanaian government, as part of a controversy over the copyrighting of folklore in the era of "world music."[106]

1928, Zanzibar–Bombay: In early 1928, a singer from the British-controlled East African island port of Zanzibar, Siti binti Saad, traveled with her group to Bombay to make the first commercial recordings of Swahili taarab for Gramophone.[107] Two years later, she was being recorded by Columbia in Zanzibar[108] and by Odeon in Mombassa: an industry report noted that "the artist Siti Binti from Zanzibar was paid 20/- per title plus travelling expenses from Zanzibar and 4/- per day expenses for food ... Ten records are being issued monthly and up to the present 108 have been issued."[109] The records were popular along the Swahili coast, selling 71,000 copies by mid-1931;[110] they made her the "most revered taarab performer" in East Africa.[111] The daughter of rural slaves,[112] Siti binti Saad had trained as a potter, migrated to the city, and learned to recite the Qur'an.[113] Her given name, Mtumwa, translates literally as slave or servant; she was given the name Siti—lady—not unlike Billie Holiday's Lady Day or the *bai* of Hirabai Barodekar, both honorific and stigmatizing—by a patron.[114] Only a handful of her recordings remain in circulation—like "Wewe Paka"* (You Cat), probably recorded in 1930, on which she is accompanied by violin, udi, and qanun[115]—but ethnomusicologists found that her songs remained central to the taarab repertoire in postcolonial Tanzania at the end of the century.[116]

January 1928, Rio de Janeiro: In 1928, Brazil's pioneering recording company Casa Edison made their first electrical recordings of the popular crooner, Francisco Alves, singing the new sambas emerging from the Afro-Brazilian favela of Estácio, among them Ismael Silva's "Me Faz Carinhos"* and Alcebíades Barcelos's "A Malandragem."[117] Silva and Barcelos (known as Bide) were among the handful of Afro-Brazilian songwriters who were to found, later that year, *Deixa Falar* (Let Them Talk), the first of Rio's legendary samba schools.

The recording of the sambas by Alves, backed by a dance orchestra, gave little sonic sense either of the parading percussion orchestras of the samba schools with their *bateria* of surdos (bass drums), tamborins (sharp drums), and cuícas (friction drums), or of the "regional" ensembles that combined guitar and cavaquinho (the Brazilian treble guitar) with percussion to play samba songs.[118] The first celebrated recording to include the sound of the *batucada*—the powerful drumming of the *samba de morro*[119]—was the 1929 "Na Pavuna" by Almirante and the Bando de Tangaras, a group of young white samba aficionados.[120] Most of the black pioneers of Carioca samba never made it to the recording studios; of the handful of recordings that were cut, the two Odeon 78s of 1931 by Estácio's Ismael Silva—"Samba Raiado"/"Louca" and "Me Diga o Teu Nome"*/"Me Deixa Sossegado"—stand as the earliest examples of the samba de morro that would come to define Brazilian modernity.[121]

July 1929, Dublin: In July 1929, a Parlophone/Columbia unit made the first commercial recordings in Ireland at Jury's Hotel in Dublin. Forty different artists were recorded; thirty-eight records were released, including the Halpin Trio's "Rogha-An-Fhile"* (Poet's Choice) and "Over the Moor to Maggie." The following year another fifty-eight discs were recorded.[122] The Halpin Trio of Limerick was one of the céilí bands of fiddles, flute, and piano that emerged in the early years of the Irish Republic—the term seems to be first used by the *Irish Radio Review* in 1927[123]—and that became emblems of Irish nationalism: the Dublin-based Siamsa Gaedheal Ceilidhe Band and Dick Smith's Ceilidhe Trio, Batt Henry's Traditional Quartet Orchestra of Sligo, and the Ballinakill Traditional Band of County Galway.[124] Their music had been deeply influenced by the earlier New York recordings of reels, jigs, and hornpipes by the Sligo fiddle players James Morrison and Michael Coleman, which not only reshaped traditional fiddle styles in the newly independent Ireland, but circulated among Irish-Americans from Boston to Chicago.[125]

1929, Shanghai: In 1929, the twenty-year-old silent film star, Li Minghui, recorded "Maomao yu"* (Drizzle), written by her father, the pioneering songwriter Li Jinhui, for Pathé.[126] Though the writer Lu Xun was said to have likened it to "a cat being strangled,"[127] "Drizzle" was to become the first "standard" of *huangse yinyue*, the popular "yellow" or "blue" music of Shanghai's cabarets in the late 1920s and 1930s in the wake of the May Fourth New Culture movement and the Shanghai uprising of 1927.[128] "Dance madness," one historian writes, "hit Shanghai like a tidal wave in December 1927 through the spring of 1928, coinciding ... with the advent of the new Nationalist regime, leaving little doubt that the larger political forces that were swirling in and around the city deeply influenced this cultural sea-change."[129]

As one of "the first women to break the Qing dynasty taboo against public performances by women in the mid-1920s,"[130] Li Minghui was at "the front lines of the New Culture Movement," according to her contemporary Wang Renmei: "the more they [conservative critics] loudly and cruelly cursed her [public appearances], the more youth who had been influenced by the New Culture Movement supported her."[131] Li had received her musical training in her father's song and dance troupe, the Mingyue (Bright Moon) Ensemble, which produced many of the stars that dominated Shanghai's popular music, including Zhou Xuan, whose recordings and film performances—most notably her version of "The Wandering Sing-Song Girl" for the 1937 film *Street Angel*—would make her China's most celebrated singer of the era.[132]

1929, Fort de France–Paris: In October 1929, the Martiniquan dance band of Alexandre Stellio, having traveled from Fort de France to Paris the previous April, made their first recordings for Odeon, performing the American ragtime tune, "Sêpent Maigre,"* in the rhythm of the beguine, with Stellio on clarinet, Ernest Léardée on violin, together with trombone, bass, and drums.[133] Stellio's band subsequently performed at the 1931 Colonial Exposition outside Paris, and, as the Martiniquan journalist Andrée Nardal wrote, "The Colonial Exhibition has introduced a new fad to the dancing public, a Creole folk-dance, called the biguine."[134] Beguine took over Parisian music halls like Stellio's own Tagada Biguine and Le Train Bleu, where the African-American journalist J. A. Rogers reported that "the orchestra, all colored, is perhaps the chief attraction. When it strikes up the beguine it is difficult to remain in one's seat, and whites and blacks of all social grades may be seen in close embrace on the tightly packed dance floor."[135]

"Odeon competes in this rush for the new music," a record reviewer for *La Revue Du Monde Noir* wrote in 1932: "Stellio's band takes once more advantage of the resources of its director's supple and dextrous clarinet."[136] Moreover, Nardel argued that beguine would not have been a dance hall success without the records: "Because of the irregularity of the accented beats, transcription is very difficult, but fortunately, the phonograph is capable of a faithful reproduction."[137]

1929, Lagos: Zonophone's West African recordings of 1928 had included the first commercial recordings of Yoruba urban popular music, made in London by the little-known singer and guitarist Domingo Justus.[138] Sometime during the next two years, Odeon responded to Zonophone's success by arranging recording sessions in Lagos, the port capital of the British colony of Nigeria.[139] By August 1931, they had released a variety of discs in Yoruba: the drum-based aṣíkò music of A. B. O. Mabinuori, the guitar-based palm-wine music of Irewolede Denge, and the Muslim sákárà praise songs of Abibu

Oluwa, including "Orin Herbert Macaulay,"* which celebrated the leader of Nigeria's anticolonial Nigerian National Democratic Party.[140] However, the crisis in the recording industry led to the absorption of Odeon into the newly formed EMI in 1931, and recording in coastal West Africa ceased soon after it began.

It was not until 1936 that Odeon's sister label, Parlophone, returned to Lagos to record nearly 150 discs including ones by the pioneering *jùjú* musician, Tunde King, and the popular palm-wine bar band, the Jolly Orchestra, whose "Abonsa" was a Yoruba version of the Gold Coast tune "Yaa Amponsah."[141] Irewolede Denge did not return to the studio until 1937, when his "Orin Asape Eko"* was one of the first releases in the new West African series that His Master's Voice launched to compete with the PO (Parlophone Odeon) discs. Denge and Tunde King would continue to record in the decades after World War II, becoming pioneers in the development of Nigerian jùjú.[142]

November 1929, Manila–New York: In the fall of 1929, Columbia, Victor, and Brunswick were recording dance bands and popular zarzuela singers like Florentino Ballecer in Manila, the leading port city of the US colony of the Philippines.[143] These followed several years of recording Filipino musicians in New York, ranging from the steel guitarist Urbano A. Zafra, who recorded "Danza Filipina"* in the fall of 1929 for Columbia's export series, and the baritone singer José Mossesgeld Santiago, who, beginning in June 1926, recorded dozens of kundiman, the Tagalog love songs that had emerged around the turn of the century and became associated with the liberation struggles against Spain, and subsequently the United States.[144]

October 1930, Johannesburg–London: In the fall of 1930, Reuben Tholakele Caluza and Griffiths Motsieloa arrived, separately, in London from South Africa to organize pioneering sessions of recordings of South African marabi and vaudeville tunes for the South African market.[145] In October and November, Caluza's Double Quartet recorded 150 songs that were released on Gramophone's Zonophone label, beginning with the popular pairing of "uBangca"* (on the elegant dandies of Durban wearing their zoot-like "Oxford Bags") and "Ingoduso," with its cautionary tale of the greenhorn migrant to Johannesburg framed for illegal liquor by rival gangs, both sung by a double quartet of male and female singers, accompanied by Caluza's ragtime piano.[146] At the same time, the actor and impresario Griffiths Motsieloa led a company of musicians in a series of London sessions for Brunswick's South African representative Eric Gallo's new Singer label.[147] They included his vocal duet with Ignatius Monare, "Aubuti Nkikho"* (Brother Nkikho) in Sesuto, with its yodels and Hawaiian steel guitar,[148] "Ndhiya eBhai," which has been called "the first Xhosa hit record,"[149] as well as the ANC anthem, "Nkosi Sikelel' iAfrika."[150] Motsieloa went on to become Gallo's musical director, recording Peter Rezant's Merry Blackbirds, a leading black dance band that played dances and fundraisers for the African National Congress and the black trade unions in the 1930s, and helped define the township jive of the black urban communities.[151]

Though Caluza came out of the Natal Christian tradition of mission school choral singing, and Motsieloa out of the the vaudeville dance bands of Johannesburg's African elite, both incorporated elements of the marabi played by itinerant pianists in slumyard shebeens that had emerged with the explosive growth of the mining metropolis of Johannesburg. Marabi was largely unrecorded: the first recordings to capture some of its sound—with piano and percussion—were the 1932 Johannesburg recordings of William Mseleku's Amanzimtoti Players and Nimrod Makhanya's Bantu Glee Singers (modeled on Caluza's Double Quartet).[152] However, both Caluza and Motsieloa recorded versions of a popular marabi number, "uTebetjana Ufana Ne'mfene" (Tebetjane Looks Like a Baboon), composed by (or in mocking tribute to) the famous but unrecorded marabi keyboardist, Tebetjane. These recordings were recalled by South African jazz composer Todd Matshikiza when he wrote the history of marabi in the pioneering black South African magazine, *Drum*, in 1951: "Looking back on the progress of Jazz Music among the African People of South Africa, I am reminded of my first little Decca model gramophone from which issued the strains of a two-step dance tune of those days—a tune with the strangely quaint title of U-Tebejana ufana ne-Mfene (Tebejana resembles a baboon). Tebejana is the name of the man who composed what was perhaps the very first African dance tune after the idiom of American Jazz."[153]

As Matshikiza later wrote, marabi did not just signify "the hot, highly rhythmic repetitious single-themed dance tunes of the later '20s": "marabi is also the name of an epoch."[154] One might say the same of the other musical idioms: son, rumba, jazz, blues, gospel, ṭarab, fasil, arabesque, rebetika, chaabi, raï, fado, mariachi, bolero, kroncong, tango, calypso, country, flamenco, cai luong, hula, tzigane, palm-wine, taarab, samba, choro, céilí, huangse yinyue, beguine, jùjú, kundiman, marabi were the names of the epoch. From 1925 to 1930, as they were etched on discs and circulated around the world, they inaugurated a musical revolution. No single book could tell the history of all of these musics. In what follows, I will explore the world they had in common: an archipelago of colonial ports (Chapter 2), a transnational recording industry and musical guild (Chapter 3), an emerging phonograph culture (Chapter 4), the birth of anticolonial movements (Chapter 5), and a sound that remade the musical ear (Chapter 6).

2

The Polyphony of Colonial Ports: The Social Space of the Vernacular Music Revolution

How do we understand these recording sessions that took place around the globe? Where did these vernacular phonograph musics come from? What if anything have they in common? Are there patterns and regularities amid the accidents and contingencies that brought these musics and musicians to regional, national, and even global renown? Was this a musical revolution, or was it simply a commercial and technical event? Perhaps the very novelty of sound recording distorts an underlying continuity in ordinary musicking. Perhaps these were not new musics, but rather new recordings of old musics that had existed for centuries before the onset of recording. This is certainly how the recordings of the 1920s were heard during their first rediscovery in the midst of the "folk music" revivals of 1950s and 1960s. To the scholars and listeners of the folk revivals, the scratchy 78s were not really artifacts of the 1920s: they were earwitnesses, capturing archaic if not timeless traditional musics just before their disappearance. The commercial 78s differed from the "field recordings" made by non-commercial folk-song collectors of the same era only in their lesser degree of authenticity, their ear to the market.

Though this remains a common perception, it is not true: as the music scholarship of the last two decades shows, virtually all the musics that assume canonic form in the recordings of the late 1920s—son, hula, tango, kroncong, samba, blues, ṭarab, jazz, palm-wine—were a product of "modern times," of the generations that lived between the 1890s and World War I. Though they came to be heard as "roots"

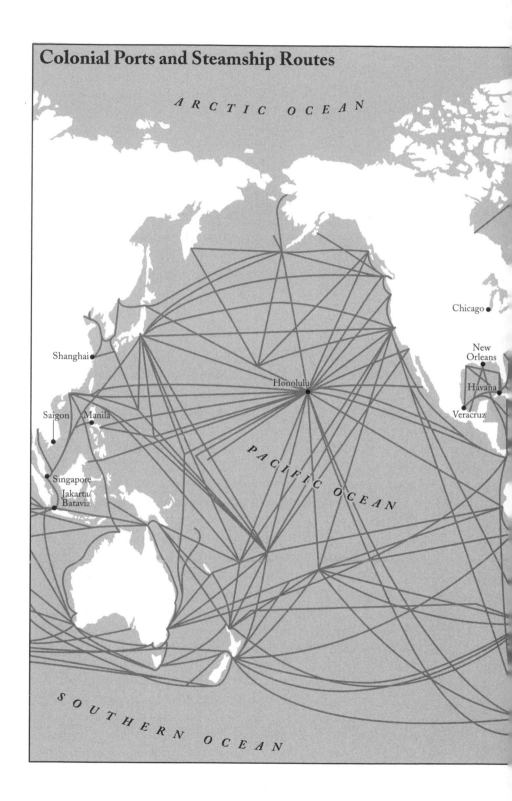

Colonial Ports and Steamship Routes

ARCTIC OCEAN

Chicago

Shanghai

New
Orleans

Honolulu

Havana

Saigon   Manila

Veracruz

PACIFIC OCEAN

Singapore

Jakarta/
Batavia

SOUTHERN OCEAN

musics in the century to come, they were as much "modern" musics as those of the Parisian and Viennese avant-gardes. The gramophone amplified a musical revolution that was already taking place in urban streets and dance halls around the world.

Because vernacular phonograph musics were not, for the most part, the musics of rural peasants and sharecroppers: they were not the "folk" musics that were coming to be collected and studied by folklorists. Nor were they the musics of the industrial working classes that had emerged in the capitalisms of the North Atlantic over the previous century: they were neither the work songs of weavers and miners, nor the parlor songs and minstrel tunes of London music halls and New York vaudeville houses. Rather, the new vernacular musics of the era of electrical recording emerged on the edges and borders of the empires of global capitalism, in the barrios, bidonvilles, barrack-yards, arrabales, and favelas of an archipelago of colonial ports, linked by steamship routes, railway lines, and telegraph cables, moving commodities and people across and between empires.

The geography of this archipelago was charted on the steamship company maps of the time; it might be figured as three great arcs linked by the Suez Canal, the Panama Canal, the Strait of Malacca, and the great fueling port of Honolulu (see map). One arc spanned the littorals of the Atlantic and the Caribbean, where fusions of African and European musics produced Havana's son sextetos, New Orleans's jazz bands, Port of Spain's calypso tents, and Fort-de-France's beguine orchestras. To the north, it stretched up the Mississippi River and the Great Lakes to the blues and gospel ports of Memphis, St Louis, and Chicago; to the south it followed Latin America's Atlantic coast to the samba schools of Rio de Janeiro and the tango *orquestas típicas* of Buenos Aires and Montevideo. These New World musics echoed across the black Atlantic to West African and South African musical worlds linked by British colonial ties and Kru sailors, as highlife and palm-wine music was taking shape in the ports of Accra and Lagos, and marabi in the ports of Cape Town and Durban and the mining capital of Johannesburg.

A second arc stretched from the coastal towns of Iberia across the Mediterranean and through the Suez Canal to the Arabian Sea and the Indian Ocean. Here the fusion of Iberian, Arabic, and Roma musical traditions—the Andalusian-Arabic as it has been called—took various timbres: from the fado of Lisbon to the flamenco of Cádiz and Seville; from the rebetika of Piraeus, played by refugees from Smyrna

(Izmir), to the Turkish, Arabic, Jewish, Greek, and Armenian musics of Constantinople (Istanbul), a key musical crossroads; from the chaabi of the North African ports of Tunis, Algiers, and Oran, to the ṭarab of Cairo, and the Swahili taarab of the East African port of Zanzibar.

A third arc stretched from the Pacific deep water fueling port of Honolulu across the Pacific to the South China Sea, and through the Strait of Malacca to the Bay of Bengal and the Indian Ocean. Here a maritime silk road spread the ʻukuleles and steel guitars of Honolulu, and linked the huangse yinyue of Shanghai, the kundiman of Manila, the kroncong of Batavia (Jakarta) and Singapore, and the popular theater musics of Bombay (Mumbai), Madras (Chennai), and Calcutta (Kolkata).

Each of these arcs was marked by a social diaspora that became a musical diaspora: the Atlantic arc by an African diaspora, the product of centuries of the Atlantic slave trade, that made "black music" central to the ports of the Americas and Africa; the Mediterranean arc by a Roma diaspora that made "gypsy music" a ubiquitous element in popular musicking; and the Pacific arc by a Polynesian diaspora that circulated "Hawaiian music" from Calcutta to San Francisco.

Why were these musics first heard in these ports? Why was samba born in Rio, hula kuʻi in Honolulu, tango in Buenos Aires and Montevideo, son in Havana, palm-wine in Accra, huangse yinyue in Shanghai, kroncong in Jakarta, jazz in New Orleans? The answer lies in the peculiar social and cultural formation of the colonial port: a volatile mix of millions of new migrants living in waterfront neighborhoods imbricated with the racial and ethnic logics of settler regimes and imperial conquests; a population dense enough to provide the critical mass to support the emerging institutions of commercial musicking, the urban industry of theaters, brothels and dance halls; a physical and cultural distance from the cultural capitals and centers of artistic prestige and power; and finally, a peculiar encounter and alliance between the "ear" musicians among the rural migrants, playing local musics on cheap, mass-produced horns, guitars, and concertinas as well as on hand-crafted drums and fiddles, and the "reading" musicians among the port's subordinated but educated elite, a "talented tenth" playing waltzes and polkas as well as sacred hymns and calls to prayer.

One might see this as a "peripheral modernity," the term Beatriz Sarlo coined in her pioneering study of Buenos Aires.[1] It was a musical culture dramatically unlike that of the learned musics of court and concert hall, the agrarian musicking of sharecroppers and tenant farmers, or even the popular parlor songs of piano sheet music. As the boundaries between sacred and secular, rural and urban, participatory and performative, polite and popular, folk and professional, were crossed or obscured, the music cultures of the colonial ports reverberated with sounds out of place, discordant noises. They embodied contradictions: urban country musics, commercial religious musics, professional folk musics, popular musics celebrated by elite intellectuals. The recorded vernacular musics were the product of this polyphony of colonial ports.

An Archipelago of Colonial Ports

This archipelago of colonial ports linked two distinct zones of the emerging world economy: the rapidly expanding settler colonial countries of the Americas, Southern Africa and Australia, and the overseas colonies and informal spheres of influence of the European and US empires—the Indian subcontinent, the Chinese treaty ports like Shanghai and Canton, French North and West Africa, British West Africa, British and German East Africa, the Belgian Congo, Portuguese Africa, the Dutch East Indies, French, British and US Polynesia in the Pacific, and the British, French, and Spanish West Indies in the Caribbean Sea.

The settler zone was for the most part formally independent. Settler colonial nations had industrial cities built around metalworking factories and textile mills, as well as vast forests, plains, and mountain ranges with mines and plantations; they each imagined their peoples divided "racially," with formal and informal distinctions between northern and western European settlers, newly recruited southern and eastern European laborers, indentured Asian workers, indigenous peoples, and the recently emancipated descendants of enslaved Africans. In many ways, Buenos Aires was a cousin to New York, Johannesburg to Chicago, and Rio de Janeiro to New Orleans.

The colonial zone was based on varieties of direct and indirect rule, backed by warships and, by the 1920s, aerial bombers. These enabled capitalist investments in colonial plantations and mines, supported by an infrastructure of railroads, ports, and telegraph cables. Color lines were firmly drawn between the relatively small European communities and the local populations, as well as between both of these and the growing numbers of indentured and migrant workers recruited from other parts of the colonial world, particularly India and China.[2]

Despite their differences, the two zones were linked by commodity chains of trade and migration. For even if these were not all *colonized* ports, they were all *colonial* ports, part of a maritime network that moved the products and people of empire around the globe. Indeed, it was in this period that geographers first began to see "maritime routes, not as autonomous links between one port and another but as clusters tied together at great ports which remained the most competitive in world shipping." Moreover, the colonial ports came to share economic, social, and cultural characteristics "because the industrialization of shipping ... was common to them all."[3]

At the center of this industrialization was the steamship. Its steel hull, steam engine, superstructure of decks, and machinery for handling freight and for steering "defined the image of modernity for contemporaries." One might amend this to say that the steamship defined two different modernities: for if the emblem of metropolitan modernity was the spectacular ocean liner—like the celebrated and doomed *Titanic*—that "offered premium service" and "sailed between a given pair of ports on a fixed schedule, usually on the North Atlantic," the emblem of peripheral modernity was the tramp steamer, which "carried the bulk of traffic between the industrialized nations of the North Atlantic and the rest of the world."[4]

From Buenos Aires to Shanghai, New Orleans to Zanzibar, Marseilles to Singapore, tramp steamers handled "colonial goods," the agricultural and mineral resources of the rural hinterlands of empire. Lands that had sustained indigenous communities were seized and put on the market—a worldwide "enclosure" of the commons—for the industrial cultivation of common foods and fibers—wheat, rice, and cotton—as well as a host of tropical plants that became everyday commodities in Europe and North America: rubber, coffee, tea, tobacco, sugar, cocoa, and bananas. Though separated by oceans and cultures, ports like Durban, Honolulu, and Havana shared the culture of sugar, as they became export centers for the plantations of Natal, Hawaii, and Cuba; similarly, the slaughterhouses of Chicago and Buenos Aires were pivotal points in a global trade in mass-produced canned meats.

The tramp steamers moved people as well. As a result, these colonial ports became crossroads in the imperial trafficking in labor, way stations in the massive migrations that historian Frank Thistlethwaite once called "proletarian globe-hopping."[5] Millions of ordinary migrants passed through these colonial ports: western and northern Europeans as settler colonists to the temperate grain belts of the world; eastern and southern Europeans recruited to steel mills and slaughterhouses; south Asians and Chinese indentured to tropical plantations, which had earlier been cultivated by slave labor.

Unlike the postmodern container ports of the present that are "huge consumers of space but employ comparatively few workers,"[6] the colonial ports of modern times were labor-intensive. The docks depended on a circulating pool of male maritime workers—crews of seamen and stokers who manned the tramp steamers, gangs of longshoremen and stevedores who loaded and unloaded goods, as well as artisans and machinists who maintained and repaired the ships and trains. Small factories grew up amid the docks and warehouses, manufacturing consumer goods for the local market: fabrics and garments, beer, cigarettes, and soaps. As centers of commerce, the port cities hosted an intricate division of service trades: domestic servants in the townhouses of the merchant and planter elites, cooks and cleaners, street sweepers and prostitutes, taxi dancers and musicians who kept the city's entertainment and leisure establishments running.

Thus, as multitudes of migrants passed through these cities, many stayed. Established ports grew by half over the two decades between 1910 and 1930. This included both the largest ones like Shanghai, Calcutta, Bombay, Buenos Aires, and Rio de Janeiro, which became cities of more than a million, and the medium-sized ones: Singapore and Batavia in the Pacific, Piraeus and Alexandria in the Mediterranean, New Orleans and Havana in the Caribbean. Smaller ports including Honolulu, Durban, Algiers, and Veracruz doubled in population (see Table 1).[7]

The waterfront districts—La Boca in Buenos Aires, La Fosse (the Ditch) in Marseilles, the Trenches and Blood Alley in Shanghai—were dominated by the flophouses and dives that fed and fleeced transients. In addition, tenement neighborhoods with a host of new names—slumyards, ghettos, barrios, favelas, arrabales—grew up near factories and slaughterhouses, often radically segregated from the older city centers. Many of their inhabitants were newly arrived from the rural provinces, dispossessed peasants as well as the children of recently emancipated slaves and serfs. If Chicago was full of "southerners" from the Mississippi River Delta and the hills of Appalachia, divided by race, Rio attracted the *nordestinos*, "northeasterners," themselves divided between the coastal Bahians and those of the arid

Table 1: Port Populations

City	1910	1930
Havana, Cuba	275,000	425,000
Port of Spain, Trinidad	no estimate	63,954
Fort de France, Martinique	20,000	27,070
New Orleans, USA	305,000	400,000
Chicago, USA	2,000,000	3,300,000
Veracruz, Mexico	30,000	70,000
Rio de Janeiro, Brazil	790,000	1,130,000
Buenos Aires, Argentina	1,000,000	1,690,881
Accra, Gold Coast (Ghana)	21,000	21,000
Lagos, Nigeria	no estimate	107,763
Durban, South Africa	69,244	127,579
Cape Town, South Africa	97,240	198,006
Piraeus, Greece	70,000	400,000
Smyrna	300,000	350,000
Istanbul, Turkey	750,000	699,602
Lisbon, Portugal	500,000	435,359
Seville, Spain	148,000	207,791
Marseilles, France	540,000	653,000
Alexandria, Egypt	230,000	444,650
Tunis, Tunisia	180,000	185,996
Algiers, Algeria	97,460	203,000
Zanzibar	150,000	187,000
Honolulu, Hawaii	39,306	113,000
Manila, Philippines	220,000	315,000
Shanghai, China	523,000	1,607,000
Batavia (Jakarta), Indonesia	105,126	384,152
Singapore, Straits Settlement	228,555	425,912
Saigon, Vietnam	200,000	200,000
Bombay, India	860,000	1,176,000
Calcutta, India	847,796	1,300,000
Madras, India	500,000	500,000

interior, the sertão. By 1931, more than a third of Lagos's people were Yoruba migrants from the Nigerian hinterlands, but there were also neighborhoods that had been settled by repatriated Yoruba ex-slaves from Cuba and Brazil.[8] In Honolulu, native Hawaiians displaced from rural taro-patch farms and immigrant Japanese and Filipino workers moving off sugar plantations settled in Kaka'ako, "an area of salt and duck ponds and mud flats … bustling with factories, workers' tenements and homes" for those who worked as seamen, fishermen, longshoremen, stevedores, laundry workers, and cannery workers.[9]

In virtually every port, the history of settler or colonial occupation had produced an urban geography segregated into districts by race and ethnicity: native towns and settler towns, as Frantz Fanon was to call them in *The Wretched of the Earth*. If this divide was starkest in the settler colonies of Northern and Southern Africa, from the Casbah of Algiers to the "townships" of Johannesburg, it nevertheless could be seen throughout the archipelago of colonial ports: in the ports of the Indian Ocean ("In Mombassa," one historian writes, "the new port city was created side by side to the traditional Swahili centre—a physical arrangement which resembled so many of the European plantings along the Asian littoral"[10]); in the treaty ports of China (Shanghai was divided between the International Settlement, the French Concession, and the Chinese municipality); and the post-slavery cities of the Americas, with African-American neighborhoods from New York's Harlem and Chicago's Bronzeville to Rio's Praça Onze, Montevideo's Barrio Sur,[11] and Havana's Belén, Jesús María, and Cayo Hueso.[12]

The circulation of peoples through the archipelago of ports also created districts dominated by diasporas (the global archipelago of Chinatowns from Havana to Honolulu, the Kru-Town settlements of Kru seamen in the coastal ports of West Africa, the *gitano* neighborhood of Triana in Seville and the gypsy ghetto of Süle Küle in Istanbul), by refugees (the post-1922 settlements of Anatolian Greeks in New Smyrna and New Ionia on the outskirts of Athens), and by mixed communities (the Creole Downtown of New Orleans, the Alfama quarter of Lisbon where the black slaves of Portugal had settled after emancipation, Batavia's Eurasian quarter of Kemayoran). In addition, the common laborers circulating around the globe on the ships of the maritime trade were a mix of "lascars" (Indian seamen on British ships), "kanakas" (Pacific Islander sailors), "Krumen" (West African sailors), and "Manilamen" (Filipino sailors). Thus these colonial ports were not only a counterpoint of products—like the Cuban counterpoint of tobacco and sugar that Fernando Ortiz figured in 1940—but a polyphony of peoples, elaborately distinguished by color, caste, language, and religion. "As a port," Rodney Gallop wrote in his pioneering 1932 essay on fado, Lisbon "has always been particularly receptive to exotic influences and, as is generally admitted, to the admixture of foreign, even non-European, blood"; "the *lisboeta* has always shown a marked liking for exotic song and dance, and in particular for those of the negroid races with which the Portuguese came into contact in Africa, and whom they transplanted as slaves not only to Brazil, but also to extensive regions in Southern Portugal which had been left empty first by the Moors and later by the American colonists."[13]

Thus, what Tan Tai Yong writes of Singapore is true across much of the archipelago of colonial ports in this period:

> From the late nineteenth century onwards, the port city was not only bustling with commerce but it stood as a centre of Malay culture and literature, of Chinese diasporic intellectual and political ferment, and of Indian debates on cultural and religious reformism. As Singapore became the centre of overlapping migrant worlds, incorporating networks of trade, labour and cultures, it developed as a key economic and intellectual node … The port city became a centre of cultural and nationalist movement … a diasporic public sphere.[14]

One might call this cosmopolitanism, but that misses the historical contingency of this cosmopolitanism—it has been persuasively argued that this cosmopolitanism is not inherent to cities or ports, but is the result of the peculiar breathing room that certain ports had as a result of the competition between empires.[15] It also misses the violence that constituted these cities. Popular memory and popular song were scarred by a host of episodes of racial violence, lynchings and massacres that triggered race riots across the first two decades of the century. These included the 1900 "bubonic plague" burning of Honolulu's Chinatown, the 1900 Robert Charles riot in New Orleans, the 1903 water riots in Port of Spain, the 1906 Dinshawai incident in Egypt when villagers were executed in retaliation for attack on a British soldier hunting pigeons on local farmers' land, and the 1912 Oriente massacre in Cuba.[16]

If this archipelago of colonial ports was created by the industrialization of shipping in the decades between the opening of the Suez Canal in 1869 and that of the Panama Canal in 1914, it was reshaped by the strikes and urban uprisings that erupted after the Great War. The worldwide crisis of 1919 was an extraordinary unsettling of social relations, as czars, kaisers, emperors, and the Sublime Porte collapsed in the wake of the bloody trench war, and revolutionary regimes emerged from the ashes of Czarist Russia, Bismarkian Germany, Hapsburg Austro-Hungary, Qing China, and the Ottoman Empire. Perry Anderson has famously argued that the "imaginative proximity of social revolution" was one of the three decisive coordinates of modernism.[17] However, if we look at the peripheral modernism of tango and ṭarab, kroncong and marabi, the imaginative proximity of revolution must be understood to include not simply the remarkable European uprisings that produced "soviets" and "councils" in the cities of eastern and central Europe, but also the worldwide wave of anti-colonial rebellions that stretched from the May Fourth Movement in China in 1919 and the non-cooperation movement Gandhi launched in the wake of the 1919 Amritsar massacre to the 1919 Wafd rebellion in Egypt, as well as the general strikes across port cities, mining towns, and plantations: the Semana Trágica of January 1919 in Buenos Aires, the 1920 strike of Japanese sugar plantation workers on Hawaii's Oahu, the 1922 Rand rebellion on South Africa's Witswatersrand, and the 1925 killing of protesters in Shanghai that provoked the May 30 movement.

Musical Cultures of the Colonial Ports

The millions of migrants who arrived in the colonial ports were a critical mass that enabled the explosion of new plebeian musical cultures in the first two decades of the twentieth century. The "migration of former slaves to uptown New Orleans created ... a huge mass of patronage for the new music, an essential element of any artistic flowering," Thomas Brothers writes of the decade when the music that would come to be called jazz took shape.

> By one count there were ten to fifteen dance halls uptown alone; between them they produced a function every night. A step or two below the dance halls were the ubiquitous honky tonks ... Twenty-five cents per dance-hall patron—that was enough, when spread through a population of some forty thousand immigrants, to nurture the new style.[18]

Throughout this archipelago of colonial ports, young musicians found that they could make a living from music in the proliferating cafés, taverns, shebeens, brothels, cabarets, "black and tans," dance halls, hotels, and vaudeville theaters catering to waterfront transients as well as well-to-do tourists, to young mill workers as well as students and clerks aspiring to middle-class respectability.

The prism of patrons produced a colorful spectrum of venues. At one end of the spectrum were the fugitive locales of plebeian drinking and dancing, like the shebeens of the South African slumyards where home-brew was sold illegally to the migrant African miners and laborers, and where the music and dances known as marabi and ndunduma developed. "Marabi: that was the environment!" the Jazz Maniacs saxophonist Wilson "King Force" Silgee recalled.

> It was either organ but mostly piano. You get there, you pay your ten cents. You get your scale of whatever concoction there is, then you dance. It used to start from Friday night right through Sunday evening. You get tired, you go home, go and sleep, come back again: bob a time, each time you get in. The piano and with the audience making a lot of noise. Trying to make some theme out of what is playing.[19]

"Ndunduma concerts were real refuse dump affairs, musically and morally," the pioneering South African playwright Herbert Dhlomo recalled in 1953.

> They were attended by degenerate young elements, the uninitiated newly arrived country bumpkins and the morbidly curious. The people danced to the accompaniment of an organ and a most cacophonic "orchestra" of small tins filled with pebbles. The atmosphere was obscene. For the first time in the history of Bantu entertainments, liquor was introduced. The functions were like nightclubs of the lowest order.

"And yet," he adds, "what naturally talented players the ragtime and ndunduma concerts had! Vampers (as they were called) who improvised many 'hot' original dance and singing numbers at the spur of the moment, and who play and accompany any piece after hearing the melody once, and did so in any key."[20]

Similar venues emerged in ports around the world, based on the cash wages of young workers. The tango violinist and bandleader Francisco Canaro recalled the cluster of bands in the Buenos Aires waterfront district of La Boca:

> We played on a narrow stage where there was barely room for the three of us and the piano ... The Café Royal, like similar establishments, was served by "waitresses" dressed in black, with white aprons, and they were much in demand by the customers. ... Opposite the Royal was a café of similar style and importance, where the brothers Vicente and Domingo Greco played. Round the corner, in Suárez Street, about thirty metres away, was the "La Marina" café. ... Roberto Firpo was playing at another café opposite "La Marina."[21]

In Honolulu, sugar plantation workers would dance at Heinie's Tavern—a well-known waterfront dive that Jack London compared to

San Francisco's Barbary Coast—to the small Hawaiian band of Sonny Cunha and Johnny Noble.[22] Palm-wine music took shape in the bars of West Africa's Gold Coast ports: "the name 'palm-wine' itself," highlife historian John Collins notes, "was derived from the low-class dockside palm-wine bars where foreign and local sailors, stevedores and dockers congregated to drink the fermented juice of the palm-tree."[23]

At the other end of the spectrum were the "hotel orchestras" that played for local elites, well-heeled tourists, and white European communities (like the "Shanghailanders" of Shanghai's International Settlement and French Concession). In elaborate ballrooms that echoed the opulence of the movie palaces of the 1920s, dance orchestras with celebrity leaders alternated established nineteenth-century dances—waltzes, polkas, schottisches—with fashionable foxtrots, tangos, and rumbas. In Shanghai, the large hotel ballrooms often featured foreign musicians, like the white American bandleader Whitey Smith (who claimed to have taught "China to dance") and the black American bandleader Jack Carter.[24] Similarly in Havana, hotels featured foreign or white musicians.[25] In Buenos Aires, tango's New Guard included hotel orchestra leaders like Julio de Caro, the "porteño Paul Whiteman,"[26] who experimented with a "symphonic tango" just as Whiteman had manufactured a "symphonic jazz." In Honolulu, Johnny Noble moved from playing for sugar plantation workers to playing for tourists when he took over the Moana Hotel Orchestra in 1919.[27]

Alongside the working-class cafés and the elite hotels were a variety of dance halls and dance academies, where local vernacular musicians played as patrons purchased tickets to dance with the young women instructors dubbed "taxi dancers" in the United States and *wunü*—dance hostesses—in Shanghai. Havana's *academias de baile* (ballroom dancing schools) mixed prostitution with taxi dancing, accompanied by Afrocuban ensembles playing son: the Septeto Nacional came to prominence performing at Habana Sport, the largest and best-known *academia de baile*, which employed more than a hundred women.[28] In Singapore,

> amusement parks became famous for their dance halls, which included stages for cabaret and *joget* (a popular Malay dance) that catered to members of the working class, invariably men. For a dance, the single man gave a ticket (costing 10 cents) to the dance hostess he fancied. The latest dances, such as the foxtrot, waltz, rumba, and slowfox, were performed in these dance halls to live music.[29]

In Rio, they were known as *dancings*, adopting the newly coined French Anglicism that distinguished them from cabarets.[30]

These venues for social dancing and commercial entertainment were distinguished not only by the laws and regulations that licensed and classified them—Havana's cabarets were sorted into first, second, or third class[31]—but also by intricate if informal markers of class and color, vulgarity and refinement, even modes of dress and forms of drink. In his 1933 account of Lisbon's "popular cafes such as the 'Luso' and the 'Victoria' where [fado] is regularly performed by semi-professional *fadistas*," Rodney Gallop noted that

> the social standing of these places seems to be largely a matter of head-gear. Entrance to the first is forbidden to those wearing caps or bérets (a fine distinction). The patrons of the second, on the other hand, many of whom are seafaring folk, seem to wear no other head-covering. The spacious rectangle of the "Luso" and the low-vaulted room of the "Victoria" are alike crowded with tables and chairs at which many men (but few women) sit drinking coffee, beer, or soft drinks with exotic names such as Maracuja or Guarana.[32]

In Lagos, the ethnomusicologist Afolabi Alaja-Browne was told, the working-class "palmwine 'depots'" were distinguished from the "exclusive gathering of the dignitaries of Lagos—men who could afford to drink 'schnapps' and 'cased beer,' not 'palmwine.'"[33] In Cuba, the world of respectable Afro-Cuban social clubs—the *sociedades de color*—forbade the working-class son and drums.[34] As Langston Hughes wrote of his visit to Havana's leading "club of color," the Club Atenas, "Then no rumbas were danced within the walls of the Atenas, for in Cuba in 1930 the rumba was not a respectable dance among persons of good breeding."[35]

Racial lines were drawn in both colonial and settler colonial cities. In Shanghai, there was a clear divide between the established hotel ballrooms of the foreign settlements that hosted the national balls of European and American Shanghailanders, and the cabarets and dance halls with Chinese hostesses and a Chinese clientele that emerged amid the "dance madness" of 1927.[36] In Havana, hotels and first-class cabarets refused black patrons and rarely hired Afro-Cuban performers.[37] In Chicago, where the large commercial dance halls were closed to African-Americans, the cabaret blues and hot jazz played by migrants from the south took shape in the "black and tans," Bronzeville night-clubs that were open to both black and white patrons, and featured black entertainers; in the decade after 1919, the Dreamland Cafe, the Royal Gardens, and the Sunset Cafe featured Alberta Hunter, King Oliver, and Louis Armstrong.[38]

If the dance halls and cabarets were the privileged venues for the early instrumentalists of son, jazz, and tango, the popular vaudeville theaters of the colonial ports held a similar place for singers, who developed their craft and their following through stage performances which combined melodramatic theater, comic sketches, puppet shows, and lyric song, all accompanied by small orchestras that combined European and indigenous instruments. In many places, theater singers were the first recording stars: Miss Riboet had been a diva in the Orion company in Batavia's stambul theater before recording kroncong songs;[39] the cai luong actress Dào Nha was one of the early singers recorded in Hanoi; the actress Habiba Messika, "a major sex symbol, the Tunisian epitome of the 'roaring twenties,'" was recorded by Pathé in their pioneering 1926 Tunis session; and Adelina Fernandes was a star of Lisbon's *revistas* before recording fados.[40] In India, the gramophone boom of the 1920s was built on the recordings of singers from the popular vernacular theater; indeed, even before film music came to dominate the popular music industry in India, recording companies were issuing elaborate multi-disc sets of songs from popular stage productions.[41] Similarly, across the Americas, many of the early recording stars came out of vaudeville, and particularly blackface, theater. In Cuba, Rita Montaner, who made her theatrical debut in 1928 singing "Ay, Mamá Inés" in blackface, became famous for her subsequent recording of that song, which made son respectable by combining it with *danzón*.[42]

The musical world of the colonial ports is vividly depicted in Claude McKay's 1929 novel, *Banjo*, a picaresque tale of young black mariner-musicians living in the Mediterranean port of Marseilles. McKay, a Jamaican poet who had spent more than a decade traveling between New York, London, Moscow, and Paris, lived in Marseilles in 1927 and 1928, haunting its waterfront district, the Vieux Port.

There any day he might meet with picturesque proletarians from far waters whose names were warm with romance: the Caribbean, the Gulf of Guinea, the Persian Gulf, the Bay of Bengal, the China Seas, the Indian Archipelago. And, oh, the earthy mingled smells of the docks! Grain from Canada, rice from India, rubber from the Congo, tea from China, brown sugar from Cuba, bananas from Guinea, lumber from the

Soudan, coffee from Brazil, skins from the Argentine, palm-oil from Nigeria, pimento from Jamaica, wool from Australia, oranges from Spain, and oranges from Jerusalem.[43]

McKay's portrait of the Marseilles waterfront captured the polyphony of the colonial ports. In every bar, restaurant, and café, "music was supplied by a tin-panny pianola and half of the night was jazzed away to its noise." The music of the cafés spilled out into the streets, "the loud voice of the pianola kicking out a popular trot rushed across the square," attracting audiences—"before the Monkey Bar, a crowd was collected in admiration of a new jangling jazz"—and clashing: "Automatically the piano-panning jumped madly out of the Anglo-American Bar to clash rioting in the square with that of the Monkey Bar."[44]

McKay carefully counterpoints the sounds, instruments, and patrons of the different venues whose names map the West Indies, North Africa, and West Africa. At the Antilles Restaurant, "whose customers were colored seamen" from the West Indies and Madagascar, "a brown jolly-faced soldier played an accordion while a Martinique guide and sweetman … was shaking a steel pipe, about the size of a rolling-pin, containing something like beans or sand grains … [which] went beautifully with the accordion." "They played the 'beguin,' which was just a Martinique variant of the 'jelly-roll' or the Jamaican 'burru' or the Senegalese 'bombé.'" At the Cairo Café, patronized by North Africans, a "slightly built Algerian rattled the drum and banged the cymbals," accompanying a woman pianist playing "a tragic imitation" of a popular Spanish cuplé singer, Raquel Meller. And, at the African Bar, "the player-piano was spitting out a 'Charleston' recently arrived in Marseilles, while Martinique, Madagascan, and Senegalese soldiers, dockers, *maquereaux*—and, breaking the thick dark mass in spots, a white soldier or docker—were jazzing with one another and with the girls of the Ditch."[45]

In the midst of this musical cacophony, McKay narrates the daily life of four "colored seamen," temporarily on shore, living by panhandling, working the docks, and playing music: Malty, from the British West Indies by way of New Orleans, the "best drummer on the beach," who could also "play the guitar right splendid, but he had no instrument"; the race man Goosey, a New Jersey high-school graduate from a "Cotton Belt" migrant family, who plays the flute, arguing that the banjo is "the instrument of slavery"; the guitarist Taloufa, a Garveyite from the "Nigerian bush" by way of Lagos, Cardiff, and New York, where he had been arrested and deported after jumping ship; and Banjo himself, who had worked "at all the easily-picked-up jobs—longshoreman, porter, factory worker, farm hand, seaman … sailing down through the Panama Canal to New Zealand and Australia, cruising cargo around the island continent and up along the coast of Africa." "A child of the Cotton Belt" and "vagabond of the lowly life," Banjo now "patrolled the magnificent length of the great breakwater of Marseilles, a banjo in hand."[46]

Banjo "dreamed constantly of forming an orchestra," and the novel—whose subtitle is "A Story without a Plot"—is loosely held together by the fleeting bands Banjo forms. The novel opens with Banjo playing "Yes Sir, That's My Baby"* (a 1925 Tin Pan Alley hit recorded by vaudeville blues diva Sara Martin for OKeh's race record label) alone at a bistro on the quay, but he thinks that the banjo "wasn't adequate for the occasion. It would need an orchestry to fix them right … I wouldn't mind starting one up in this burg." His first chance comes when he and Malty meet "a crew of four music-making colored boys, with banjo, ukulele, mandolin, guitar, and horn" from a cargo boat; their impromptu band plays "Shake That Thing"* (a popular race record of 1925 by Chicago banjo songster Papa Charlie Jackson) at the Café African where the "Senegalese boys crowd the floor, dancing with one another," then at a "love shop" where "all the shop was out on the floor … strutting, jigging, shimmying, shuffling, humping, standing-swaying, dogging, doing, shaking that thing," eventually ending up at a "drinking hole-in-the-wall … chock-full of a mixed crowd of girls, seamen, and dockers."[47]

This band dissolves into the night: as Banjo says, "the fellows with instruments never stay long in port."[48] However, when the *patrone* of a café gives Banjo and his friends "a free option on the comfortable space at the rear for the use of their orchestra," a new ensemble of guitar, banjo, tin horn, flute, singers and dancers takes shape, playing "a rollicking West African song, whose music was altogether more insinuating than that of 'Shake That Thing': 'Stay, Carolina, Stay'"* (a song later recorded in Sierra Leone by Freetown's Leading Sextet). "It was, perhaps," the narrator writes, "the nearest that Banjo, quite unconscious of it, ever came to an aesthetic realization of his orchestra. If it had been possible to transfer him and his playing pals and dancing boys just as they were to some Metropolitan stage, he might have made a bigger thing than any of his dreams."[49]

"The bigger thing" remains elusive; "the group began to break up, every man to his own dream!"[50] Banjo even loses his instrument—his livelihood—and has to get a job on the docks, working in coal. By the novel's end, even though Banjo has managed to buy a "second-hand instrument" and the band briefly reunites at the café to reprise "Shake That Thing," the dream of an orchestra is as distant as ever.

None of McKay's musicians made it to the "Metropolitan stage," and none of them are brought into a recording studio (it was not until three years later, in 1931, that Odeon and Pathé went to Marseilles to record musicians from Madagascar and East Africa[51]). However, McKay's portrait of music-making in Marseilles captures the world of cafés and dance halls in the colonial ports that produced the recording artists of the vernacular music boom of the late 1920s.

For most of these recording artists, we know little of their lives; some are only a name on a record label and a voice preserved in shellac. The lives of a handful of the most celebrated have been tracked, though their stories are often a fusion of history and legend: figures like Cairo's Umm Kulthūm, Buenos Aires's Carlos Gardel, New Orleans's Louis Armstrong, Zanzibar's Siti binti Saad, Havana's Ignacio Piñeiro, Rio's Ismael Silva, Port of Spain's Atilla the Hun, and Athens's Salonikiós.

They were a generation born near the turn of the twentieth century (see Table 2). Some grew up in the barrios of the ports: steel guitarist Sol Ho'opi'i in Honolulu's Kaka'ako, the son of a rat catcher and neighborhood minister;[52] jazz trumpeter Louis Armstrong in New Orleans's Storyville, the son of a domestic servant; tango singer Rosita Quiroga in La Boca of Buenos Aires, the daughter of a seamstress;[53] palm-wine guitarist Kwame Asare in Cape Coast, the son of a storekeeper who sold carpenter's tools;[54] and Cuban bassist and songwriter Ignacio Piñeiro in Pueblo Nuevo on the outskirts of Havana.[55] Others were attracted from the rural hinterlands: ṭarab singer Umm Kulthūm moved from a poor rural village in the Nile Delta to Cairo; taarab singer Siti binti Saad, the daughter of slaves, was a migrant to Zanzibar.

Many had worked on the docks. Piñeiro had been a stevedore on Havana's docks; the rebetika bouzouki pioneer Márkos Vamvakáris loaded coal on the docks of Piraeus, and the Hawaiian steel guitarist Freddie Tavares was hired to the orchestra at Honolulu's Royal Hawaiian Hotel "from a job of sacking onions, down at the pier."[56] One researcher tracking the West African musicians who were recorded by Zonophone in the late 1920s notes that "the only address entered on the recording contracts is that of Daniel Acquaah (from

Table 2: Birthdates of Musicians (and Associated City, Region, or Country)

1880: Siti binti Saad (Zanzibar), Ramón Montoya (Madrid), Rabbit Brown (New Orleans)
1883: Salonikiós (Anatolia)
1885: Sadettin Kaynak (Istanbul), Alexandre Stellio (Martinique)
1888: Ignacio Piñeiro (Havana)
1889: Cheikh Hamada (Mostaganem)
1890: La Niña de los Peines (Seville), Cirilo Marmolejo (Mexico City), Carlos Gardel (Buenos Aires)
1892: Atilla the Hun (Trinidad), Dalgás (Istanbul), Johnny Noble (Honolulu)
1894: Bessie Smith (Chattanooga)
1895: María Teresa Vera (Havana), Wilmoth Houdini (Trinidad), Reuben Tholakele Caluza (South Africa), Antonio Menano (Coìmbra)
1896: Adelina Fernandes (Lisbon), Griffiths Motsieloa (Johannesburg), M. K. Moke (Honolulu), Rosita Quiroga (Buenos Aires)
1897: Hafiz Burhan Bey (Istanbul), Jimmie Rodgers (Mississippi), Cheikh El-Afrit (Tunis), Blind Willie Johnson (Texas)
1898: Mike Hanapi (Honolulu), Francisco Alves (Rio), Sara Doughtery Carter (Virginia), Heitor dos Prazeres (Rio)
1900: Miss Riboet (Jakarta)
1901: Udi Hrant (Istanbul), Louis Armstrong (New Orleans), Paulo da Portela (Rio)
1902: Alcebiades Barcelos "Bide" (Rio), Sol Ho'opi'i (Honolulu)
1903: Kwame Asare (Kumasi, Ghana)
1904: Umm Kulthūm (Cairo), Niño Ricardo (Seville)
1905: Ismael Silva (Rio), Guty Cárdenas (Yucatán), Hirobai Barodekar (Bombay), Márkos Vamvakáris (Piraeus)
1907: Sofka Nikolić (Belgrade)
1908: K. B. Sundarambal (Tamil Nadu), Cartola (Rio)
1909: Oscar Alemán (Argentina), Li Minghui (Shanghai)
1910: Django Reinhardt (Roma encampments near Paris)
1918: Zhou Xuan (Shanghai)

[Ben] Simmons' ensemble), in Liverpool—Caryl Street, Toxteth, hard by the docks."[57] Others, like the calypsonians Wilmoth Houdini and Atilla the Hun, had been merchant seamen; Atilla had also worked as a clerk in a coal company on the Port of Spain wharfs.[58]

And many worked in the mills, factories, and small workshops of the ports: Vamvakáris worked in a slaughterhouse, Piñeiro had been a cooper, smelter, cigar maker, and mason, and Gardel recalled his time "as a cardboard maker, in a jeweler's, and as an apprentice linotypist."[59] In his account of early country music, Patrick Huber notes that "Piedmont textile workers made up the single largest occupational group to sing and play in front of radio and recording studio microphones before World War II."[60] In Africa, Chris Waterman concluded, popular styles were often "pioneered by members of an intermediate urban wage force that includes laborers, artisans, drivers, sailors, railway workers, clerks, and teachers ... cosmopolitan individuals ... adept at interpreting multiple languages, cultural codes, and value systems."[61]

These young musicians were shaped not only by the dance musics of cafés and dance halls, the proliferating venues, refined and risqué, of the commercial entertainment districts, but by forms of subaltern neighborhood musicking, sacred and secular. Many first learned their craft in storefront churches, mosques, and religious ceremonies, leading to the dialectic between the sacred and the secular that one finds throughout these musics. Umm Kulthūm began singing in a family musical group—led by her father, an imam in a village mosque—that performed pious *tawshih* and *qasida* about the life of Muhammad at weddings and celebrations; she developed her phrasing during three years studying Qur'anic recitation.[62] Similarly, Siti began by learning to recite the Qur'an. In Istanbul, Sadettin Kaynak not only studied theology, but also worked in mosques throughout his career, and made the first recording of the Turkish call to prayer.[63]

Several early African recording artists came out of mission school choirs and recorded hymns: this was true of the pioneering South African recording artist Reuben Caluza. The first West African Zonophone recording, of Christian hymns in Yoruba, was made in 1922 in London by the Rev. J. J. Ransome-Kuti (the grandfather of Fela, the Nigerian singer of the 1970s); they were followed by Roland Nathaniels's 1925 recordings of Christian hymns, which he sang in Ewe and Latin to his own organ accompaniment.

In the Gold Coast, the Fante language hymns of the "singing band movement" associated with the pioneering Ghanaian composer Ephraim Amu not only "offered a new platform for Christians both to perform music outside the strict confines of the church and to Africanize church music," but "extensively influenced the development of popular music in Ghana" and the recording business on the Gold Coast: many early Odeon and Parlophone recordings from the Gold Coast were of these Christian "singing bands."[64]

In Hawaii, North American missionaries had been translating hymns into Hawaiian and organizing church choirs since they arrived in the 1830s. As a result, songs based on hymn forms—*himeni*—had become a major part of Hawaiian music by the early part of the twentieth century. Not only were the late nineteenth-century Sankey-style gospel hymns composed by the Reverend Lorenzo Lyons—collected in *Ka Buke Himeni Poepoe* of 1872—common throughout Hawaii, but "by the 1870s, elite Hawaiians in Honolulu had begun to compose secular Hawaiian songs whose melodies were modeled on the gospel hymns then in vogue."[65] As a result, many of the early recording artists were well versed in hymn forms, and had often been part of church choirs. An example is Helen Desha Beamer, member of the well-known Desha Beamer *'ohana*, or kin group, of hula dancers, musicians and composers, who was recorded by Columbia in the landmark 1928 Honolulu sessions; she was also an organist for the Haili Church Choir of Hilo, which regularly won choir contests through the 1910s and 1920s.[66]

Many of the musicians were also shaped by the plebeian parading associations that made music in the streets of the colonial ports: brass bands, dance troupes, *comparsas*, calypso tents, and samba schools. Many were informal associations like those of Banjo and his friends in Marseilles. In the ports of the Gold Coast, *osibisaaba* was a street dance that combined local percussion with guitars and accordions: "*osibisaaba* outings began in the town center, where revelers organized together, formed a small mobile caravan, and paraded through town in order to attract other participants. Eventually, the gathered group settled in an open space on the town periphery where musicians played with unabated energy and dancers organized into a ring."[67] Similarly, in Batavia, street or "walking" kroncong groups—*kroncong jalan*—"wandered the *kampung* (residential neighborhoods) at night, singing verses to the accompaniment of a *kroncong* lute and whatever other instruments they had available—violin, flute, guitar, and tambourine are usually mentioned."[68]

Marching brass bands emerged throughout the colonial ports. In South Africa, every mission station had a brass band, and the Tswana and Pedi had developed autonomous brass bands in the late nineteenth century; by the 1920s and 1930s, local brass bands marched through the townships on Sundays, in support of the stokvels and shebeens.[69] "In the 1920s," one historian notes of the West African ports, "many prominent trading firms ... set up brass bands and used them to signify their wealth and advertise their businesses."[70] In Lagos, the Calabar Brass Band "utilized Western instruments to perform a music essentially modeled on European military band tradition, and spiced with African and Afro-American features."[71]

There were also large choral groups, like the Cuban *coro de guaguancó*, Los Roncos, which was led by the young Ignacio Piñeiro,[72] and dance troupes, like the *ronggeng* of Malaya, described by the editor of the *Straits Echo* in 1932:

> Every public ceremony … concludes with a *ronggeng*. People sit round a brightly illuminated open space under the shade of trees in a large garden, close to the main road. A native orchestra, consisting of two violinists, a drummer, a tambourine player, and gong beater take their work seriously, while two Malay girls, well dressed and made up, sing and dance for hours and hours. Occasionally they dance towards a Malay or Chinese and challenge him to keep step with them. The dancing is painfully monotonous to watch, but the Orientals greatly enjoy the *ronggengs*.[73]

In West Africa, the sákàrá and *aṣíkò* dances of Lagos (the former associated largely with Muslims, the latter with Christians) were described by the Yoruba writer Isaac Delano in 1937:

> The dancing of "Sakara" is very easy and graceful, and is usually performed by groups of four men on one side and four women on the other. They dance together, meeting in the center of the ring, and sometimes returning, sometimes crossing. The expert dancers enjoy the variations of music introduced by the drummer, who watches the dancer, and is in turn watched by him … The drum is the major instrument, the diameter of which is not more than nine inches. The opposite side is open, and a variety of tunes is obtained by pressing the face of the leather with the left-hand fingers while beating the drum with the right … In the band also are three calabashes and three beaters, and the string instrument … [which] resembles a violin in appearance but is only about a quarter the size.

In the aṣíkò dance, "the dancing is done by pairs, two ladies and two gentlemen facing each other … No stringed instruments are employed, only drums and a carpenter's saw, used occasionally to make a kind of noise on its sharp edge, as an embellishment. Sometimes a bottle is also used, a nail beating time on it, for the same purpose."[74] These percussion-based dances of Lagos were a "local variant of a type of syncretic street drumming found in port towns throughout Anglophone West

Africa."[75] In South Africa, a variety of competitive dance troupes were organized by migrant workers: the IsiBhaca gumboot dance done in Wellington boots by dockers, the Ukukomika dance parodying military drills, and the ingoma ritual stick fighting.[76]

Perhaps the most celebrated of these musical street associations were the barrio-based carnival bands throughout the Americas. In Cuba, carnival activities had been prohibited during the war of independence; when they were reinstated in 1902, Afro-Cuban carnival street bands organized by barrio, known as *comparsas*, took part using "stave drums of various sizes and shapes, bells, frying pans, tire rims, trumpets, and other brass instruments, and the *corneta china*": "The inclusion of *comparsas de cabildo* in pre-Lenten carnival seems to have been considered one of their newly won 'rights' as citizens of Cuba libre."[77] In Trinidad, calypso emerged as a carnival music, as "syndicates" set up tents made of bamboo and palm fronds for their bands and singers—chantwells—to practice in the weeks before the carnival that preceded the Christian season of Lent. In 1919, a reporter for the *Trinidad Guardian* covered two of these syndicates: a Woodford Street tent with a string band that "consisted of four pieces—a violin, flute, cuatro, and guitar, their blending soft and low being very good indeed"—and a George Street tent with a "bamboo band" where "the musical paraphernalia were confined to the popular 'instruments' of the proletariat, which consisted of lengths of hollow reeds of bamboo, a small grater operated on by a musician with a stick, a 'chac-chac,' and the inevitable empty gin flask with a tin spoon as the beater."[78]

In Brazil, the celebrated samba "schools" of Rio de Janeiro—the favela-based music and dance associations that paraded during carnival—were first formed in the late 1920s in the neighborhoods of Afro-Brazilian migrants from the coastal cities of Recife and Salvador in the northeastern states of Bahia and Pernambuco. In 1928, the young Afro-Brazilian sambistas of the neighborhood of Estácio—Ismael Silva, Nilton Bastos, and Alcebíades Barcelos (Bide)—formed *Deixa Falar* (Let Them Talk), which, historian Carlos Sandroni writes, "is believed to have been the first to parade in the carnival to the sound of a percussion orchestra made up of surdos (bass drums), tamborins (sharp drums), and cuícas (friction drums), to which tambourines and rattles were added," an ensemble that came be called a "bateria."[79] This Estácio samba became "Carioca samba par excellence" and led to competing samba schools: a year later, in 1929, the second samba school—Estação Primeira de Mangueira—was formed by Cartola

(Angenor de Oliveria) and Carlos Cachaça, and Mangueira's great rival, Portela, was founded in 1935 by Paulo da Portela and Heitor dos Prazeres.[80] Samba school competitions took place in Praça Onze, which Heitor called a "Little Africa," which bordered on the Cidade Nova, a quarter that had been built around 1870 to house emancipated slaves and immigrants from inland.[81]

The competitions between these parading associations and dance troupes often embodied and expressed the social antagonisms within the colonial ports: rivalries and animosities between musical associations were tied to the intricate social differentiations based on color and class, religion and occupation, ethnicity and language that structured the plebeian neighborhoods of ports and mill towns. "Ingoma dancing," the musicologist Veit Erlmann writes, "was the cultural correlative of the 'political economy of tribal animosity' among migrant workers."[82] "There had always been a most pronounced system of class differentiation in the choice of chantwells for carnival bands," Atilla the Hun writes in his autobiographical account of the kaiso tents. In an analysis that echoes C. L. R. James's famous account of Trinidad's cricket clubs, Atilla delineates the spectrum of chantwells and bands: "Norman Le Blanc, a store walker, who earned fame as the first to sing a complete kaiso in English, was chantwell to Shamrock Syndicate, a band of whites and persons described as near-whites. The Duke of Marlborough, George Adilla, who was a senior shop assistant, was chantwell to Crescent, a band composed from the coloured middle class and persons described as near-whites ... Kaisonians like Red Box, Lord Baden-Powell, and Conquerer could not in their wildest dreams aspire to become chantwells of such bands."[83]

The parading associations were sometimes mobilized by competing political parties: in Cuba, white political candidates hired Afro-Cuban comparsas to perform campaign songs like "La Chambelona": "In addition to soliciting and promoting their own political songs, each major party frequently paid musicians to parade through the streets playing parodies of the rival party's songs."[84] Despite these occasional involvements with urban politics, the parading associations usually found themselves engaged in an unending struggle with the local and colonial state for the right to the streets. In Trinidad, the canboulay riots during the 1881 carnival led to two decades of struggle, as the government tried to regulate and ban drum dances, "noisy instruments," and "indecent ballads" during carnival;[85] in Cuba, a 1900 Havana ordinance prohibited the use of all "drums of African origin, in all types of public meetings," though it was "enforced only sporadically."[86] Nonetheless, the participation of Afro-Cuban comparsas in carnival remained controversial, and "by 1916, the suppression of the *comparsa* ensembles in Havana was nearly total," a ban that Machado extended throughout Cuba in 1925.[87] In South Africa, ingoma dances were banned after the 1929 beer riots.[88]

However, in the midst of these struggles, the parading associations were also becoming part of the world of commercial entertainment in the 1920s. In his autobiography, Atilla the Hun recalled the "first time that visitors were charged a fee in a Syndicate's tent" (probably 1926): "From the moment that charges were imposed by King Fanto to defray expenses of his tent, the public has had to pay to attend kaiso performances. A small fee of one penny was first charged for admission to Fanto's tent. Other Syndicates at once emulated the vogue started by Red Dragon [Fanto's Syndicate] and before the season was over, the price of admission had climbed to four cents." This led to

> a complete reversal of the kaisonian's status in relation to the carnival band. Now instead of being under the dominance of the band, he emerged as the dominant partner in the chantwell-carnival band alliance. Whereas before the leaders of the band gave a miserable stipend to the kaisonian, for example a few charitable shillings and a carnival band costume for his services on carnival day, the shoe now found itself on the other foot.

"By the end of the thirties," this had led to the separation of the chantwell and the carnival band.[89]

Counterpoint of Musicians

Thus, across this archipelago of ports, music-making had become a way of making a living, part of the urban division of labor. However, for the most part, music-making in the colonial ports was not yet the routinized job it was becoming in the musical factories of London, Paris, New York, and Berlin, where instrumentalists held regular chairs in dance bands and theater pit orchestras (and, by the late 1920s, in radio orchestras and recording-studio house bands) and were beginning to form powerful unions to set standards for their profession and fight the competition of recorded, "canned," music.[90] In contrast, in the colonial ports music-making was either a casual, itinerant street occupation, a way of supplementing day labor and occupying periods of unemployment, or a traditional skilled trade, a craft whose knowledges and secrets were handed down through families, ethnic networks, and informal guilds.

In many ways, the musical revolution that produced the vernacular phonograph musics of the late 1920s was a product of the counter-point between these two classes of musicians: on the one hand, an array of ear-trained street musicians, the children of migrants from agricultural plantations, tenant farms, and mining towns, adapting folk tunes and playing styles to urban streets and dance halls; and, on the other hand, a caste of formally trained, often ethnically defined, artisan musicians—"reading musicians"—who occupied a niche in early twentieth-century ports not unlike other artisans in fine and luxury crafts, serving the needs of the city's merchant elite.

The accounts of rural migrants bringing new musics to the city run throughout this period. Legend has it that son arrived in Havana from the rural eastern provinces of Cuba—the *Oriente*—together with the army. In the ports and mining towns of the Gold Coast, migrants "set up their own bands for the enjoyment of their own forms of music. Such immigrant bands are to be found in Accra, Kumasi, in mining and commercial areas, and in many Zongo quarters."[91] Umm Kulthūm recalled that her own success lay in part in her rural origins: "Compared to the Cairo singers, I was more well known to the rural audience. When someone from the country came to Cairo it was natural that he would buy the recording of a singer whom he had heard and seen before."[92]

The artisan musicians, like other artisan trades, often came from families that had long practiced the craft: the Hawaiian steel guitarist Mike Hanapi came from a family of musicians; Kwame Asare's father played the concertina[93]; the father and grandfather of Salonikiós were both Ottoman violin craftsmen, and his father was also a popular wedding musician.[94] Just as other trades and occupations were eth-nicized by a combination of restricted labor markets and family traditions, so musical trades often became associated with particu-lar peoples. Throughout Europe, the itinerant Roma people—known variously in this period as gypsies, *manouches*, Sinti, *gitanos*—were not only associated with several musical idioms from flamenco to tzigane, but Roma musicians were regularly recruited to popular dance orches-tras. Similarly, across the Pacific, there was a diaspora of versatile Filipino musicians, who played in Hawaiian orchestras and jazz bands in Shanghai, Japan, the Dutch East Indies, and Malaya: "Filipino orchestras are the interpreters of jazz on the Pacific Ocean liners," a journalist wrote in 1922. "Where music is concerned, Filipinos are known as the Italians of the East."[95]

If particular ethnic groups became associated with the musical trades, playing a wide range of idioms, it was also the case that musical genres became ethnicized by the recording industry. Musics from rumba to hula became so associated with particular racial, ethnic, or national groups that some musicians "passed" as that nationality: there were Puerto Rican musicians who were known as "Cubans," Tahitians who performed as "Hawaiians."[96]

Like other artisans, these musicians constantly faced the threat of "deskilling," as musical machines from the player piano to the gramophone, the radio and the sound film, automated their work and displaced live performances. They also faced new struggles over the legal ownership of their music, as the forms of musical copyright developed in the first decades of the century.

In many circumstances, these two classes of musicians would have little to do with each other; indeed the early metropolitan musicians' unions rarely included "unskilled" ear musicians. But in the colonial ports, the artisan "reading" musicians were often themselves part of a subordinated elite, either the "talented tenth" of the city's colonized or racially subordinated community or members of a mixed-race or ethnically defined in-between community. In some, though not all, cases, this led to collaborations that brought together musical idioms, rough and respectable, rural and urban.

It is a story vividly played out across the Caribbean. In New Orleans, there was often great tension between the established Downtown Creole musicians and the street musicians of the growing Uptown community of African-American migrants from Delta plantations. As Thomas Brothers has argued, the two classes of musicians were distinguished less by repertoire than by sound. For the Creoles of color, music was an artisanal trade, and their occupational, even class, identity was based on their clean, pure tones, the product of a polished and professional technique. The ear-trained street players, in contrast, distinguished themselves by their powerful volume and idiosyncratic "freak" effects.[97] New Orleans's distinctive jazz was the product of those figures who crossed the urban boundary and counterpointed the styles: Creole musicians like Sidney Bechet and Jelly Roll Morton, and Uptown African-Americans like King Oliver and his young protégé, Louis Armstrong.

In Cuba, the national recognition of Afro-Cuban musics was, Robin Moore has argued, the result of the efforts of two distinct groups: "professional, conservatory-trained musicians"—salon composers and singers like Eliseo Grenet and Rita Montaner—and "working-class and underclass Afro-Cuban performers" like the son composer Miguel Matamoros.[98] In Trinidad, calypso grew out of a similar counterpoint, as carnival celebrations set the songs—"calindas"—of the rough stick-fighting bands of the barrack yards alongside the fancy masquerade bands of the English-speaking Creole middle class.[99]

A similar counterpoint was central to the emergence of urban vernacular musics in the ports of Africa. In South Africa, there was, as David Coplan has argued, a tension between the mission-based African culture, encompassing clerks and small farmers, that developed from Christian hymns accompanied by the harmonium, and the black urban proletarian culture that adopted the guitar and concertina but not Christianity. By the 1930s, however, the prestige of African-American jazz led to the fusion, in the township dance bands, of the mission music of the educated African elite and the marabi of the shebeens.[100] In Lagos, Chris Waterman argued, "the distinction between 'refined' and 'crude,' or 'civilized' and 'bush' musical styles" not only reflected "a social boundary between a literate bourgeoisie and a large population of migrant workers from the rural hinterland," but also served to protect the cultural and economic position of a Creole elite "vis-à-vis the European colonists." In the face of this divide, "the early *jùjú* practitioners were cultural brokers … [who] fashioned an expressive code that linked clerks and laborers, immigrants and indigenes, the modern and the traditional, within a rhetorical framework deeply grounded in Yoruba values."[101] And in the Gold Coast, highlife music grew out of three streams of musical and social life: the working-class guitar bands of the palm-wine bars, the *adaha* brass bands that had developed from colonial military bands, and the dance orchestras of the Christianized black elite, which played waltzes, polkas, foxtrots, and tangos. By the mid-1920s, even the music of the palm-wine bars and the mission schools began to connect, as the mission-school composer Ephraim Amu wrote new lyrics to the popular palm-wine song, "Yaa Amponsah," and the dance orchestras added palm-wine tunes to their repertoire: "the poor people who congregated outside prestigious black elite clubs in Accra like the Merry Villas and the Palladium Cinema suddenly began to hear their own local street music being orchestrated by sophisticated bands and they gave this music the name 'highlife.'"[102]

It is not a surprise that the colonial ports, with their mix of classes, races, and ethnicities, became a privileged site for the encounter between these two classes of musicians, self-taught ear players ("routine" musicians, as they were called in New Orleans) and skilled musical artisans reading scores and crafting instruments. But the colonial ports were also a privileged site for these musical counterpoints because of their distance from the major cultural capitals, the consecrated hubs of established metropolitan culture like Paris, London, Vienna, Berlin, and New York. Though the new vernacular musics would travel to the cabarets and recording studios of these imperial capitals, they did not develop in them, nor were they rooted in the popular styles of the metropolitan working classes—the Parisian café-concert, the London music hall, the Berlin cabaret, the New York vaudeville.[103]

This is a crucial point about the vernacular revolution of the 1920s: the musics of the metropolitan working classes had little resonance outside their home cities, in marked contrast to the earlier worldwide impact of the European dance crazes of the revolutionary era of 1789–1848 that made the waltz and the polka ubiquitous. By the late nineteenth and early twentieth century, the plebeian "popular style" of the metropolitan working classes had been subordinated to the concert musics of the metropolitan elites, the world of Italian opera and Viennese sonata, and did not have wide-ranging reverberations.

In the colonial ports, in contrast, the plebeian musical culture that emerged from commercial dance halls and theaters as well as parading associations and street festivals attracted the attention of city elites, who were all too aware of their own distance and isolation from the centers of imperial culture. Though many were repelled by the music of the streets, and allied themselves ever more closely to metropolitan standards of "civilized" and "respectable" culture—accompanied by the carrot of uplift and the stick of censorship—this "colonial mimicry," as it has been called, was always aware of the artificial, abstract, and "misplaced" character of the transplanted metropolitan culture. In retrospect, those members of the urban elite who embraced the music of the streets and the dance halls in the name of an independent cultural identity—creating modernist urban renaissances, often nationalist and populist in tenor—have seemed more significant. A classic instance comes from Brazil with the legendary 1926 "evening of guitar music"—analyzed in Hermano Vianna's *The Mystery of Samba*—at which a group of modernist intellectuals including the anthropologist Gilberto Freyre and the composer Heitor Villa-Lobos met the sambistas Pixinguinha, Donga, and Patrício Teixeira.[104] For a decade after the celebrated Modern Art Week of 1922, many of Brazil's artists and writers—most notably Mário de Andrade—heard the vernacular musics of choro and samba as the sound of a Brazilian nationality.[105]

This meeting of subaltern musical worlds and the vanguardist intellectuals and artists of modernist renaissances is repeated around the world: in the *Afrocubanismo* of Havana, associated with the musicologist Fernando Ortiz and the writer Alejo Carpentier; in the invocations of blues and jazz among the writers and artists of the Harlem Renaissance, particularly Langston Hughes and Alain Locke; in Shanghai's radical New Culture Movement, which attracted musicians like Li Jinhui, Ren Guang, and Nie Er; and in the organization of the 1922 Granada Concurso de Cante Jondo by the composer Manuel de Falla and the poet Federico García Lorca, which presented La Niña de los Peines, among others, in an attempt to revive flamenco's deep song, the cante jondo. Each of these encounters triggered debates about music, race and nation that would, as we will see, surround the vernacular music recording boom.

To visitors, the soundscape of the colonial ports—street festivals and calls to prayer, refined hotel orchestras and dance-hall bands—seemed more like cacophony than polyphony. A characteristic impression is that of the French novelist Paul Morand, who visited Cholon, the Chinese section of Saigon in what was then French Cochin-China, in 1925: "The Chinese inns—full of noise, outcries, murderous turmoil, and the mah-jong tiles clattering all night like hail on a tin roof. The theatres—cymbals clanking, gramophones wailing, operetta singers adding their strident notes to the infernal din."[106]

But the voices each had their own logic, and as a result, the polyphony of the ports produced a music that was, I would suggest, richer and more complex than the segmented high and low musics of the metropolitan capitals, the isolated musics of rural peasantries, or those of the single-class mining and mill towns dominated by an industrial logic. This, I would suggest, is the answer to the oft-pondered mysteries of why samba was born in Rio[107] or jazz in New Orleans, as well as the equally mysterious roots of rumba and hula, highlife and marabi.[108]

These were the local urban musical cultures that the recording engineers of the great multinational record companies encountered when they began to lug their equipment from port to port in the mid-1920s. Out of the counterpoint of recording engineer and vernacular musician came a worldwide dissemination of vernacular phonograph musics on disc, and a revolutionary remaking of the world's musical space.

3

Phonographing the Vernacular: Remaking the World of Music

Beginning in the mid-1920s, the vernacular musics of this archipelago of colonial ports began to be recorded by the engineers of the great imperial companies that had survived the upheavals of World War I: among them, the Gramophone Company based in the United Kingdom, the Victor Talking Machine Company based in the United States, Carl Lindström A. G., based in Germany, and Pathé, based in France. The result was a recording boom. "In almost every country, from North America to Portugal, from Greece to Argentina," the music writer and discographer Paul Vernon noted, "a massive explosion of recording activity occurred from 1926 onwards, one that would last for almost five years!"[1] "1929 was a boom year everywhere," writes Pekka Gronow, who has done the closest study of record production and sales statistics. "The industry was well established in Europe, Asia, and the Americas, but now it also expanded to Africa south of the Sahara."[2] The global nature of this recording boom is perhaps best registered in the dramatic expansion, and the equally dramatic decline, of record exports, as the European and North American companies shipped millions of discs to port cities around the world (see Figure 1, p. 75).

This worldwide recording boom not only revived an industry that had staggered through the Great War (and whose postwar recovery had been short-lived), but it also had two dramatic and far-reaching consequences for the world of music. In what one might think of as twin Copernican revolutions, it established new centers of the musical universe. On the one hand, electrical recording placed recorded music, hitherto a relatively minor aspect of the business of music, at the center of the music industry; on the other, the turn to the vernacular made popular musicking, which had rarely been notated and was on the periphery of the industry, the center of modern music.

Why did this happen? Why was the music of the colonial ports recorded? Why did record companies seek out these little-known musics and musicians? And why did these records have such dramatic and far-reaching effects on the world of music? In this chapter, I will suggest that the combination of electrical recording and vernacular music constituted a new sound formation: an electric era of microphone and loudspeaker that united phonograph, radio, and sound film, based on the dissemination of vernacular musics. Together they created, not a "world music," but a radically new configuration of world musical space, a new musical world-system.[3]

This world musical space can be plotted along two different axes, one economic and one symbolic. On the one hand, there is the economic structuring of world musical space, the worldwide production and marketing of musical commodities that make up the "music industry," an industry that dates from the seventeenth-century alliance of concert promoters and sheet music publishers and that grew to include instrument manufacturers, recording companies, and royalty collection agencies.[4] On the other hand, there is the symbolic structuring of world musical space, an imagined "world musical guild" shaped by an economy of prestige and established hierarchies, in which certain musics, places, and institutions are consecrated as centers of cultural value, whether as instances of the ancient or the modern, the classic or the avant-garde. The recording boom of the late 1920s was not simply a passing episode in the industry's boom and bust cycle because it marked a profound shift along both axes: for the first time, the sale of recordings became the center of the music industry, displacing not only the sale of printed music but even live performance; and, for the first time, the vernacular musics captured on recordings created a new imagination of the constellation of musics around the world, and became the symbolic currency of a world musical guild.

The Music Industry in the Age of Electrical Recording

To get a sense of the distinctiveness of the sound formation of the electric era, it may be helpful to place it in a longer history of sound recording, which can be divided into four distinct periods: the acoustic era (1900–25), the electric era (1925–48), the tape era (1948–80), and the digital era (1980 to the present). Though the technologies serve as a useful shorthand, this is not simply a history of new machines; each "technology" is a sound formation, a mix of economic forms, spatial relations, ideologics, and justifications that structure the social relations of music.

During the acoustic sound formation, the first three decades of sound recording, one sang, spoke, or played directly into a recording horn, and the sound vibrations cut the grooves on cylinders or discs; the gramophone reversed the process. Recording was a difficult technique, and it remained on the margin of the music industry. For one thing, the inventors of sound recording—notably Edison—did not think of recorded music as its primary function; for another, the musical world saw the phonograph as a novelty device, and was initially more interested in automated musical instruments, particularly the player piano.

These decades did begin to see what David Suisman has called "the musicalization of the phonograph,"[5] and a wave of musical recordings took place around the world in the first decade of the twentieth century, triggered by Fredrick Gaisberg's landmark Milan recordings of the Italian opera tenor, Enrico Caruso, for Gramophone in 1902. But the experiment was cut short by the Great War, and the early years of the recording industry were hardly a tale of steady progress; rather, struggles over technical formats and conflicts over patents left a business history of bankruptcies and takeovers, arcane divisions and consolidations among the recording companies.

The music industry in the acoustic era was based not on recordings but on the link between the public concert and the publication of printed sheet music. New York's Tin Pan Alley (West 28th Street) and London's Denmark Street developed as streets of music publishers, with piano-playing song pluggers persuading popular performers to adopt new tunes in order to sell the sheet music. Amateur pianists often collected and bound their favorite songs in albums. In this way, piano-extract sheet music forged a link between the parlor piano and touring vaudeville troupes, minstrel shows, brass bands, opera companies, and orchestras. Printed music also dominated the emerging fascination with folk music at the turn of the century, as can be seen in the classic collections, from Francis J. Child's *The English and Scottish Popular Ballads* (1882–98) to John Lomax's *Cowboy Songs and Other Frontier Ballads* (1910).

The electric sound formation—which lasted from the middle of the 1920s to mid-century—was more than a new kind of record player; it marked the symbiotic relation between electrical recording, sound film, radio broadcasting, and mass public-address systems, what Steve Wurtzler called "electrical acoustics."[6] All these new devices of the 1920s were enabled by the forging of a link between the microphone and the loudspeaker, the former turning sound waves into electric signals, and the latter reversing the process. The devices differed in the ways they linked microphone and loudspeaker, some storing the sound-turned-current on discs or film for later presentation, others broadcasting it live over wires or to antennas. Even the "live" performance of music was electrified, as the microphone and loudspeaker transformed both singing—with the emergence of the "crooner," whose instrument was the microphone—and instrument playing—with the emergence of amplified instruments, notably the electric guitar.

Around 1950, a third sound formation began to take shape, based on magnetic tape and sound editing. Though consumers continued to use discs—the 78 rpm discs were gradually phased out as companies divided their products between the 45 rpm single for popular songs and the 33 1/3 rpm long-playing discs (LPs) for more extended works—it was the development of magnetic tape recording during World War II that constituted the real conceptual break: henceforth sound could be recorded not only accurately, but flexibly. The ability to splice and mix recordings, to bounce and layer tracks, and to create effects in the studio, led to an era that was less about recording specific musical performances than about making musical recordings.[7] If the electric era had seen the expansion of "location" recording, capturing musics as they were performed, both in concert halls and in the "field recordings" of folk performers, the tape era witnessed the creation of recorded musical works that had never been performed "live." New forms of listening emerged, as car radios, jukeboxes, and portable transistor radios played pop 45s, while high-fidelity stereo systems and FM radios played LPs in living rooms.

A fourth, digital, sound formation began to take shape in the

1970s and early 1980s with "music's reduction into a universal code that can be recombined at will."[8] Though the proliferation of digital devices to produce and reproduce music—from portable keyboards, drum machines, and samplers to the CD and the mp3, from karaoke machines to computer sequencers—underscores the importance of technology to this sound formation, it would be wrong to see it simply as an effect of digital technology. For the real breakthrough preceded digitization: it was less the digital coding of sound than the use of already-recorded sound as the raw material of musical composition— as in the dub versions produced by Jamaican sound system engineers, or the turntablism of the early hip-hop DJs—that opened up a sound formation based on sampling.[9]

In each of these moments, not only does recorded music change; so, too, does the meaning of "live" performance. Just as the microphones and loudspeakers of the electric era became musical instruments, amplifying and mediating the live performance, so the onstage monitors and mixing boards of the tape era allowed musicians and engineers to edit and balance live sound, eventually using the system's feedback as a musical device. The live performances of the digital era have fully incorporated samplers, loops, turntables, and laptops, at times making the DJ—an instrumentalist who manipulates recorded sound— the central performer. Moreover, like earlier sound formations, the digital era is marked not only by new forms of sound production and reproduction, but also by new forms of listening, particularly the simultaneous rise of individualized, private, mobile listening (from the Sony Walkman to the iPod) and of mass public listening through powerful sound systems (the earlier rock festivals like Woodstock were mythic successes but technical failures).

To return to the second of these moments, the electric era, we see that it dramatically changed the place of recording in the music industry in several ways. First, it transformed the sound of the 78 rpm shellac discs, altering the dimensions of their sonic space in volume, range, and depth. As Peter Doyle notes in his fine history of echo and reverb, "gramophone records now played back much louder than before; the recordable frequency range was immediately extended by two and a half octaves, [and] … recordings became capable of picking up room ambience—of carrying, in other words, significant sonic information about the spaces in which they were made."[10] Instruments and voices that had not recorded well—plucked strings like the guitar, drums and other percussion instruments, as well as women singers with their higher range—could now be heard, and small groups could project a larger sound. Despite the skeptics (both Compton Mackenzie, the editor of the leading British review, *The Gramophone,* and German music critic Theodor Adorno argued that acoustic recordings were superior to electrical recordings),[11] in general the audio fidelity of the electrical process meant that listening to recordings was to become a central form of musical experience.

But electrical recording was not simply a matter of audio fidelity. It also marked a new relation between the music industry and the interlinked culture industries of recording, film, and radio, a "new era in electrical entertainment," as David Sarnoff of RCA (Radio Corporation of America) put it in 1929.[12] Recorded music became the center of the music industry, overtaking music publishing, instrument manufacture, and even live music entertainment: "the talking machine industry is entitled to first place among the music industries," the head of Columbia said in 1926, "as the retail turnover of this section is today larger than any other section."[13] The music publishing industry collapsed as a producer of mass commodities—sheet music—and had to reinvent itself as a licensing or copyright industry, collecting royalties from radio, film, and recording. Live performance, which had expanded in the first quarter of the century, began to decline in the face of "canned" music. The silent film and live radio of the acoustic era had both depended on working musicians: many new jobs had been created in the theater orchestras that accompanied silent films and in the radio orchestras that filled the airwaves of live broadcasts. However, these jobs disappeared as the film industry quickly adopted electrical recording techniques to produce sound films (beginning with *The Jazz Singer* in 1927), and as the radio industry gradually turned to broadcasting recorded music, provoking, in the United States, the American Federation of Musicians' long and unsuccessful recording strike in the early 1940s.[14]

If the microphone and loudspeaker figured the technological transformation of the music industry in the 1920s, the recording and sale of vernacular musics was an equally fundamental transformation of the music industry, and perhaps equally unexpected. It is true that multinational recording companies had developed local records for local markets two decades earlier: from the early years of the acoustic era, recordings of local artists were outselling foreign recordings in most parts of the world, though it is not clear, as Pekka Gronow, the pioneering historian of the recording industry, writes, "how the decision to make local recordings in all important markets was made."[15] However, since the Victrola gramophone was, like the parlor piano, a piece of expensive furniture throughout the acoustic era, these local recordings were limited to the high-status, cultivated musics of local elites.

It is hard to pinpoint the turn to vernacular musics exactly. In some cases, it may have been a response to the competition from the new independent labels that briefly flourished in the wake of World War I, when the early recording patents expired and the US courts ruled against the patent cartel. In the United States, for example, the recording of African-American musicians for an African-American audience—what came to be called "race records"—was pioneered by the short-lived Black Swan label, founded by the African-American music publisher Harry Pace. "In the second half of 1922, Black Swan recorded as many African-American blues artists as all the other labels combined," the historian David Suisman notes; however, the larger firms quickly entered the new market and "within six months Black Swan's artists were outnumbered four to one."[16] In the Middle East and North Africa, the independent Baidaphone label was established by the Baida Brothers of Beirut and "appealed to recording artists and customers as a national rather than foreign enterprise."[17] In a number of places, the postwar US independent label Brunswick turned to vernacular recording: it was one of the first to record Afro-Cuban musicians in Cuba,[18] and it was a Brunswick distributor, the Italian immigrant Eric Gallo, who developed the first South African label, "selling American hillbilly records to working-class Boers."[19] In most cases, it was the local, largely autonomous labels affiliated with the German firm Carl Lindström (Odeon) that initially sought vernacular music markets to compete with the more prestigious artists that had been signed by Victor and Gramophone: these included Federico Figner's Casa Edison (the Odeon affiliate in Brazil), Max Glücksmann's Discos Nacional (the Odeon affiliate in Argentina), Otto Heineman's OKeh in the United States, an early pioneer of "race records," Tio Tek Hong (the Odeon distributor in Batavia), Blumenthal Brothers (the Odeon affiliate in Istanbul), and Saraswati Stores (the Odeon label in Madras).[20] A. V. Meiyappan of Saraswati Stores, who pioneered the recording of popular Tamil singers, later recalled that "it occurred to them at the time that they needed to come up with a musical product other than classical Carnatic music in order to cater to a wider market and appeal to the music tastes of common folk (in Tamil, *paamara-makkal*)."[21]

In any case, by the middle of the 1920s, even the Gramophone Company recognized the vernacular music market and heeded the advice of their local representatives. For example, in July 1924, Gramophone's agent in the Middle East, Karl Friedrich Vogel, reported back to the head office in Hayes that they needed to record, not more performers in the operatic vein, but "more common" performers who could "render popular songs as the mass is accustomed to hear them."[22]

This explosive rise of the new vernacular gramophone musics between 1925 and 1929 is registered in export statistics, since record-pressing capacity remained concentrated in the large factories of Britain, Germany, and the United States. Exports soared between 1925 and 1929, particularly to areas where the new vernacular gramophone musics were being recorded and marketed. For example, overall British gramophone record exports grew by about 75 percent from 1925 to 1929, from about 8.5 million to about 15 million (see Figure 1).

However, the raw numbers mask a dramatic shift in destinations. In 1925, more than half of British record exports went to Australia and New Zealand; the export trade was thus largely an extension of the home market to white Anglophones. By 1929, in contrast, Australia and New Zealand accounted for only 1 percent of British record exports. The bulk of exports were to areas where the new musics were being recorded and marketed (although the records were still pressed in Britain). The rise of popular Arabic song, figured by Umm Kulthūm, paralleled a sixfold increase in exports to Egypt; the recording of rebetika in Athens accompanied a fivefold rise in British record exports to Greece; and the twentyfold increase in exports to Turkey was a sign of Istanbul's musical cosmopolitanism, with recordings of Greek, Turkish, Arabic, Armenian, and Jewish musics. In British West Africa, where the Zonophone African series was marketed, record imports grew sevenfold from 1925 to 1928; and the popularity of kroncong accompanied a similar fourfold growth in exports to Java and the Straits Settlements. The recording of Lisbon and Coimbra fado paralleled a fiftyfold leap in British record exports to Portugal.[23]

German record exports grew even more dramatically, from about one million in 1925 to 14 million in 1929, almost equaling the 15 million of the British companies. As in the British case, the destinations of the records also changed. In 1925, Germany's four largest markets were its European neighbors (the Netherlands, Sweden, Czechoslovakia, and

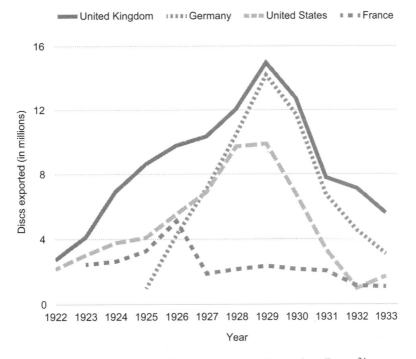

Figure 1: Exports of Discs during the Recording Boom[24]

Switzerland), and they accounted for about half of the total exports. The only non-European destinations that were significant enough to be listed were Egypt and the "rest of Asia." By 1929, exports to the four European neighbors were a smaller proportion of the total. Not only had German exports to Egypt grown more than sixfold, but two East Asian markets—not even enumerated in 1925—were each as large as the total exports of 1925: the Dutch East Indies and China. In all three areas, German labels substantially outsold British labels. In addition, German exports were of the same magnitude as British exports in the other non–German-speaking countries where Lindström labels were competing with Gramophone to record local musics: Greece, Portugal, and Turkey. There were also significant German record exports to Argentina and Brazil, even though the Lindström-affiliated local pressing plants dominated those markets.[25]

US record exports more than doubled, from about 4 million in 1925 to nearly 10 million in 1929. This was less than either Britain (15 million) or Germany (14 million); with a continental home market, US record companies depended less on exports than their British and

German competitors (on the other hand, US labels also had a smaller network of offshore pressing plants). In both years, about two-thirds of the US exports were to Latin America and the Caribbean, with the largest numbers to Mexico, Cuba, Colombia, and Argentina. Between 1925 and 1929, exports more or less doubled to Mexico, Colombia, and Peru. Systematic recording of Cuban son and Argentine tango had already begun by 1925, so the growth of exports to Cuba and Argentina were more modest. But exports to Brazil, Chile, and Venezuela grew four to sixfold. Meanwhile, the other major region of US record exports—East Asia—also saw remarkable growth: exports to the Philippines and China tripled from 1925 to 1929, and exports to Hong Kong expanded sevenfold.[26]

The transformation of the musical marketplace by the vernacular phonograph records was also registered in the record catalogs issued by the companies. For example, as Robin Moore has shown, the 1923 Victor catalog in Cuba largely featured "semiprofessionally trained *trovadores* … whose repertoires were heavily influenced by European art song, or classically trained singers … Musical representations of Cuba's blacks, *guajiros* (Hispanic peasants), and other working-class groups are largely absent. Within ten or fifteen years, however, genres prominent in the 1923 Victor catalogue were fading from popular memory, having been largely supplanted by *sones, guarachas*, stylized congas, rumbas, *afros*, and other Afro-Cuban–inspired compositions."[27]

The combination of electrical recording and vernacular music turned the industry that exported these millions of vernacular music discs, as well as the inexpensive gramophones that played them, from Europe and North America to the colonial ports and railway towns around the world, into one of the characteristic modern global consumer goods industries—not unlike textiles, garments, beer, and cigarettes.[28] Like the other transnational consumer-goods industries, the recording industry was remarkably centralized and concentrated: at the beginning of the recording boom in 1925, it was dominated by five transnational corporations. The two largest companies—the US-based Victor Talking Machine Company and the UK-based Gramophone Company—rarely competed with each other, having agreed to divide the world market in a way that reflected the imperial influence of the US and Britain. "Out of the great Camden plant Victor supplied the United States, Mexico, South America, China, Japan, and the Philippines," a journalist wrote in 1932. "The rest of the world it tapped through a half-interest in the Gramophone Company of London, whose business extended over Europe, Africa, Asia, India, and Australia."[29] They shared the famous "His Master's Voice" emblem and slogan, and each marketed the other's records in their respective spheres of influence: when Gramophone distributed Victor's Cuban records in West Africa, they labeled them "Gramophone Victor" records. The late 1920s were a boom time for both companies: Gramophone hit a peak of worldwide profitability in 1928,[30] while Victor celebrated "how a great industry came back" in March 1928.[31]

In many markets, however, Victor or Gramophone faced competition from one or more of three major European rivals: Polyphon, Carl Lindström A. G., and Pathé. Polyphon Musikwerke had acquired the German affiliate of the British Gramophone, Deutsche Grammophon, after it was seized during World War I; their export label in the 1920s was Polydor, and in late 1926 they signed a joint marketing agreement with the third-largest US recording company, Brunswick.[32] Carl Lindström A. G. was a Berlin holding company that had emerged as an international force by buying out, and continuing to market, a host of prewar independent labels, notably Odeon, Parlophon, and Beka; Lindström's success during the recording boom led the company's shares to reach their highest value in 1930.[33] Pathé was a pioneering French company whose distinct technology of vertically cut ("hill-and-dale"), rather than laterally cut, discs gave it a substantial, though declining, segment of the market.

The dramatic explosion in the record industry in the late 1920s led to the formation of a number of smaller companies, as well as a variety of takeovers and consolidations. These produced one more major multinational, the UK-based Columbia which rescued its failing US parent company Columbia in 1925, took over Lindström in 1926, and bought out Pathé in 1928: "During the industry's last boom year [1929]," one recording industry historian writes, "the British Columbia became the world's largest phonographic company."[34]

The crisis of 1929 hit the recording industry hard as record sales collapsed: in the US, they dropped from 65 million discs in 1929 to 10 million in 1932 (Victor dropped from 30 million to 3 million);[35] in the UK, from 59 million discs in 1930 to 24 million in 1934;[36] in Germany, from 30 million discs in 1929 to 8 million in 1933;[37] in South Africa from 2.3 million to .7 million, in the Dutch East Indies from 1.9 million to .5 million.[38] Within a few years all of the six major recording companies—legacies of the acoustic era—had been taken over by the emerging radio- and electrical-manufacturing corporations: the US-based RCA (Radio Corporation of America) bought out Victor, creating RCA Victor; the British-based EMI (Electric & Musical Industries) took over Gramophone and British Columbia (thereby getting most of Lindström and Pathé as well); and Telefunken took over Polyphon/Deutsche Grammophon.[39]

During the boom, each of the major recording companies established an intricate network of traveling recording engineers, local agents, and musical directors that facilitated the recording of vernacular musicians for local markets. Gramophone, Victor, Lindström/Odeon, and Pathé sent engineers on regular tours of the colonial ports, supervising recording sessions arranged by the company's agents as well by local merchants, who handled the imported phonographs and records and often recruited the artists. Much of our knowledge of these early recording sessions comes from the field reports these engineers sent back to Hayes and Camden.

The recording engineers would travel through a region for three to six months, recording in a city for two weeks before moving on. The major cities of this musical archipelago would be visited once or twice a year; the master recordings would be shipped back to central pressing plants, and the shellac 78s would be re-exported for sale in the local markets, handled by dry goods dealers and furniture stores. In his memoir, the Victor recording director H. O. Sooy not only noted the recording of "some Hawaiian & Mexican vocal selections" during a June 1924 trip to Los Angeles, but he also tracked the departures and returns of Victor engineers going to East Asia and Latin America in 1924 and 1925:

June 24th, 1924: The Lindermans & Elsasser sailed from San Francisco, Calif., on the S.S. President Pierce, one p.m. for the purpose of making a repertoire of records in Shanghai, Tientsen, Pekin, Hong Kong, Canton, and in French Indo China. They returned June 10th, 1925.

October 20th, 1925: C. S. Althouse and Elmer Raguse left for Havana, Cuba, to make another repertoire of Cuban records. These being the first records we have made in Cuba electrically. (They returned November 10th.)

During July, 1925, H. O. Sooy received orders from the front to arrange to send a recorder to Buenos Aires to relieve George K. Cheney who had been ordered by the Victor Company to return. (Cheney originally sailed to Buenos Aires, December 22, 1923, to erect a Pressing Plant and act as manager of the new venture.)[40]

Electrical recording technology made location recording easier, and the recording expeditions increased dramatically in 1927 and 1928. In US "race records," the turn to field recording by Victor, Columbia and Brunswick really begins in early 1927; OKeh had begun slightly earlier but their sessions also take off in 1927 and 1928.[41] By 1928, a record reviewer was noting that "it is the pleasant occupation of Ralph S. Peer to go on expeditions throughout the South looking for such as Rabbit [Brown], and inducing them to sing their songs for Victor records on the spot."[42] Indeed, Peer's now-legendary series of recording sessions of "hillbilly" and "race" music in the southeastern United States for Victor were one circuit among many; half of the location recording sessions took place in Piedmont cities led by Atlanta and Charlotte.[43]

Recording expeditions to Latin America also took off during the recording boom, and were featured in the industry trade journal, *Talking Machine World*. Columbia's John Lilienthal spent ten months in 1927 and 1928 visiting "dealers and distributors in some fifty South and Central American cities." His account makes a marketing tour sound like high imperial adventure: "I have traveled thousands of miles by steamer, river boats, railroad, automobile, motorcycle, horseback, and cable lines, and have been in treacherous climates, where one had to use the utmost precaution regarding food, insects, and animals." Nonetheless, he found "an excellent market in these countries": "the Latin Americans have an inborn love for music" and "the phonograph industry has a vast field to work upon."[44] At the same time, Brunswick's export manager Z. E. Salisbury returned from a sales trip to Latin America and announced a "recording expedition to Havana ... the first journey outside of the continental limits of the United States of a Brunswick recording outfit," noting that "both American and European capital has been invested in Chile, Argentina, and Brazil in order to manufacture records ... made with 'local color' and from native music in order to satisfy the very normal desire of these nations that their own cultural efforts may be perpetuated on records, not only for their own enjoyment but for the ever-increasing demand by other countries for the typical music which all of these nations possess."[45]

Brunswick also recorded across the Pacific. In March 1928, the Brunswick engineers Elmer Avery and Francis H. Winters arrived in Honolulu for a week of recordings, the first electrical recording sessions in Hawaii. "The recording apparatus, consisting of a 'mike,' many hundred feet of wires, the 'cutting machine,' and other technical instruments, has been at work night and day in the Gold Room at the Young Hotel," the *Honolulu Advertiser* reported. "A canvas room was constructed to eliminate echoes and extraneous noises."[46]

If the US recording engineers of Victor, Columbia, and Brunswick focused on Latin America, the Caribbean, the Pacific, and East Asia, the Gramophone Company sent engineers around the Mediterranean and to West and South Asia. The discographer and historian Paul Vernon has tracked the travels of the Gramophone engineers, and his account of the travels of Edward Fowler is representative of their commercial "field recordings" of the late 1920s. Fowler joined Gramophone in August 1924 and worked for two years at their headquarters in Hayes (outside London), and then in Paris. Between April and September 1927, he visited Tunis, Athens, Cairo, and Istanbul; he returned to Athens and Istanbul in 1928. In the spring of 1929, he was in Cairo to record Umm Kulthūm:

> We are experiencing great difficulty in making arrangements with Omm Koulsoun, she came to the studios on Friday last at 9.30 after making an appointment for 7 o'clock. At 10.30 she started singing. After making one title which took an hour to rehearse she decided it was no good. This is the usual procedure and we are accustomed to it. Having decided she would sing no more that night she left saying she would not come again until the 4th of May. This evening she has telephoned saying she will start recording again on the 29th. You will understand it is impossible to give any date as to when we are likely to finish.[47]

In 1930, he returned to Paris to produce cabaret, jazz, and Hawaiian records, as well as the French K series of North African musics of Algerians, Moroccans, and Tunisians. He spent most of the 1930s in Naples.[48]

Though Victor and Gramophone rarely entered each other's recording spheres, both faced competition from the major continental European firms as well as smaller independent firms. The success of one company in a city quickly drew other engineers: within a few years of Gramophone's pioneering East African Swahili recordings of 1928, Columbia was recording in Zanzibar and Dar es Salaam, Odeon was recording in Mombassa and Kampala, and Pathé was bringing Swahili musicians to Marseilles.[49] When Brunswick organized the first electrical recording session in Honolulu in March 1928, OKeh/ Columbia quickly followed in May.[50] Victor's success in East Asia spurred Brunswick's recording expeditions in Canton and Manila in November 1929.[51]

Odeon/Lindström was a particularly important competitor because it pioneered local recording, preceding Gramophone in Athens by a year, and making the earliest Yoruba records in Lagos.[52] In a number of port cities, Odeon's agents—often immigrant entrepreneurs from Europe—used their position to establish local recording companies: in Argentina, Odeon's agent was the Ukrainian Jewish immigrant Max Glücksmann, who opened a pressing plant in Buenos Aires in 1913, and became virtually autonomous during World War I, issuing pioneering tango records like Carlos Gardel's "Mi noche triste" (1917) on the Discos Nacional label. Glücksmann was, Paul Vernon argues, "an independent producer and distributor, certainly the first in Latin America and arguably the first in the world to successfully concentrate on a specific format."[53] In Brazil, Odeon's representative was the Czech-born immigrant from the US, Fred Figner, who had created Casa Edison in 1900. Figner opened the first record-pressing plant in Rio in 1912, Fábrica Odeon, made the legendary first samba recording, Donga's "Pelo Telefone" (1917), and dominated Brazilian recording until the late 1920s.[54] In the US, Odeon's partner was Otto Heinemann, a German-speaking immigrant entrepreneur, who founded the OKeh label that pioneered the recording of blues and jazz: Ralph Peer was OKeh's recording director in New York from 1920 to 1925, before moving to Victor.[55] In India, Odeon became the leading label in vernacular musics by developing regional links with independent stores—Ruby Records in Bombay, Saraswati Stores in Madras, Taylor's Gramophone Salon in Calcutta, Tas-O-Phone in Madurai: "each of these agents organized the recording sessions in their region and made the decision as to which recordings were to be released and how frequently."[56] In Batavia, Odeon's early partner was Tio Tek Hong, who created his own Tio Tek Hong Records around 1925.[57]

The masters made at these recording sessions were usually shipped back to Europe or North America for pressing. The factories manufacturing gramophones and pressing shellac discs required large capital investment, and at the beginning of the recording boom, they were virtually all owned by the major companies and located in industrial districts outside their home metropolises: the Gramophone factory was in Hayes, Middlesex, just outside London; the Victor factory was in Camden, New Jersey, outside Philadelphia; the Polyphon factory was in Hanover; the Lindström factory was in Weissensee, outside Berlin; and the Pathé factory was in Châtou, outside Paris. The major exception to this pattern was Gramophone's Calcutta factory. Opened in 1908, just after Gramophone's Hayes factory (1907), it was the center of Gramophone's production not only for colonial India but also for China, Southeast Asia, and East Africa.

The electrical recording boom of the 1920s led to the opening of new pressing plants around the world: Victor's Argentine subsidiary—the Pan American Recording Company—established a pressing plant in Buenos Aires in 1924;[58] in 1928, Gramophone moved its South Asian production to a new record-pressing complex in Dum Dum, on the outskirts of Calcutta; and the Pathé factory in Shanghai was the "most important and biggest record factory in China until RCA built its factory in Shanghai at the beginning of 1930 and became Pathé's strongest competitor."[59]

Independent record labels often contracted the pressing of their discs to the larger multinationals. For example, Baidaphone, the independent record company in the Middle East and North Africa, had their discs manufactured at a Berlin record factory.[60] By the early 1930s, a number of independent labels in India—"private recorders" as they were known—were using Gramophone's Calcutta plant, and similar locally owned labels in China—known as "pocketbook" companies—contracted recording and manufacturing to the Pathé and RCA Victor facilities in Shanghai.[61]

To set up the recording sessions and to market the records, the recording engineers depended on local agents, usually dry goods or furniture merchants for whom a supply of records promoted the sale of record players. They issued catalogs every few months, which often included song lyrics, biographies, and pictures of the artists, as well as lists of the recordings.

However, the most important figure in these sessions was the musical director. A key intermediary between the traveling engineers, the local merchants, and the musicians, the musical director united the distinct worlds of electrical recording and vernacular musicking. He—I have not found a woman in this role—recruited the musicians, drew up the arrangements, and even transcribed the music so it could be filed for copyright.[62] In addition, the musical director and his band often accompanied the singers being recorded. If the engineers and managers were often foreign, agents of the overseas company, the musical director was local, a product of the musical institutions of the colonial port. The most successful musical directors were those who bridged the worlds of cultivated music, commercial dance halls, and rural folk styles, formally trained "reading" musicians who also knew the vernacular idioms.

In Brazil, for example, by the late 1920s, Odeon, Victor, Columbia, and Brunswick not only "employed foreign general managers [and] technicians (the 'gate-keepers')" but also a "few local maestros (as 'artistic directors') and musicians to care of the 'local colour' of the music."[63] It was these local maestros—among them Pixinguinha and Radamés Gnattali—who, Wander Nunes Frota argues, "tried to integrate local music with the new foreign technology and as a result ended up devising a sort of local trademark orchestration for their recordings."[64] The choro flutist Pixinguinha, who had become celebrated after traveling to Paris with his band, Os Oito Batutas, in 1922, became an arranger and conductor for Victor, while the classical composer Gnattali served in a similar role for Columbia. Similarly, in Argentina, the classically trained pianist Adolfo Carabelli became Victor's artistic director in 1926, leading the label's house tango orchestra, the Orquesta Típica Victor, and overseeing the label's tango and jazz recordings.[65]

"The recording companies," Nicholas Pappas observes of Athens, "had been quick to realize that the best way to foster talent among the seemingly inexhaustible ranks of the refugee community [from Anatolia] was to appoint as their recording directors the community's foremost performer." As a result, the early stars of rebetika including Róza Eskenázi and Ríta Abatzí "owed their quick rise to prominence after 1930 to musical directors of the three great recording companies."[66] The "director in charge at Columbia at that time was Dimítris Sémsis or Salonikiós (the best violin in the Balkans), who was among the top-ranking musicians playing popular music," a contemporary, Stellákis Perpiniádis, recalled:

> Once we went together somewhere to eat and drink and then when we got in high spirits, he fetched the violin and began playing a variety of tunes: Turkish, Arabic, Serbian, Spanish, Romanian, Hungarian, Bulgarian, Gypsy. Immediately all the wallets of the customers present were emptied on our table. When he played all the gods climbed down to watch him, when he played your heart would bleed.[67]

In Istanbul, the Armenian musician and composer Kanuni Artaki Candan-Terzian played a similar role as recording director when the Turkish division of His Master's Voice—Sahabinin Sesi—was established in 1925; Artaki was not only a distinguished kanun player who accompanied various singers, but knew music theory and could "read the old neumatic notation."[68]

It seems that Zonophone's series of West African recordings in London in 1927 were organized by Roland Nathaniels,[69] a West African student, pianist, and organist who had earlier recorded Christian hymns (in Latin as well as Ewe translation) as well as Ibo folk songs and dances for Zonophone, and by the guitarist and concertina player George Williams Aingo: one discographer writes that Aingo's "influence is most heard throughout the series itself, as a featured vocalist in a number of dialects, as accompanist to other artists, as the musical director of a number of sessions and, one is led to suspect, general advisor to Zonophone on West African musical matters."[70] Similarly, after Griffiths Motsieloa made the pioneering trip to London from South Africa to record in 1930, he became a musical director and talent scout for Gallo's Singer label; to compete, Columbia hired the classically trained music critic Mark Radebe.[71] And in North Africa, the "staid" and "elegant" classical singer Mahieddine Bachtarzi, the "Algerian Caruso,"[72] was recruited by Gramophone to record artists in Tunisia, Algeria, and Morocco.[73]

In the United States, the creation of separate "race record" divisions by the recording companies also depended on such musical directors, including Thomas Dorsey, Mayo Williams, and Lonnie Johnson.[74] A representative and ubiquitous figure was Clarence Williams, a New Orleans Creole piano player, the son of a bassist, who started a black-owned music publishing house in New Orleans with A. J. Piron, before moving to Chicago, and then to New York, where he became the race record director and talent scout for OKeh from 1923 to 1928. Williams organized the early sessions of the pioneering New Orleans jazz instrumentalists Louis Armstrong and Sidney Bechet, as well as of urban vaudeville blues singers like Bessie Smith, often accompanying the musicians on piano.[75] "I guess that I've been on or else made about five thousand records," he later recalled. "There was one time I figured I was losin' money being under contract to OKeh, and so I recorded under lots of different names, the Blue Five, Lazy Levee Loungers, the Blue Four, Washboard Footwarmers, Jazz Kings, and many others."[76]

When Brunswick brought electrical recording equipment to Honolulu in 1928, they recruited the songwriter Charles E. King as musical director and hired Johnny Noble, the director of the Moana Orchestra, to assemble "artists from all over the island group" and supervise the recordings in Honolulu. "'We want this music recorded exactly as it is played here in Hawaii, and not as the theatrical manager back in New York would probably suggest,' said [Brunswick representative E.] Avery, before sailing. 'We are also selecting old-time standard numbers, because they have proven their popularity, and they will be enduring.'"[77]

These musical directors served to link the two classes of musicians—the ear-trained itinerant street musicians and the artisan "reading" musicians—that were central to the new vernacular phonograph musics. Indeed, in their involvement with the recording industry, the conservatory-trained world of orchestras and opera, and the music of the streets and dance halls, figures like Pixinguinha, Salonikiós, and Johnny Noble stood at the fault lines of the world of music at a time when cultivated, popular, and folk musics were all undergoing profound change.

Vernacular Phonograph Music and the World Musical Guild

If the sound recordings of vernacular music transformed the "music industry," the economy of world musical space, it also transformed the symbolic system that structured world musical space, that imaginative world-system that mapped the musical places of the world. Analyzing the symbolic world-system of literature, Pascale Casanova wrote of a "world republic of letters," in which certain consecrated places of accumulated literary capital serve as a "Greenwich meridian of literature." "The world of letters," she writes, "is a relatively unified space characterized by the opposition between the great national literary spaces, which are also the oldest—and, accordingly, the best endowed—and those literary spaces that have more recently appeared and that are poor by comparison." It has its own "literary economy ... based on a 'market' ... in which the sole value recognized by all participants—literary value—circulates and is traded."[78] There is no exact musical equivalent for the literary notion of a "republic of letters," but perhaps the notion of a "musical guild"—a term that has, over the centuries, referred to the medieval craft organizations of musicians, the early

modern concert-giving groups sponsored by aristocrats and coffee-
houses, the families that produced generations of musicians, the late
nineteenth-century benevolent societies that offered singing classes
to working-class men and women, and the twentieth-century labor
unions of musicians—captures the sense of a musical space as an
autonomous field with its own systems of value.[79]

In the nineteenth century, there were distinct musical guilds with
little or no overlap or intersection. The European musical guild was
built around two centers of transcendent value: Italian opera with its
symbolic home at Milan's La Scala, and the German symphonic tradition figured by Mozart, Haydn, and Beethoven. This cultural field was
structured by an elaborate hierarchy of concert halls and opera houses,
musical academies and publishers, and was echoed in European settler
colonies around the world. At the edges of this musical world were the
peasant musics of agricultural villages, part of the "national" soundscape at least since the folk-song collectors of the early nineteenth
century and the polka craze of the 1840s: folk airs and dances were
regularly incorporated into refined music by a variety of composers.[80]
"Lighter" forms—from Viennese waltz to Parisian operetta—took
their place in this musical field, as did the popular styles of urban cafés
and dance halls of varying degrees of refinement.[81]

Across Asia and Africa lay other guilds often tied to aristocratic or
courtly circles or to religious orders: the learned traditions of Arabic
maqam, the ragas of North India, the Carnatic tradition of South India,
the opera traditions of Canton and Beijing, the gamelan orchestras of
the East Indies. Each of these musical guilds had large repertoires and
its own "common practice" that required long apprenticeship to master.
Though these musical guilds were aware of each other through travelers' accounts, imperial conquests, and the great world's fairs—iconic
encounters range from the 1871 world premiere of Verdi's *Aida* in the
new Khedivial Opera House in Cairo to the landmark performance
of a Javanese gamelan orchestra at the 1889 Paris Exposition—few
musicians moved from one sonic space to another.

The initial emergence of sound recording in the acoustic era did not
significantly unsettle these established musical guilds, largely because
the acoustic recording boom in the decade before World War I concentrated on the most cultivated and consecrated musics. This was as
true in Istanbul, Havana, and Bombay, as in London and New York.
The apparatuses of cylinders, discs, and talking machines were initially
marketed as parlor furniture for the households of the established and

cultivated classes. The prestigious "Red Label" series of Gramophone and Victor, which featured opera stars as well as virtuoso pianists and violinists, set the tone among elite listeners throughout the archipelago of colonial ports. Thus, the celebrated recording trips that Fred Gaisberg took around the world after 1901 led him to record musics patronized by local elites, whether in England or China, Russia or India. Gaisberg's classic 1902 recordings of the great opera singers who had appeared at Milan's La Scala—the Italian tenor Enrico Caruso and the Russian bass Feodor Chaliapin—were accompanied in the same year by his recordings of the celebrated Hindustani singer Gauhar Jaan.[82] The only exception was Gaisberg's trip to record Tartar music, and he himself emphasized its unusual and unwelcome nature: "the better-class Tartars adapt European music to their native idiom," he wrote. "So to the working-man's cafés and to the low-class brothels we went, since they were the only avenues for the Tartar songs we wished to record. Altogether it was an unsavory business that we concluded as quickly as possible before our return to Moscow."[83]

This pattern of recording cultivated musics continued throughout the acoustic era. Columbia was recording Cantonese Opera from 1903, and beginning in 1908, Pathé began "a massive schedule of recording in China," covering almost all of Beijing and Cantonese Opera performances.[84] In Cairo, the local Sama al-Muluk (Choice of Kings) label recorded court musician Yusuf al-Manyalawi between 1908 and 1911[85]; in Istanbul, Gramophone's William Sinkler Darby recorded Ottoman court music, including the *taksims* of the virtuoso Tanburi Cemil Bey;[86] and, in Bombay, Gramophone recorded the learned court musicians of North India, like Abdul Karim Khan.[87] "Of all south Indian music genres deployed by the Gramophone Company during the 1910s," the historian Stephen Hughes writes, "classical Carnatic music held the key to reaching their targeted upper-class south Indian audiences. The privileging of Carnatic music was, at least in part, a commercial strategy to tap into the existing networks of elite patronage and music appreciation."[88]

At the same time, folklorists and ethnographers used acoustic sound recording to capture the "folk" musics of peasants and indigenous peoples: in 1907, Frances Densmore began recording American Indian musics for the Smithsonian Institution, and in 1908 Béla Bartók began recording Magyar peasant songs.[89] But these recordings did not transform the musical guild, for they were still subordinated to the publication of printed transcriptions of folk songs. These field recordings were not released commercially, but were intended either as documents in ethnological museums—like the Berliner Phonogramm-Archiv founded by Erich von Hornbostel in 1905—or as raw materials for cultivated composers like Bartók.

In contrast, the twin Copernican revolutions of vernacular phonograph records in the mid-1920s—placing sound recordings and vernacular music at the center of the musical universe—had profound and unsettling effects on the world's musical guilds. Foreshadowed by the "dance crazes" on the eve of the Great War, when the maxixe, the tango, and the foxtrot stormed the cultural capital of Paris in 1912 and 1913, and then reverberated back to polite society in Rio de Janeiro, Buenos Aires, and New York, the overlapping waves of recorded tango, jazz, hula, and rumba in the 1920s challenged the symbolic hierarchies of the musical world-system. These "modern dance musics" created new musical capitals, as Paris, London, and Vienna appeared to be conquered by Havana and Honolulu, New Orleans and Buenos Aires.

The upheaval in the symbolic space of the musical guild can be sensed in the controversies and debates over what to call the new sounds and how to hear them. Often these musics were simply called "jazz," a capacious term that came to encompass all forms of "modern dance" from the foxtrot to the tango. As a result, the intense metropolitan debate over the nature of "popular music" triggered by the vernacular phonograph musics—a debate that has reverberated for nearly a century—usually focused on "jazz." In London, Paris, New York, Berlin, and Vienna, composers, conductors, and music critics argued the merits of "jazz": from *Ballets Russes* orchestra conductor Ernest Ansermet's well-known appreciation of the Southern Syncopated Orchestra with Sidney Bechet in 1919, to the French composer Darius Milhaud's 1924 account of his encounter with jazz in New York;[90] from the pioneering analyses by American composers Virgil Thomson (in *American Mercury* in 1924) and Aaron Copland (in *Modern Music* in 1927), to the polemical interventions of European critics like André Schaeffner (the author of the first French study of jazz, *Le Jazz,* in 1926) and Theodor Adorno (the 1928 "The Curves of the Needle" inaugurated his lasting critique of the effects of recording and radio on popular musics).[91]

However, the use of the term "jazz" by writers at the time can be misleading. It does not capture the difficulty felt by the young South African Zulu writer B. W. Vilakazi as he tried to describe the music of his countryman Reuben Caluza, which had been recorded by His Master's Voice in 1930: "There is no name in music libraries for purely Caluza music but for lack of an apt word we call it jazz. Jazz music is somewhat inferior to the sort of music found in Caluza's compositions."[92] Similarly, when the Yoruba writer Isaac Delano describes the popular Yoruba dances of Lagos, he draws on jazz analogies, noting that "The music for the 'Sakara' dance is like that of a jazz band," whereas "the 'Ashiko' dance is ... rather quicker than the 'Sakara' or the Blues, and resembles a fox-trot."[93]

Thus, it would be wrong to understand these vernacular phonograph musics as simply versions of US jazz, marking the emergence of a "jazz planet."[94] Though US jazz was one of these vernacular phonograph musics, and had worldwide reverberations, its relation to the other musics was often contested. Some musicians adopted jazz standards and created lasting musical fusions: one thinks of the gypsy jazz of guitarist Django Reinhardt or the hula blues of the Hawaiian steel guitarist Sol Ho'opi'i, who recorded "St Louis Blues" as well as "Aloha Oe." But such fusions often provoked resistance. Pixinguinha, the Brazilian *chorão*, faced criticism throughout the 1920s for becoming *jazzificado*—jazzified—after taking up the saxophone (he had become famous on flute) and incorporating foxtrot rhythms.[95] In Hawaii, two of the most celebrated songwriters took contrary positions: Johnny Noble became well known in the early 1920s for his attempt to bring jazz into Hawaiian music, figured by his song "Hula Blues." "The younger set had been infected with the jazz rhythms of the mainland bands," he recalled in 1944. "I was trying to keep up with the times and decided that if I didn't change the style of playing Hawaiian music my band would be just another Hawaiian orchestra."[96] In contrast, Charles King, the Hawaiian bandleader and composer, criticized the mixing of jazz and Hawaiian songs: "Compose your own jazz and swing music, but let our native melodies remain as they are in their special niche," he said on a Honolulu radio broadcast in the late 1930s. "Let us have enough pride in our own music to keep it pure."[97] Similarly, in Cuba, the composer Emilio Grenet worried, in a 1939 publication sponsored by the Cuban government, about the influence of jazz on local styles: "jazz submerged our *danzón* into the most absolute oblivion." He added the qualification that "cultivation of the jazz made possible the triumph of our *rumba*. Cuban music with the American accent of the saxophone was as interesting a melodic element for Americans as their trombone glissades and their acrobatic drumsticks had been for us."[98]

This confusion about the term "jazz" has also bedeviled discussions of the figure who has come to epitomize the battle over the vernacular phonograph musics: the German philosopher and music critic Theodor Adorno, whose essays of the 1920s and 1930s denounced jazz, popular music, and radio music. Defenders of jazz have long criticized Adorno for his dismissal of it; in response, his supporters have often argued that what he called "jazz" was not what the jazz critics thought of as jazz. This led to a recurring debate: was Adorno thinking of the "symphonized syncopations" of Paul Whiteman's hotel dance band, or of the improvisations of Louis Armstrong? If he meant Whiteman, perhaps he was right; if he meant Armstrong, surely he was mistaken. However, casting the debate about Adorno simply around US jazz is misleading.

Like many of his contemporaries, Adorno began from the ambiguity of the term "jazz," and used it to sum up all of the modern dance musics that emerged in the wake of the Great War: "jazz … is that type of dance music … that has existed since the war and is distinguished from what preceded it by its decidedly modern quality … Musically, this 'modernity' refers primarily to sound and rhythm," to vibrato and syncopation. For Adorno, as for many listeners and many musicians, jazz, rumba, hula, and tango were part of the same musical world: in his 1933 essay, "Farewell to Jazz," he writes of jazz's "world-economic resonance in cheap foreign locales that could be imported at will from Montevideo, Waikiki, and Shanghai"; in the famous 1936 essay, "On Jazz," he explicitly writes of tango as a music "accepted as jazz," and includes "the first rumba" side by side with "hot music" and Duke Ellington.[99]

One could conclude that Adorno was confused or ignorant. However, Adorno's perception was shared by many contemporaries. For example, the 1922 account of "jazz latitude" by the American foreign correspondent Burnet Hershey, often cited as an image of US jazz conquering the planet, conveys this wider sense of "jazz":

> Every ship the traveler takes today throbs with the staccato cacophony of jazz and every stop at a port is punctuated by the syncopation of jazz. Jazz latitude is marked as indelibly on the globe as the heavy line of the equator. It runs from Broadway along Main Street to San Francisco to the Hawaiian Islands, which had lyricized it to fame; to Japan, where it is hurriedly adopted as some new Western culture; to the Philippines, where it is royally welcomed back as its own; to China, where the mandarins and even the coolies look upon it as a hopeful sign that the Occident

at last knows what is music; to Siam, where the barbaric tunes strike a kindred note and come home to roost; to India, where the natives receive it dubiously, while the colonists seize upon it avidly; to the East Indies, where it holds sway in its elementary form—ragtime; to Egypt, where it sounds so curiously familiar and where it has set Cairo dance-mad; to Palestine, where it is looked upon as an inevitable and necessary evil along with liberation; across the Mediterranean, where all ships and all shores have been inoculated with the germ; to Monte Carlo and the Riviera, where the jazz idea has been adopted as its own *enfant-chéri*; to Paris, which has its special versions of jazz; to London, which long has sworn to shake off the fever, but still is jazzing and back again to Tin Pan Alley, where each day, nay, each hour, adds some new inspiration that will slowly but surely meander along jazz latitude.[100]

Hershey's "jazz" clearly refers to the vernacular dance musics generally ("lyricized" to fame by Hawaii), rather than to the African-American jazz of Sidney Bechet, King Oliver, and Louis Armstrong that was first recorded the following year. Even in the 1925 essay "Jazz at Home," in the landmark anthology of the Harlem Renaissance, *The New Negro*, the African-American journalist J. A. Rogers linked jazz to a variety of vernacular musics:

> In its elementals, jazz has always existed. It is in the Indian war-dance, the Highland fling, the Irish jig, the Cossack dance, the Spanish fandango, the Brazilian *maxixe*, the dance of the whirling dervish, the hula hula of the South Seas, the *danse du ventre* of the Orient, the *carmagnole* of the French Revolution, the strains of Gypsy music, and the ragtime of the Negro.[101]

To understand why hula was heard as jazz, we need to suspend *our* sense of the lines between jazz, tango, son, and hula, each informed by carefully tended, nationally defined canons.

For it is not simply that "jazz quickly became a global music," as Jeffrey Jackson argues, gaining "listeners in Britain, Germany, Italy, Eastern Europe, the Soviet Union, and beyond."[102] Rather, "jazz" was a metaphor for the musical revolution taking place, as the recordings of popular dance musics created a "world-economic resonance" of "cheap foreign locales," to use Adorno's infelicitous phrase. Paris's Pigalle, Michael Dregni argues, was a melting pot of the world's music: "the finest tango *orquestas típicas* outside Buenos Aires and Montevideo, Tzigane bands serenading the Russian cabarets, and other bars with bands playing West Indian and Latin beats driving fashions for dances from the beguine to the zamba."[103] The Parisian music halls that helped "make jazz French," Jackson notes, "exhibited an international character, offering listeners the chance to hear polkas, South American tangos, Russian folk music, Spanish songs, music from Asia, and popular music from the United States, including jazz."[104]

But such accounts suggest that these musics were distinct and unconnected; in fact, the same musicians may well have played in several of these bands, participating in an interconnected network of musical idioms. Consider the world inhabited by the guitarist Oscar Alemán. Born in Argentina in 1909, but orphaned in Santos, Brazil, Alemán began by playing the Brazilian *cavaquinho*, and then joined Gastón Bueno Lobo in a group called Les Loups, recording "Hawaiian" tangos like "La Cumparsita"* and foxtrots for Victor in Buenos Aires in 1927 and 1928. They went to Europe in 1929 as a Hawaiian duo but Alemán went on to lead a swing quintet, recording sambas and rumbas; he was also in the band that backed Josephine Baker.[105] Alemán might be seen as a marginal figure to each of these musics, neither jazz nor Hawaiian, neither samba nor tango; alternately, he might be taken as a quintessential figure of the new music, mediating between the exotic and the vernacular, Paris and Rio, by way of Honolulu, Havana, and Harlem.

"Jazz" is thus perhaps best seen as one of the riot of new names for vernacular musicking that emerged in the first two decades of the century, names that were used to categorize the sounds and make them understandable, "hearable." "The very act of naming a genre … may … be a declaration of cultural consolidation," Christopher Waterman argued in his study of West African musics, since "musical style may articulate and define communal values in heterogeneous, rapidly transforming societies."[106] From the first emergence of the vernacular phonograph musics, aficionados as well as scholars argued over the meanings and etymologies of these new names: tango, samba, rebetika, shi dai qu, jùjú, kroncong, marabi, rumba, calypso, jazz, ṭarab.

Since "the tango is the most widely known Argentine accomplishment," Jorge Luis Borges wrote in 1927, "we should investigate its origins and construct for it a genealogy that will lack neither deifying legends nor ascertainable truths."[107] However, decades of subsequent controversy have hardly separated legend from truth: tango, we are told, might be derived from an African word for a place, a Portuguese word meaning to touch, or simply an onomatopoeic representation of a drum-beat; in any case, it seems to appear throughout the

Spanish-speaking world as a term for black dances.[108] Celebrating these multiple meanings, Robert Farris Thompson concludes that "the creole word *tango* ... refers to drums, dance, and place."[109]

Samba had its commercial birth when Donga registered "Pelo Telefone" as a "Samba Carnavalesco" in 1916; but the word has been plausibly traced to a half-dozen different African languages, usually referring to a dance, rhythm, or skip: "the very richness and multiplicity of these variants spread over a wide area of Africa," one historian writes, "may well have helped to establish the word 'samba' as a stock term for a cluster of dances."[110]

"Perhaps the two most convincing etymologies" of rebetika, a recent scholar writes, "are Turkish and ancient Greek, one possible root being the Turkish *rembet*, meaning the untamable one, the rebel, and another being the ancient Greek *rembomai*, a verb meaning to be unsteady, to act at random." However, another scholar argues that the term was the invention of the European and American record labels marketing the music in the mid-1920s.[111] In China, the music came to be known as *shi dai qu*, "modern songs," though one scholar argues that this term was only used in Hong Kong, and insists on *huangse yinyue*, "yellow music" (which, yet another scholar argues, is better translated as "blue music").[112] In Nigeria, there are several popular etymologies for the term *jùjú*: one account says it was coined to imitate the sound of the tambourine played by Tunde King's percussionist; another sees it as a satiric reversal of the colonizer's contemptuous name for traditional Yoruba practices.[113] Kroncong emerged as both the name of an instrument—the small plucked lute with four or five strings—and an onomatopoeia for the sound of strumming or the jangling of ankle bells or tambourines; it later came to refer to the ensemble, the repertoire, and the idiom itself.[114] Marabi was a word applied not only to a musical style but to a dance, a social occasion, and the rough characters who attended marabi parties: its etymologies include a Sotho phrase for flying around, a Pretoria district where domestic workers lived, and the Sotho slang for gangsters.[115]

Sometimes the names took shape as the music migrated: though "rumba" signified a particular dance in Cuba, commercial music publishers adopted it to refer to all Cuban music as recordings circulated to Lagos and Paris, Kinshasa and Singapore.[116] "Without fear of exaggerating," the Cuban musician Emilio Grenet wrote in 1939, "we can say that the typical Cuban *rumba* is not known abroad where the music known as *rumba* is in reality a *son* with a faster tempo than required by the eastern dance."[117] In a similar controversy, the calypso singer Atilla the Hun insisted that "every competent writer on the subject is agreed that the term calypso is a misnomer," the "result of irresponsible journalese" in the 1930s; unlike calypso, associated with "Greek mythology," he suggested that kaiso might derive from "an African word meaning bravo or well done."[118] "Jazz" itself was controversial. Though it seems to have emerged in the 1910s as New Orleans bands—the Creole Jazz Band and the Original Dixieland Jass Band— traveled the vaudeville circuit,[119] the music's most celebrated early innovators—Louis Armstrong and Sidney Bechet—did not use the term, calling their music "ragtime."[120]

There is a striking antinomy in many of these names: on the one hand, they are marketing categories, emerging commercial genres that segment audiences as consumers; on the other hand, they point to emotional states provoked by the music or to musical actions, ways of playing, that elude naming ("It don't mean a thing if it ain't got that swing," as the title of a 1932 Duke Ellington recording put it). *Tarab* was not only the name for the urban secular Arabic music, but named the "ecstasy" the music created in performers and auditors alike.[121] Kaiso also had this double meaning: "Kaiso was used to describe the song when sung," Atilla noted, "as well as a means of expressing ecstatic satisfaction over what was in the opinion of the audience a particularly excellent kaiso."[122] One even sees this antinomy in Clarence Williams's claim that he was "the first to use the word 'jazz' on a song." While claiming commercial precedence—"On both *Brown Skin, Who You For?* and *Mama's Baby Boy*, I used the words 'jazz song' on the sheet music"—he also acknowledges its wider meaning as a form of musical ecstasy: "I don't exactly remember where the words come from, but I remember I heard a woman say it to me when we were playin' some music. 'Oh, jazz me, baby,' she said."[123]

If the coining of new names was one sign of the musical revolution taking place, another was the common perception that all this "jazz" was "noise." A Dutch journalist reported that the name of the kroncong singer Miss Riboet meant "noisy" in Malay—"hardly the stage name to be chosen by a European Star."[124] "The word 'jazz' signifies noise in America and is in no way a dance," the 1922 edition of the *Encyclopedia Britannica* pronounced.[125] In New York, a *New York Times* journalist referred to jazz musicians as "the masters of noise acrobatics."[126] In Paris, jazz was heard as "le tumulte noir"—black noise;[127] a historian of jazz in France notes that "many simply equated jazz with 'noise.'"[128]

Similarly, "in Japanese mass media," E. Taylor Atkins has noted, "the word *noise* (*sōon*) was often used to describe jazz's sound and, conversely, the word *jazz* was synonymous with *noise* ... [and] came to represent not only dance music but also the constant indecipherable noise generated by machinery, phonographs, and radios."[129] The South African music critic Mark Radebe looked "forward to a time when our eardrums will not be shattered by a pandemonium of horrible noises," and referred to jazz as "noise-drunk."[130]

It is tempting to dismiss these complaints, but that would miss the centrality of noise in the history of music, a point insisted upon by Jacques Attali in his powerful polemic, *Noise*. The history of music is, he suggested, "a succession of orders ... done violence by noises ... that are prophetic because they create new orders, unstable and changing."[131] The controversy over noise in the 1920s is particularly interesting, because it involved two different senses of noise. On the one hand, noise in the 1920s was often associated with the upsetting industrial sounds of machines and new technologies: "the jazz band," a French critic wrote in 1922, "is the panting of the machine, the trepidation of the automobile, the train that squeaks on the rails, the tramway that passes shaking the clock."[132] On the other hand, noise was associated with the musics and sounds of the "primitive" and the "exotic," the musics of colonized Africa and Asia. "The music of blacks ... has been judged, even by the least severe critics, as more deafening than beautiful," the Cuban folklorist Israel Castellanos wrote in 1927; "the majority of their instruments tend to make noise rather than agreeable sounds."[133] These two conceptions of noise mark the twofold nature of musical revolution taking place, at once technological and vernacular. The new musical idioms were not "agreeable sounds" but were the creation of new musical orders out of the noise of the machine and the noise of the unruly decolonizing crowd.

The upheaval in the symbolic space of the musical guild was also registered in a cluster of landmark essays and musical congresses that appeared in these years across the Atlantic, Mediterranean, and Pacific arcs. In Latin America, the young Argentine writer Jorge Luis Borges published what has been called the "first mythology" of tango, "Genealogy of the Tango," in 1927;[134] the Brazilian poet, Mário de Andrade, not only published his *Ensaio sobre a música brasileira* in 1928 but began a series of short newspaper articles on new phonograph discs;[135] and the Martiniquan writer Andrée Nardal published "Notes on the Biguine Créole" in 1931.[136] The revaluation of Afro-Cuban musics was marked by the early essays of the folklorist Fernando Ortiz—"El estudio de la música afrocubana" (1929) led to his series of monographs on Afro-Cuban music beginning in 1935[137]—and of the poet Alejo Carpentier, whose "Los valores universales de la música cubana" (1930) foreshadowed his pathbreaking *Music in Cuba* a decade later.[138] In the US, Alain Locke's "The Negro in American Culture" (1929), which led to his pioneering book of 1936, *The Negro and His Music*, and poet Sterling Brown's "The Blues as Folk Poetry" (1930) inaugurated the debate among African-American writers over the "seculars," the popular blues appearing on "race records" in the United States.[139] Across the black Atlantic, the young black South African music critic Mark Radebe began a series of articles on Bantu music in *Umteteli wa Bantu* in 1930.

At the same time one finds a similar cluster of interventions on the musics of the Mediterranean arc. The Spanish poet Federico García Lorca delivered his famous lecture on flamenco in New York in 1930, and the Andalucian nationalist Blas Infante wrote a series of essays on the origins of flamenco between 1929 and 1933.[140] At the 1932 Cairo Conference on Arab Music, Arab musicians and composers debated the use of European instruments and notation with European musicologists including Erich Hornbostel and Curt Sachs; the singer Umm Kulthūm performed at the Congress's evening concerts, and Mansûr Awad and Béla Bartók directed the recording by Gramophone of nearly two hundred discs of musicians from across North Africa and the Middle East.[141]

The Cairo congress echoed similar movements for musical reform in Asia that combined rhetorics of modernization and nationalism while grappling with the remaking of world musical space by the gramophone. A series of All-India Music Conferences that debated issues of notation, recording, and sound led to the formation of the Madras Music Academy in 1928, a key part of the renaissance in South Indian Karnatic music;[142] and a wave of music reformers associated with the May Fourth Movement in China led to the formation of the Shanghai Conservatory in 1927.[143] And in the Pacific, the young Hawaiian ethnographer Mary Kawena Pukui began her pioneering studies of traditional hula in the early 1930s.[144]

In these essays and conferences, a generation of young modernist intellectuals in the colonial ports began to develop the aesthetic lenses through which the vernacular musics were viewed, or rather, the aesthetic woofers and political tweeters through which they were heard.

In these controversies within and around the musical guild, three common figures emerged as ways of comprehending the new noise: "folk music," "gypsy music," and "light music."

The first framework for hearing the new vernacular records was "folk music," drawing on a century of established ideologies of the "folk."[145] Lisbon's fado was, Rodney Gallop wrote in 1933, "the spontaneous music of the plebeian populace of Lisbon, just as much as the folk-songs are that of the peasants, and, like the *chansons vécues* of the French artisan, may perhaps most fairly be defined as 'urban folk-song.'"[146] Similarly, Alejo Carpentier wrote in 1930 that son was "a product unique to us, as authentically Cuban as any *danza* or bolero ... [it] has created by means of its *lyrics* a style of popular poetry as genuinely creole as peasant *décimas* could ever be ... A whole Antillean mythology ... lives in those couplets."[147]

The "folk" framework was particularly attractive because folklorists had seized on recording to collect rural musics in ever-expanding field expeditions: Béla Bartók across Eastern Europe, Turkey, and North Africa from 1906 to 1918 (and later in 1932 and 1936),[148] Helen Roberts in Hawaii in 1923–1924,[149] Hugh Tracey in Mozambique and Rhodesia in 1929,[150] Yusuf Ziya Bey in Anatolian Turkey between 1926 and 1929,[151] Marcel Griaule across West Africa in the 1931 Dakar–Djibouti mission,[152] Alan Lomax across the US South and the Caribbean beginning in 1931,[153] and Mário de Andrade in the Brazilian northeast in 1938.[154] As the US composer Aaron Copland noted in 1937,

> In this field the phonograph is well-nigh indispensable. There is an immense difference between taking down an indigenous song by means of our imperfect system of notation and hearing the same from the lips of the native singer. It is not always realized what a small portion of the world's music is familiar to us. With the phonograph one can listen to new worlds of sound: the sonorous languor of a Balinese gamalang, the dulcet flutes of the Incas of Peru, the astonishing virtuosity of the flamenco singer of Andalusia. It would be difficult to exaggerate the importance of these new fields of musical exoticism opened by the phonograph.[155]

Even the commercial companies invoked this rhetoric, as when Victor insisted that

> Victor specialists have travelled to the lofty heights of the Andes, where the traditional music of the Incas has been preserved for all time by

Victor records. The weird music of the African jungle, as preserved by the negroes of the West Indies, has been recorded. But by far the most important achievements have been the successes of our specialists in penetrating the remote provinces of China, Japan, and Korea.[156]

However, the vernacular phonograph musics did not fit easily into the framework of "peasant musics," the traditional folk practices of rural agricultural communities. The emerging ideology of folk music led many collectors and folklorists to discount the urban and commercial musics, lamenting the corruption and commercialization of folk music as both repertoire and instrumentation changed. "It is my belief that city-Arab music generally is far behind Arab peasant music with regard to animation and originality," Bartók wrote in his 1933 reflections on the Cairo congress. "The urban music frequently sounds stilted, affected, and artificial; the peasant music, on the other hand, gives the impression of being a far more spontaneous and vivid manifestation despite its primitiveness."[157] "So it is in East and South Sumatra," the Dutch musicologist Jaap Kunst lamented in 1936,

> where, also as a result of Western economic expansion, the Javanese music in less cultivated forms has superseded the original music; so it is with the monotonous and empty ditties, known as Stambul and krontjong music, which estrange the Indonesians from their own art; elsewhere the influence of the Christian missions has killed the old songs and dances, but in most cases the decay increases because European music, assisted by gramophone and wireless, and usually in its worst productions, proves too strong for the native art, which in an increasing tempo is degenerating or disappearing altogether.[158]

In South Africa, the pioneering black music critic Mark Radebe saw the creation of a Bantu National Music as threatened by the popular marabi of the townships: "The problem of African music must be solved by Africans. The 'marabi' dances and concerts and the terrible 'jazz' music banged and wailed out of the doors of foul-smelling so-called halls are far from representing real African taste. They create wrong impressions."[159] Radebe did not object to the gramophone, and indeed made a number of recordings for Columbia; he thought the gramophone would give "lastingness to the untrained Bantu voice" and preserve Africans' "most treasured cultural resource."[160] For "music to be truly national," Radebe wrote in another essay, "it must be based on the idiom of the people ... the only real Bantu music, namely, its folk music," the foundation for "a golden age of national Art."[161]

Similar complaints echoed across the Americas: Mário de Andrade, who would later collect the rural folkloric music of the Brazilian northeast, attacked what he called "*popularesca*" music, a "sub-music, fodder for the radio and records ... with which factories, businesses and singers sustain themselves."[162] As one historian notes, Andrade "lamented that samba was an urban genre. Its roots in the city, among a fluid population subject to the blandishments of radio stations, condemned it to inconstancy."[163] In Mexico, the composer Manuel Ponce struck a similar note: "I have been in an hacienda very far from the railroads, but where there is a radio, and the boys there sing these 'sun-drunk palms' [boleros] and just like that they have killed the vernacular music."[164] In the US, folklorist Newman I. White complained in 1928 that "the folk blues and the factory product are today almost inextricably mixed ... Most blues sung by Negroes today have only a secondary folk origin; their primary source is the phonograph."[165] The African-American intellectual Alain Locke saw jazz as "a vulgarization" of "pure and serious forms of Negro art." Jazz is not, he wrote in 1929, "a pure Negro folk thing"; rather, "'Jazz' is one-third Negro folk idiom, one-third ordinary middle class American idea and sentiment, and one-third spirit of the 'machine age' which, more and more, becomes not American but Occidental."[166]

For those drawn to the emerging ideology of folk music, the new vernaculars were suspect. Part of the suspicion sprang from the commercial nature of these musics; unlike rural folk performers, these musicians were involved in a thriving entertainment industry, where singers, dancers, and instrumentalists struggled to earn a living and songs were exploitable commodities, subject to copyrights and licenses. Even defenders of the new musics worried about their commercial exploitation.

Not only did these musics emerge from the unrespectable worlds of popular theater and dance, they also had close ties to the worlds of illicit sexuality and intoxication. Since working-class neighborhoods often bordered on vice and entertainment districts, the world of working-class musicking—from street singers to house rent parties, from carnival parading groups to ethnic benefit society and union halls that hosted festivals and weddings—bled into the dance halls, cabarets, and brothels run by gangsters and patronized by metropolitan and colonial leisure classes and tourists. As early as 1926, Lisbon's fado was condemned as "an unhealthy emanation from the centres of corruption, from the infamous habitations of the scum of society."[167] In subsequent decades, the "born in the brothel" story became part of the mythology of many of these musics. "My advisors agree on one essential fact," Borges wrote in 1955, "that the tango was born in the brothels."[168] "It is no accident that the modern Mexican bolero was born in a brothel," a recent historian writes, noting that the classic bolero composer, Agustín Lara, began as "a pianist who played tangos in several Mexico City brothels."[169] The brothel pianist—most famously Jelly Roll Morton—recurs in the account of the birth of jazz in New Orleans's Storyville. Indeed, in South Africa in 1933, Mark Radebe referred to "King Jazz" as "brothel-born."[170]

Defenders of the music often tried to dispel the link to illicit sexuality. "The mixture of indecency in modern times is not the fault of the dancers but of the disreputable persons who have money to spare and bring in this element for their own enjoyment," the hula ethnographer Mary Kawena Pukui wrote. "It is the dollar that has brought low the *hula* of *Hawaii nei*."[171] And the Martiniquan critic Andrée Nardal wrote that "it is to be deplored that the biguine should be presented to Parisians only under an obscene interpretation when it can express both a langourous grace and an extreme liveliness according to the changes in its tempo."[172]

Finally, these musics were rejected as folk musics because of their character as mixed-race, inter-tribal, or immigrant musics. In the Dutch East Indies, kroncong was associated with the Eurasian community—a music neither Javanese nor European; similarly, in Hawaii, the guitar-based commercial music, based on adopted hymn forms—*himeni*—was often referred to as *hapa haole* (half white), and distinguished from the traditional chants being collected by folklorists like Helen Roberts.[173] In Cuba, the folklorist Eduardo Sánchez de Fuentes y Peláez rejected urban son for its "bastard" origins, contaminated by Afro-Caribbean immigrants from Haiti as well as by US jazz.[174] In Greece, rebetika was long associated with the influx of Anatolian refugees in the early 1920s, and rejected for its "Oriental" character.

Similarly, a young Jorge Luis Borges blamed the decline of tango— "this regrettable contemporary episode of low-life elegies in a studiously *lunfardo* dialect, complete with *bandoneones*"—on its immigrant practitioners.[175] Three decades later, he recalled and criticized the anti-immigrant nationalism of his younger self:

Around 1926, I remember blaming the Italians (particularly the Genoese in the Boca) for the tango's decline. In that myth, or fantasy, of our "native" tango corrupted by "foreigners," I now see a clear symptom of certain nationalist heresies that later devastated the world—coming from the foreigners, of course. It was not the concertina, which I once ridiculed as contemptible, nor the hardworking composers who made the tango what it is, but the whole republic. Those old "natives" who engendered the tango, moreover, were named Bevilacqua, Greco, de Bassi.[176]

In his influential 1928 essay on African music, Erich Hornbostel rejected the hybrid commercial musics emerging in Africa in the 1920s: "a Negro brass band instituted by the German missionaries at Usambaraand," he noted, "left to themselves during the war added to their repertoire European street songs which the Negro conductor had picked up from an Indian merchant's gramophone record." "The mixture of 'white' and 'black' music, with a kind of musical pidgin as result, would be, if not impossible, yet most undesirable."[177] Hornbostel's arguments against such "musical pidgins" were, as Christopher Waterman has argued, part of an "anti-Creolization ideology evident in much scientific writing, art, and literature of Western Europe in the late nineteenth and early twentieth centuries, grounded in a fundamental ambivalence concerning Western-educated people of color."[178] Indeed, even the black South African critic Mark Radebe shared this view, though he thought that the record companies could preserve African music from "hybridization."[179]

The fact that these urban commercial dance musics seemed to evade the dominant understandings of folk music as rural and non-professional meant that a second powerful framework was often adopted in thinking about these musics: the discourse about "gypsy music." For Roma musicians, like African-American musicians, had long been characterized in nineteenth-century European discourse not as a rural national peasantry with a folk music, but as outcast urban entertainers, virtuoso improvisers on other people's music. Indeed, Bálint Sárosi has argued that European society's "contemptuous and condemning attitude toward entertainers" in part enabled the emergence of gypsy bands in the late eighteenth century:

What counted as humiliation and degeneration for those more strictly belonging within the framework of society meant for the gypsies a way of entering society and the best way towards success. By the end of the eighteenth century, with the first successful appearance of the gypsy bands they really had reached the stage where music-making became the highest of gypsy occupations (it used to be the craft of smithery), and the occupation which was most attractive to the gypsies themselves.[180]

Gypsy musicians were thus seen less as "folk" musicians than as commercial musicians, and Franz Liszt's 1859 book on gypsy music triggered a wide-ranging controversy over whether gypsy musicians were original or imitative.[181] This ideology explicitly reappeared in writings about the tzigane dance bands of the recording era, not least in Béla Bartók's 1931 essay, "Gypsy Music or Hungarian Music?" Bartók argued that "what people … call 'gypsy music'" was neither gypsy music nor folk music: "The music that is nowadays played 'for money' by urban gypsy bands is nothing but popular art music of recent origin." For Bartók, "gypsy musicians are merely the propagators and performers of a certain type of popular music."[182] Since the urban gypsy bands were distinguished by their performance styles, not their repertoire, they were, for him, imitators:

> In the folksong, text and music form an indivisible unity. Gypsy performance destroys this unity because it transforms, without exception, the vocal pieces into purely instrumental ones. This alone suffices to prove the lack of authenticity in gypsy renderings of music, even with regard to popular art music … This circumstance furnishes indirect proof to substantiate our contention that the gypsies could not be the authors of popular art songs attributed to them.[183]

By privileging the "indivisible unity" of the song over any element of performance style, Bartók's ideology of the "folksong" led to a discounting of the remarkable remaking of folk songs and printed sheet music by the performers. In retrospect, the gypsy orchestras' "renderings" of popular Hungarian tunes, turning the rudimentary melodies and piano accompaniments of the sheet music into fiddle and cimbalom improvisations, are as strikingly original as the jazz improvisations on Tin Pan Alley songs that musicians like Louis Armstrong pioneered in the late 1920s.[184]

Bartók insisted that he was not attacking this urban commercial music: "nothing is farther from our mind than to condemn gypsy musicians, the purveyors of this mass article. On the contrary, we wish them to hold fast to their position against the onslaught of the jazz and salon orchestras; we wish that they may continue to cling to their old repertory with its original coloring and physiognomy, without the admixture of waltzes, song hits, jazz elements, and whatnot."[185] Nevertheless, the terms of his argument paralleled those of contemporary musicologists like George Pullen Jackson, who argued that Negro spirituals derived from white sources.[186]

Moreover, the idea that urban dance musics, unlike rural folk musics, were deracinated and imitative recurred in the debates across the colonial ports and mill towns. In the Pacific, Filipino musicians were regularly characterized through this period as able practitioners of modern dance musics—from jazz to Hawaiian—but, like gypsy musicians, were said to lack an original music.[187] The folklorist and collector Hugh Tracey characterized the urban music of the black South African townships as a "drab proletarian grey in imitation of others."[188]

The parallels between these representations of gypsy music and African-American music were noted by the pioneering scholar of popular music Peter Van der Merwe, who argued that

> gypsy music and jazz had so much in common that it is tempting to see them as successive stages in a single historical process. Both were vigorous forms of urban popular music, in touch with folk tradition but assimilated to the Western mainstream. Both were created mainly, though far from exclusively, by outcast races with darker skins. Both specialized in exhilarating syncopation on the one hand and minor-mode gloom on the other.

These parallels led, he suggests, to the peculiar European jazz that Adorno and his generation encountered:

> So close, indeed, was the resemblance, that in the Germany of the 1920s, Gypsy (or at any rate eastern European) musicians were able to fabricate an ersatz jazz out of little more than instruction books and scores, both imported from the United States. It was this Teutonic "jazz," rather than the genuine American article—least of all the *black* American article— that captivated both bright young things and composers like Krenek, Hindemith, Weill, and Berg.[189]

It was out of this European reception of tzigane and jazz that the third framework invoked to understand these new musics emerged: "light music." Contrasted with "serious music," light music was a term that had emerged in the late nineteenth century to characterize the repertoire of hotel and seaside resort orchestras and was adopted by radio broadcasters from the BBC to All-India Radio; it carried many of the connotations that would later cluster around the idea of "easy listening."[190] Indeed, in 1931, Bartók characterized tzigane as an example of "so-called 'light music'":

> The role of this popular art music is to furnish entertainment and to satisfy the musical needs of those whose artistic sensibilities are of a low order. This phenomenon is but a variant of the types of music that fulfill the same function in Western European countries; of the song hits, operetta airs, and other products of light music as performed by salon orchestras in restaurants and places of entertainment ... The half-educated multitude of urban and semi-rural populations wants mass products; let us be pleased that in music at least they are partial to domestic factory articles and do not let us indulge in Utopian dreams for a quick improvement since they are unattainable.[191]

The idea of "light music" was central to Adorno's critical project, particularly in his early years in Germany. As early as 1928, he insisted on the importance of studying

> the entire realm of "light music," of kitsch, not only jazz but also the European operetta, the hit tune, etc. In doing so, one ought to adopt a very particular kind of approach that ought to be circumscribed in two senses. On the one hand one must abandon the arrogance characteristic of an understanding of "serious" music which believes it can completely ignore the music which today constitutes the only musical material consumed by the vast majority of all people. Kitsch must be played out and defended against everything that is merely elevated mediocre art, against the now rotten ideals of personality, culture, etc. On the other hand, however, one must not fall prey to the tendency—all too fashionable these days, above all in Berlin—to simply glorify kitsch and consider it the true art of the epoch merely because of its popularity.[192]

Adorno followed through on this project in his classic 1932 essay "On the Social Situation of Music," which concluded with a powerful account of "the vast realm of '*light*' music," which lies "below the realm of 'musical life,' below education and representation," and "satisfies immediate needs, not only those of the bourgeoisie, but of all of society."[193] Thus, when Adorno turned to jazz in "Farewell to Jazz" (1933) and "On Jazz" (1935), he viewed it through the lens of light music.

Both Bartók and Adorno assimilated the sonic challenge of the new phonograph musics into the familiar world of late nineteenth-century parlor piano sheet music and waltz orchestras. But if these were merely forms of light music, "satisfying immediate needs," why did they so often seem to be an unbearable and incomprehensible noise? The idea of "light music" (or "light popular music," a phrase Adorno often uses in his later English-language essays while in exile in the United States) was unable to capture the radical discontinuity between a musical universe in which "light" and "serious" music shared sonic idioms and timbres, and the new musics whose idioms and timbres were less "easy listening" than noisy disruptions of the familiar soundscape.

Subsequent accounts of twentieth-century recorded musics recognized this break, and largely abandoned the notion of "light" music for a notion of "popular music." In a particularly powerful recent version, the Brazilian ethnomusicologist Rafael José de Menezes Bastos argues that "popular music" is "the third 'musical universal' of the West, the nucleus of which was consolidated between 1930 and 1960 around the jazz-rock axis ... a global system specifically linked to the entertainment industry and to show business." Menezes Bastos makes three key arguments about this "popular music." First, though "a global phenomenon of recent modernity" extending "from India to Mexico, from Brazil to England, from Italy to the USA, from Egypt to Germany, from Turkey to Argentina, from Spain to Cuba," it was fundamentally tied "to the construction of the identity of modern nation-states" and became "an expression of the concert of nations." Second, this popular music was disseminated and made possible by "the technological-industrial establishment through phonography, beginning with the record, the radio and the talking cinema." (Thus he excludes what he calls "the archaeological phase of popular music, which is linked to sheet music, music halls, parlours, etc.") And third, he argues that we should see "jazz and rock as a single continuous language ... In this language, the classical-romantic tonal theory of western music, the theatricality and the operatic way of singing and the centrality of interpretation (far more than the composition itself) are as important as their local African-American base." Popular music "does not only incorporate art and folk musics into its mythology of origins, it also reinvents them ... It is this frame that gives consistency—at once global, local, regional, and national—to such genres as the tango, the habanera, the samba, the fado, the blues, etc."[194]

Though Menezes Bastos rightly sees a common frame to "genres" like tango, habanera, samba, fado, and blues, neither the notion of "popular music" nor the sense of "jazz and rock as a single continuous language" captures the complexity of the musical revolution that spawned these disparate "genres." Instead I would suggest that the notion of vernacular music, which emerged at this time, better captures this contradictory situation. Though there were a few uses of the phrase "vernacular music" in the nineteenth century,[195] it is in the wake of the recording boom of the 1920s that the concept of the vernacular begins to extend beyond its reference to language.[196] It was adopted by several Popular Front music critics and composers, including Charles Seeger, Wilfrid Mellers, Aaron Copland, and Marc Blitzstein, to refer to the new urban commercial musics—what Seeger called "the musical vernacular of the 'common man.'"[197]

The notion of vernacular music carries two useful connotations. First, like the notions of folk or popular, vernacular suggests the forms of everyday common musicking, as opposed to the formal learned traditions of musicking. The word's Latin original signified domestic, native and indigenous; it was built from a root—*verna*—that meant a home-born slave. However, unlike notions of popular, folk, ethnic, or national music, which yoke music directly to the "folk" or the "people," the "race" or the "nation," and suggest that music directly represents, or belongs to, a particular people, the term vernacular inserts a linguistic detour between art form and people, reminding us not only that music is a kind of language but that there are recognizable idioms of musicking.[198] Languages—like musics—are linked to peoples and nations, and individuals often inhabit a "mother tongue." Nonetheless, languages and musics travel across borders and oceans; they give rise to pidgins, creoles, and dialects. Individuals learn and adopt other languages and musics, though not without difficulty.

Moreover, the concept of vernacular has a particular relevance to the musical revolution of the 1920s. For vernacular carries the connotation of a *spoken* language, which stands somewhat apart from a sacred universal *script* such as Latin, Hebrew, Arabic, or Sanskrit. Thus, like the vernacular languages of Eurasia—the Romance languages of Europe or the Aryan languages of India—which inherited common forms and structures from Latin or Sanskrit and yet remained distinct languages, the vernacular musics that arose in the age of sound recording inherited musical forms and technologies from the notated tradition of European philharmonic music—common practice tonal harmony and the song form, as well as industrially produced instruments—while developing distinctive, even unmistakable, timbres, rhythms, and articulations. A musician raised in one vernacular did not effortlessly "speak" another, though many "bilingual" musicians emerged, and "translations" of songs from one idiom to another abounded.

Though jazz, samba, marabi, tango, and kroncong came to be defined as commercial genres linked to particular peoples and nations, it is perhaps more accurate to think of them as distinct vernacular languages or idioms, each of which was marked by characteristic instrumentation and repertoires, rhythmic timelines and harmonic cadences, vocal timbres and articulations. These musical vernaculars were not simply imports, imitations, or echoes of US jazz; rather, like jazz itself, each of them embodied a particular articulation of African, Arabic, Asian, European, and American musics. These sonic syncretisms cannot be understood as either the simple adoption of exotic sounds and rhythms, as in European philharmonic orientalism, nor as the continuation of the aristocratic or folk traditions of Africa and Asia. Rather they were new counterpoints, often emerging in the borderlands and contact zones of the colonial ports, not unlike the commercial pidgins.

It was precisely this scandalous and cacophonous counterpoint—the barbarous accents and incomprehensible noises of these idioms—that led to the moral panics of the era. The ideologies of folk music, gypsy music, and light music were valiant if failed attempts to understand the twin Copernican revolutions that were taking place in the world of music, as recorded music moved to the center of the music industry and vernacular music to the center of the musical guild. These revolutions not only reconstituted the worlds of art music and folk song, and circulated new timbres and new performance styles; they also reshaped the terrain of musicking generally, creating a new musical culture, a "phonograph culture," that was to spread far beyond the colonial ports in which it began.

4

Phonograph Culture: The Remaking of Vernacular Musicking

The electrical recording of vernacular musics not only transformed the music industry (making sound recording its center rather than live performance and printed music) and the world's music guilds (giving a new symbolic primacy to urban popular musics); it also profoundly changed the vernacular musical cultures of the colonial ports. This was true both for audiences, as listening to records became a part of everyday musicking, and for musicians, as recording became an essential element in acquiring musical skills, a new kind of musical labor, and, eventually, a new form of artistic expression. A new phonograph culture emerged. On the one hand, it was manifest in the simple ubiquity of discs and record players in the popular quarters: as Theodor Adorno wrote in the midst of the recording boom, "the downtrodden gramophone horns reassert themselves as proletarian loudspeakers."[1] But this phonograph culture was also a profound remaking of the time and space of music. "Although a phonograph record is recorded at a special time and a special place," Adorno noted, "it is no longer bound to this special time and place."[2]

Of course, musics had long circulated as musicians traveled with their instruments; moreover, the mass printing of sheet music was a powerful form of musical circulation, even though it relied on relatively arcane and incomplete notations. But the circulation of records meant that music's sound moved without the performers; it created an entirely new relation between sound and space, music and territory.[3] Even radio broadcasting was not as mobile as the gramophone record:

as Adorno pointed out, the radio listener was tied to the moment of the broadcast and the reach of the signal. "The phonograph record destroys the 'now' of the live performance and, in a way, its 'here' as well," Adorno wrote. The ubiquity of "music pouring out of the loud-speaker" meant that listeners came to hear the sound captured on recordings as the sound of music. Even the expression "canned music," which had emerged in the early years of recording to denote a poor, factory-made substitute for fresh, homemade music, peaked relatively quickly.[4] As songs and dances became "records," records became music. This new dialectic between performing and recording changed the meaning of both musical practice (the place of music in the daily life of a community) and the musical work (the enduring notation of a musical composition).

A World of Record Players

The emergence of this popular phonograph culture was a product of the dramatic leap in working-class access to phonographs. "The porta-ble wind-up gramophones of the late 1920s were certainly not beyond the resources of the average worker," the record industry scholar Pekka Gronow noted,[5] and this trend was recognized by both industry leaders and social researchers. "The popularity of the phonograph," the head of Columbia, Louis Sterling, concluded in 1927, "is probably due to the fact that the phonograph is one of the few products that have not increased in price proportionately with the rate of wages earned by the average working man in Europe."[6]

As a result of declining prices and portable models, gramophones and records were becoming part of ordinary working-class life in colonial ports and mill towns across Asia, Africa, and the Americas. In British Malaya, whereas in 1911 "only the urban rich—including British officers, plantation and mine owners and some Babas (interpreters and clerks for the British) and Jawi Peranakan (mainly traders and merchants)—could afford to buy the gramophone player and discs," by the 1920s, "records also became more accessible to the urban dwellers of principal towns such as Penang, Singapore, and Kuala Lumpur due to the postwar record boom."[7] Similarly in British India, the "coming of the gramophone to Tamilnadu in the early 1920s was," S. Theodore Baskaran argues, "something in the nature of a revolution. It was the first time that music was accessible to all, irrespective of caste or class

… through the gramophone, even people in interior villages without electricity could listen to famous musicians."[8] This trend accelerated in the late 1920s when gramophones began to be assembled in India from inexpensive Japanese parts: the price of gramophones fell by more than half in about five years from the late 1920s to the early 1930s.[9]

In Egypt, the magazine *Rūz al-Yūsuf* noted in 1926, "the phonograph has spread among all classes of people after its price went down and it became possible for any family of moderate means to acquire one along with some records to fill the home with music."[10] That same year, Gramophone's S. H. Sheard found the business thriving in Istanbul and Baghdad but placed Tehran outside of gramophone culture: "the large majority of people here are so poor that the purchase of a gramophone is out of the question. After seeing the country and the people I am amazed that the Company ever had a branch in Tehran and venture to say that it was, and is, impossible for a branch to be made to pay there."[11] By 1937, an Algerian police agent reported that "there is hardly a *café maure* or family—however modest their condition—that does not have a phonograph and a collection of popular songs."[12]

On the east coast of Africa, a Gramophone agent noticed in 1931 the "large demand" among migrant miners for the records Odeon made "in all the principal languages" in the Mozambiquan ports of Lourenço Marques (present-day Maputo) and Beira:

> I have been unable to obtain any statistics in proof of the large sales claimed in Lourenço Marques, but it is probably true on account of the natives in the area having money by reason of the fact that they go to Johannesburg to work in the gold mines where they earn good wages. It is stated that there are 100,000 of these natives always working in the mines and after working out their contract period they return to their native lands and are replaced by others. In common with all natives on the East Coast they spend liberally when they have money in their possession.[13]

In southern Africa, one historian writes, "by the 1920s, the gramophone had installed itself as a fairly common feature in the homes of black people living in the cities";[14] in 1929, a black South African newspaper writer complained that "nowadays the dance craze has taken hold of the Native masses and they play or vamp whatever they hear from gramophones."[15] In West Africa, the evidence is sketchier:

in Nigeria, one musicologist writes, "gramophones were owned pre-dominantly by Europeans, Saro, and Western-educated African civil servants, since their cost (from about two to six pounds sterling in 1930) placed them out of the reach of most traders, artisans, and laborers."[16] In Ghana, on the other hand, one historian notes that "as a result of lucrative cash-crops, many Ghanaians, even farmers, could afford wind-up gramophones" in the 1920s.[17]

In the Americas, one sees a similar adoption of the phonograph. In the United States, phonographs spread throughout immigrant and African-American working-class communities in the 1920s; by 1927, phonographs were found in 60 percent of households in large cities.[18] L. L. Sebok, who took over Brunswick's foreign recording in 1927, recognized "the tremendous market represented by the foreign record field" among European immigrants to the US: "despite immigration restrictions thousands of people are coming to America every year … America is said to be the 'melting pot,' but the 'melting' process does not make the newcomer to our shores forget his home melodies and folk songs. European people are more or less music lovers and spend their money liberally in comparison to the average American."[19] In their classic study of Muncie, Indiana, *Middletown*, Helen and Robert Lynd found that a quarter of working-class families had purchased phonograph records over the preceding year; a larger proportion owned phonographs.[20] In the mill towns of the Carolina and Georgia Piedmont, a sociologist noted in 1934, "installment sellers convinced the workers that they wanted their houses fitted up with phonographs, parlor suites, and player pianos"; surveys found that a third of families owned phonographs.[21] The folklorist Zora Neale Hurston came across phonographs in Florida turpentine camps;[22] even in the Mississippi Delta, 30 percent of households had a phonograph in 1930.[23]

"Often as not, the Victrola was the sole source of musical enter-tainment for working-class Puerto Ricans," historian Ruth Glasser notes. When she interviewed guitarist Francisco López Cruz, he said of his *compatriotas* living in New York in the 1920s and 1930s: "If they had to give up eating, they gave up eating in order to buy records."[24] The anthropologist Manuel Gamio, studying the communities of Mexican immigrants in the United States in 1926 and 1927, found phonographs not only in established working-class households— "nearly always"—but also in tenements and even the huts of transient workers: "very frequently even in a poor house there is a phonograph." Moreover, on examining the records of customs officials, he found that phonograph records were the most common item brought back to Mexico by returning migrants.[25] In Argentina, the cost of a record player dropped by half from 1920 to 1929, though the historian Donald Castro argues that it remained beyond the means of ordinary workers;[26] nonetheless, in the late 1920s, the folklorist Juan Alfonso Carrizo found that Argentine sugar workers were buying gramophones and tango records.[27]

Taking part in phonograph culture did not necessarily require the purchase of a gramophone, because records were heard not only, or even mainly, in the home. Rather recorded music remade the local spaces of musicking, as phonographs became public "musical instruments." Gramophones were regularly played in bars, coffee shops, bodegas, barbershops, and in the street. "What a state Istanbul was in!" the satirist Refik Halid Karay wrote. "On streets lined with coffee houses, the cacophony of forty-odd gramophones playing all at once will gnaw your ear, scratch your heart, and blow your head up."[28] In Kirkuk, Iraq, a Gramophone agent in the late 1920s found coffee-house gramophones playing records of local Kurdish music.[29] A Puerto Rican musician later recalled that the first gramophone he saw was in 1927, a wind-up Edison playing on the back of a truck that carried merchandise to the town's central market.[30] In Cairo and Beirut in the 1920s, street entertainers "carried a phonograph from one public place to another, playing discs upon request, and charging a certain fee per playing."[31] Similarly, in Athens, "those who could not afford the luxury of a gramophone relied on … those who wandered the streets and markets and played songs for a fee on their portable gramophone machines … These individuals were particularly important to the refugees [from Smyrna], many of whom lacked the necessary capital to acquire a gramophone."[32]

In China, "records were widely sold in urban areas and were played publicly in hotels, nightclubs, restaurants, bars, and shops";[33] a 1929 novel of colonial Shanghai opens with a character listening to a phonograph in a bathhouse.[34] Similarly, in Malaya, "By the mid-1930s, recorded music was played in public places especially in shops … [and] at amusement parks … thus gramophone music also became accessible to the general urban population who could not afford the gramophone itself."[35] In Nigeria, gramophones were used in "two primary contexts: private homes, where a group of men might gather to drink beer or palmwine and hear the latest sounds, and public bars, where they were utilized to attract patrons."[36] The first important musicological account of West African gramophone music—that of J. H. Nketia—did not appear until the mid-1950s, but it summed up the emerging phonograph culture:

> I need hardly point out that the Gramophone is, in many places in the Gold Coast, growing in popularity. People are drawn to it wherever it is played in village or town, just as people would gather around a wayside musician. Many drinking bars find it a useful means of attracting customers ... The popularity of the gramophone has been fostered by the availability of a variety of recordings which meet the taste of the literate and the illiterate, the young and the old.[37]

The time of popular musicking was also remade by the record player. As J. H. Nketia noted of the Gold Coast, the gramophone was "not subject to customary control. Whereas certain forms of music are performed on prescribed occasions only—at funerals, festivals, worship, and celebrations, recordings of such occasional music may be listened to at any time."[38] Records became a way of extending the celebrations of daily life. "Everyone from the countryside in whose home or at whose wedding I sang," Umm Kulthūm recalled, "bought my records in order to be able to say to his friends, 'Come and listen to the girl who sang at my daughter's wedding.'"[39] They also commemorated public festivals, as popular songs of each carnival season were released on disc. The songs of the beguine "used to remain popular only during the Carnival time in the Antilles," Andrée Nardal noted in 1931. "Then they were rapidly forgotten, but thanks to the phonograph, now-a-days certain ones are being revived such as the biguines formerly played during the delirious Carnival of St. Pierre, the city swallowed up by the volcano Mount Pelée."[40] Gramophone records could cross social boundaries that restricted musicians: in Istanbul, the recording served as a kind of shellac veil, allowing some women singers who would rarely perform publicly to became widely heard.[41]

In some cases, this breaching of the boundaries of space and time provoked moral panics. "In our Singapore suburbs," a newspaper reporter noted in the midst of a 1934 noise controversy, "with their open houses and different nationalities, the gramophone, especially the electrical type, can be a very real nuisance." When the Singapore legislative council prohibited the playing of gramophone music after midnight, the newspaper reported that "an outraged house-holder, unable to listen any longer to Miss Riboet's ditties in the neighboring servants' quarter" could now invoke the law against her.[42]

This working-class phonograph culture of the colonial ports was first constructed as a local culture. For the most part, even when the vernacular phonograph records were recorded and pressed in imperial metropolises, they were circulated in the cities and towns where the musicians worked. Visiting East Africa in 1931, the Gramophone agent H. Evans reported that "the bulk of the sale of Swahili records already placed on the market has been among the Swahilis themselves and very little has been purchased by others."[43] A decade later, the US critic Paul Bowles wrote that

> it has been impossible to buy recordings of North African music other than in the record shops of the regions producing the particular kind of music desired. Records of Kabyle music are found only in the coast towns of northern Algiers, whereas Chleuh music is not sold at all in Tangier and Rabat, but only farther south. Interest is particularly centered on local stars, who sing songs of local significance.[44]

This led the well-known British music critic, Constant Lambert, to complain that "one's exasperation with the excessively drab catalogues issued recently by the gramophone companies is increased by the knowledge that the very same factory ... is at the same time producing records of the greatest interest which are destined to be immediately sent abroad."[45] Even those records that did travel the world—like Cuban son, African-American jazz, and Hawaiian hula—were originally made with local audiences in mind.

As a result, despite being dominated by the transnational recording companies, the emerging phonograph culture of these local segregated markets often marked the beginning of an industrial decolonization. Gramophone records linked dance halls and cabarets to furniture dealers and radio stations and became the heart of a local consumer goods industry, marketing local products to working-class consumers, and "substituting"—like the other import-substitution industries of the era—for the more "prestigious" European and North American musical imports. "The Brazilian recording industry," historian Brian McCann notes, "was one of the most successful Latin American cases of import-substituting industrialization in the 1930s."[46]

The emergence of these local record markets was, however, a contradictory process, particularly in the settler colonial states where national cultural sovereignty often coincided with racial disenfranchisement. One sees this in the uneven history of the recording of black musics. In the United States, on the one hand, the recording boom produced the distinct marketing of "race records" to African-Americans. As a result of this segregated market, hundreds of African-American musicians recorded jazz, blues, and gospel records in the era of electrical recording, even as white musicians adopted these forms. Similarly, many Afro-Cuban musicians recorded secular dances and songs both in Havana and New York (though the traditional rumba itself was not recorded in Cuba during the first half of the century[47]). In South Africa, in contrast, "aside from an effort by Zonophone (the Gramophone Record Company) to market some records by black South Africans in 1925 there were no records by local blacks available" as late as 1929.[48] In Brazil, where no separate "race records" industry aimed at Afro-Brazilian consumers developed, relatively few of the Afro-Brazilian musicians who created the samba schools of Rio's favelas were recorded at the time. For example, Cartola—the founder of Mangueira samba school in 1929, whose compositions were recorded by all of the leading vocalists of the era and who would later be central to the samba revival of the 1950s and 1960s—was recorded only once in the 1920s and 1930s, more or less anonymously as part of Stokowski's famous 1940 "field recording," *Native Brazilian Music*.[49] The samba became a national rhythm through the popular recordings by light-skinned Brazilian crooners like Chico Alves and Mario Reis.

If the economy of gramophones and records was designed to tap local musical markets, it is also clear that records circulated throughout the archipelago of colonial ports, carried by sailors and maritime workers, and imported by music stores. As Paul Gilroy noted, ships made possible "the movement of key cultural and political artefacts: tracts, books, gramophone records, and choirs."[50] In many cases, diaspora communities of migrant workers imported records from homelands across oceans. After decades of indentured workers—*girmitiyas*—migrating from South Asia, Indian records circulated in the East Indies as well as the West Indies. Parlophone's Tamil-language discs followed workers to ports and plantations across Southeast Asia, advertised in the Tamil press (a Tamil gramophone song compendium was published in British Malaya through the 1920s); meanwhile, as early as 1929, East Indians in Trinidad were importing records from India, and by the 1930s the ghazals of K.L. Saigal and the bhajans of K.C. Dey were popular among Indo-Caribbeans.[51] Some early African recordings echoed across the black Atlantic; the African-American music critic Maud Cuney-Hare took note of the Kumasi

Trio's recording of Fante tunes in London and the London appearances of South Africans Griffiths Motsieloa and Reuben Caluza.[52]

The vernacular phonograph musics of the Americas—calypso, jazz, hillbilly, samba, and son—reverberated widely. Trinidadian calypsos moved quickly across the Atlantic to West Africa, in part by way of London, as can be seen in the 1929 Zonophone recordings of the West African Instrumental Quintet that included both "Kara So," a Trinidadian carnival song and "Tin Ka Tin Ka," a version of "Sly Mongoose," which had been recorded a few years earlier by Trinidadian singers Lionel Belasco and Sam Manning.[53] The impact of African-American jazz on the urban communities of Africa and Latin America was equally important: the distribution of African-American records made "jazz maniacs" of the musicians who created the marabi of Cape Town and Johannesburg. In Brazil, Louis Armstrong's "West End Blues" was imported immediately by Parlophon.[54] (This might be contrasted to France and Germany where, as many critics and historians have noted, the "race" records of Louis Armstrong were generally unavailable, and "jazz" meant the hotel orchestras of Paul Whiteman and Britain's Jack Hylton.) The blue yodels of the US singer Jimmie Rodgers, hardly noticed in the US outside the South, had remarkably wide reverberations elsewhere, particularly in Africa: as early as 1930, record advertisements in South Africa's black press put the "Dixie Records" of Jimmie Rodgers and the Carter Family side by side with Zonophone's Zulu records, and the black South African writer Es'kia Mphahlele later recalled that "at Christmas-time, Jeemee Roe-Jars (Jimmy Rodgers), then in fashion, yodelled plaintively from various parts of the village."[55] Rodgers's records influenced palm-wine guitarists in Lagos and rumba musicians in Kinshasa, and, in 1932, the Durban singer William Mseleku recorded songs directly modeled on Rodgers's blue yodels.[56] By 1950, Hugh Tracey was noting "the widespread influence [of] gramophone records of Brazilian music" on the East African coast: "Dance bands in all East African towns are playing Africanized versions of Brazilian rumbas, congas, and sambas."[57]

Afro-Cuban son had an even wider circulation. The popularity of Cuba's "El Manisero"* has long served as a figure for the travels of these musics to metropolitan capitals. Recorded in 1928 and 1929 by the cabaret singer Rita Montaner, by Miguel Matamoros's son trio, and by the hotel orchestra of Don Apiazu (a recording that was released in France, Spain, Italy, and Scandinavia, as well as Brazil, India, Australia, and West Africa), "The Peanut Vendor" crossed the world, a *son pregón* packaged as a "rumba" for European and North American audiences.[58]

But Cuban music was celebrated not only in Paris and New York; it reverberated across the archipelago of colonial ports. In the Dutch East Indies, Takonai Susumu notes, "Kroncong Rumba was a fusion of Kroncong music and rumba, a Cuban music which had world-wide popularity following the 1930 hit 'El Manisero.'"[59] In Africa, the recordings of "El Manisero" were among the earliest of hundreds of recordings of Cuban music released when Gramophone repack-aged Victor's Cuban recordings as the African GV—Gramophone Victor—series in 1933.[60] "From Senegal to the Congo, [the record of 'El Manisero'] had a pronounced influence on the development of African popular music," the musicologist Richard Shain notes:

> It shaped regional styles (as in Ghana) and sometimes constituted the very foundation of national musics (as in Senegal) … Distributed in francophone West Africa by the Compagnie Française d'Afrique Occidentale, the records were heard in Senegal at a number of different venues. Some Senegalese heard Cuban music at dry good stores in Dakar that began selling records and gramophones in addition to their regular stock. To stimulate business, these stores sometimes played "the latest" music for their customers while they were shopping.[61]

In Lagos, the Latin American GV series were "the most influen-tial recordings" among palm-wine musicians.[62] In the Congos, these recordings of Cuban soneros triggered the emergence of a Lingala rumba in the migrant riverside cities of Leopoldville (Kinshasa) and Brazzaville in the 1930s. As a Congolese musician recalled, "South American music, the records we had here, especially on the GV label, distributed works that Congolese people picked up on right away."[63] The first Congolese recordings, often just of guitar and voice, used the melodies and chord progressions of GV recordings.[64] Indeed, there are stories of musicians calling out the songs by their GV number, rather than their Spanish title.

The reach of commercial Hawaiian music—the product of a colonial plantation economy that forced together Asian, Pacific and Atlantic peoples and cultures—was as wide and influential as that of US jazz or Cuban son. It was heard not only in the colonial capitals of New York, Paris, London, and Tokyo, but throughout the archipelago of colonial ports.[65] Ernest Kaai's Royal Hawaiian Troubadours had left Hawaii in 1919 for a three-year tour across Pacific and Asian ports from Batavia and Manila to Shanghai and Calcutta; he published *Hawaiian Songs* in Java—where two members of his band stayed—in 1921, and recorded in Tokyo in 1923.[66] A few years later, Kaai's troupe was followed by steel guitarist Tau Moe—born in Samoa and raised in Hawaii—who toured Japan, China, Southeast Asia, the Philippines, India, Burma, and Indonesia from 1928 to 1934 as part of Madame Riviere's Polynesians (they recorded in Tokyo in 1929).[67]

In the wake of such tours, Hawaiian music was intertwined with the emerging vernacular phonograph musics of the Pacific and Asia. In India, there were Hawaiian groups in the 1930s, and the Hawaiian steel guitar became an element of Hindi film music.[68] In Java's Batavia, Hawaiian music reverberated in kroncong, as "Hawaiian" served to name a genre of popular music that used the same instrumentation as kroncong but was sung in Hawaiian or English.[69] By the 1930s, the kroncong recordings of Miss Ninja—recorded in Calcutta for distribution in both British Malaya and the Dutch East Indies—featured her "Hawaiian Orkest 'Sweet Java Islanders'" with Hawaiian steel guitar and 'ukulele, and these Hawaiian/kroncong bands—like "The HMV Combined East & West Java Kronchong Orchestra & Hawaiian Rhythm Kings"— were performing in Singapore.[70]

Hawaiian records not only traveled to Latin America (the hula records of Kalama's Quartet were imported to Brazil by Parlophon in 1929), but Hawaiian-style ensembles—like Oscar Alemán's Les Loups in Argentina—performed and recorded.[71] In the United States, Hawaiian music was not simply the Tin Pan Alley fantasy of the South Seas; a number of the vernacular musicians who came out of the recording boom incorporated the sounds of Hawaiian music, collaborating with Hawaiian musicians. Country singer Jimmie Rodgers recorded with the Hawaiian steel guitarist Joseph Kaaaia Kaipo in the fall of 1929, and jazz trumpeter Louis Armstrong later recorded several sessions with a Hawaiian band led by Andy Iona.[72] Hawaiian music also had remarkable reverberations across the ports of Africa. Hawaiian guitar records not only influenced the palm-wine music of Lagos,[73] but when Griffiths Motsieloa arrived in London from South Africa to organize an early session of recordings of South African marabi and vaudeville tunes for the South African market, his first recording, a duet with Ignatius Monare, "Aubuti Nkikho" (Brother Nkikho), featured Hawaiian steel guitar.[74] Hawaiian guitar eventually became so influential that the term Hawaiian—*hauyani*—was adopted into Bantu languages.[75]

Other musics did not travel as widely. Indeed, in 1933, a journalist remarked on the difference between the global diffusion of Hawaiian music and the local nature of kroncong: "If the Hawaiian songs have become popular throughout the world, and appear in a variety of compositions, the *Lagu Krontjong* has remained unchanged and unspoiled."[76] However, the circulation of records of US jazz, Cuban son, and Hawaiian hula across the archipelago of colonial ports is not only a story of specific musical influences and echoes. Rather it is also the sign of the emergence of a new world musical space, a transnational phonograph culture, in which words like "jazz," "rumba," and "Hawaiian" were often attached to idioms that bore little sonic resemblance to their "originals."[77]

The changing time and space of phonograph culture also changed the way music was learned and passed on. Though musical apprenticeships with teachers continued, a host of idioms that had not been notated and were learned largely by ear were now available to musicians well out of earshot. Umm Kulthūm "learned songs from the records she heard at the home of her schoolmate, the *'umda*'s daughter"; she even remembered specific records she had heard, including those of Shaykh Abū al-ʿUlā Muhammad.[78] Louis Armstrong recalled getting "one of those upright Victrolas, which we were very proud of," and he purchased a copy of *Livery Stable Blues* (one of the early 1917 recordings of the Original Dixieland Jazz Band).[79] Armstrong's own records, in turn, had a powerful effect on younger jazz musicians: "My greatest inspiration," Danny Barker recalled, "was the regular flow of Armstrong records on OKeh, each to me and the other young jazz musicians a masterpiece in jazz playing … I went to Dave Karnosky's South Rampart Street record store and listened to records and checked on when Louis's next great record would be released and arrive in New Orleans." Rex Stewart said he and his friends played Armstrong's recording with King Oliver "until our arms were worn out from working the phonograph handle, the record was worn out and our souls were on fire."[80] Legend had it that the flamenco guitarist Sabicas, a teenager at the time of the recording boom, taught himself from gramophone records because no one in his home town of Pamplona could play flamenco.[81] "In a country without a tradition of written musical publication," the Ghanaian musicologist J. H. Nketia wrote, "the importance of the disc cannot be overemphasized."[82]

But recordings not only influenced apprentices in a particular idiom; they also became the key avenue for the exploration of musical idioms across oceans. There are many stories like those of the bands in the West African port of St. Louis like Grand Diop, St. Louis Jazz, and La Lyre Africaine who taught themselves Cuban music from the GV records;[83] of the young tzigane and musette guitarist Django Reinhardt in Toulon, listening to the jazz 78s of Duke Ellington, Eddie Lang/JoeVenuti, and Louis Armstrong;[84] or of the young Murakami Kazunori—who would become the first major Japanese performer of Hawaiian music—learning steel guitar in Tokyo in the early 1930s from the 78s of Sol Ho'opi'i.[85]

Recording also transformed the lives of musicians, as recording sessions become a part of their work, less as a way to make a living than as a form of advertising and promotion. Some of the early vernacular music discs were made by musicians who migrated to colonial metropolises before entering recording studios, as exemplified by the parallel but separate careers of two Honolulu-born steel guitarists: Sol Ho'opi'i left Hawaii for California at age seventeen in 1919, and rarely returned, becoming well known both for his recordings in Los Angeles and for playing in Hollywood's "Hawaiian" films; Buckie Shirakata left Hawaii for Japan at age twenty-one in 1933, recorded Hawaiian records for Columbia's Japanese label, and became the leading Hawaiian musician in Japan over the next three decades.[86]

Most of the recordings took place in the colonial ports themselves, as record company agents set up sessions in hotel rooms and makeshift studios. However, some musicians used local success to become migrant workers in the global music industry, traveling to national or colonial metropolises and recording in state-of-the-art studios: the Cuban Septeto Nacional recorded in Madrid as well as New York; Johnny Noble's Hawaiians went to Los Angeles after their first Honolulu sessions. A few of the early recordings occurred when companies brought artists to London, Paris, or New York for specific recording journeys. One of the rare musical narratives of these overseas recording journeys was the Kumasi Trio's song "Asin Asin."[*87] Accompanied by palm-wine guitar and *frikyiwa* (the West African iron castanet), Kwame Asare sings that "we were in Kumasi for a funeral. I heard DC officials were in town, looking for Kwame Asare, Ocansey and Biney [the three members of the Trio] ... they took us to the white man's office, he said Sunday morning we'd set sail, to record Fanti songs abroad, for the good of the people." The song then becomes a praise song for the black man who helps them in England, Kweku Yankson, a "charming personality ... a hard worker ... our guardian." Yankson, they sing, has been accepted by the whites in England; nonetheless, "some of the whites are evil ... they killed his kid brother."[88]

Few musicians made much money from these sessions, despite the hyperbole of journalists like E. V. Solomons who reported that Miss Riboet "has made a fortune from the royalties paid to her by Gramophone companies for her *Krontjong* and other song records."[89] In 1931, a Gramophone agent wrote of the Odeon recording sessions in east Africa that "the cost of the recording is stated to be small as the artists were only paid nominal sums and the average per title is 10/-."[90] Meanwhile, in Mombassa, the agent noted, "the artist Sitti Binti from Zanzibar was paid 20/- per title plus travelling expenses from Zanzibar and 4/- per day expenses for food."[91] In Lagos, Parlophone paid the highlife singer Tunde King five shillings for each side.[92] In many cases, these payments had no provision for royalties: Cuba's pioneering son group, the Trio Matamoros, apparently never received any royalty payments from their Victor recordings.[93] "When I was first recorded in the year 1932," the popular Bombay Bhavageet singer G. N. Joshi later wrote,

> I was lured to the studios to record only two of my most popular songs. At the recording session, I became so involved and excited at the prospect of being recorded that instead of just two songs, when the recording session was wound up after about six hours, I discovered that I had actually recorded fourteen songs! These songs, when released in the market, received such unprecedented support that literally thousands of disks were sold. Artists are by nature very simple, sentimental, and temperamental. When I received such a tremendous following and public favour, I did not care that I had not been paid a single penny for the first fourteen songs![94]

The role recordings were coming to play in the public image of musicians was dramatized in the occasional incorporation of the recording apparatus in live performances: blues singer Bessie Smith sometimes performed alongside a large recording horn, and her rival Ma Rainey, according to her pianist Thomas Dorsey, emerged on stage from a giant Victrola.[95]

Given the development of this phonograph culture, one of the curiosities of the intellectual debates over these vernacular musics in the late 1920s is how rarely actual records were mentioned. The record review was only just emerging as a genre, so with only a handful of exceptions, the early controversies over the vernacular phonograph musics were conducted through discussions of performances and books, particularly published song collections. This was true of both those who celebrated the musics and those who condemned them. Carpentier's account of son in *Music in Cuba* mentions a half dozen classic songs and compares them to the compositions of Stravinsky, but names no son recording artist; for Carpentier, son remains an anonymous folk dance on the way to the learned compositions of Roldán and Caturla. Bartók's dismissal of gypsy music took place in a book review of a folk song collection. The US debate over African-American spirituals, jazz and blues in the 1920s almost entirely ignored specific recordings. There were a handful of exceptions—both Irving Brown's 1929 account of flamenco, *Deep Song*, and Alain Locke's 1936 study, *The Negro and His Music*, had short appended discographies of commercial recordings—but for the most part phonograph culture had not penetrated the literary culture of music.

In contrast to the music critics and folklorists, who rarely analyzed the commercial recordings they deplored, there were a handful of figures who heard these records with new ears, in large part because they were reviewing the records themselves, rather than the printed songbooks. Two of these figures, Abbe Niles and Rodney Gallop, are particularly interesting because the trajectory of their magazine articles captures the tensions between print and recording, rural folklorism and urban commercialism, and marks the emergence of this phonograph culture.

Abbe Niles's year-long series of monthly articles in *The Bookman* were perhaps the first regular reviews of vernacular phonograph records in US journalism. Niles, a young lawyer and blues aficionado, had visited the songwriter W. C. Handy at his New York publishing office in 1925, intending to write a profile for the *Wall Street Journal*; within a year he wrote an introduction to Handy's pathbreaking collection *Blues: An Anthology*, and began reviewing books on American vernacular musics for the *New Republic* and the *Nation*. In early 1928, he took up an offer by the monthly magazine, *The Bookman*, to review contemporary "popular music":

> In speaking of "popular music" ... I shall not imply the assertion that it *is* music, nor by this disclaimer do I confess that it is not. The term will be used in the narrow sense which denotes the songs and other pieces on which royalties are paid (or left unpaid), which generally escape mention

in the purer musical circles, and which, together with American folksong and the slender but growing literature of both, will be among our major subjects.[96]

When he embarked on his monthly surveys in February 1928—titled "Ballads, Songs and Snatches"—he focused mainly on printed music: song collections and the best-selling sheet music. However, by the June 1928 survey, he was recommending phonograph records, and by the September 1928 installment he had abandoned sheet music entirely, and was discussing the recording company's expeditions to the southern mountains. In the final January 1929 article, he concluded that he had, over the last year, "listened to a substantial proportion of the current 'popular' records of five leading phonograph companies."[97] The recording boom faltered in the wake of the Crash of October 1929, and Niles never returned to record reviewing (though he did contribute the occasional *book* review on popular music to the *Nation* and the *New Republic*). So the dozen articles Niles wrote in 1928 stand as a remarkable, unparalleled survey of the US side of the revolution in recorded vernacular music.[98]

Niles's counterpart across the Atlantic was Rodney Gallop, a young British diplomat stationed in Belgrade, Athens, and Lisbon in the 1920s and early 1930s. An amateur folklorist, Gallop had begun collecting Basque folk songs in his early twenties—in a 1928 letter to *The Gramophone* he inquires about obtaining "a recording machine, preferably fairly portable, to take direct records of folk-songs from the peasant singers"[99]—and he wrote essays on Basque and Portuguese folk song for *Music & Letters* and the *Musical Quarterly* throughout the 1930s. However, in June 1928, while in Athens, he began a decade-long series of record reviews of the vernacular gramophone musics with a notice of the "new HMV Greek Records" in *The Gramophone*.[100] If Niles mapped the musics of North America's periphery, from the African-American South to the colony of Hawaii, Gallop mapped the musics of the European periphery, stretching across Greece, Albania, Serbia (the tzigane singer Sofka in Belgrade), Hungary (drawing on the work of Bartók and Kodály), the Basque country, Andalusia (*cante jondo*), Aragon (*jota*), Catalonia (the Sardana dance), Galicia (bagpipes), rural Portugal (the *cantos regionais*), and Lisbon and Coimbra fado. Later, Gallop reviewed recordings from Mexico, Java, and Japan, but they were not central to him; nor did he ever focus on the Celtic fringe, aside from an article on Scottish bagpipes. It was the "gypsy and Moorish ingredients" in the vernacular gramophone musics that captured his attention.

Like most of those of their generation interested in folk music, Niles and Gallop began with a focus on *songs*, paying more attention to the history and variations of particular songs than to individual performers or performances. Gallop was very much a folk-song collector, transcribing words and music of songs he heard, whereas Niles was a collector of printed sheet music as well as folk-song collections. And they retained elements of the folklorist's disdain when they approached commercial recordings: reviewing a recording by José Luis de la Rica, Gallop noted that it "contains examples of what Basque song should and should not be. [One side] is one of those misapplications of five-eight time to a drawing-room ballad tune which are unfortunately so popular in the larger coast-towns. [The other side] is a perfectly lovely and genuine Basque folk melody." Sounding like Bartók, he wrote that "the other two [records] are perfect examples of unaccompanied folk-song performed by real peasants with all the shades and inflections which only the untutored folk-singer can give."[101]

Unlike many folklorists, however, they sensed the way recordings shifted attention from the song to the performer's style. If Niles's articles begin by tracking variants of topical songs—like ballads of the Titanic—with only a casual mention of the recorded performer, they increasingly shift to describing the performance style and timbre on the records, as when he writes of "Blind Willie Johnson's violent, tortured, and abysmal shouts and groans and his inspired guitar in a primitive and frightening Negro religious song, 'Nobody's Fault but Mine.'"*[102] Similarly, Gallop defends "the services which the gramophone companies have rendered the cause of music in recording the folksongs of many and divers nations" because "it is the original singers whose voices are recorded with all the subtle inflections and mannerisms of performance without which folksong loses so much of its value and charm."[103]

Both Gallop and Niles recognized that these recordings were aimed at local audiences, and were rarely available to mainstream metropolitan audiences. "Few owners of gramophones realise that these records, although recorded in Greece by Greek artists, are printed at Hayes, and can be obtained in England, if specially ordered," Gallop wrote in his first review in *The Gramophone* in June 1928;[104] that same month, Niles found it necessary to define "race records" for the readers of *The Bookman*: "'Race records,' here indicated by the letter 'r,' are those made for colored consumption. Most dealers haven't them, but all can obtain them. Listening to race records is nearly the only way for white people to share the Negroes' pleasures without bothering the Negroes."[105]

Both also recognized the significance of the commercial field recordings: "It is the pleasant occupation of Ralph S. Peer," Niles wrote, "to go on expeditions throughout the South looking for such as Rabbit [Brown], and inducing them to sing their songs for Victor Records on the spot."[106] Nonetheless, he asked in exasperation: "Why should recording managers of phonographic companies remain ignorant of the mine which [the folk-song collector Carl] Sandburg has opened up? They contribute to knowledge by their expeditions into the Southern mountains, where they pick up the country's least sophisticated songs and dances at their source, but the resulting hill-billy records are ninety percent trash, fit only to sell back to the hill-billies."[107] Despite his condescension to "hill-billies," Niles praised the recordings of Jimmie Rodgers, Ernest Stoneman's Mountaineers, Gid Tanner and his Skillet Lickers, and Bascom Lunsford, all of which have come to be regarded as the "roots" of modern country music. For his part, Gallop noted that "Not only do scientific expeditions and individual collectors arm themselves with recording apparatus and thus make permanent record of the words and music of folk-musicians the world over, with all their vocal and instrumental mannerisms, but the big recording companies, while pursuing purely commercial aims, have made similar records forming a valuable contribution to musical scholarship."[108]

Niles and Gallop stand out not only for their early practice of the record review, a form that would flourish over the next century, but for their recognition and defense of the new phonograph culture taking shape. "I have been waiting for someone to take up the cudgels on behalf of the gramophone," Gallop wrote in 1934, "and proclaim the respects in which 'canned' music may be preferable to the real article. Since no one has done so, I now feel constrained to enter the lists myself," noting that "we can summon up native performers from every quarter of the globe with their 'strange music' and stranger instruments and voice production."[109]

From Song and Dance to Records

If phonograph culture transformed audiences and musicians, it also transformed the musics themselves, turning songs and dances into "records." At first glance, the vernacular phonograph musics seem to be made up of a repertoire of songs and dances: the labels on the discs almost always carried a song title and usually included a dance title. But song and dance are such universalizing terms that it is worth reflecting on the nature of the songs and dances found on these "records," particularly since the word "record"—now as much an emblem of twentieth-century vocabulary as the "triple-decker" novel is of the nineteenth century—came to mean not simply the disc one purchased, played, and collected, but the "piece" of music it contained.[110] The characteristic musical unit of the vernacular phonograph record was three minutes of recorded sound, set by the approximate limits of a ten- or twelve-inch disc rotating at 78 revolutions per minute, more or less.[111] These three-minute extracts were ripped from musical practices built on longer durations, and did not match the variety of existing song and dance forms. There were many musicians like the flamenco singer Aurelio de Cádiz (Aurelio Selles), recorded in a 1929 Polydor session, who "disliked records, saying they never allowed the singer to get going."[112] As a result, the vernacular phonograph musics were constituted by the tension between the record and the song, the record and the dance.

In addition, it might seem that song and dance have always been part of everyday life, and that everyday life is itself a transhistorical phenomenon. However, if everyday life is, as social theorists from Henri Lefebvre on have argued, a modern invention, the consequence of the capitalist division of workplace and household, of "making a living" and "living," then the songs and dances of vernacular phonograph music—forms radically distinct from earlier art songs and work songs, court dances or folk dances—were, I would suggest, the first great medium that articulated and constituted the "everyday." The songs and dances on the "record" evaded the terms of musicology's classic dichotomy of functional and absolute music. They were neither functional, deeply embedded in social activities at specific times and places, the way work songs, sacred songs, or wedding dances were, nor were absolute, the object of an autonomous aesthetic contemplation, disconnected from the world of utility, like the modern art musics. Records simply inhabited modern daily life, an omnipresent soundtrack to household and neighborhood. They were, to borrow Walter Benjamin's way of understanding the arts of daily life (his examples were architecture and film), musics for distraction rather than contemplation, musics that one lived with rather than musics that separated themselves from daily life.[113]

Moreover, though dance and song are in many times and places intertwined, one of the peculiarities of the vernacular phonograph musics was the way they encompassed but separated dance and lyric. Almost all of these musics had two distinct recorded repertoires: the one an instrumental dance music with characteristic rhythms performed by ensembles, the other a lyric song form with characteristic commonplaces, performed by individual singers with spare accompaniment. Thus highlife in Lagos encompassed both a dance style with roots in marching brass bands, and the guitar-based lyric "palm-wine" style spread by Kru sailors;[114] tango on the River Plate was both a driving instrumental dance played by the sextets of Francisco Canaro and Roberto Firpo (two violins, two bandoneons, piano, and bass), and a lyric song—*tango canción*—made famous by Carlos Gardel, often accompanied by two guitars.[115] Samba encompassed the parading style dominated by the percussive batucada as well as a lyric samba—*samba cancão*—accompanied by guitar and matchbox; the blues could mean either the virtuoso "hot jazz" played by the young Louis Armstrong or Sidney Bechet, or the blues lyrics sung by Bessie Smith or Blind Lemon Jefferson. To those outside the idiom, it was sometimes difficult to see the two branches as related. By separating, analytically, lyrics from dances, we can see how the new song topoi refigured the commonplaces of everyday life, while the new dance steps remade the rhythms of everyday life.

The hybrid "songs" of the vernacular phonograph records came out of the intersection of, and tension between, the professional ballads and theater songs that had become the mainstay of the sheet music publishing industry over the previous century, and the practice of performing linked lyric commonplaces that characterized the vernacular musics of the colonial ports. At the time, this uncertain relationship between commercial sheet music and lyric commonplaces was viewed through the lens of folk song, provoking controversies over whether or not samba, fado, jazz, and the like were folk musics. Reflecting on fado's relation to folk song, Rodney Gallop concluded that it was "urban folk song"; in the US, the composer Virgil Thomson insisted that jazz was not folk song but urban and urbane.[116] Three elements seemed to distinguish these musics from folk song: they were urban, not rural; they were played by professional musicians, not ordinary members of a community; and they appeared as authored songs, not simply variants on an oral tradition. In retrospect, it is clear that the recorded vernacular songs were not "folk songs," as that term was understood at the time; indeed a host of historians and musicologists have revealed that many songs which appeared to be "authentic" folk songs had their origins less in the "oral tradition" than in the circulation of commercial sheet music. However, the rejection of the "folk" nature of vernacular phonograph music has often obscured the hybrid nature of these "songs," and it would be an equal mistake simply to assimilate them to the established paradigm of printed sheet music.

Since the commodity sold was a disc rather than the printed song, the musical unit of the commodity usually had a unique lyric component, which was often confused and conflated with the commercial "popular song." Moreover, since the circulation of records quickly led to the practice of "covering" popular tunes from distant regions, this helped reify the "song" as the central musical unit. However, in most cases, the lyrics sung on these records were less composed songs with standard sections—verses and refrains, choruses and releases—than improvised combinations and recombinations of lines, couplets, and verses drawn from a body of lyric commonplaces that were used and reused. This was true of the *coplas* of flamenco, of the *largos* and *montunos* of son, of the *pantuns* of kroncong, of the *mele* of hula, of the ṭarab phrases repeated and extended through vocal melismas, and of the blues couplets of early jazz and blues. These lyric commonplaces were often tied to particular rhythms, as in the various *palos* of flamenco; to melodic shapes, as in the "tumbling strain" of the blues or the maqam of ṭarab; or to chord changes: for example, the classic West African "song," "Yaa Amponsah," is really a particular rhythm and set of chord changes.[117] The resulting songs often had little thematic or narrative unity. "The first two lines of a *pantun* very seldom have any connection with the following two lines," a contemporary wrote of kroncong's Malay lyric, "they are simply placed there for the purpose of rhyming. To those who understand Malay, it is an easy matter to appreciate the construction of a *pantun*, but it is no easy task to render a correct translation in a foreign tongue."[118] Thus, these songs were neither closed organic forms, like the folk songs Bartók collected—"in the folksong, text and music form an indivisible unity"—nor closed compositions like commercial sheet music; rather they lie in the open quotidian realm of the proverb, "equipment for living," in Kenneth Burke's words.[119]

Nonetheless, since "songs" had, through the world of publishing, become commodities on which songwriters staked claims to ownership, the issue of the "author" of vernacular music was highly contested. Commercial bandleaders arranged commonplaces, both melodic and lyric, turning them into commercial "songs." When they copyrighted and published the arrangements, they were often taken to be the author of the song: W. C. Handy did this with blues commonplaces, as did Johnny Noble with "ancient" hulas and chants.[120] The early Afro-Brazilian sambistas regularly sold the sambas they had written to white singers who recorded them: Ismael Silva sold many sambas to Francisco Alves, and Cartola later remembered being told in 1931 that "Mário Reis [a popular singer] wanted to buy one of my sambas … Buy a samba? For what?" "He's going to make a record," was the reply, so Cartola met Reis, "sang the samba [he] wanted to hear," and sold it for 300 *contos*.[121] In turn, many early record producers like Ralph Peer insisted that vernacular musicians record musical works made up of such lyric commonplaces rather than commercially printed songs; in this way, they not only avoided paying royalties, but also, by copyrighting these "new" songs in the name of the record producer, they generated new income for the record producer's music publishing firm.[122] After a period of chaotic claims and counter-claims to songs in the early years of the recording boom, a host of legal challenges to the copyright of particular songs emerged in the 1930s, and the battles continued through the rest of the century.

When the popular song of commercial sheet music did intersect vernacular phonograph records, it often led to the remarkable musical transformation that is central to the vernacular revolution in music: the elevation of the recorded improvised performance over the song itself, a tendency that can be seen in tzigane's treatment of Hungarian sheet music and in jazz's treatment of Tin Pan Alley tunes. As Béla Bartók noted of tzigane, "Gypsy performance destroys" the "indivisible unity" of text and music "because it transforms, without exception, the vocal pieces into purely instrumental ones. This alone suffices to prove the lack of authenticity in gypsy renderings of music, even with regard to popular art music."[123] What Bartók understood as "lack of authenticity" could as easily be understood as a "re-functioning" of the popular song, to use Benjamin's term, creating a new, performance-based rather than song-based, idiom. Such a re-functioning is close in spirit to the remarkable innovation of Louis Armstrong when he first adapted Tin Pan Alley songs to the idiom of jazz in 1928. This was a radical break with the repertoire of hot jazz and race records; indeed, one might think of this as the moment of a shift from "race records," on which black musicians recorded a black repertoire for black audiences (figures like Bessie Smith or Blind Lemon Jefferson in the 1920s), to "race covers," on which black musicians recorded covers of mainstream popular hits for a largely black audience (figures like Billie Holiday in the 1930s). Nonetheless, each of these mark a powerful decolonization of the ear, as mainstream forms were subjected to new timbres and new rhythms, often leaving the source song behind.

Just as the mass production of printed sheet music in the nineteenth century created "songs" as commodities to be sold, so the proliferation of printed dance manuals at the turn of the century created "dances" as commodities, as the waltz, polka, schottische, and mazurka were joined, in ports around the world, by the dances of the Americas: the tango, the maxixe, the foxtrot, the Charleston, the beguine, the rumba. "When the *tango* made its appearance in the old world in 1910, it released a dance frenzy, almost a mania, which attacked all ages and classes with the same virulence," the pioneering German musicologist Curt Sachs wrote, as he summed up the history of his generation in his 1933 *World History of the Dance*:

> The adoption of American Creole and Negro steps corresponds exactly to the assimilation of Spanish and Slavic dances in earlier centuries, ... Since the Brazilian *maxixe* of 1890 and the *cakewalk* of 1903 broke up the pattern of turns and glides that dominated the European round dances, our generation has adopted with disquieting rapidity a succession of Central American dances, in an effort to replace what has been lost to modern Europe: multiplicity, power, and expressiveness of movement to the point of grotesque distortion of the whole body. We have shortly after 1900 the *one-step* or *turkey-trot*; in 1910, inspired by the Cuban *habanera*, the so-called "Argentine" *tango* with its measured crossing and flexing steps and the dramatic pauses in the midst of the glide; and in 1912 the *fox trot* with its wealth of figures. After the war we take over its offspring, the *shimmy*, which with toes together and heels apart contradicts all the rules of post-minnesinger Europe; the grotesquely distorted *Charleston*; in 1926 the *black bottom* with its lively mixture of side turns, stamps, skating glides, skips and leaps; and finally the rocking *rumba*— all compressed into even movement, all emphasizing strongly the erotic element, and all in that glittering rhythm of syncopated four-four measures classified as *ragtime*. One can hardly imagine a greater contrast to the monotony of steps and melody of the latter part of the nineteenth century.[124]

These modern dances were thus neither folk dances nor society dances. "When talking about mambo," the Cuban critic Alejo Carpentier wrote, "it's a matter of not mixing up or confusing dance music, the fruit of urban life, with folklore. The two are never the same. Dance music of the cities is not a pure outburst of popular inspiration, like the *son*, for example, rural song, regional dance, and so on. It is the product of what in all times is called 'modern life.'"[125] This was true as well of the modern hula that emerged in late nineteenth-century Hawaii: the "hula kuʻi," "the most democratic of the hulas," which, in the words of a turn of the century observer, "became all the rage among dancing folk, attaining such a vogue as almost to cause a panic among the tribunes and censors of society."[126] The modern dances were, one might say, a product of the circulation of commercial "dances" marketed in printed dance manuals and dance schools, and the popular practice of mimicking and satirizing society dances and folk dances alike in the colonial ports.

However, as these urban dances were recorded, they were further transformed. Their iterative forms had to be fitted to the three-minute limits of the disc; one finds, for example, that the commercial recordings of Irish dance tunes—with their repeating and alternating eight-bar sections—often assembled medleys of three different tunes. And if the printed dance manuals had illustrated the dances as a disciplined and regularized set of steps that could be taught and learned, with competitions and exhibitions codifying them, sound recording tended to transform the vernacular dances—whether the tango or the foxtrot, the beguine or the hula—from a set of steps into a characteristic rhythm. As a result, phonograph "dances" were more abstract if just as visceral, increasingly autonomous from social dancing, recorded rhythms that reverberated around the world.

In addition to turning songs and dances into records, the commercial and technical context of recording had profound effects on the repertoires and musical styles of vernacular musicking. The commercial impulses of the recording producers reshaped the musics in ways of which we, as listeners to the existing recordings, may not be aware. In some cases they restricted the recorded repertoire of performers to specific commercially defined genres, as when the blues recording boom led race-record labels to package black songsters with wide-ranging repertoires as blues singers.[127] In other cases, recording engineers changed the characteristic instrumentation of vernacular idioms: Christopher Waterman notes that a recording engineer added a violin and keyboard to an early *jùjú* recording, though these instruments were not part of performed *jùjú*.[128]

The technical limits and freedoms of recording had profound effects on musical styles. "There is a wide difference between hearing an air in the propitiatory surroundings of a dance hall and the listening to the same as emitted by a mechanism of pitiless precision," Gisèle Dubouillé wrote in a review of the early beguine recordings. "The microphone requires the sacrifice of the allurement of improvisation and the embellishments of a pre-arranged orchestration."[129] But the microphone also opened up new and more intimate vocal styles—"crooning"—and changed the relations between singers and instrumentalists. "The microphone and audio amplifier facilitated the coordination of guitar and voice in flamenco performances," flamenco scholar William Washabaugh argues.

> Prior to the mike, the guitarist and the *cantaor* formed a mismatched pair. The guitar was a quiet, introspective instrument, generally incapable of projecting anything but vague percussive sounds over long distances. The *cantaor*'s voice, however, had formed in early nineteenth-century Andalucía under the influence of Italian operatic styles, and was a powerful projective instrument.[130]

Finally, electrical recording led to a wave of experiments with techniques of altering sonic space. Precisely because recording separated music from its place of performance, recording engineers began to reinsert a sense of place in the recording. At first, this took the form of audio captioning, as artists were introduced at the start of the disc; later, as radio broadcasting accustomed audiences to listening from afar, singers would open a recording by setting the scene. As recording engineers began to experiment with reverb and echo, they could create imaginary audioscapes; indeed, Peter Doyle has suggested that a repertoire of "spatial sonic production practices" were invented, not at the heart of the recording industry's best practices, but in the less prestigious "shadow" recording of Southern blues and hillbilly music. The first use of "managed reverb," he argues, was the landmark 1927 recording of Jimmie Rodgers's "Blue Yodel No. 1" in RCA's Camden studio in Trinity Baptist Church.[131] In the process, recording became an art in itself.

The feedback loops created by the schizophonia of recorded sound, combined with a worldwide industry that inadvertently circulated the vernacular musics of the colonial ports, not only reconfigured local and regional music practices, but created a new phonograph culture. Whereas musical performances in the era before recording usually functioned in specific social worlds and spaces, vernacular sounds on shellac discs not only transgressed those boundaries but created a new world soundscape. And this new soundscape was more than a musical revolution. Just as earlier musical revolutions were harbingers of political transformations, so this remaking of world musical space was a harbinger of the remaking of the world's social and political space, a herald of the anticolonial revolutions of the twentieth century.

5

Decolonizing the Ear: The Cultural Revolution of Vernacular Phonograph Musics

What were the political consequences of this phonograph culture? The recording sessions between 1925 and 1930, which rendered a musical revolution on discs of shellac, coincided with a vogue for primitivism and exoticism among the modernist counter-cultures of the imperial capitals. Dance "crazes" broke like waves over the cabarets of Paris, New York, and Berlin, beginning with the tango and the foxtrot just before the Great War, and followed by the Charleston, the rumba, and the beguine in the decade after the war. The modern "night-club" assumed a colonial shape, from Paris's Bal Nègre to New York's Cotton Club. Empire was displayed and performed for metropolitan audiences in the series of world's fairs and colonial expositions, which featured the "exotic" musics of the colonies. Hawaiian musicians performed at the 1914 Taishô World Exposition in Tokyo and the 1915 Panama-Pacific International Exposition in San Francisco, African and Caribbean musicians at the 1924–25 British Empire Exhibition at Wembley, Cuban son sextetos at the 1929 Ibero-American Exposition in Seville, Martinique beguine orchestras as well as musicians from Algeria, Madagascar, and Indochina at the 1931 Paris International Colonial Exposition in Vincennes, Mexican mariachi bands at the 1934 Century of Progress exposition in Chicago, and black South African dance bands at the 1936 British Empire Exhibition in Johannesburg.

But the recording sessions also coincided with the first stirrings of anticolonial activism and thought. In February 1927, nearly two hundred pioneering anticolonial activists from Asia and Africa met in Brussels to form the League Against Imperialism. They were members of a host of anticolonial organizations: the Étoile Nord-Africaine in Algeria, the Destour in Tunisia, the South African National Congress, the Indian National Congress, the Comité de Défense de la Race Nègre. Moreover, the Brussels conference was just one of a series of such meetings that took place in various imperial cities in the decade after the Great War: the three Pan-African Congresses in Paris, London and Brussels between 1919 and 1923 initiated by W. E. B. Du Bois among others; the Baku Congress of the Peoples of the East in 1920, which marked the anticolonial turn in Communist theory and practice; the congress of the Union Intercoloniale in Paris in 1921, which brought together activists from the French colonies including a young Ho Chi Minh; the First Continental Anti-Imperialist Congress in Buenos Aires in 1925; and the Pan-Asian People's Conferences in Nagasaki in 1926 and in Shanghai in 1927.[1] These meetings of young intellectuals and activists were themselves reverberations of the protest and unrest that ranged from the massive Chinese student demonstrations in 1919 (that became known as the May Fourth Movement) to the non-cooperation campaigns in India that brought Gandhi to international attention, and from the Egyptian uprising of 1919 to the Rif War of the early 1920s and the Sandinista rebellion in Nicaragua in 1927.

Were the vernacular phonograph records simply another face of the metropolitan dance crazes, a commercial exploitation of the imperial fascination with the exotic colonial "other"? Were they a form of colonial mimicry, a derivative discourse not unlike the ubiquitous minstrel shows of modernism? Or were they more akin to the fugitive meetings of anticolonial intellectuals, musical leagues against imperialism, part of the revolution against colonialism that was to shape the course of the twentieth century? The links between literature and anticolonialism have often been noted—Ngugi wa Thiong'o's classic *Decolonizing the Mind* addressed the politics of language in African literature—and Fanon pointed to the role of the radio in the anticolonial struggle in Algeria. In this chapter, I want to suggest that the phonograph was equally important to decolonization: that vernacular gramophone music was a herald of decolonization, part of a cultural revolution that made possible the subsequent political revolutions.

For these vernacular phonograph musics not only captured the timbres of decolonization; the emergence of these musics—hula,

rumba, beguine, tango, jazz, samba, marabi, kroncong, ṭarab, chaabi—
was decolonization. It was not simply a cultural activity that *contributed*
to the political struggle; it was somatic decolonization, the decolonization of the ear and the dancing body. Decolonization, I will suggest,
was a musical as well as political event. Moreover, this decolonization
of the ear preceded and made possible the subsequent decolonization
of legislatures and literatures, schools and armies. The global soundscape was decolonized by the guerrilla insurgency of these new musics
before the global statescape was reshaped.

There are three reasons why it may be difficult to hear these vernacular phonograph musics as a decolonization of the ear. First,
there was often a profound gap between decolonization as a political revolution—the winning of formal political independence, and
the indigenization of state apparatuses from legislatures and schools
to armies and police—and decolonization as a cultural revolution—
the iconoclasm that smashed the aesthetic and philosophical idols of
everyday life, the ordinary hierarchies and inequalities that depended
on common-sense ideologies of "race," "color," and "civilization." For
every brief moment of convergence between the political and cultural revolutions, there are long stretches where they seem completely
separate. Antagonism and mutual suspicion were perhaps more characteristic than solidarity and alliance between the forces of political
and cultural decolonization; anticolonial political activists and thinkers were often tone-deaf when hearing these new musics.

Second, there is a gap between the biographical time of individual musicians making recordings—and the remarkably brief window
in time when the recording industry was open to these vernacular
musics—and the *longue durée* of cultural revolution, a remaking of the
very structure of feeling, as new sensibilities and new aesthetics become
new ways of living. If, over generations, these musics did decolonize
the ear, it remains difficult to register this in particular recordings by
particular musicians. It was never self-evident what the decolonization
of music would sound like, and what musics were or were not part of
the colonial order. But this gap is not different in kind than the parallel
one between the *longue durée* of political decolonization and the biographical time of political actors; the debates over figures like Umm
Kulthūm, Louis Armstrong, Johnny Noble, and Carmen Miranda are
not dissimilar to those over Gandhi and Bose, Nkrumah and Senghor,
Mao and Ho Chi Minh, who struggled among themselves over the
strategies and idcologies of anticolonialism.

Third, these were not unequivocally musics of liberation. Unlike the "movement musics" that sustained later liberation movements, like *chimurenga* in Zimbabwe or *nueva cancíon* in Latin America, these musics appear to be simply the apolitical commercial musics of the barrios and favelas. Moreover, as nationalist critics recognized early on, these musics did not easily fit into nationalist garb; they were creolized, mixed-race musics from the start. The subsequent attempts by post-revolutionary and postcolonial regimes to mobilize these music as nationalist "audiotopias," often taking particular regional musics as metonymies of a whole nation, was a complex process, and, when successful, often ended up succumbing to an official state nationalism.

Thus if we interpret these musics solely in a frame of national liberation, we miss the fact that the circulation of these records, to Rio and Shanghai as much as to Paris and Berlin, was fundamental to their decolonization of the ear. The antinomies that haunt the debates over these musics—their initial appearance as an exotic "craze" abroad and a disreputable "noise" at home, and their subsequent vindication as a music both "national" and "popular"—depend on a too-simple geography, which reads home as the nation and abroad as the imperial metropolis. I want to suggest that the recent re-thinkings of the space and time of decolonization allow us to recast our understanding of these musics.

The pioneering accounts of decolonization generally narrated the winning of political independence by peoples in colonized territories, and the emergence of new postcolonial nation-states. They focused on the era after World War II, the age of Three Worlds, and in them, as Martin Shipway puts it in his fine synoptic history, decolonization was seen "*either* as a composite of the individual national narratives of each of the hundred or so ex-colonies' paths to independent statehood, *or* as the 'bigger' story of the breakdown of a number of imperial systems against the backdrop of a major structural shift in the international system."[2] National historians narrated the emergence of an independent state, as anticolonial politics and culture fused in popular mobilizations; imperial historians chronicled the international conflicts and metropolitan political struggles as they diagnosed the end of the European empires.

However, the various forms of "postcolonial" critique (which range from Edward Said's *Orientalism* to *Subaltern Studies* to the notions of colonial modernity in Aníbal Quijano and Enrique Dussel) have shifted our sense of decolonization in both space and time. The spatial recasting accents the transcolonial and diasporic character of decolonization. If one reads the conjuncture of mid-twentieth-century decolonization less in the light of the nation-states that resulted from it and more in the light of the uneven history that produced it, we see the crucial importance of Frederick Cooper's insistence that "the success of anticolonial movements ... cannot be explained on a colony-by-colony basis"; rather it depended on "territory-crossing politics" like the pan-Arab and pan-African movements.[3] This is particularly true of the hinge decade after the crisis of the Great War, when the colonial empires seemed at their "zenith,"[4] and when the utopias or promised lands of home rule, self-rule (*swaraj*), independence, a Negro World, an intercolonial union emerged. "Black internationalism," Brent Edwards writes of this moment when the term is coined, "is not a supplement to revolutionary nationalism, the 'next level' of anticolonial agitation. On the contrary, black radicalism necessarily emerges through boundary crossing—black radicalism *is* an internationalization."[5]

The temporal recasting suggests that, even if the conjuncture of decolonization in the era of the United Nations remains a fundamental punctual history—the extraordinary emergence of more than one hundred new nations in the three decades between the end of World War II and the defeat of the Portuguese in Angola and Mozambique in the mid-1970s—it must nevertheless be read against the longer *durée* of colonial modernity, during which colonial conquest and anticolonial resistance overlapped, and which has still not ended. Since this longer history created, as Fanon argued, a Manichean world in which "settlers" dispossessed "natives" of their land, decolonization is racked by the interference between "settler" decolonization and "native" decolonization. Moreover, since colonial economies were built on plantations and mines worked by enslaved and indentured populations, often recruited across oceans and continents by ship and railway, decolonization was complicated by the interference between the emancipation struggles of slave and post-slave populations, the land struggles of dispossessed indigenous populations, and the justice struggles of contracted and indentured migrants from the east and the south of Europe and Asia alike.

To understand the decolonization of the ear, we need a parallel reconceptualization of these vernacular phonograph musics. They, too, have often been understood either as distinct and unconnected national musics, linked in complex ways to regional folkloric musics, or as an episode in the remarkably concentrated and centralized multinational recording industry, part of the emergence of a transnational, Western popular music industry. To argue that decolonization is a musical event, that a musical decolonization preceded and prefigured political decolonization, suggests that empire and colonialism was itself a musical event. The vernacular phonograph musics grew out of the colonization of music, and they were enmeshed with the institutions and spectacles of colonial culture. These musics and records shared the ambiguity of the colonial ports and railway towns in which they took shape: they were two-faced musics, objects of suspicion, intimate with both colonial and indigenous forms and instruments. However, as we will see, these recorded musics were quickly mobilized in anticolonial struggles, and became part of the emerging cultures of resistance. Even when these musics carried no apparent political meaning, their disruptive noise challenged not only the musical codes of empires and racial supremacy, but also the improving and uplifting ideologies of many colonial elites. And their embodiment of the commonplaces of daily life in the colonial ports gave them hidden meanings, what the Hawaiians called the *kaona* of the hula. As they reverberated across the archipelago of colonial ports, they came to figure the utopian promise of decolonization itself, heralding a Third World.[6]

His Master's Voice? Colonizing the Ear

There are two reasons one might be skeptical of the claim that these vernacular phonograph musics were heralds of decolonization. First, the musics were deeply influenced by colonialism's musical project, its colonization of the ear. Second, as these musics were performed in colonial ports and metropolitan capitals in the 1920s and 1930s, they were often subordinated to the work of tourism and imperial display. As a result, anticolonial militants and intellectuals were suspicious of musics that seemed a product of colonial domination and exploitation. For many critics, the slogan emblazoned on so many of these discs in a variety of languages—"His Master's Voice"—aptly captured the meaning of these colonized musics.

There is no doubt that these musics were products of the colonial era. As Kofi Agawu has persuasively argued, colonialism was a musical event.[7] The imperial conquest and colonization of territory was "accompanied" by the musical occupation of the space, and the projection of a new colonial order in sound. The vernacular phonograph musics were as deeply indebted to colonial music practices as they were to the street parading ensembles of the colonial ports. Two colonial legacies were particularly important: the worldwide spread of Protestant missionary hymns and choral singing, and the worldwide creation of military brass bands. Together they sponsored the diffusion of European musical instruments and practices as well as the imposition of European common practice tonality.

The remarkable missionary energy invested in the propagation of Christian hymn singing suggests that musical conversion is a necessary condition for religious conversion: to learn to sing is to learn to pray and to "believe" in a new way. A central part of colonial missionary work was the translation of Christian hymns into local languages and the formation of local choirs. In Hawaii, songs based on hymn forms—*himeni*—had become a major part of Hawaiian music by the early part of the twentieth century. Many of the earliest African recording artists came out of mission school choirs, figures like South Africa's Reuben Caluza, Ghana's Ephraim Amu, and Nigeria's J. J. Ransome-Kuti.[8] In his influential 1928 essay on African music, Erich Hornbostel characterized the mission-school propagation of hymn music as a form of colonialism, and lamented that Africans "would rapidly forget their own music, and Africa would become what North, Central, and large parts of South America and Polynesia (and of Africa itself) already are: that is, a mere European colony as far as music also is concerned."[9]

Similarly, the building of colonial forces of order—colonial police and armies—depended on their musical "auxiliaries"—the military brass bands and police bands that were developed around the globe.[10] "The brass band was a small-scale metaphor for the colonial process itself," a study of bands from Ghana and Tanzania to Surinam and Nepal concludes: "a single foreign bandmaster exerting authority over numerous native bandsmen who were expected to abandon their traditional ways of making music in favour of more 'civilized' European ways."[11] Many of the musicians recorded in the late 1920s received their training in military bands,[12] and several of these colonial brass bands were themselves recorded, including the band of the King's African Rifles, the British colonial regiment in East Africa.[13]

In these ways, the new musics of colonialism instituted new disciplines of the body—new ways of singing, of dancing, of marching, of playing instruments. Almost all of the vernacular phonograph musics adopted the mass-produced musical instruments of the European and American metalworking factories that had been marketed throughout the colonial world, not only the harmoniums and concertinas of hymn music and the trumpets and trombones of the military bands, but the ubiquitous guitar. This musical discipline also involved what Kofi Agawu has called the "violence of imposing harmony": "tonality was part of the 'civilizing mission' from the 1840s," which denied sovereignty to African languages, religions, and musics.[14] To speak of the colonization of the "ear" is thus a metonymy, for the reshaping of the musical subject is not only a reshaping of the individual's musical muscles—the articulated flesh and bones that make up the singing voice, the instrument-playing hands and lips, the dancing feet and hips; it is also the reshaping of the order of the group. The creation of marching bands and church choirs was a colonization not only of the body, but of articulated bodies.

Gandhi himself gives a good example of this when, in his *Autobiography*, he writes that his youthful attempt to become an "English gentleman" was as much about music and dance as language and elocution. "I thought I should learn to play the violin in order to cultivate an ear for Western music. So I invested £3 in a violin and something more in fees." He also "decided to take dancing lessons"; it was, he writes, "beyond me to achieve anything like rhythmic motion. I could not follow the piano and hence found it impossible to keep time." Though he gave up this attempt to cultivate a colonial ear and to keep colonial time, he later recalled that "the National Anthem used to be sung at every meeting that I attended in Natal," and he felt that he "must also join in the singing." "With careful perseverance I learnt the tune of the 'national anthem' and joined in the singing whenever it was sung." "I likewise taught the National Anthem to the children of my family," and "to students of the local Training College." Only later did the text begin to "jar" on him: "As my conception of *ahimsa* [nonviolence or non-harming] went on maturing, I became more vigilant about my thought and speech."[15]

There is no question that this musical colonization was an unfinished project, not least in the eyes of the colonizers. Musical cultures around the world remained a battleground between different musical codes, and in some places, there was little colonization of musical culture: "with the significant exception of military marching bands," David Lelyveld writes, "one is hard pressed to find any effort to introduce European music to India."[16] The musical codes of European colonialism took root mainly in the official musicking of schools, armies, and churches in the urban ports and colonial capitals. But it was precisely in the shadow of these urban schools, armies, and churches that the vernacular phonograph musics took shape.

If the vernacular phonograph musics were shaped by the colonization of the ear, much of their international celebrity was due to the apparatuses of imperial exhibition and tourism in Paris, Berlin, London, New York, and Tokyo. As early as 1933, Theodor Adorno argued that the apparent triumph of "'black jazz' as a sort of a brand-name" in "the European-American entertainment business" was "merely a confusing parody of colonial imperialism": in "the manufacture of jazz ... the skin of the black man functions as much as a coloristic effect as does the silver of the saxophone."[17] So it is not surprising that anticolonial activists and militants were deeply suspicious of these new commercial musics. On some occasions, this suspicion was shared by the musicians. In China, for example, Nie Er, the radical young songwriter and violinist of a Shanghai huangse yinyue ensemble, turned against the music of his mentor Li Jinhui, arguing that "erotic sex appeal and revealing passion are the 'achievements' of song and dance during the past dozen years ... Can't you hear the masses of people desperately crying out? You must go down to those people, because therein lies fresh material to create a new and fresh art." Nie left the Bright Moon Song and Dance Troupe but continued to work for Pathé, writing popular "mass songs" that incorporated Chinese work chants and folk tunes into huangse yinyue.[18]

Across the Americas, black activists and intellectuals often distanced themselves from black vernacular musics because these existed amid vaudeville theater's embrace of blackface minstrelsy, stage primitivism, and tourist exoticism. This tension is dramatized in Claude McKay's 1928 novel, *Banjo*, where musical episodes are regularly counterpointed against political conversations among the black sailors about racism and colonialism, Garveyism and seamen's unions. The clash of music and anticolonial talk culminates on the novel's final night in the Seaman's Bar in Marseilles. When Banjo and his fellow musicians arrive at the bar, the West African guitarist Taloufa is talking with an Indian seaman about being refused entry into England: "Colored subjects were not wanted in Britain. This was the chief topic of serious talk among colored seamen in all the ports. Black and brown men being sent back to West Africa, East Africa, the Arabian Coast, and India, showed one another their papers and held sharp and bitter discussions in the rough cafés of Joliette and Vieux Port." In the midst of this conversation, Taloufa is lured into joining the band: "You come right along and make that mahvelous music and fohgit the white man's crap," he is told. Taloufa abandons the political discussion and plays "a tormenting, tantalizing, tickling tintinnabulating thing that he called 'Hallelujah Jig' ... 'Lay off the coal, boy, and scrub you' hide / Jigaway ... jigaway. / Bring me a clean suit and show some pride / Jigaway ... jigaway. / Step on the floor, boy, and show me that stuff / Jigaway ... jigaway.'" Meanwhile, "above the sound of the music the Indian was emphasizing the necessity for all colored people to wake up and get together."[19]

For those in the bar, Taloufa's music and the Indian seaman's politics are at odds: one character stops listening to the Indian, because "the jigaway music was pounding in his ears ... There was no resisting it." Eventually the Indian seaman gives up: "it was dismaying to him that those boys with whom he had just been conversing so earnestly should in a moment become forgetful of everything serious in a drunken-like abandon of jazzing. 'Just like niggers,' he muttered, turning away."[20] McKay does not share the seaman's contempt for jazzing: it is worth noting that Taloufa's call to the dance floor—"lay off the coal ... and show some pride"—is itself a version of the Indian seaman's call to "colored people to wake up." And the novel's most powerful image of "the necessity for all colored people to wake up and get together" is Banjo's repeated attempt to form an orchestra. Nonetheless, as the novel ends, there seems to be an irreconcilable gap between "serious talk" and "jazzing."

Those who forged the very notion that decolonization was a cultural as well as a political revolution felt a profound ambivalence about these musics, as one can see in the fraught reflections on beguine, jazz, and "national music" that occur in the writing of the Martiniquan anticolonial thinkers who came of age in the era of vernacular gramophone music: Frantz Fanon and Édouard Glissant. According to his biographer, Fanon enjoyed the beguine of Alexandre Stellio, whose popular Martiniquan dance band first recorded in 1930.[21] However, Fanon's only reference to beguine comes in the 1955 essay "West Indians and Africans," where two periods in West Indian consciousness are delineated in an almost autobiographical sketch: "Before 1939, the West Indian claimed to be happy, or at least thought of himself as being so. He voted, went to school when he could, took part in the processions, and drank rum and danced the beguine."[22] Fanon's dismissal of vernacular music as part of an unreflective colonial daily life recurs when he writes that the French radio station in Algeria, Radio-Alger, was "listened to only because it broadcast typically Algerian music, national music."[23]

Fanon did take an interest in jazz, though a friend later said it was more sociological than musical.[24] In his writings, he is always *over-hearing* jazz and blues: rather than responding directly to the music, he responds indirectly, through another's audition, as in his account of Mlle B., the white patient whose "fear of imaginary black men" had its origins in the radio programs of black music to which her Colonial Service father listened. A similar parable of listening to jazz is at the center of Fanon's ambivalent claiming and disclaiming of "European culture" and "black civilization" in the conclusion to *Black Skin, White Masks*: replying to "an article that literally likened jazz to cannibalism irrupting into the modern world," Fanon writes that, "in the case in point, I didn't have to defend black music against white music; rather, I had to help my brother get rid of an unhealthy attitude."[25]

Fanon's overhearing the white reception of jazz and blues haunts his two famous talks on culture delivered at the Congresses of Negro Writers and Artists (in 1956 and 1959). In the earlier one, he writes that the "blues ... was offered up for the admiration of the oppressors. This modicum of stylized oppression is the exploiter's and the racist's rightful due. ... Still today, for many men, even colored, Armstrong's music has a real meaning only in this perspective."[26] Three years later, he returns to the way

the colonialists ... become the defenders of indigenous style. A memorable example, and one that takes on particular significance because it does not quite involve a colonial reality, was the reaction of white jazz fans when after the Second World War new styles such as bebop established themselves. For them jazz could only be the broken, desperate yearning of an old "Negro," five whiskeys under his belt, bemoaning his own misfortune and the racism of whites. As soon as he understands himself and apprehends the world differently, as soon as he elicits a glimmer of hope and forces the racist world to retreat, it is obvious he will blow his horn to his heart's content and his husky voice will ring out loud and clear. The new jazz styles are not only born out of economic competition. They are one of the definite consequences of the inevitable, though gradual, defeat of the Southern universe in the USA. And it is not unrealistic to think that in fifty years or so the type of jazz lament hiccupped by a poor, miserable "Negro" will be defended by only those whites believing in a frozen image of a certain type of relationship and a certain form of negritude.[27]

For Fanon, a new music was a consequence, not a cause, of the struggle against colonialism; for him the music of Stellio and Armstrong remains "frozen" in the colonial and Southern universe.

Fanon's contemporary, Édouard Glissant, used a more sanguine view of jazz to mount a withering critique of beguine in colonial Martinique. When jazz accompanies the migration of blacks in the US to "the great sprawling cities," he writes, "black music is reborn": "This music progressively records the history of the community, its confrontation with reality, the gaps into which it inserts itself, the walls which it too often comes up against. The universalization of jazz arises from the fact that at no point is it an abstract music, but the expression of a specific situation." In contrast, beguine represents the suspended state of Martinique where the plantation system has collapsed and "nothing replaces it." "The 'beguine' is the true voice of Martinique, from the plantations to the intense activity of the town of St.-Pierre. But from 1902 ... it no longer develops," leaving Stellio in the limbo of the commercial dance band. "The universalization of the beguine was real," Glissant writes, "(it is even possible that it exercised a profound and more durable influence on Europe, for example, than do salsa and reggae today), but this music is soon worn out." "Musical creativity, cut off from the imperatives of reality, becomes folkloric (in the worst sense) ... You must 'do things' in your country to be able to sing about it. If not, musical creativity is reduced to a numbing, neurotic practice that contains nothing but the capacity for disintegration."[28] For Glissant, beguine remains caught in colonial stasis, folkloric in the worst sense.

In the wake of Fanon and Glissant, postcolonial critics have accented the ways that rumba, tango, beguine, and hula were exploited by imperial entertainment industries. The international transculturation of stage or cabaret rumba in this period, Robin Moore argued, inaugurated the worldwide vogue of exotic musics, the "globalization of marginal culture."[29] The world circulation of tango, Marta Savigliano argued in her classic postcolonial critique of tango, was part of the logic of colonialism, "a trackable trafficking in emotions and affects that has paralleled the processes by which the core countries of the capitalist world system have extracted material goods and labor from, and imposed colonial bureaucratic state apparatuses and ideological devices on, the Third World (periphery)." This "imperialist circulation of feelings" produced a form of "emotional capital—Passion—accumulated, recoded, and consumed in the form of Exotic Culture"; these exotic representations then returned and ended up "becoming symbols of national identity" in a kind of "autoexoticization."[30] Similarly, discussing Odeon's marketing of beguine for the gramophone, Brent Hayes Edwards concluded that "the commodification of recorded beguine is simultaneously the commodification of the colonies ... another way for the European to appropriate *La France d'outre-mer*."[31] "In the hotel version of the *hula*," the native Hawaiian sovereignty activist Haunani-Kay Trask writes, "the sacredness of the dance has completely evaporated." It is, she writes, "a measure of the depth of our mental oppression ... [that] even those who have some glimmer of critical consciousness do not generally agree that the tourist industry prostitutes Hawaiian culture."[32]

The Coming Combat

Despite these powerful critiques of the exploitation and commodification of vernacular musics by a culture industry saturated in the racisms of colonial regimes as well as white-supremacist settler societies, there was also a sense among anticolonial thinkers that shifts in popular arts like music and dance anticipated the psychic and cultural transformation that was beginning to take shape. "Well before the political or armed struggle," Fanon wrote,

> a careful observer could sense and feel in these arts [dance, song, rituals, and traditional ceremonies] the pulse of a fresh stimulus and the coming combat. Unusual forms of expression, original themes no longer invested with the power of invocation but the power to rally and mobilize with the approaching conflict in mind. Everything conspires to stimulate the colonized's sensibility, and to rule out and reject attitudes of inertia and defeat. By imparting new meaning and dynamism to artisanship, dance, music, literature, and the oral epic, the colonized subject restructures his own perception. The world no longer seems doomed. Conditions are ripe for the inevitable confrontation.[33]

Perhaps the "dance crazes" in which "exotic" dances and songs conquered Europe and North America were only a surface turbulence obscuring a more fundamental transformation taking place across the archipelago of colonial ports.

The most striking—if atypical—examples of this anticipation of the "coming combat" appeared in the places where the electrical revolution in sound coincided with anticolonial struggles, as in the Indian subcontinent, in parts of the Caribbean, in East and Southeast Asia, and in North Africa, or with social upheavals in settler colonial societies, as in Cuba, Brazil, South Africa, and the United States. Here the links were so direct as to be misleading, as both militants and authorities connected the circulation of records with the circulation of opposition. Vernacular recording artists allied themselves with militant movements, joining anticolonial and radical organizations and participating in benefit concerts, as well as recording satirical attacks on the colonial regime, praise songs for movement leaders and martyrs, and nationalist anthems of the land and people.

A number of musicians allied themselves with anticolonial movements and played benefit concerts; a few even joined movement organizations. In Egypt, the popular theater singer Munīra al-Mahdiyya, one of the first Egyptian women to record, was closely aligned with the anticolonial movement: as the musciologist Virgina Danielson notes, "her company frequently performed nationalistic songs that were summarily censored by the British, giving rise to the slogan, 'Hawá 'l-ḥurriyya fī Masraḥ Munīra al-Mahdiyya' (There is love of freedom in the theatre of Munīra al-Mahdiyya)." These songs and performances were part of "the widespread public attitude of resistance to foreign rule that permeated city and countryside throughout the first quarter of the century." As early as 1921, the young Umm Kulthūm was featured in a concert honoring the Egyptian Wafd leader Zaghlul Pasha, and in 1928 she was singing at a benefit concert sponsored by the Egyptian feminist and nationalist Hudá Sha'rāwī.[34]

In Shanghai, popular "yellow music" and left-wing nationalist music were intertwined. Li Minghui was, according to one of her contemporaries, at "the front lines of the New Culture Movement ... the more they [conservative critics] loudly and cruelly cursed her [public appearances], the more youth who had been influenced by the New Culture Movement supported her."[35] In India, the Civil Disobedience campaign that Gandhi led in 1930 and 1931 attracted the support of popular singers, particularly in Tamil south India, where the local branch of the Odeon company, Saraswati Stores, produced records by popular Tamil artists supporting the Civil Disobedience campaign.[36]

Perhaps the most celebrated example was K. B. Sundarambal. Born in 1908 to a poor family, she became a popular Tamil theater singer despite having no formal musical training, and first recorded for Columbia in 1926. She was drawn to the Congress movement in the mid-1920s and began wearing khadi, the hand-spun and hand-woven cloth that became an emblem of the boycott of British goods and of Indian self-sufficiency, "swadeshi." In the late 1920s, K. B. Sundarambal and S. G. Kittappa staged a performance of their celebrated Valli-Thirumanan (Valli's Wedding) for Madras women activists. When, in 1931, Gandhi was released from prison and invited to the Second Round Table talks in London, Sundarambal released a record celebrating it: "Gandhi has Reached London/Let Us Honor Him."* She campaigned actively for Congress in 1937, and, after independence, was elected to the Madras state legislature.[37]

In South Africa, the dance bands that came out of the culture of marabi were linked with the emerging movements of black South Africans: the Merry Blackbirds played benefits for the African National Congress and the South African Communist Party through the 1930s and 1940s, as well as recording together with Makatshwa's Choir, a working-class choral group sponsored by the leading black labor organization, the Industrial and Commercial Workers' Union.[38]

For some musicians, these benefit concerts were just another gig: the Merry Blackbirds' leader Peter Rezant later recalled that he "had no political leanings in any way," and a member of the Pitch Black Follies recalled that Griffiths Motsieloa "never wanted to be involved ... [but] always wanted to be on the ... good side of the law." On the other hand, there were others, like John Mavimbela's Rhythm Kings, who explicitly endorsed the ANC in 1935.[39] In the United States most of the well-known jazz bands, including those of Duke Ellington, Cab Calloway, and Count Basie, played benefit concerts for the key Harlem political campaigns of the late 1920s and early 1930s, particularly the defense of the Scottsboro Nine.

In Cuba, many musicians were associated with the anti-Machado movement that led to the revolution of 1933. After Machado extended his presidential term in 1928, many musicians left Cuba; the songwriter Eliseo Grenet was forced to emigrate in 1932, when his popular "Lamento cubano" was deemed subversive.[40] Moreover, since the musicians' union would not accept son musicians as members, some son musicians joined Communist labor activists to form the Asociación Cubana de Conjuntos Típicos e Instrumentistas in 1932.[41]

Others became close to the Cuban Communist Party, including the trumpet player Julio Cueva, who had gone to Paris with Don Apiazu's band in 1932, and fought in the Spanish Civil War before returning to Cuba in 1939 and leading a popular mambo band. As a result of these connections, in "a unique chapter in broadcasting in the Western Hemisphere," the Communist Party operated one of the major radio stations in Cuba, Mil Diez, beginning in 1943; it emphasized Cuban music and culture, and featured leading Cuban musicians including the most popular bands of Arsenio Rodríguez and Antonio Arcaño: "Working at a Communist station," the historian Ned Sublette notes, "often had little to do with a musician's political affiliation. Some were enthusiastic Communists, but the intensive working schedules of most musicians suggested that they spent all their time in the world of rhythm and harmony and had little time or inclination for political involvement."[42]

In Argentina, an anticolonial interpretation of tango had emerged by the 1920s and 1930s.[43] In 1936, a pioneering social history of tango by the brothers Héctor and Luis Bates, based on their radio shows, argued that Paris, in adopting tango, an "exotic thing ... to exhibit ... before the astonished eyes of its tourists," did not realize that "instead of being the conquerer, it would end up conquered by our popular dance."[44] Tango musicians ended up on all sides of the political struggles that resulted in the rise of the populist Juan Perón in the 1940s. The bandleader Osvaldo Pugliese joined the Popular Front Communist Party in 1936, and was imprisoned several times by Perón; the singer Libertad Lamarque opposed Perón, and went into exile in Mexico.[45] The lyricist Homero Manzi, on the other hand, was a populist nationalist who began with the Radical Party in the 1930s and ended up a Peronist; and the lyricist Enrique Santos Discépolo, whose songs had been censored in the 1930s, gave radio talks for Perón.[46]

In some cases, insurgent movements—populist, nationalist, and communist—began to pay attention to the new sounds, and anticolonial activists became supporters of the new musics. In Nigeria, musicologist Christopher Waterman argues,

> early *jùjú* was a musical correlate of the tenuous political networks linking elite nationalist leaders such as Herbert Macaulay to a Yoruba-speaking wage-earning population that included civil servants, merchants, skilled craftsmen, and laborers ... Descendants of the nineteenth-century literate black elite had split into two major political groups: cultural

nationalists, who supported Macaulay's Nigerian National Democratic Party and the exiled Prince Eshugbayi Eleko, and sought to associate themselves with hypostasized Yoruba traditions; and a collaborationist faction ... which allied itself with the British administration. The former group provided a crucial source of support for *jùjú* music, while the latter generally regarded *jùjú* practitioners as insincere or incompetent converts performing an aesthetically displeasing hodgepodge of European and African musical elements.[47]

In South Africa, the leader of the Natal Industrial and Commercial Workers' Union, A. W. G. Champion, was a supporter of the vernacular musics, organizing a concert to welcome Caluza's Double Quartet back from London after the 1930 recording session.[48] In Tamil-speaking South India, the leader of the Congress Party, S. Satyamurthi, forged alliances with a number of popular singers, even though the rest of Congress was suspicious, and he hailed the "democratisation of musical tastes": "In days of old it was only the rich people that could afford the luxury of good music. But today, modern development and discoveries had brought it to the poorer classes by means of the gramophones and the radio."[49]

These links are not surprising, because the young musicians of the recorded vernacular musics often came from the same milieu as the young anticolonial activists. They lived in the colonial ports, working as shipping and railway clerks or seamen and dockers, and were mediators between the establishments of the local elites and the plebeian quarters. Like the anticolonial activists, they were often intercolonial migrants: indeed, in 1931, the South African Communist activist (and editor of the newspaper *Umsebenzi* [Worker]), Alfred Nzula, managed to travel from Cape Town to Moscow by "posing as one of Griffiths Motsieloa's singing group going to London for recording."[50]

In a few cases, anticolonial activists were themselves occasional musicians: such an overlap between anticolonial activism and vernacular recording can be seen in the figure of Ladipo Solanke, the Nigerian law student living in Britain who cofounded the West African Student Union in London in 1925, and published *United West Africa at the Bar of the Family of Nations* in 1927. The WASU not only sought to "foster a spirit of national consciousness and racial pride among its members,"[51] but combatted racism against West Africans in Britain. In 1925, Solanke took time from his activism to record for Zonophone a series of discs of unaccompanied Yoruba songs, as well as tracks of Yoruba proverbs and aphorisms, on which Solanke breaks into song, exclamation and chant: as the Zonophone advertisement noted, "Mr Solanke is a close Student of his country's laws and customs, and welcomes the opportunity of making a permanent record of some of the old ballads and sayings of the Yoruba-speaking nation, which otherwise might become lost in the course of time."[52] One sees a similar trajectory in the Trinidadian singer Sam Manning, who had recorded since the mid-1920s, leading the West Indian Rhythm Boys band in England, and then became a member of the executive committee of the International African Friends of Abyssinia, the pioneering anticolonial organization formed in London in 1935 by C. L. R. James and George Padmore.[53]

As a result of these links, a number of recordings explicitly expressed political sentiments, usually cast in one of the three main forms: satirical attacks on the colonial regime, praise songs for movement leaders and martyrs, and nationalist anthems of the land and people.

Satirical attacks on the colonial regime were perhaps the least common, though one finds them echoing throughout Trinidad's calypso in the 1920s and 1930s. When stevedores in Port of Spain went on strike in the fall of 1919, backed by the nationalist Captain Cipriani and the Trinidad Workingman's Association, the calypsonian Connie Williams recorded two songs about the strike; the following year's carnival saw what has been called the "first political cariso," by Patrick Jones, known as Oliver Cromwell, the Lord Protector. As calypso singer Atilla the Hun later recalled, "Oliver Cromwell, the Lord Protector, sang a kaiso that in the opinion of the audience was a castigation of colonialism: 'Class legislation is the order of this land/ We are ruled by an iron hand/Britain boast of equality/For the dominant race in this colony/But all British coloured subjects/In perpetual slavery.' He gained the second prize."[54]

Praise songs, on the other hand, were a particularly prominent genre for anticolonial sentiments. In addition to her song about Gandhi, K. B Sundarambal recorded a tribute to Congress leader Motilal Nehru on his death in 1931, as well as one of the many songs recorded about the March 1931 execution of the revolutionary nationalist Bhagat Singh in Lahore.[55] In post-revolutionary Mexico, the vernacular phonograph music boom led to the recording of many corridos about revolutionary leaders—the musical equivalent of the murals of Rivera, Siqueiros, and Orozco.[56] The earliest Yoruba recordings in Lagos, released by Odeon in 1931, included praise songs for Herbert Macaulay, the pioneering anticolonial activist who had led a successful mass campaign for the return of the Eleko, the traditional ruler of Lagos, from exile in 1931. After the Eleko returned "amid scenes of jubilation unprecedented in the history of Lagos,"[57] both the sakara musician Abibu Oluwa and the *jùjú* singer Tunde King recorded tributes to Macaulay.[58] And, in South Africa, the pioneering 1930 London recording session by Reuben Caluza included a praise song for John Dube, the first president of the African National Congress.[59]

A host of such praise songs came out of the strike wave that erupted across the British Empire in the mid-1930s. In Nigeria, the Jolly Orchestra, a popular working-class palm-wine band led by a Kru sailor and pennywhistle player, recorded a praise song, "Wallace Johnson," about I. T. A. Wallace-Johnson, the West African Marxist anticolonialist who had helped to form the African Workers' Union in Lagos, and was forced to flee Lagos when the police raided his house.[60] Meanwhile, in Trinidad, the strike wave that led to the 1937 "Butler riots" (and a major colonial investigation) became the subject of a series of calypsos recorded by Atilla the Hun, who had become the voice of ordinary Trinidadians over the previous decade—not only in the annual competitions among bands in the carnival tents, but on Decca recordings made in New York and shipped back to Trinidad for carnival season.[61] Atilla's first recording was a straightforward critique of the colonial commission's report, but the record was banned in Trinidad,[62] as he himself later wrote,

> another aspect of state interference which presented a terrifying proposition to the kaisonian was the banning of his records. Arising out of the 1937 riots and the visit and report of the Forster Commission, a kaiso record of the song on the strike was made for the Decca Recording Company, but it was banned and not allowed entry into Trinidad. The offending passage ran: "A peculiar thing about this Commission/And its 92 pages of dissertation/Is that there never arises the question/Of capitalistic exploitation/Read through the lines and there is no mention/Of the worker and his tragic position/Which leads one to entertain the thought/And wonder if it's a one-sided report." The kaisonian lost his royalties.[63]

In response to the ban, Atilla recorded two songs that ventriloquized his critique of the colonial commission by praising the colonial officials who had been dismissed or transferred for defending the workers.[64] In the following weeks, he also recorded and released a carefully worded narrative of "The Strike"*—"Different versions have been stated/As to

how the strikes originated/Well you may draw your own conclusion/
Atilla will reserve his opinion"—as well as a praise song for Butler
himself, who was still in hiding.[65]

If the praise songs were topical and timely, vernacular recording
artists also recorded songs that became nationalist anthems, praising the land and its people. A good example is the 1930 recording
of Ignacio Piñeiro's "Incitadora Región"* by the Sexteto Nacional,
which celebrated the beauties of "splendid Havana" "in spite of the
tyrant."[66] In China, the left-wing composer Ren Guang was hired as
the Pathé Asia musical director in 1928, and he "became instrumental
to the release of almost fifty leftist screen songs and national salvation
anthems from 1932 to 1937"; similarly, the radical songwriter Nie Er
wrote "most of his compositions … either for the musical screen or for
gramophonic reproduction," including "The March of the Volunteers,"
a film song that was to become the national anthem of the People's
Republic.[67]

In Vietnam, Dinh Nhu, a participant in the Nghe Tinh uprising
of 1930 who is credited with having written the first modernized
Vietnamese song—"Cung nhau di Hong Binh" (Let's Go Together
to Hong Binh) (1930)—set anticolonial lyrics to French popular
songs like "La Madelon" as well as to the French national anthem,
"La Marseillaise."[68] In Egypt, Umm Kulthūm's nationalist songs like
the 1936 "Ljmay Ya Misr!"* (Egypt, Let's Gather Together) became
emblems of Egyptian anticolonialism, both through recordings and
through her immensely popular monthly radio broadcast concerts.[69]

Both of the South African musicians at the London sessions of
1930 wrote and recorded these kinds of nationalist anthems. Griffiths
Motsieloa recorded "Nkosi Sikelel' iAfrika,"* the 1897 Xhosa
Christian hymn that had been adopted in 1925 as the anthem of the
African National Congress; and Reuben Caluza recorded "Umteto we
Land Act,"* his 1912 anthemic protest of the Native Lands Act that
had dispossessed black farmers: "We are the children of Africa/We
are crying for our land/Zulus, Xhosas, Sothos unite over the Land
Act issue."[70] Similarly, the Akropong Singing Band from the Gold
Coast made a 1931 Parlophone recording of "Yen Ara Asase Ni" (This
Is Our Own Land), the 1920s nationalist lyric by the choir leader
and composer Ephraim Amu which later became "Ghana's unofficial national anthem."[71] There were also anticolonial versions of the
socialist and communist anthem, the "Internationale": Ho Chi Minh
set it to Vietnamese words in 1925 and an instrumental version played

by two guitars, an eight-string banjo, ʻukulele or cavaquinho, and percussion, was issued in 1929 by the West African Instrumental Quintet
under the title "Bea Tsin No. 2."[72]

Nonetheless, the political stances taken by musicians and their lyric
commentaries on the politics of anticolonialism are perhaps the least
significant part of the cultural revolution worked by these musics. The
anticolonial meaning of a record often lay neither in the politics of
the musician nor of its lyrics, but in the way its very sound disrupted
the hierarchical orders and patterns of deference that structured colonial and settler societies. "Insurgency was a massive and systematic
violation of those words, gestures, and symbols which had the relations of power in colonial society as their significata," Ranajit Guha
argues in his classic account of the elementary forms of subaltern
struggle. "This was perceived as such both by its protagonists and their
foes. The latter were often quick to register their premonition of an
uprising as a noise in the transmission of some of the more familiar signals of deference."[73] The vernacular phonograph musics were
such a noise—disruptive and unsettling—and were heard as a violation of the musical order, an active challenge to the social "harmony."
Their sound carried political connotations. For example, kroncong, a
hybrid Eurasian genre that was initially associated with Jakarta youth
gangs—"kroncong crocodiles"[74]—became, as a result of gramophone
records and radio broadcasting, an emblem of resistance to Dutch
colonialism; kroncong, the Indonesian novelist Pramoedya Toer later
wrote, had "the vitality of a nation that was not yet free."[75]

This disruptive noise was met with a variety of forms of official
repression. "Post-midnight noises in the Colony" were banned by a
1934 ordinance in Singapore, which prohibited gramophone music as
well as "any drum or tom-tom, or blows [of] any horn or trumpet, or
beats or sounds [of] any brass or other metal instrument or utensil."[76]
"State interference in kaiso," the calypso singer Atilla the Hun wrote,

> conforms to the general accepted thesis that conquering powers, in their
> effort to consolidate their rule, have always sought to suppress native
> cultures and wage a withering war of ideas against the cultural mani-
> festations of native peoples. Kaiso has not escaped this common fate
> and the cultural ramparts have been … the scene of many skirmishes
> and battles between the conquerors and the conquered even down to the
> present day.[77]

Indeed, the vernacular phonograph musics often inherited a history of repression, since forms of percussion, dance, and public parading had been subjected to censorship and bans throughout the first quarter of the century. In his study of the censorship of Ghanaian popular performance, John Collins notes that popular musics regularly attracted the attention of both colonial authorities and missionaries: in 1908–09, Cape Coast brass bands were forbidden from playing "objectionable native tunes or airs"; the drums of an *aṣíkò* group were confiscated for playing "obscene songs"; and *osibisaaba* players were jailed for playing "a banned dance associated with social protest."[78]

In Hawaii, there had been a series of attempts to ban the performance of hula through the middle decades of the nineteenth century—in part because of missionary objections to its morality, in part because it was thought to encourage idleness—and "editorials against the hula continued to run in the newspapers and establishment press until as late as 1918."[79] Atilla the Hun recognized that the repression of kaiso was connected to the long battle over carnival celebrations: "That kaiso has been and is inextricably bound up with carnival is an accepted fact. Any measure affecting one has affected the other. In the war of derision and suppression against kaiso and carnival the trinity of state, press, and pulpit were united in a common crusade of condemnation."[80]

In white-dominated settler nations, the recording and circulation of the musics of post-slavery black populations appeared as a genuine musical revolution, as these musics had long been the object of repression. In Cuba, son musicians were occasionally jailed in the 1910s, and "throughout the 1910s, police routinely confiscated or destroyed instruments associated with son music."[81] This was part of the larger repression of Afro-Cuban culture in the first quarter of the century, which led to prohibitions of Afro-Cuban drumming and dancing by the Zayas administration in 1922.[82] The Sexteto Boloña, the son ensemble who were members of the Abakwa secret society and who had recorded in New York, were given jail sentences for disturbing the peace. During Machado's second term, at the height of the recording boom, he prohibited carnival *comparsas* and the playing of son in public, and in 1929 the mayor of Santiago even banned bongos and congas.[83] In Brazil, there are many accounts of the repression of Afro-Brazilian musicking. Though Marc Hertzman has recently challenged this "punishment paradigm," arguing that musicians were rarely targeted as musicians, he nonetheless vividly shows how sambistas were regularly jailed for vagrancy.[84] In South Africa, "noise" was invoked as a pretext for police raids on the slumyard shebeens where marabi was played: "the police used to come there just to stop the noise," recalled marabi pianist Ernest "Palm" Mochumi.[85]

This history of musical repression was closely linked to a history of anti-black race riots and massacres. Scholars have found persuasive if often silent connections between, for example, the 1900 Robert Charles riot in New Orleans and the culture of New Orleans jazz, and between the 1912 Oriente massacre in Cuba and the rise of Havana's son among communities of migrants from Cuba's eastern provinces.[86] In the nations of the Americas and Southern Africa whose independence had resulted from a *settler* decolonization, the "noise" of black music marked a powerful challenge to the sonic order. Throughout the ports of the settler colonial societies, controversies raged over the "blackness" of popular phonograph musics, since, as Gisèle Dubouillé wrote in 1932, "most of the modern dance music—from the tango to the rag-time, passing through the biguine and the blues—proceeds from the sources of African songs."[87]

Within these debates, two distinct ideologies took shape: on the one hand, a valorization of black musics, usually as a component of a mestizo or mulatto national identity, or, on the other, a rejection of black musics in favor of a valorization of the musics of rural white settlers, particularly ranchers and farmers, what might be called the "country" ideology. In Argentina, Vicente Rossi's *Cosas de Negros*, published at the height of the recording boom in 1926, argued, in the words of Borges's review, that "the tango has black blood." "The child of the Montevidean *milonga* and grandchild to the *habanera* ... it was born in ... a Montevidean warehouse used for public dances attended by *compadritos* and blacks ... [and] emigrated to the Buenos Aires Bajo, ... (where it was received by blacks and camp followers)."[88] In Cuba, the composer Eduardo Sánchez de Fuentes argued that there were "no African elements of any sort" in the Cuban *danzón*. "Sánchez de Fuentes's repugnance in admitting the black rhythms in Cuban music," Carpentier wrote in 1940, "can be understood as a reflection of a general outlook during the first years of the republic." The Afro-Cuban music movement "provoked a violent reaction from those opposed to anything black," he argued. "*Guajiro* music was pitted against Afro-Cuban music, the former purveyed as representative of white music, more noble, melodic, pure." In contrast, Carpentier insisted that "attempts to create a work of national expression always return, sooner or later, to Afro-Cuban and mestizo genres or rhythms."[89]

The new phonograph culture emerged in the midst of these battles over popular musicking. But phonograph records had a different relation to the social order of the colonial ports than either street parades or hotel ballrooms. Though the musical idioms were shared, there were three ways in which the shellac discs being sold in colonial ports and mill towns around the world constituted a different musical culture than the live performances in the streets or in the metropolitan music halls.

First, phonograph culture itself was less of a colonial culture than other aspects of music. To say that the "gramophone goes east," as the pioneering record producer Fred Gaisberg put it,[90] suggests that recorded sound was received, not only as a Western invention, but also as a Western practice. But this was not really true. Earlier mass-produced musical commodities distributed around the world had been accompanied by implicit musical cultures and practices. The export of sheet music and hymnals had depended on the acquisition of literacy in European musical notation. Mass-produced musical instruments carried with them implied ways of playing, in some cases fixed or standardized tunings, even if musicians adapted and transformed them. In contrast, when the phonograph appeared around the world, there was not a right way to record music nor to play a phonograph. Rather, as a historian of the gramophone in China has argued, the "shock" of the new technologies of recorded sound "took place nearly simultaneously in both Europe and Asia, Paris and Shanghai." Since recorded music circulated "roughly at the speed of the steamships that plied the colonial trade routes," it was not seen as "an ineffably and unalterably foreign cultural form."[91] Moreover, just as the first commercial musical recordings of the acoustic era took place in rapid succession around the world at the turn of the century, so the electrical microphone-loudspeaker complex—radio, electrical recording, and sound film—spread equally quickly in the 1920s.

Second, the circulation of phonograph records often evaded control by colonial authorities. In the Gold Coast, gramophone records were a way around the pass laws: "the legacy of British rule has made it impossible in some towns for musicians to perform in public since they must always obtain a 'pass,'" J. H. Nketia noted, "Fortunately one does not need a 'pass' to play the gramophone."[92] In India, colonial authorities did not immediately recognize the influence of gramophone records. "Only towards the end of the Civil Disobedience Movement, by which time there were already hundreds of gramophone records of patriotic songs in circulation, did the government seem to wake up to their importance," historian S. Theodore Baskaran notes in his discussion of the place of song in the Indian anticolonial movement. In contrast to the popular song booklets that were proscribed under press censorship laws, "there was no specific law which could be used against gramophone records," and few were banned.[93]

Even where they were censored or banned, it was more difficult to monitor discs than print or film. In Algeria, the historian Rebecca Scales notes, "the staff of the Bureau of Native Affairs … began to transcribe and translate the lyrics of hundreds of Diamophone records (and those of other labels), underlining particularly subversive passages with red ink." When a record of a "piano solo," issued by the North African company Rsaissi, was discovered in 1937 to contain no piano solo but rather a singer calling on Algerians to join Messali Hadj's recently formed Algerian People's Party, the colonial authorities tracked the distribution of the record from Algiers to cafés, market stalls, and brothels in tiny villages, seizing records and closing cafés.[94] In the British Caribbean, the calypso singer Atilla the Hun captured the contradictions of the colonial censorship of calypso. Trinidad's Theatre and Dance Halls Ordinance

> set up the benighted police and more particularly alien high-ranking officers as the supreme authority over the kaiso, a most anachronistic situation in 1934, bearing in mind the difficulty if not impossibility of an itinerant Englishman understanding the subtleties, innuendos, insinuations, and nuances connected with this art medium. The kaiso singer was now at the mercy of the police … In addition to this, the Colonial Secretary, usually another bird of passage, reserved the right to ban kaiso records.[95]

Third, though there is no doubt that the metropolitan music industry exploited the labor of colonial musicians in the recording studio as much as in hotels or nightclubs, the movement of gramophone discs was, as we have seen, paradoxically both narrower and wider than the live performances. On the one hand, it was more narrowly focused on the local market in the colonial ports; on the other, it was more open to accidental and contingent distributions and appropriations around the world.

Like the copies of Marcus Garvey's *Negro World*, George Padmore's *Negro Worker*, and Ho Chi Minh's *Le Paria*, gramophone records were carried around the world by sailors and students, militants and migrant workers. For example, a region-wide market in Arabic-language records developed, just as movements for independence—the Wafd in Egypt, the Destour in Tunisia, the Étoile Nord-Africaine in Algeria— emerged across North Africa in the wake of the Great War and the Rif anticolonial uprising in northern Morocco. Noting that the imported Baidaphone records disseminated "the official and unofficial songs of the different Muslim countries," an Algerian agent in the Bureau of Native Affairs wrote: "while this might appear anodyne, in fact they inculcate in the native the idea that there exist in the world peoples having his faith ... who have kept more or less the façade of Arab states and who proclaim their desire for liberty in their maternal language and not in that of a foreign *Marseillaise*."[96] The records of Umm Kulthūm not only traveled across North Africa and the Middle East but, by the mid-1930s, they were also being broadcast on the radio in the Dutch East Indies, making up much of the Arabic programing.[97]

Often the most innocuous songs and sounds carried anticolonial and nationalist connotations in the eyes of the population and of the authorities. This is particularly true of one of the most common song forms, the romantic lyric tribute to the land, often built on the simple musicality of place names. An example is the classic kroncong river song, "Bengawan Solo," written in 1940: "Because [it] described the historic beauty and magnificence of Central Java's river Solo, it qualified as an 'Asia for Asians' song," the musicologist Margaret Kartomi writes. "Under the Japanese Occupation and ensuing Indonesian revolutionary independence struggle, the song assumed national importance and spread from village to village in Java and then throughout Indonesia via Republican and private radio stations. President Soekarno himself told Indonesia's Ambassadors from the 1950s on that they should sing and promote the song in all their overseas postings."[98] Such songs of the land made up much of the repertoire of commercial Hawaiian music and are usually interpreted as versions of a tourist picturesque, the aural equivalent of the popular color postcards of the early twentieth century.

Indeed commercial Hawaiian music stands as a central instance of the contradictory relation between the vernacular phonograph musics and decolonization. The international vogue for Hawaiian music seems the perfect example of the expropriation of a music for a colonial and tourist exoticism. After all, Hawaiian music came to international attention through its presentation at Tokyo's Taishô World Exposition in 1914 and at the 1915 Panama-Pacific Exposition in San Francisco, which celebrated the US's recently acquired Pacific empire. Traveling theatrical troupes exploited the allure of sexualized Hawaiian women dancing the hula; the cult of the hula dancer echoed the cult of Josephine Baker in Paris. There is no doubt that much of the 1910s Tin Pan Alley boom in pseudo-Hawaiian songs fit a paradigm of tourist music. Moreover, by 1927, "Hawaiian Records" had become a separate category in the US recording industry journal, *Talking Machine World*, alongside "Race Records," "Old Time Tunes," "Dance Music," "Vocal Music," and "Instrumental Music." Unlike most records of vernacular musics that were mainly exported and sold to local markets, Hawaiian records were clearly being purchased by metropolitan audiences.

Moreover, the commercial Hawaiian music of Kalama's Quartet and Sol Ho'opi'i with its steel guitars and 'ukuleles seemed far removed from the traditional meles and chants that were being collected and recorded at the same time by the folklorist Helen Roberts, whose *Ancient Hawaiian Music* lies in the ethnographic tradition of folk-music documentation. When one of the characteristic timbres of the commercial Hawaiian music of the 1920s—that of the steel guitar—was almost immediately adopted by US country music (not least by Jimmie Rodgers, who hired Hawaiian musicians to accompany him), it was separated from Hawaiian music and was often heard as an artificial or inauthentic sound of Hawaii.[99] As a result, commercial Hawaiian music has usually been interpreted by anticolonial critics as a form of Orientalism, and, unlike the blues, it has rarely been given much attention or respect by historians of popular and vernacular musics.[100]

The ambiguous situation of Hawaiian vernacular records is, I would suggest, a consequence of timing. In Hawaii, the recording boom of the 1920s coincided not with the initial stirrings of anticolonial sentiment but with a deep trough in the wave of decolonization. It was at once too late and too early: a generation after the anticolonial struggles that erupted around the colonial conquest of Hawaii (from the settler-imposed Bayonet Constitution of 1887 to the 1893 coup that created a settler-dominated "republic" and the 1898 annexation by the United States); and a generation before the explicit project of cultural and political decolonization in the Hawaiian renaissance of the 1970s and the sovereignty struggles that followed. Ironically, the modern

hula with 'ukulele and steel guitar accompaniment—hula ku'i—originally had clear anticolonial meanings. It had taken shape in the 1880s
and 1890s as part of the effort, sponsored in part by Hawaii's king,
David Kalākaua, to preserve and revitalize Hawaiian culture in the
face of colonial dispossession. In the crisis that followed Kalākaua's
death in 1891, a strike by members of the Royal Hawaiian Band was
a significant symbolic gesture of resistance to the 1893 overthrow and
imprisonment of the new queen, Lili'uokalani, herself a well-known
composer. A number of musicians refused to sign a loyalty oath to the
new US-backed settler regime, and formed a new band, the Hawaiian
National Band, led by José Libornio; their resistance was embodied
in a well-known song, "Kaulana Nā Pua" (Famous Are the Flowers).
When the band performed the song on the anniversary of the strike,
it had, according to an imprisoned Hawaiian, "on the Hawaiians the
effect of the 'Marseillaise' on the French."[101] This explicitly anticolonial song was not recorded or re-published until the 1950s, even
though it remained "a favorite political statement of bitterness and
rebellion for the people of Hawai'i who seek a return to sovereignty"
through the twentieth century.[102] When it was included in a pathbreaking 1970 collection of Hawaiian songs, the editors wrote that it
was "the only bitter song in this collection."[103] Thus the hula ku'i that
was recorded in the 1920s was a music without "Kaulana Nā Pua,"
a music of a moment of defeat, unable to express explicit bitterness
even in the midst of significant social struggles, particularly the strikes
of the multiracial working class of plantation workers who had been
recruited from Japan, the Philippines, and Madeira.

However, as the early scholar of hula Mary Kawena Pukui pointed
out in 1940, the chants of hula always had a "*kaona*, or 'inner
meaning'": "The inner meaning was sometimes so veiled that only
the people to whom the chant belonged understood it, and sometimes so obvious that anyone who knew the figurative speech of old
Hawaii could see it very plainly."[104] And there may well be a political
kaona in the many songs recorded through the 1920s that praise the
land itself, like the well-known place name chant "Nā Moku 'Ehā"*
(The Four Islands), recorded by Sol Ho'opi'i, by Kalama's Quartet,
and by William Ewaliko (at the historic 1928 Columbia sessions in
Honolulu).[105] At first glance, the verses of "Nā Moku 'Ehā" seem to
have little political meaning, alternately invoking the flower lei of each
island and its characteristic mountain—"Majestic Maui, rose is the
lei/The beautiful mountain is Haleakalā"—before concluding with the

simple "This is the end of my song/Of the four islands of the Pacific."[106] However, if one recalls that the verses of "Kaulana Nā Pua" (Famous Are the Flowers) alternated the song's political dissent—"No one will fix a signature/To the paper of the enemy/With its sin of annexation/And its sale of native civil rights"—with a simple place-name chant—"Hawai'i, land of Keawe answers/Pi'ilani's bays help/Mano's Kauai lends support/And so do the sands of Kakuhihewa"—it seems likely that the place names carried their own *kaona*, the shadow of an unsung, unwritten verse.[107] Place songs are not only "an extension of preexisting practices of using place names in poetry," hula scholar Amy Ku'uleialoha Stillman argues. They are also "a logical extension of nationalist sentiment at a time when national sovereignty had been usurped."[108] Given the centrality of land in colonial dispossession, and given the unambiguous association of many of Hawaiian lyrics, including the oft-recorded "Aloha Oe," with the deposed and imprisoned Lili'uokalani, the reclaiming, in the Hawaiian language, of the winds, waters, and rains of Minnehaha and Hanalei, may have been as powerful an anticolonial lament as Atilla's humorous calypsos about the Butler riots.

If the political revolution of decolonization was the assertion of political independence and sovereignty, it depended on a cultural revolution of decolonization, the countless small declarations of cultural independence in subaltern daily life that Adria Imada, writing of hula, has called counter-colonial tactics.[109] The circulation and social recognition of vernacular musics was a fundamental part of this cultural revolution, as recording became a form of subaltern self-representation. What Walter Benjamin said of the crowd scenes of early film might be said of the vernacular phonograph records: they embodied "the human being's legitimate claim to be reproduced."[110]

Thus an aspect of these records that was recognized by many contemporaries, their lyric invocation of everyday life, may have been as political an act as any explicit protest. It was said of Umm Kulthūm that "her voice was full of our everyday life."[111] The sonero, the musician Ismael Rivera said, "is like a poet of the people. He has to make up a story from a chorus that is given to him, without departing from the theme. He must know the vernacular, because he has to inject things from our daily life. He has to come from a humble background in order to touch people. He has to use the words that one uses on street corners."[112] And Atilla the Hun wrote that Chieftain Douglas, the barrack-room kaisonian, was "kaiso's novelist ... his themes were

poor people, resentment to catching and destruction of stray dogs, …
landlord and tenant relationships, police court matters, rows between
neighbors, the eternal triangle, the whole gamut of topics from every
life, but street walkers or jammette girls were his favorite themes."[113]

The lyrics of beguine, Andrée Nardal notes in an early record review,
"written to comment upon a political or sentimental adventure … are
satirical or of a certain wistfulness always relieved by a shade of humor.
In their dialect, the crudeness of the words often offends decency." [114]
Tango lyrics "form a vast, unconnected *comédie humaine* of Buenos
Aires life," Jorge Luis Borges wrote in his "A History of the Tango."
They are "the true poetry of our time."[115]

The lyrics of the vernacular phonograph musics captured the lan-
guage of the barrios and slumyards; their commonplaces mapped the
colonial ports and gave voice to their characteristic inhabitants. In
South Africa, Reuben Caluza's "best-known song" sang out the call of
Durban's ricksha driver;[116] in Argentina, Carlos Gardel's "Organito de
la Tarde"* was a tribute to the organ-grinders of the streets of Buenos
Aires;[117] and in Shanghai, Zhou Xuan's famous "Tianya Genü"* (The
Wandering Songstress) was a lament of a Shanghai "sing-song girl."[118]
Bessie Smith's recording about a common urban inhabitant, the
bedbug, was singled out by reviewer Abbe Niles in 1928 for his "own
periodical prize for a contemporary American lyric. Comparing it to
classic rural songs about the boll weevil, he wrote: "On the Columbia
record 14250-D the Negro Empress of the Blues, Bessie Smith, raises
her immense voice, and, in tones of great bitterness and haunting
sadness, … and to the accompaniment of the strangest sounds known
to the banjo, she sings in part: 'A bedbug sure's evil, he don't mean
me no good.'"[119]

Perhaps the most characteristic inhabitant of the port cities was the
migrant, and the topoi of the migrant lament are pervasive in these
country-haunted city musics. There are tales of migrant singers, like
the Trio Matamoros's "Mamá, Son de la Loma,"* with its juxtaposi-
tion of eastern Cuba and Havana—"They're from the hill, and they
sing on the plain";[120] tales of migrants who go wrong, like Reuben
Caluza's "Ingoduso,"* which tells of a brother who is framed, beaten,
and jailed in Johannesburg, after forgetting his fiancée at home;[121] and
tales of migrants who return, as in George Williams Aingo's "Akuko
Nu Bonto,"* a Fante lyric backed by highlife guitar, castanets, and a
chorus that sings "Old man Bonto/I've brought money home/Back
from abroad/Living is hard, ayeee."[122]

The lyric commonplaces mapped the social divisions of the city's geography. In Rio, the very genre of samba came to be divided between the *samba de morro* (the samba of the hills, the favelas) and the *samba da cidade* (the samba of the middle-class neighborhoods). In Buenos Aires, tango not only celebrated the city in anthems like "Mi Buenos Aires Querido," but also invoked the working-class *arrabales,* as in the 1926 recording of Celedonio Estaban Flores's "La Musa Mistonga" (The Muse of the Poor) by Rosita Quiroga, who, Flores said, had a "colloquial tonality": "The muse of the poor in the *arrabales*/Writes in a droll fine vernacular/ … Unaware of the glories/Of life in Versailles,/ She goes out happy, when the night comes,/To watch the boys' street games/To study the smiles of couples sitting down/And the face of heaven, turning dark with the stars/And listen to old tunes/An organ-grinder plays."[123] "There is no one who doesn't feel that our word *arrabal* is more related to economics than to geography," Jorge Luis Borges wrote in 1927:

> *Arrabal* is any tenement in the Centro. *Arrabal* is the last corner on Uriburu, with the final wall of the Recoleta cemetery, bitter *compadritos* standing in an entryway, a broken-down store, and the whitened line of low houses waiting in calm expectancy—I don't know if they're waiting for social revolution or the organ-grinder. *Arrabal* are those empty, vacant neighborhoods where Buenos Aires collapses into disorder in the west and where the red flag of auction—sign of our civil epic about brick kilns, monthly payments, and bribes—reveals the reality of our America. *Arrabal* in Parque Patricios is the anger of workers and the setting to words of that anger in shameless newspapers.[124]

The meaning of these geographical and linguistic commonplaces has been much debated: were they an integral part of the popular idiom, or merely local color added for tourists and visitors? For example, Borges argued that the use of the argot of *lunfardo* (the criminal slang that became a Buenos Aires dialect) was the result of the commercialization of tango in the 1920s: "The first tangos, the old, wonderful tangos, never had *lunfardo* lyrics." Rather, he continues, "the common people don't have to add local color to themselves … The substance of the snappy *milonga*" (a style that preceded the tango) was the soul of the *arrabales* "combined with a vocabulary that belonged to everyone … international banality and an underworld vocabulary are what we have in today's tango."[125]

More recently, the musicologist Carlos Sandroni has made a

similar argument about the recorded sambas of 1930. The lyrics of "Na Pavuna," the celebrated recording by the young white middle-class band led by Almirante, were a catalog of Afro-Brazilianisms, and functioned, like the studio use of the batucada on the same recording, to signal their identification with Afro-Brazilian culture. The lyrics of the less well-known recording of Heitor dos Prazeres's "Vou Te Abandonar," sung by Paulo da Portela (a founder of the Portela samba school), were more typical of samba songs, even though they appear less local and apparently more universal, dealing with the ruptures of love.[126]

One can see this same paradox in one of the emblematic songs of the era: the Cuban *son-pregón* "El Manisero" (The Peanut Vendor), which, as I noted earlier, has long served as a figure for the trans-national reverberations of the vernacular musics. The English lyrics recast the song as a form of exotic and racist local color: "In Cuba, each merry maid/Wakes up with this serenade ... If you're looking for a moral to this song/Fifty million little monkeys can't be wrong."[127]

But the song was actually built around the call of a street vendor selling peanuts—"Peanuts, peanuts/If you want a snack/Eat a handful of peanuts"—elaborated into a double-entendre of seduction: "Young girl, don't go to bed/Without eating a paper cone of peanuts/When the street is empty/Sweetheart/The peanut vendor sings his song/And if the girl listens to this tune/She will call him from her balcony."[128] Street vendor calls were an ordinary part of the urban neighborhoods of the colonial ports: in 1933, Rodney Gallop transcribed one of "the *pregões* (cries) with which the street vendors of Lisbon hawk their fish, fruit, vegetables, and even lottery tickets. If many of these are no more than raucous cries, or a recitative on two notes, others, within their limited register, are little gems of song, such as the cry of a seller of Setubal oranges who passes my house every day."[129] In Shanghai, one historian notes, "nightclubs frequently played ... songs sung by street vendors for selling fried dough (*youtiao*) and newspapers."[130] Such cries became the kernels of popular recorded songs, including the Cuban Ignacio Piñeiro's "Échale Salsita"—put a little sauce on it—which praises the sausages sold by a street vendor,[131] and the song that launched the career of the Bahian samba composer Dorival Caymmi, "A Preta do Aracajé"* recorded by Carmen Miranda, which uses the cry of an Afro-Brazilian *acarajé* (beancake) vendor.[132] These musical street traders are a figure not only for the routines of daily life, but for the place of gramophone music in daily life, itself a kind of street singer, calling out its wares in commonplace double entendres.

Trans-Colonial Reverberations

Music constitutes subjects as social subjects: the rhythms of songs, dances, and marches merge bodies and voices. Thus one might say that a people or movement must be constituted musically before they can be constituted politically. If, as Benedict Anderson suggested three decades ago, the nationalisms of the eighteenth and nineteenth centuries depended on the books and newspapers of "print capitalism," one might conclude that the popular movements of the era of decolonization depended, ironically, on the electrical acoustics of a "sound capitalism," and on the new, urban, plebeian musics they circulated around the world. The new song topoi refigured the commonplaces of everyday life, the new dance steps remade the rhythms of everyday life, and the new sounds were a noise uprising.

Nonetheless, the relation between the vernacular gramophone musics and decolonization cannot be captured by a single overarching narrative in which music gave birth to the nation. Rather there are several reverberating trajectories in which these musics and the conflicts over them constituted the relations between colonial intellectuals, the migrant workers of ports and railway centers, and the masses of rural peasants, miners, and plantation workers. Though there is no clear separation between a moment when the ear was "colonized" and when it was "decolonized," the battle over the ear was central to the struggle over colonialism, as one can see in the ambiguous formulations of the theorists of decolonization themselves.

However, these vernacular phonograph discs were, in their very sound, a "working out of the social order to come," an improvisation of a postcolonial world. They were not utopian in the classic sense; they rarely projected a perfected world, unlike, for example, some of the musical utopias imagined in the early Soviet Union, with their leaderless, unconducted orchestras. Rather the records often prefigured the contradictions to come, the trials and tribulations of the decolonizing movements and states: the divide between a democracy of improvisation, and a cult of populist stars and bandleaders; the divide between male instrumentalists, inheriting the craft ideologies of artisan music-making, and a now open, and openly sexualized, ambivalence toward the woman singing star; the divide within new territories, as the musics of particular regions and peoples became emblems of the nation; and the political metaphysics of rhythm— the inversion of the disparagement of rhythm and "rhythmic" peoples into the celebration of a sometimes essentialized, naturalized somatic rhythm.

If these musics figured anticolonial opposition, they did not nec- essarily figure anticolonial space—home rule, *swaraj*, the Negro World—as national space. Rather, like the forms of black and anti- colonial internationalism, these vernacular phonograph musics took shape in an archipelago of colonial ports and mill towns, on an impe- rial commodity chain whose links were not only banana boats and coal trains, but gramophone records and steel guitars. And, as in the case of anticolonial thought, we should not see the musical cultures of this archipelago through a model of center and periphery, source and echo. It was commonly thought at the time that these musics were simply echoes of US jazz. But this is no more accurate than the analogous idea that anticolonial movements and theories were simply echoes of Soviet revolution. Jazz was a central instance of the new vernaculars, but the fact that contemporaries heard the new musics as forms of "jazz" is really more akin to the equally common perception that every anticolonial activist was a "Bolshevik"—even Gandhi, in the eyes of some British colonial officials.

Rather than this image of jazz echoing around the planet, in various delayed repetitions, one might adopt Ron Radano's use of "resonance": resonance, he writes, is "the sounding after an unlocatable origin ... the 'afterlife' of a negative sonic inception, the 'absent cause' represented in the audible outer world."[133] However, in the era of electrical recording, the gramophone seems less like a resonant instrument, sympathetically vibrating, than a reverb unit. Reverberation—the "acoustic context of a sound"[134] constituted by the multiple and overlapping repercussions from the surrounding surfaces of the sound's space—suggests the timbral chaos and sheer noise of the gramophone boom.

Just as different spaces amplify certain frequencies and deaden others, so the trans-colonial soundscape amplified some musics over others. There is no necessary or direct relation between the size and resources of a colonial territory and the influence of its music. Glissant may have been accurate in his sense that beguine did not develop as richly as jazz, but his oddly direct sense of the relation between com- munities and musics is misleading. Just as a handful of Caribbean intellectuals, from George Padmore and C. L. R. James to Aimé Césaire and Frantz Fanon, had a disproportionate impact on anticolonial thought, so particular musics seem to have had disproportionately long reverberation times. Paradoxically, it was precisely the musics that seemed most entwined with tourist ideologies of exotic tropical resorts—those of Cuba and Hawaii, island outposts of empire—that had the widest trans-colonial reverberations.

The commercial names these musics acquired—rumba, hula, jazz, beguine—do stand as signs of their expropriation by the cultural apparatuses of empire. But as these musical signifiers reverberated across the colonial ports, they were reappropriated to name new and unexpected trans-colonial hybrids that linked the black Atlantic, the gypsy Mediterranean, and the Polynesian Pacific: "kroncong rumba," "hula blues," "flamenco tango," and "gypsy jazz." These unlikely reverberations were, one might say, a musical Bandung conference (the historic Afro-Asian political gathering of 1955), the sound of the transcolonial political and cultural project that was to be called the "Third World."

6

"A Noisy Heaven and a Syncopated Earth": Remaking the Musical Ear

What does it mean to remake the ear? In his early manuscripts, the young Karl Marx suggested that "the *forming* of the five senses is a labour of the entire history of the world." Marx drew his example of the history of senses from music: "only music awakens in man the sense of music … the most beautiful music has *no* sense for the unmusical ear."[1] Thus the musical ear has a history: new modes of music awaken a new sense of music, a new musical ear. But this is not the history so often imagined by early musicology, an evolutionary progress from "primitive" to "civilized" musics. Rather, the history of the musical ear, its making and remaking—like the forming and reforming of the five senses in general—is the fundamental labor of cultural revolutions, those contradictory upheavals in the habits and manners, jokes and prayers, sounds and smells of daily life that accompany the struggle between modes of production, regimes of labor, technological grids, economies of sexuality, structures of domination and representation, and modes of emancipation and exploitation.[2]

Every mode of production has its sound, as F. Murray Schafer suggested in his visionary book, *The Soundscape*, its own divide between music and noise, and the conflict between modes of production—whether in the fast violence of war and political revolution or the slow violence of displacement and expropriation over decades or generations—is registered in the struggle between ways of hearing, between the sound of the dominant machines and the sound of the subaltern masses.

So what did this cultural revolution sound like? At first glance, this seems a simple empirical question: what did these musics sound like? Moreover, since many recordings survive, the sound of the music is accessible in a way unparalleled for earlier musics, whether learned or popular. Indeed, a new musicology is developing techniques of musical analysis, transcribing recorded performances and analyzing their musical structures and rhetoric. But it is a more complex issue for three reasons.

First, since recordings became the fundamental vehicle of the rise and spread of these musical vernaculars, it is worth stressing that the question "what did these musics sound like?" must be recast as "what did these recordings sound like?" The recording process was not transparent, and recorded musics were always an artifact of the recording process, their sound shaped by engineers and producers as well as musicians. Moreover, recording often changed musical cultures around the world, creating a gap between performed music and recorded music, a gap that can be often obscured if one assumes the transparency of recording.

For this reason, historians and ethnomusicologists interested in understanding the practices of musicking have long held a justified suspicion of commercial recordings: it is easy to misread musical practice by assuming that recorded music represents that practice accurately. In some cases, the technological limits and capabilities of recording create these misreadings: the limits of recording time gives a distorted sense of the length and structure of musical works, and the fact that different voices and instruments were more or less suited to recording meant that recorded performances often diverged radically from live performances by the same musicians. In other cases, decisions made by record producers created the gap: the demand for particular types and genres of music, both on the part of folklorists seeking "traditional" genres and on the part of commercial recorders seeking "saleable" genres, have long given a sense that musicians had more limited or restricted repertoires than was actually the case. Thus one must be careful in deducing musical practices from recordings; recordings are not transparent documents, mere evidence of an underlying musical culture.

Second, since twenty-first-century auditions of these records may be quite different to those of the 1920s and 1930s, the question "what did these musics sound like?" must be recast as "how were they heard?" It is difficult to hear these 78s as they were heard at the time, because our ears are the product of the very success of these recorded vernacular musics over the last hundred years. In some cases, the adoption of certain musics as national musics has contributed to the routinization of their sounds, making it difficult to hear the original "noise"; our boredom is, as Fredric Jameson has noted of aesthetic boredom generally, less an index of the music itself than a sign of our own resistance to its now conventional sounds.[3] In other cases, timbres have been adopted and popularized by other idioms: as I noted earlier, the pervasiveness of the steel guitar in US country music has made it more difficult to hear the distinctiveness of the early Hawaiian recordings. As a result, the question "what did they sound like?" must further be rephrased as "what did people say they sounded like?" Thus Theodor Adorno's very revulsion at the sound of the modern dance musics is a powerful sign of the remaking of the musical ear. Adorno recognized the timbres of the new musics—"the muted distortions of the horns, the chirping and vibrating tonal repetitions of the plucked instruments, the banjo and the ukulele, and even the harmonica"— but found them "unbearable" (he used the word in relation to the Wurlitzer organ).[4] The "guitar, ukulele, and banjo, as well as the accordion" were, he insisted, "infantile instruments in comparison with the piano."[5] He hated the twang and the vibrato, the beat and the syncopation, of the dance musics. He saw—and deplored—their connection to military marches, but thought it was a connection to fascism rather than a legacy of colonial brass bands.[6] Adorno's hearing of the new sounds should be understood not simply as his individual "taste" but as a Geiger counter, registering the scale of the musical revolution taking place.

Third, the question "what did these musics sound like?" raises the question of whether it makes sense to group the sounds of these vernacular musics together. Even if these new musical vernaculars shared a common social and historical situation—their place in the working-class barrios of colonial ports and their relation to the migrations and movements, unsettlings and uprisings in the wake of the Great War—and even if the global recording industry remade world musical space around these musical vernaculars, can we conclude that they had a common sound? Did the records sound alike? Were they heard to sound alike? This, too, was contested in the polemics of the day. If it is a mistake to lump all of these musics together as "jazz," "light" music, or "popular" music, it is equally misleading to separate them into entirely distinct and unconnected "national" or "ethnic" traditions.

Rather, the sound of the records circulating through the archipelago of colonial ports was inflected by the sounds of three diasporas: a black Atlantic sound that emerged out of the slave trade and the post-slavery migrations of African-American communities from Brazil to the United States; a gypsy Mediterranean sound that emerged as the Roma diaspora inflected musics from flamenco to tzigane; and a Polynesian Pacific sound that resonated across the ports of the Pacific and Asia.

Moreover, I want to suggest that the sound of the vernacular phonograph records in each of the three arcs also depended on a new kind of ensemble, a "dance band"—the phrase in English dates from the 1920s[7]—a *bando regional* or *orquesta típica.* These vernacular recording ensembles were based on a musical division of labor between a front line of melodic instruments and a "rhythm section," a term that also emerged at this time.

The sound of these "dance bands" was characterized by four distinctive and controversial elements that remade the musical ear: the "noisy" timbres of their instruments and voices; their "syncopated" rhythms; their "weird" tonalities; and their "recorded" improvisations. They were, as a journalist wrote at the time, "prophets of a noisy heaven and a syncopated earth."[8]

Noisy Timbres

As the repeated invocation of noise indicates, the recorded vernacular musics were first distinguished by the timbres of their characteristic ensembles, their instruments and voices. It is not surprising that these were heard as noise, because timbre is the product of the specific noise of an instrument: in acoustic terms, timbre consists both of the harsh sound of the attack, the first pre-pitched moment of the sound envelope, and of the peculiar mix of overtones or partials that color the fundamental frequency as the sound resonates and decays.[9] Timbre long seemed an accidental and ephemeral aspect of music, escaping notation and evading the mathematics of harmony and rhythm; but recording gave new substance to timbre, as the sheer noise of voices and instruments reverberated even when the harmonies or rhythms seemed rudimentary.

The vernacular ensembles that recorded were, for the most part, neither the large hotel, theater, or concert orchestras of the city's cultivated classes, nor the large collective singing and parading groups of the city's workers and poor—the church and union choirs, the *coros de clave* and *coros de son*, and the carnival percussion paraders. Rather, they were mainly small bands of three to seven musicians—trios and quartets, "hot fives" and "hot sevens," "sextetos" and "septetos"—that accompanied singers and performed instrumental dance numbers. Table 3 lists some of the characteristic lineups of the vernacular phonograph musics. Their timbres varied, but two aspects of these ensembles were particularly evident.

First, these ensembles usually combined instruments with distinct and often clashing timbres, and much of their musical interest lay in this timbral counterpoint. For example, the takht of modern ṭarab—associated with the early recordings of Umm Kulthūm—was, the musicologist Ali Racy argues, "a collection of *khāmāt ṣawtiyyah*, 'sound timbres' ... Incorporating one of each type of instrument, for example one 'ūd, one qānūn, one nāy, one violin, and one riqq, the takht amounts to a few layers of discernible timbral-acoustical lines." Racy contrasts these multi-timbral ensembles with "'unitimbral' but register-separated combinations, such as Europe's Renaissance recorder or viol consorts, or for that matter the classical string quartet."[10] Similarly, a recent jazz historian has argued that "the polyphonic basis of New Orleans jazz made a small number of melody instruments of differing timbres desirable."[11] Such collections of instruments with distinct timbres were common to the vernacular phonograph musics, spanning quite distinct musical idioms. Indeed, as early as 1924, the American philharmonic composer Virgil Thomson noted that "jazz"—by which he meant modern dance music with a syncopated melody over a foxtrot rhythm—"does not require balanced timbres," being "contrapuntal rather than homophonic."[12]

However, it was not simply this multi-timbral texture that generated the sounds so often heard as noise: almost all of the vernacular ensembles also juxtaposed mass-produced musical instruments, imported from European and American metalworking factories, with artisan-crafted indigenous instruments. A social as well as timbral counterpoint emerged, as imported industrial instruments—often with standardized tunings—joined the host of regional soundboxes which had arrived with rural migrants. The immense variety of these hand-crafted flutes, fiddles, scrapers, rattles, and drums led ethnomusicologists of the time, notably Curt Sachs and Erich Hornbostel, to develop the arcane vocabulary of modern "organology" (the science

Table 3: Idioms, Ensembles, and Instruments

Musical Idiom	Reeds, Flutes	Brass	Bowed Strings	Plucked Strings	Keyboards, Zithers	Free Reeds	Percussion	Number
son		trumpet		tres, guitar, bass			bongo, clave, maracas	trio, sextet, septet
jazz	clarinet, saxophone	trumpet, cornet, trombone, tuba		banjo, guitar	piano		drum set	quintet, septet
ṭarab	nāy, flute		violin	ʿūd	qānūn		riqq	quartet, quintet
fasil			kemence	ud	kanun			
rebetika			violin, lyra	guitar, mandola, lauto, bouzouki, baglamás		accordion	cembalo, santouri	
chaabi, rai	gasbas		violin	ʿūd	qanun		tār, bendir, guellals	
fado			violin	guitarra, viola da França				duo, trio
South Asian theater music			violin			harmonium	tablā	
mariachi		trumpet	two violins	guitarrón, 2 guitars, 2 vihuelas				septet
kroncong	flute		violin	kroncong, guitar, ʻukulele			rebana	

genre	winds	brass	bowed strings	plucked strings	keyboard	free reed	percussion	ensemble
tango	clarinet, flute		two violins, bass		piano	two bandoneons		sextet or guitar duo
calypso	clarinet, flute		violin	cuatro, guitar, cello, banjo			vera, chac-chac	quartet
country			fiddle	guitar, banjo	autoharp			
flamenco				guitar			castenets	
cai luong	bamboo flute		two-stringed fiddle	two-stringed lute			bell	
hula kuʻi				steel guitar, ʻukulele, harp-guitar, guitar			ipu, uliʻuli, pahu	quartet
tzigane	clarinet		violins, cello, bass				cimbalom	
palm-wine, highlife	kazoo			guitar	piano	concertina	castenets	
taarab			violin	udi	qanun			
samba, choro	flute, clarinet			guitar, cavaquinho			surdo, tamborin, cuícas, pandeiro	
céilí	flute		fiddle		piano			
huangse yinyue	clarinet, saxophone		violin		piano			
beguine	clarinet, saxophone, bamboo flute	trombone	bass, violin	banjo	piano		chacha, tibwa, drum kit	
jùjú				guitar, banjo			shekere, jùjú	
kundiman				guitar				
marabi				guitar	piano			

of classifying musical instruments): chordophones, aerophones, membranophones, and idiophones.

In the Pacific ports, the early Hawaiian hula ku'i ensembles combined guitars and 'ukuleles with the *ipu*, the Hawaiian gourd drum;[13] there are also fusions like Vietnam's cai luong, which featured, as Jason Gibbs notes, two ensembles: one with Vietnamese instruments playing pentatonic melodies on plucked and bowed stringed instruments, and a second with Western military band instruments, playing "fanfare music."[14] In the Atlantic ports, one finds palm-wine music "created by coastal West African musicians who combined local stringed and percussion instruments (including the *gombey* frame-drums) with those of foreign sailors; that is, portable instruments used aboard ships such as the guitar, mandolin, banjo, harmonica, accordion, and concertina."[15] "Whereas old style music keeps to indigenous or traditional instruments," J. H. Nketia wrote in one of the first musicological accounts of West African commercially recorded music, "new style music is more daring in its choice of medium. Bottles, cigarette tins, adaptations of the Western side drum, guitars, saxophones, clarinets, and other sound instruments are pounced on. Many bands attempt a 'syncretism': traditional drums are brought in company with guitars, castanets, and gongs or with tins, bottles, and so on."[16] To traditionalists everywhere, this was a sonic as well as ideological challenge.

One set of voices in this counterpoint were the imported industrial instruments, whose numbers grew exponentially in port cities in the early decades of the century. By the turn of the century, stocks of "melodeons, concertinas, mandolins, and guitars" were being exported to Africa;[17] meanwhile, in China, "Cantonese folk musicians began to incorporate guitars, banjos, and saxophones into their regional music."[18] These brash mass-produced commodities of a growing musical-instrument industry were sold in standardized "models" in urban music shops and by mail-order catalog, together with cheap "method" books. They were usually portable chordal instruments, inexpensive, with little prestige. Plucked strings and free reeds resonated throughout these ensembles. The guitar was ubiquitous in the vernacular idioms, as were its near and distant relatives: the mandolin, son's *tres*, samba's *cavaquinho*, calypso's *cuatro*, fado's *guitarra* and *viola da França*, rebetika's *lauto* and *bouzouki*, Hawaii's *'ukulele*, kroncong's *kroncong*, mariachi's *vihuela* and *guitarrón*, as well as the four- and five-string banjos of New Orleans jazz and Piedmont old-time music, and the *'ūds* of tarab and chaabi. And there were a host of manufactured free reeds, including accordions, concertinas, harmonicas, harmoniums, bandoneóns, and melodeons.

As the guitar, a soft-spoken parlor instrument in the European and North America musics of the late nineteenth century, was adapted to factory-made steel strings in the 1880s and 1890s, inexpensive models proliferated and they became indigenous instruments throughout the Polynesian Pacific, the gypsy Mediterranean, and the black Atlantic. In Hawaii, King David Kalākaua's 1880s patronage of the guitar—introduced to Hawaii by Mexican cattle herders—had made the instrument central to the new hula ku'i, an emblem of Hawaiian cultural resistance. By the early twentieth century, Hawaiian guitarists had not only developed a variety of "slack key" tunings (in which strings were loosened to make patterns matching major or minor triads), but also invented a new playing style, sliding a steel bar over the strings of a lap-held guitar to create striking glissandos. This "steel guitar" (*kika kila*), usually attributed to Joseph Kekuku, a student at the Kamehameha School for Boys in the 1890s, became one of the major guitar timbres of the vernacular phonograph records of the 1920s and 1930s, not only in the recordings of Hawaiian virtuosos like Sol Ho'opi'i, Mike Hanapi, and David Napihi Burrows, but on recordings in Jakarta, Calcutta, Johannesburg, Athens, and Atlanta.[19]

In Andalusia, guitar playing—*toque*—emerged as an ever more central part of the flamenco tradition, taking its place alongside singing (*cante*), dance (*baile*), and handclaps (*palmas*), in large part because of the technologies of electrical recording that allowed the guitar to carry melodic leads as well as rhythmic accompaniments. "In 1925," a flamenco scholar notes, "with the development of the microphone and the audio amplifier, the guitar came into its own. Amplification released it from its acoustic constraints, and the guiding hand of musical geniuses such as Ramón Montoya led it to new heights."[20]

Meanwhile the guitar was also adopted across Africa, becoming an African instrument. "What sense does it make," Kofi Agawu asks, "after a century and a half of regular, continuous, and imaginative use, to describe the guitar as a 'foreign' instrument in Africa?"[21] "In the late 1920s and early 1930s," musicologist Christopher Waterman writes of Lagos, "a 'box' guitar could be obtained for one pound, a price within the reach of many regularly employed wage-earning Africans."[22] "For those with cash to spare," the collector Hugh Tracey noted of South Africa, "the guitar takes over the accompaniment with drums and rattles as before and a kind of Bantu *calypso* is the response to this now universal instrument."[23] It rarely earned respectability—Kwaa Mensah recalled that his uncle Kwame Asare "learned to play guitar against his father's wishes, who thought only ruffians played guitar."[24] However, despite the fears of folklorists, it did not undermine vernacular music making. In some cases, the playing techniques of indigenous stringed instruments were transferred to the guitar: Michael Veal has pointed to the ways African guitarists used techniques of the likembe, nyatiti, and kora.[25] In other cases, new techniques were developed to gain desired timbres. Kru seamen, originally from Liberia but living in "Kroo-town" settlements in West African ports, developed a two-finger playing style that spread up and down the coast: the Kumasi Trio's guitarist Kwame Asare claimed "to have learned the basis of the two-finger style known as *dagomba* from a Kru sailor."[26] Not only playing techniques but even distinctive tuning systems traveled widely: "common Hawaiian slack-key tunings in C, G, F—for example—'taro patch' (5-1-5-1-3-5, ascending)—are identical to tunings used by Lagosian guitarists," Christopher Waterman notes. "The international distribution of such tuning systems along trade routes has yet to be adequately investigated."[27]

Equally important, and equally controversial, were the relatively new family of free reed instruments, manufactured boxes with flexible metal tongues—"reeds"—that vibrate as a result of air pressure or suction, usually mouth- or bellows-blown. These "squeezeboxes" emerged across Europe and North America in the decades of the first Industrial Revolution, influenced by the appearance of the Chinese mouth organ, the *sheng*, in Europe in 1777: first the accordion and harmonica in 1820s Vienna, followed, over the next three decades, by the English, or Wheatstone, concertina, the melodeon, the German *Konzertina*, later renamed the bandoneón, the cheaper diatonic Anglo-German concertina, and the French harmonium.[28]

Some had buttons, other keys; some were diatonic, with only the notes of a single key, others were chromatic. In general, their fixed tunings and "closed systems" that prevented the playing of dissonant chords made them relatively easy to master; in addition, they were loud and portable, enabling one-man dance bands.[29] As a result, the historian Stuart Eydmann notes, "the 1870s and 1880s saw many working-class musicians turn to the more versatile and robust free-reed instruments which were being developed on the continent."[30] The free reeds followed labor migrants to settler colonies around the world: legend has it that the bandoneón was brought to Buenos

Aires by German sailors.[31] By the early twentieth century, the largest importers of accordions were the United States, Argentina, and Brazil.[32] The "cheap ten-key Anglo-German concertina" was particularly popular in South Africa,[33] and the 1927 Zonophone recordings of the West African George Williams Aingo included several concertina tracks.[34] Meanwhile, in 1875, a Calcutta instrument maker added drone stops and a hand pump to the French harmonium: "By 1913, India had become the richest market in the world for harmoniums— for church services, for missionaries in the field, for accompaniment of urban musical dramas, and, increasingly, for playing in Indian classical music."[35]

The free reeds were controversial everywhere. On the one hand, they were modern and urban; in Buenos Aires, the guitar was associated with the countryside, the bandoneón with the city.[36] In India, the shift from the traditional bowed *sarangi* to the harmonium occurred not only because it was easier to play but also because it didn't have the traditional association with courtesans.[37] On the other hand, free reed instruments were shunned by the respectable, the cultivated, and the traditional.

"The harmonium has attracted more elite contempt than any other instrument in the history of Indian music," the historian Matt Rahaim writes. Gandhi lamented the "execrable harmonium, concertina, and the accordion." "All-India Radio banned the harmonium from its airwaves for over thirty years, and it has long been banished from the South Indian classical music stage."[38] In South Africa, Africans associated with mission education avoided the concertina, choosing piano and brass instruments.[39] "The musical establishment throughout Europe was unified in the dismissal of the popular squeeze boxes," historian Christoph Wagner notes.[40] "The accordion," Theodor Adorno wrote, "is a very primitive instrument" on which the "player strikes ready-made chords in a quasi-improvisatory manner." Noting that it was known in Germany as a "sailor's piano" and in the US as a "gypsy piano," he argued that "its role may be roughly defined as a piano fit for camp life or collective life of any sort, involuntarily antagonistic to the private apartment."[41] Traditional musicians also found themselves threatened by the new technology: the Auvergne piper Antoine Bouscatel, the star of the turn-of-the-century Parisian *bal musette*, was challenged by the arrival of immigrant Italian accordionists: "The days of my bagpipes are numbered, and those of your hurdy-gurdy too! This character with his accordion carries with him our ruin! ... The accordion is a miracle that falls from the sky. It is a revolution on the way. Did you hear? It is complete, it is hot, it is alive. And it is a whole orchestra, this instrument of the devil!"[42]

But it was also the sound, the timbre, the noise of these instruments that offended. The harmonium—argued its critics, English and Indian—could not glide between notes; its tuning was wrong, and it was un-Indian.[43] Accordionists of the early decades of the twentieth century often used a "wet" tuning—"one reed tuned precisely to a note and supplemented by the other two reeds tuned sharp and flat around it"—which gave players, in the words of Michael Dregni, "the trademark plaintive sound with 'vibration' surrounding every note in a sentimental quavering like a street singer's crooning."[44] It was this wavering intonation—characteristic of bent guitar strings as well—that Adorno heard in all the varieties of "jazz."

The "American accent of the saxophone"—as Cuban composer Emilio Grenet put it— was also a distinctive timbre of the vernacular phonograph records, and, in many cases, an emblem of "jazz."[45] "In Europe," Adorno wrote, "the saxophone is considered representative of this sound [of jazz], the instrument against which the resistance has concentrated its forces."[46] To adopt the saxophone was to link oneself symbolically with jazz, as when the bandleader Pixinguinha brought the saxophone into Brazilian choro in 1923, when steel guitarist Sol Ho'opi'i recorded with Andy Iona in 1928 in one of the earliest hula sessions that incorporated saxophones, and when guitarist Ramón Montoya recorded with Fernando Vilches in 1933 on one of the first flamenco sessions with a saxophone.[47]

If the timbres of these industrial instruments reverberated from the vernacular phonograph discs, so, too, did the remarkable variety of vocal timbres. Unlike printed sheet music, which stripped the voice from words and melodies, the phonograph captured a semblance of the vocalist's timbre, what Roland Barthes later called "the grain of the voice."[48] At the time, musicologists and folklorists noted that this was important not simply for accuracy but also because singers themselves privileged timbre. "Phonograms are immensely superior to notations of melodies taken down from direct hearing," the German musicologist Erich Hornbostel argued, because "the singers themselves attach as much importance to the timbre of the voice and the mode of recitation as to anything else, and very often more."[49] Similarly, reviewing the early recordings of Portuguese fado, Rodney Gallop argued that "it is precisely in the manner of singing of *fadistas* such as Alberto Costa and Filipe Pinto, which no musical notation, but only the gramo-phone, can convey, that the chief character and charm of the *fado* lie."[50]

The centrality of timbre in recorded music was also responsible for the then surprising shift in which the singer, rather than the song, became the center of the music industry. After all, ever since the explo-sion of the mass circulation of sheet music in the 1850s, the music industry had depended on the popularity and sale of songs. Publishers would try to attract a number of singers to put across the song in their live performances, and this model continued in the early days of recording. A striking example of the reversal from song to singer is noted by recording industry historian Alan Sutton: before 1926, Victor "would scout the South not for performers but for songs, with the idea of 'refining' the compositions, copyrighting them, and then handing them off to professional studio performers in New Jersey and New York." However, the unexpected success of the southern Piedmont singer Ernest V. Stoneman and his family string band on the OKeh, Edison, and Gennett labels in 1925 and 1926 led Victor to sign Stoneman and begin seeking singers rather than songs; a few months later, they sent Ralph Peer, with Stoneman's help, to find local singers in Bristol, Tennessee, resulting in the landmark recordings of Jimmie Rodgers and the Carter Family.[51] One can also see this rever-sal in the writing of Abbe Niles: whereas his early essays focused on songs and their variants, his record reviews of 1928 called attention to the voice rather than the song. "Crave you Hawaiian singing," he writes, "try 'He Manao Healoha,' or words to that effect by Kalama's Quartet"; he also recommends Jimmie Rodgers's "engaging, melodi-ous and bloodthirsty 'Blue Yodel' ... which started the whole epidemic of yodeling blues that now rages," and Bessie Smith's "immense voice" with its "tones of great bitterness and haunting sadness."[52]

Many of the recordings of the late 1920s became famous for the vocal timbres they circulated: the yodeling of Jimmie Rodgers, the scat singing of jazz vocalists like Louis Armstrong, and the Hawaiian fal-setto of singers like Mike Hanapi of Kalama's Quartet.[53] "In modern songs of considerable range one very often hears a peculiar break due to the slipping of the vocal cords which in a modified way resembles yodelling," Helen Roberts wrote of Hawaiian singing in 1925. "This is so commonly encountered that it may be described as a feature of modern Hawaiian singing. Coupled with a habit, which is to be defi-nitely traced to the ancient hula music, of gliding swiftly from a tone finished to the one to be attacked, slightly in advance of its normal appearance, it imparts a peculiar quality to the music which is quite foreign to our manner of singing."[54]

In some cases sound recording circulated established vernacular singing styles; however, the adoption of the electric microphone also enabled a new range of intimate vocal timbres that came to be known as "crooning." If the best-known crooner was the young Californian Bing Crosby, nonetheless versions of crooning emerged in a variety of vernacular idioms, perhaps most notably in the tremendous success of tango's Carlos Gardel and samba's Francisco "Chico" Alves.

The circulation of these distinct vocal timbres by recording led to their appropriation by the raciologies of the day, as folklorists and musicologists took timbre, like rhythm, to have a basis in the racialized body. "Timbre and recitation appear to be racial characteristics deeply rooted in physiological functions," the German musicologist Erich Hornbostel argued in 1928, "and give therefore valuable evidence of anthropological relations and differences. Peoples and their music, then, are not so much distinguished by what they sing as by the way in which they sing."[55] The connection between race and vocal timbre ran throughout popular journalism. "The somewhat nasal singing of a native Don Juan or his female counterpart may not, at first hearing, find favor in ears trained to Western music," E. V. Solomons wrote of kroncong records in 1933. "But, if one is prepared to listen to *Krontjong* music without prejudice, one will be forced to admit that the language of love is universal."[56] Abbe Niles argued that race records illustrated how "jazz draws on the timbres and accents of the Negro voice, weaving it into its fabric, contrasting its shrill or throaty melancholy with the voices of wood and brass, imitating, imitated by it, catching its tricks of expression, translating them, throwing them back again." His praise for the recordings of Jimmie Rodgers was punctuated by the remark that Rodgers was a "white man singing black songs."[57]

The association of vocal timbres and peoples—whether defined by race or nation, language or religion—was long-lasting, in part because of the materiality of sound recording's schizophonia. In many cases the political and cultural meanings of the vernacular phonograph musics depended on the symbolic power of their vocal timbres. In some cases, singers turned the local idiom of a vernacular language into an emblem of a nation or a people. Umm Kulthūm's resonance as the "voice of Egypt" lay not simply in her vocal power, both in volume and range, but, as Virginia Danielson has shown, on the clarity of her diction in Arabic—often remarked on by contemporaries—and on the color of her voice, its *ghunna* or nasality, and its *bahha* or hoarseness.[58] Similarly, a recent critic has argued that Zhou Xuan's diction in Beijing Mandarin was an important part of the making of Mandarin as the national language in China.[59] In Hawaii, the recording of Hawaiian-language songs in vocal timbres drawn from traditions of chant were crucial to the survival of the language through decades of suppression; indeed, the ethnomusicologist Mantle Hood once noted the paradox that whereas, outside Hawaii, the timbre of the steel guitar became the emblem of Hawaii, inside Hawaii it was the vocal timbre of the sung words that was considered the most important aspect of the music.[60]

These recorded vernacular voices stood apart from the timbres of classically cultivated voices, and often validated an emerging vernacular aesthetic, constituting a "modern" voice. In her discussion of the "subaltern voice" in the Indian subcontinent, Lakshmi Subramanian notes the importance of the new timbres of Tamil vernacular singers like K. B. Sundarambal: though

> what kept such voices outside the domain of classical music was in part a lack of training, and in part the way they interpreted music and its intentionality, ... for some of the protagonists [in the debate over Tamil music], the preference lay with spontaneous full-throated singing unmediated by constructed notions of refinement and containment. A taste for this was developed by the circulation of commercial recordings and the growing popularity of early film songs, which became the logical site for Tamil music at the most immediate level. Singers like K. B. Sundarambal and Kittappa in particular embodied this register.[61]

Similarly, the fadista, Rodney Gallop wrote in 1933, "sings in the curiously rough, untrained voice and simple unpretentious manner which are dictated by tradition ... The fado does not lend itself to bel canto, and the opera singer with his cultivated voice and professional manner would never be tolerated by the critical audience." Rather, Gallop goes on, "against the strict common time of her accompaniment, the fadista maintains a rhythm as free and flexible as that of the jazz-singer, with whom she shares certain tricks of syncopation and suspension of the rhythmic beat which give the song a lilt as fascinating as it is difficult to reproduce."[62] Here we see the appearance of the second element that characterized the new ensembles of recorded phonograph music: their syncopated rhythms.

The Servants' Hall of Rhythm

If the vocal and instrumental timbres—the music's "noise"—marked these phonograph discs, so, too, did their "syncopated" rhythms. Virtually every commentator on recorded vernacular musics called attention to their rhythms, linking their syncopations to subaltern and colonized peoples, and seeing them as figures of social and sexual upheaval. "Down in the basement" of the "house of music," a New Orleans journalist wrote in 1918, there is "a kind of servants' hall of rhythm. It is there we hear the hum of the Indian dance, the throb of Oriental tambourines and kettledrums, the clatter of the clogs, the click of Slavic heels, the thumpty-tumpty of the negro banjo, and, in fact, the native dances of the world."[63] The vernacular musicians and ensembles often appropriated the term themselves: there were "Rhythm Kings" in Batavia, Buenos Aires, Johannesburg, Port of Spain, and New Orleans.

Others were more skeptical; the German critic Theodor Adorno discounted the originality of "those achievements of jazz in which people thought they perceived elements of a fresh beginning and spontaneous regeneration—its rhythms." "The rhythmic achievements of jazz are mere ornaments above a metrically conventional, banal architecture, with no consequences for the structure, and removable at will," he argued, "… the apparent variety of rhythmic constructs can be reduced to a minimum of stereotypical and standardized formulae."[64]

Were these "rhythm kings" expressing a desire for freedom or simply playing standardized formulae? The intensity of this controversy over rhythm was as great as that over timbre. In part, it marked the emergence of a new ideology of rhythm deeply entwined with modern, colonial notions of race, one that continues to inform musical thought and practice. But it also grew out of the distinctive form and structure of the vernacular phonograph musics, figured by the centrality of their "rhythm sections." Far from being "mere ornaments," the rhythmic constructs were central to the architecture of the music.

The ideological link between rhythm and race that has inflected much musical discourse over the last century was forged during the modernist generation. In his essay, "The Invention of 'African Rhythm,'" Kofi Agawu noted the "way rhythm as a separate dimension is singled out for special mention" in the influential essays on African music published by Erich Hornbostel and William Ward in the late 1920s.[65] Both the German musicologist Hornbostel (working from phonograph recordings) and the British collector Ward (who worked with training college students in the Gold Coast) insisted on the radical difference between African and European conceptions of rhythm, and both maintained that African rhythm was more advanced: "African rhythm springs from the drummer's motions and has far out-stripped European rhythm, which does not depend on motion but on the ear," Hornbostel wrote;[66] while Ward argued that "in rhythm Africa is two centuries ahead of Europe … The sight of a native dancer keeping with different sets of muscles five different rhythms at once almost makes one believe that Africans have not merely cultivated their sense of rhythm far beyond ours, but must have started with a superior sense of rhythm from the beginning."[67]

The invention of this idea of an "African rhythm"—spanning the peoples and cultures of the continent—was part of a modern racial discourse about rhythm that was historically quite new, as Ronald Radano has shown. In the nineteenth century, the sacred singing of the African-American jubilee groups had made vocal and melodic elements the "signature of race"; however, "within the space of thirty years … that perception would change dramatically. By the 1920s, when Americans imagined black music, they thought first of rhythmic practices, particularly in instrumental settings … the bodily affect-ing power of black rhythm consumed the attention of reporters and readers alike."[68] This rhetoric was often adopted by African-American critics discussing the new musics: in his pioneering essay on jazz in *The New Negro*, the journalist J. A. Rogers wrote of "that elusive some-thing, for lack of a better name, I'll call Negro rhythm. The average Negro, particularly of the lower classes, puts rhythm into whatever he does, whether it be shining shoes or carrying a basket on the head to market as the Jamaican women do."[69]

However, this ideology of rhythm and race stretched beyond Africa and the African diaspora. The discourse about "gypsy rhythm" went back to Liszt's assertion in 1859 that "the liberty and richness of its rhythms … more than anything else, tends to increase the admira-tion in which Gipsy music is held": they were "distinguished both by a multiplicity and a flexibility nowhere else to be met with in the same degree."[70] And there was a parallel "invention of Polynesian rhythm," as musicologists singled out rhythm in their accounts of the musics of the Pacific. "The hall-mark of Hawaiian music is rhythm," Nathaniel Emerson wrote in his pioneering 1909 study of the hula, "for the Hawaiians belong to that class of people who cannot move hand or foot or perform any action except they do it rhythmically."[71] Similarly, the anthropologist Helen Roberts, who made field record- ings of traditional chants in the mid-1920s, insisted that the proof that Hawaiians were "inherently musical" was "their excellent rhythm, about which even the earliest travelers to their shores remarked when witnessing their *hulas* and hearing the accompanying chants."[72] By the 1920s and 1930s, this association had become a commonplace, articu- lated in academic journals—the *Musical Quarterly* noted that "Drums were of utmost importance in all Hawaiian music, which was rhyth- mic rather than melodic"[73]—as well as popular journalism: the popular music writer Sigmund Spaeth wrote that missionaries to Hawaii had "found a heathen race musically addicted to rhythm and little else," while *Time* reported that "contrary to popular belief, 'Hawaiian music' is not a pure racial product. Natives invented the rhythm, foreigners the melodies."[74]

But the link between rhythm and race was not an eternal trope of racial thinking; nor was it a result of the encounter between traditional ceremonial musics of cultivated elites around the world. Rather the peculiarly modern notion of race and rhythm emerged alongside the eruption of the unsettling plebeian phonograph musics in the colo- nial ports; it offered a genealogy of these "mixed-race" musics. It is striking that both Erich Hornbostel and William Ward arrived at their sense of the radical difference between "European" and "African" rhythm through the mediation of the New World musics—blues, jazz, ragtime—which Ward dismissed as "a false and feeble imita- tion of the mixture of African and European music that developed among the American negroes." For Ward, the popularity of jazz is "due solely to its rhythmic appeal; to the device, taken from West Africa to the Southern cotton-fields, and thence to Tin-Pan Alley, of superposing on the heavy regular dance beat a multitude of shifting, changing, shimmering subsidiary rhythms."[75] Similarly, both Emerson and Roberts arrived at their sense of Hawaiian rhythm through reflections on the contemporary vogue for commercial renditions of hula kuʻi.

For many, the distinctive nature of these new rhythms was captured in the notion of "syncopation," a more or less technical term for the displacement of accents to the weak or off beat, that emerged, in these years, as a keyword in the popular discussion of the new rhythms. By 1928, at the height of the recording boom, the new edition of *Grove's Dictionary of Music and Musicians* noted that "syncopation has become a general term for all that class of twentieth-century dance music which has sprung from the American adoption of rag-time."[76] "Syncopation is the reigning feature of both" the beguine and the rumba, the Martiniquan critic Andrée Nardal noted.[77] But "syncopation" was also extended beyond its common connection to ragtime and jazz to the Polynesian musical arc and the gypsy musical arc. As early as 1909, Nathaniel Emerson wrote that Hawaiians had an "inclination to lapse from their own standard of rhythm into inexplicable syncopations," the product of "an emotional susceptibility and a sympathy with environment."[78] Syncopation, the well-known "music appreciation" commentator Anne Shaw Faulkner wrote in 1921, "is found in its most intense forms among the folk of all of the Slavic countries, especially in certain districts of Poland and Russia, and also among the Hungarian gypsies."[79] And by 1933, the black South African critic Mark Radebe was defining "jazz" as "a perversion of some of the remarkable syncopating rhythms to be found in the Native music of many races."[80] As a result, syncopation came to have social and political, as well as musical, connotations. "Syncopation, this curious rhythmic accent on the short beat, is found in its most highly developed forms in the music of the folk who have been held for years in political subjection," Anne Shaw Faulkner argued. "It is, therefore, an expression in music of the desire for that freedom which been denied to its interpreter."[81]

The commonplace notion that the rhythms of these musics could be understood through the category of "syncopation" led many to hear them as simple ornaments and to dismiss their originality; "syncopation is new for popular music," Adorno writes, "but by no means for art music."[82] However, as Carlos Sandroni has argued, the very term "syncopation" was less an adequate way of understanding the rhythmic character of the musics—he is writing about samba—than a metaphor that mediated between the vernacular musics and the dominant musical discourse. A concept drawn from Western musical theory, where it denoted a sense of rupture or dislocation and depended on the non-syncopated, it was an uneasy match for musics where the "irregular"—the variety of asymmetrical formulae—was the rule. Despite its inadequacy, the notion of syncopation was, he argues, adopted into the local knowledge of the music, giving it a musicological sanction and becoming a seal of authenticity: syncopation should be seen less as a scientific concept than a kind of "native-imported category like café or mango."[83]

Thus the new rhythms of the vernacular phonograph records must be understood as more than simple syncopations, and less than the essence of a people or a continent. Rather, I would argue, they were the product of a new hybrid musical form: the "rhythm section." For the distinctiveness of these vernacular ensembles derived not only from their vocal and instrumental timbres, but also from their characteristic divide between a front line of melody instruments and a "rhythm section" of bass and chordal instruments as well as drums and percussion instruments. The importance of these "rhythm sections" was noted at the time; the phrase first appears in English in 1924.[84] There are analogous formations in other idioms: in the popular Cantonese opera of the 1920s, Su Zheng notes, the musical ensemble was called *pai he/paak woh*, "beat and accompaniment."[85] In Brazil, the sambistas who played percussion were known in the 1920s as "rhythmists."[86]

The newness of the rhythm section involved four distinct if overlapping connotations: the appearance in the music industry of a range of traditional percussion instruments; the invention of the drum set; a structural divide among the instruments of the ensemble; and a formal principle of these vernacular idioms. First, the idea of the "rhythm section" marked the eruption into commercial music of the wide range of percussion instruments—ṭarab's riqq, son's bongos, hula's ipu, samba's pandeiro—that had been part of these new urban musical cultures, and that stood in sharp contrast to the mass-produced industrial instruments imported from Europe and North America as well as the aristocratic instruments fashioned by highly skilled artisans. "We still remember the marvelous stupor," Alejo Carpentier wrote, "with which the people of our generation greeted, one fine day, the instruments that came from the eastern provinces, and that today are heard, poorly played, in all of the world's cabarets ... the bongo, on whose hide were heard the most sonorous glissandi with the palm of the hand; the creole *timbales*, secured between the knees, so nervous and mischievous, as they were struck with one or more fingers; the *econes* or *cencerros* (cowbells), little bells made of dull-sounding metal, played with a metal stick; the *botijuela*, a potbellied clay jar, with a narrow neck, from whose lips pour forth a sound analogous to the pizzicato of a bass."[87]

These percussion instruments were often seen as uncouth noisemakers, sometimes banned from street festivals and excluded from the musical stage. In Cuba, son is generally taken to be the first music to "incorporate an Afro-Cuban drum (the bongo) performed with bare hands."[88] However, as late as the mid 1920s the bongo was banned from urban performances, though the Septeto Habanero was allowed to use it in private shows for Machado himself.[89] "Thanks to the *son*," Alejo Carpentier later wrote, "Afro-Cuban percussion, confined to the slave barracks and the dilapidated rooming houses of the slums, revealed its marvelous expressive resources, achieving universal status."[90]

As a result of these exclusions, the "first" recordings of particular drums and percussion instruments have achieved legendary status, symbolic markers of the recognition of vernacular musics in many places. In Cuba, it is said that Eliseo Grenet's productions of the late 1920s were "the first to adopt conga drums into stage entertainment."[91] In Brazil, the surdos, tamborins, and pandeiros of the samba schools first appeared in a recording studio, according to legend, in 1930 when the Bando de Tangarás, a group of young, middle-class whites, mainly amateur musicians, from Vila Isabel, fronted by the singer and radio host Almirante, recorded "Na Pavuna."[92] In Hawaii, the first commercial recordings of the *ipu* (a gourd drum), the *uli'uli* (a gourd rattle), and the *pahu* (a wooden drum) were also between 1928 and 1930, most famously when Kalama's Quartet decided to record "ancient chants" and fused their steel guitar hula ensemble with the traditional Hawaiian gourd drum.[93]

In another respect, the "rhythm section" marked the emergence of a new percussion apparatus, the "drum set" or "traps." The development of pedals in the 1890s enabled drummers to combine a variety of percussion instruments into a mechanical drum machine that could be played by a single individual, thereby cutting labor costs in live entertainment industries. It seems to have first become a musical fixture in New Orleans: according to Royal Hartigan, the "snare and bass drums of the concert and marching bands in New Orleans provided a base to which, from 1900 to 1930, other accessories, or 'trappings'—hence the name *traps*—were added."[94] "The trap-drummer of the early part of the century," percussion historian James Blades notes, "... was connected with various forms of light entertainment, including the dance hall, the travelling show, the circus and the theatre pit. In the dance hall, he and the banjo constituted the rhythm section of the ragtime and early jazz bands."[95]

By the early 1920s this mechanical combination of drums and cymbals had become an emblem of "jazz." The "jazz-drum," the 1922 *Encyclopedia Britannica* stated, "needs some explanation ... The drummer uses a side drum, a big drum, and cymbals played with the feet, and various other instruments on which he beats a tattoo with his drum-sticks in alternation with the side drum. He is in fact a sort of one-man band in himself and adds considerably to the rhythm of the ensemble."[96] This "jazz-drum" turned up in vernacular dance ensembles around the world, regardless of their musical idiom: when it was adopted in the accordion-led musette bands of Parisian music halls, it was called "*un jazz*."[97] "Every jazz band in Asia, Africa, or Europe starts with the drum-and-trap accessories as a nucleus," a *New York Times* reporter wrote in 1922. "This constitutes the jazz, the rest merely band."[98]

But if the machine had its origins in New Orleans, the drum set was itself a hybrid of several vernacular traditions across the colonial ports. Chinese and Ottoman diasporas had brought percussion instruments of East and West Asia to the Caribbean and the Mediterranean, where they were assembled into the drum kit. Chinese percussion instruments were central to the early drum kit: "early drummers," Royal Hartigan notes, "adopted the instruments they heard played by Chinese immigrants in urban areas in the late 19th and early 20th centuries, like the small Chinese cymbal (Bo), large gong (Da Luo), woodblock (Ban), temple blocks (Mu-Yu), and the first tom-tom (Bangu), usually a thick painted pigskin drum head tacked on to a red painted wooden shell."[99] Cymbals had entered European and American musics from the Turkish military bands of the Ottoman janissaries, and Istanbul—a key musical crossroads—remained a center of cymbal production, particularly by the Zildjian firm.[100] Moreover, many of the drum sets that emerged included local percussion instruments as well as newly improvised sound-makers: "Nowhere else in the world, outside of New York, have the cymbals, bells, sirens, motor horns, cow bells, and all the clap-trap of the original ragtime bands been abandoned," the *New York Times* journalist reported.[101] "The trap-drummer was not only the metronome of the band," drummer and historian James Blades concludes: "his purpose was to colour it with every sound possible from the instruments at his disposal, and to give the combination style with his *ad lib* syncopation."[102]

Nonetheless, if the drum set turned up in "jazz" dance bands from Bombay and Shanghai to Rio and Cape Town, it was not adopted by all of the vernacular idioms. The drum set never became important in Hawaiian music where the rhythm section was dominated by a strummed 'ukulele, often playing the *olapa* rhythm that had been associated with the ipu. Few of the gypsy-inflected idioms of the Mediterranean adopted the drum set; in tzigane, the hammered cimbalom was the key to the band's rhythm section. Even in the Americas, one sees, as Matthew Karush notes, the "refusal of many tango bands to incorporate the drum set."[103] Noting that the drum set would later enter Cuban music via Cuban jazz bands, Ned Sublette points out that "the bass-snare-cymbal combination, so closely identified with African-American music, was never an important part of Cuban popular music which used timbales and African-derived percussion." Thus it would be a mistake to conflate the spread of the drum set with the wider emergence of "rhythm sections."[104]

For the rhythm section signified more than the eruption of local percussion instruments in the recording studio, or the spread of the drum kit. It was also the wider appearance of analogous forms of ensemble in modern dance bands—like the *bando regional* of Brazilian samba or the *orquesta típica* of Argentine tango—that were distinguished from both the street-parading percussion troupes and the violin-based "universal" orchestras of the hotel ballroom and concert hall. In Brazil, for example, recorded samba was based, as Carlos Sandroni has argued, on a "new instrumental synthesis of elements from Afro-Brazilian traditions and elements from the music played by middle-class urban groups," which was called "'regional,' abbreviation of 'regional orchestra,' in the recording studios and the radios, to distinguish it from the 'universal' orchestra based on string and bow." The "regional" ensembles combined what Sandroni calls a "chamber batucada," in which the percussion, or batucada, of carnival parades was "reduced to a surdo, a pandeiro, one or two tamborins," with "an instrumental ensemble of the type called 'choro' at the start of the century, that is, a harmonic base provided by guitars and cavaquinho joined by one or two soloists on the flute, clarinet, or mandolin."[105]

The sambas recorded by these "regional" ensembles with their "chamber batucada"—one thinks of the recordings by Estácio's Ismael Silva, or Noel Rosa's 1930 recordings with the Bando Regional and Grupo Regional—differ in timbre and texture, as well as rhythm, from the orchestrated sambas of popular crooners like Francisco Alves and Mário Reis. It is a divide analogous to that between the "hot" jazz of Louis Armstrong's Hot Fives and Hot Sevens and the "sweet" jazz of the hotel orchestras like that of Paul Whiteman, or between the steel guitar and 'ukulele hulas of Kalama's Quartet and the *hapa haole* film and hotel music of Harry Owens and His Royal Hawaiians. In each of these cases one sees a divide between the distinctive new ensembles of the vernacular phonograph musics, with their "rhythm sections," and the incorporation of elements of the vernacular idioms into the "light music" mainstream of the commercial music industry, which remained dominated by the "universal" orchestra.

However, the "rhythm section" was not just a form of ensemble but also an informing principle of the music, the key to the structure and organization of the vernacular phonograph musics. The different idioms of vernacular phonograph musics were usually distinguished by the patterns woven by their rhythm sections, composite rhythms that established the overall feel or groove. For their rhythmic character was not simply a matter of a single rhythm, a single voice. Rather, rhythm, like harmony, is constituted by the relation between multiple voices. Just as the idiomatic harmonies of these musics involved "voice leading" from one combination of voices (a chord) to another, as well as the underlying modes or keys (or, more abstractly, pitch classes) that the voices share, likewise their idiomatic rhythms were constituted by the interlocking of relatively fixed voices—the high-hat or the claves—and the relatively variable ones, all working within an underlying grid or frame that held them together.

Alejo Carpentier identified this dialectic between "rhythmic regularity" and "rhythmic variation" when he wrote one of the earliest analyses of the Afro-Cuban son. The passage is worth quoting at length, because it captured—far more than the idea of syncopation or the ideologies of race and rhythm—the musical revolution of these new rhythm sections:

> The great revolution of ideas instigated by the *son*'s percussion was in giving us *the sense of a polyrhythm subjected to a unity of time.* Up until then, one spoke of *the* rhythm of the *contradanza, the* rhythm of the *guaracha, the* rhythms of the *danzón* (admitting to a plurality within that succession). The *son*, on the other hand, established new categories. Within a general tempo, each percussive element assumed an autonomous existence. If the function of the *botijuela* and the *diente de arado* was rhythmic regularity, that of the *timbales* was to enact rhythmic variation. If the *marímbula* worked on three or four notes, marking the harmonies with the insistence of a basso continuo, then the *tres* furnished a cadence. The *bongo* acted more freely, using a more direct percussiveness or a glissando technique. The other percussive instruments would manage themselves according to their tonal registers and possibilities, according to the performer's imagination, as long as the singing—all of the musicians sang—was sustained by the percussion.[106]

This dialectic between "rhythmic regularity" and "rhythmic variation" that Carpentier pointed to in the son is echoed in many of the vernacular phonograph musics, whose composite rhythm depends on the interplay between a relatively fixed, often cyclic, ground or grid, kept by the "rhythm section," and the more fluid and varied figures and inventions of the solo voices, whether singers or instrumentalists. And these composite rhythms become the basis for the distinct "rhythmic dialects" of the vernacular idioms. "Much of the expressive essence of Latin music," musicologist Peter Manuel writes, "lies in the intricate composite rhythm created by the percussion, bass, and piano. ... This composite rhythm is the product of a set of standardized accompanimental ostinatos."[107] The real difficulty in crossing idioms, a jazz musician once said to me about playing with a clave-based Afro-Cuban band or with a Brazilian band using samba rhythms, lay less in the melodic or harmonic material than in "feeling the time," inhabiting the interplay of individual rhythms that constitutes a particular rhythmic dialect.[108]

The different rhythmic voices were often highlighted by contrasting timbres: "distinct timbres," Thomas Brothers notes, "help the ear distinguish the layers."[109] This is a structural reason for the prominence I noted earlier of multi-timbral rather than uni-timbral ensembles in these musics; it also accounts for the curious centrality of instruments that were often taken to be simple noise-makers, "percussion instruments of sharp and penetrating timbre," in Sandroni's phrase. A striking example is the Afro-Cuban claves, the pair of wooden dowels that sound the distinctive rhythmic timeline—also called the *clave* in Cuban music—that organizes the idiom.[110]

In recent years, musicologists analyzing these idioms have developed several ways of expressing this dialectic of "rhythmic regularity" and "rhythmic variation," distinguishing between the "fixed" and the "variable," the "background" and the "foreground," the "ground" and the "figure." Thomas Brothers insisted on the "basic distinction of fixed and variable" in his account of the New Orleans jazz of King Oliver and Louis Armstrong, arguing that "the technique depends on a division of musical labor: one group of instruments or voices (or just a single part) maintains a fixed rhythmic pattern; the other plays in variable rhythms, with the intention of creating a pleasing mix of agreement and disagreement with the foundational pattern."[111] Kofi Agawu called attention to "the essential tension between a firm and stable background and a fluid foreground" in his discussion of

West African dance musics.[112] Jeff Pressing distinguished "a figure–ground relationship … with the rhythmic patterns the figure, and the ground defined either by pulse, meter, or timeline" in his account of "the rhythmic devices of African diasporic music [that] typically rely on the support of a firmly structured temporal matrix, typically called a 'feel' or 'groove.'"[113] Louise Meintjes also used the notion of figure and ground in her study of South African *mbaqanga*: "The figure is a motive that is subject to ornamentation, to variation in repetition, over a more or less steady (bass) line, termed the 'ground.'" Linking social theory with musical theory, she argues that figuring is "a process of arguing musically, by means of repeated and varied motives, over ideas about social relations." These analyses are not identical: some stress the interplay between the ground established by the rhythm section and the figuring of the soloists; others emphasize the interlocking of rhythmic patterns and underlying pulse within the rhythm section that establishes the music's feel.[114]

Oddly, Adorno's hostile account of the rhythms of "jazz" was itself based on an analogous recognition of this divide between the fixed and the variable: "rhythmically free, improvisational constructions complement each other in such a way that, taken together, they fit back into the unshaken schema after all. Hence, for example, to cite only the simplest and most frequent case in point, two measures in three-eight and a measure in two-eight are combined sequentially to make a four-four measure, as marked out by the drum."[115] Unlike recent musicologists, however, Adorno does not find in it a "pleasing mix" (Brothers), or an "essential tension" (Agawu). Rather, for Adorno, the fixed schema—"stereotypical and standardized formulae"—turn the variable figures—the "rhythmically free, improvisational con-structions"—into "mere ornaments … with no consequences for the structure, and removable at will."[116] Adorno's sense that the rhythmic figures were less essential to the music's structure than the rhythmic ground, or that the ground was banal precisely because it was a fixed grid, seems strange to postmodern ears: a sign not only of his unwill-ingness to acknowledge the distinct structural principle embodied in the modern dance musics, but also of the aesthetic revolution taking place at the time.

Throughout the vernacular phonograph musics, there are common rhythmic grids or frames, which are often associated with a dance. Record labels on the 78 rpm discs of the 1920s prominently dis-played the dance genre of the recording alongside the song title and musician's name. A similar phenomenon is found on the flamenco discs of the 1920s, where the *palo* of the recording—the classification as *seguiriya, bulería, soleá,* among many other styles characterized by rhythm and mode—was usually more prominent than the "title"— often little more than the opening words of the song. Thus, one might think of the tango and the foxtrot, the hula and the samba, not only as specific dances, but as forms of musical time: tango-time, foxtrot-time, hula-time, and samba-time might be thought of the way one thinks of waltz-time or march-time.

In addition to the proliferation of names of dances and rhythmic styles, two different principles run through the dance-like grids played by the rhythm sections of the vernacular ensembles: timelines and chord cycles.[117] Timelines are distinctive rhythmic figures or cells, repeated throughout a performance or composition. The term was developed by ethnomusicologists discussing the West African dance rhythms that are often played on a metal bell.[118] A timeline, Kofi Agawu writes, "is a distinctly shaped and often memorable rhythmic figure of modest duration that is played as an ostinato throughout a given dance composition."[119] Well-known Ghanaian timelines include the "standard" timeline, the *kpanlogo,* and the *Gahu.*[120] However, the term has been extended beyond West Africa by theorists of rhythm: the principle of the timeline can be seen in the rhythmic cells at the heart of the African-American vernacular musics of Latin America—the *tresillo,* the *cinquillo,* the *son clave,* the *habanera* or tango rhythm, and the bossa nova—as well as the *compás* of the flamenco of Andalusia, the *talas* of South Asia, and the Turkish *aksak* rhythms of the Balkans.[121] Though the timeline was articulated in different ways—with metal bells, wooden sticks (*claves*), or accented hand claps—these periodic rhythmic figures are fundamental to each musical idiom. "The key to understanding the structure of a given topos" or timeline, Agawu argues, "is the dance or choreography upon which it is based … No one hears a topos without also hearing—in actuality or imaginatively—the movement of feet."[122]

The principle of the timeline was adopted by many of the vernacular music ensembles not only because they inherited the traditional practices, but because, as Godfried Toussaint points out, "timelines act as an orienting device that facilitates musicians to stay together and helps soloists navigate the rhythmic landscape offered by the other instruments."[123] The timeline was usually articulated by an instrument in the rhythm section, like the claves in son or the matchbox in samba, or by an element of the drum set, like the snare or cymbal.

However, the ostinato of the timeline was usually combined with a second rhythmic principle that grew out of the new rhythm sections in which not only percussion instruments but bass and chordal instruments served as timekeepers: the chord cycle. The chord cycle was a commonplace series of chords played by the rhythm section to establish a periodic harmonic rhythm, a harmonic ostinato. Such chord cycles are found throughout the vernacular phonograph musics across each of the musical arcs of the colonial archipelago. Across the black Atlantic, one finds the palm-wine patterns of West Africa like the "Yaa Amponsah" cycle;[124] the four-bar chord ostinato of South African marabi;[125] the twelve-bar blues cycle that structured not only recorded blues but much of early jazz and country recording in the United States; the thirty-two-bar "rhythm changes," the chord cycle of George Gershwin's "I Got Rhythm," which was adopted by jazz musicians in the early 1930s; and the beguine chord cycle that, Prieto argues, played "a role similar to the Blues or Rhythm changes … for the biguine of Stellio's era."[126] Across the gypsy Mediterranean, they include the Andalusian cadence of flamenco,[127] and the chord oscillation between relative major and minor chords in the rebetika of Piraeus.[128] Across the Pacific, they include the ten-bar hula cycle played on the 'ukulele,[129] as well as the thirty-two-bar *kroncong asli* chord cycle that was, in the words of musicologist Philip Yampolsky, "an inescapable harmonic-melodic pattern" in Indonesian popular music: "Imagine if *I Got Rhythm* were the only set of changes available to jazz musicians."[130] Like the timeline, these chord cycles served both to mark time and to enable improvisation within the idiom.[131]

The distinctive new rhythms and "syncopations" of the idioms of the vernacular phonograph musics were thus a product of the interplay of timelines and chord cycles in the rhythm sections of these "dance bands" and "orquestas típicas." Some musics were based mainly on time lines: in Cuban music, the timeline of the clave was so omnipresent that the composer Emilio Grenet wrote of its "rhythmical tyranny." When a composition passes into "popular hands," he argued, "the rhythm almost always recovers its predominance. In the language of the people this is called *meter en los palos* (to put into the sticks)." The sound of the wooden claves dominates the music with "relentless authority"; "the steps of our dancers … follow the *claves* as closely as the shadow follows the body."[132] Other musics were based more on chord cycles: as the gourd pattern of the ipu gave way to the strummed chords of the 'ukulele, the ten-bar harmonic ostinato dominated the recorded hula ku'i of the 1920s and 1930s. However, the circulation of phonograph records led to hybrids of the two principles. Musics based on timelines developed a repertoire of commonplace chord cycles when they were adapted to chordal instruments like the guitar, while musics based on chord cycles—like African-American blues and jazz, often distinguished by musicologists by the absence of timelines[133]—began to incorporate timelines: though Latin timelines rarely structured entire jazz performances, the *tresillo*, *cinquillo*, and *clave* became, as Chris Washburne has argued, ubiquitous in jazz.[134] In the United States, as David Schiff puts it, "the clave pattern wore a variety of disguises."[135]

Moreover, unprecedented syntheses, hybrids, and transformations of the timeline and the chord cycle appeared. Ghanaian highlife, for example, was rooted in dance forms based on timelines, but it developed a distinctive timeline with fewer attacks, one that, Kofi Agawu suggests, expressed a distinctive modern ethos.

> The Highlife ethos is essentially different from that of the traditional dances (like Agbadza or Atsiagbeko) … it is more committed to exploring—with a mixture of optimism and irony—the recent urban or modern turn in African history. Highlife is inflected by European ways of musical doing; it enshrines syncreticism as a creative force. This bundle of attributes may be read into the Highlife timeline, which occupies a lighter register in the hierarchy of African expressive forms."[136]

But if highlife had a distinctive timeline, it also developed a repertoire of chord cycles drawn from early recordings like the Kumasi Trio's 1928 "Yaa Amponsah." In one of the earliest analyses of the vernacular phonograph musics, Robert Sprigge showed how the melody of "Yaa Amponsah" incorporated both the rhythm of the clave and the chordal patterns produced by Jacob Sam's two-finger guitar style.[137] In this way, the timbral and rhythmic syncretism of "Yaa Amponsah" leads to the third element of these new musics, their "weird" harmonies.

Weird Harmonies

The pervasiveness of these deceptively "simple" chord cycles led to a curious paradox in the way the harmonies of the vernacular phonograph idioms were discussed. On the one hand, their harmonies were routinely discounted as rudimentary, hardly worth mentioning; on the other hand, they were often heard as strange or, in English-language commentary, as "weird." It is not difficult to collect accounts dismissing the harmonies. The blues were, Abbe Niles wrote in 1926, "unconsciously so constructed that if the singer wished to accompany himself, he need know only three chords."[138] The sense that these idioms were harmonically simple was, as I have suggested, often based on a misunderstanding of the rhythmic centrality of the chord cycles: they are less "chord progressions," leading voices to modulate and resolve, than "changes," as the jazz tradition called them, marking time, and serving, as we will see, as a framework for improvisation. "If repetition of a harmonic progression seventy-five times can keep listeners and dancers interested," Kofi Agawu argues, "then there is a power to repetition that suggests not mindlessness or a false sense of security (as some critics have proposed) but a fascination with grounded musical adventures."[139]

The paradox is that these apparently simple chords often sounded weird, producing strange blends that fit neither the framework of common practice harmony nor that of the traditional modes. As a result, they offended the ears both of those trained in common practice and of those trained in traditional modes, maqam, and ragas. Perhaps the most celebrated early example of the resulting clash was in gypsy music: "the civilized musician," Franz Liszt wrote in 1859, "is at first so astounded by the strangeness of the intervals employed ... that he can find no other way of settling the matter in his mind than that of concluding the dissonances to be accidental; that they are mere inexactitudes; or, to be quite frank, faults of execution." Nonetheless, "the harmony acquires a strangely dazzling character," and Liszt went on to theorize a "gypsy" scale.[140] The sense that different musical idioms could be defined by specific notes and scales was fundamental to the musicology of the period: it ranged from Carl Engel's coining of the term "pentatonic" to characterize folk music scales in the 1860s[141] to the early twentieth-century debates over the differences between European and Indian scales, as in A. H. Fox Strangways's influential 1908 essay on "The Hindu Scale." "The measurement of scales," musicologist Matt Rahaim observes, "had become a sort of sonic phrenology."[142]

In the decade before the recording boom, another celebrated example of these strange intervals emerged: the "blue note." The blue note was apparently first named during the blues "craze" of the 1910s: an early use cited by the *Oxford English Dictionary*—"The lank trombone ... unburdens its pent-up soul and sobs to high heaven the unspeakable agony of the famous 'blue note'"—is particularly interesting, because it indicates that the term was both already famous and yet still unusual enough to put in quotation marks.[143] The blue note was immediately heard as "weird": "the weirdest blue notes ever heard," a writer in the *Dramatic Mirror* noted in 1919, "began to flow ... from the clarionet"; and W. C. Handy, the self-proclaimed "father of the blues," called the blues guitar sound he encountered in Tutwiler, Mississippi, in 1903 "the weirdest music I had ever heard."[144]

However, the "gypsy" scale and the blue note were less marks of distinctive "folk" scales, than the product of the clash between modal traditions and the common practice harmony embodied in printed popular sheet music. So-called gypsy notes were not part of the traditional musics of the Roma peoples of the European subcontinent, as Bálint Sárosi showed. Rather, they emerged in the "verbunkos idiom," the popular urban Hungarian music, disseminated by sheet music with parlor piano accompaniments, but usually played by gypsy musicians in small orchestras built around a violin lead with a rhythm section anchored by the cimbalom, a hammered dulcimer. This fusion was heard as "gypsy music" from the time of Liszt to the era of Bartók; it was a major idiom of the 1920s recording boom, recorded and marketed as "tzigane."[145] The resulting clash between the common practice harmonies of the Hungarian popular sheet music and the performance practices of the gypsy violinists and cimbalomists—"the emphasis is never on what but on *how* they perform," Sárosi writes—generated the characteristic "gypsy" notes.[146]

Similarly, the "blue note" was less a specific note in African-American folk singing than, as Abbe Niles noted in his introduction to W. C. Handy's 1926 collection of sheet music "blues," Handy's influential solution to the problem of representing the blues singing he had heard in the terms of commercial sheet music. "Writing down his tunes with the memory of how the Negroes had sung, Handy was first met by the problem of perpetuating the typical treatment of the tonic third—the slur of the voices, whatever the song. This aberration he chose to represent by the frequent introduction of the minor third into melodies which ... exhibited a prevailing major." Handy's "interpolated minor third"—which "acquired a name of its own: 'the blue note'"—figured the clash between the traditional bending and worrying of African-American modes of singing and the parlor piano harmonies of Tin Pan Alley sheet music.[147]

However, this clash between common practice harmony and forms of singing shaped by intonational languages and modal musical practices was not only the product of the friction with the notational conventions of the sheet music industry. It was also a fundamental part of the colonization of the ear, as part-singing and solfège (the use of the do, re, mi syllables as training in common practice melody and harmony) were instituted in colonial choirs and choruses around the world, part of what Kofi Agawu has called the "violence of imposing harmony."[148]

As a result, in all three arcs of the colonial archipelago, the new vernacular idioms were shaped by a clash between two practices of pitch. Early New Orleans jazz embodied, Thomas Brothers argued, the musicians' response to the contradiction between blues training and solfège training: "blues finds expressive depth through subtle shading and dramatic bending of pitch, while solfège is designed with just the opposite goal in mind—to internalize the distance between pitches with such precision that there is absolutely no deviation from the measured scale." Though "Baptist hymns, Sousa marches, and Ragtime songs were rigidly shaped … with the Eurocentric harmonic system in mind," Brothers suggests, "it must have been perfectly fine to sing the hymns and popular songs with complete disregard for their harmonic implications."[149] Thus the "blue note" might be seen not only as the result of the attempt to notate the blues for commercial sheet music, but also as a sign of the tension between a blues ear and a well-tempered ear, a tension that marked the two worlds of New Orleans musical culture. For the Creole musicians as for Handy, Brothers argues, "Eurocentric harmony is a primary system of pitch syntax that must not be violated"; for Louis Armstrong and the emerging jazz tradition, on the other hand, "Eurocentric harmonic syntax is secondary and subservient."[150]

In an analogous situation, many African musicians were caught between traditional African pentatonic sound fields and melodic shapes (beginning at a high point and coming down) and European cadences (with their stepwise melodic ascents and descents); composing under a tonal regime meant the grafting of one tonal system onto another or trying to inflect the tonal system.[151] "Highlife melody," Agawu writes, "is in a perpetual state of tension, seeking to balance the pull of an intonational language-based pattern against that of an invariant, harmonically driven, precompositionally determined one."[152]

Hawaii was likewise the scene of a clash between the vocal glissan-dos of Hawaiian mele and hula that were imitated by the steel guitar, and the common practice harmonies of the Sankey gospel hymns that had been translated into Hawaiian. "In a century of acquaintance with harmonized European music the Hawaiians have learned to sing in parts," the anthropologist Helen Roberts noted in 1925, "but unless they have been well schooled in choral singing, or are singing from notes, one frequently hears harmonies which are unorthodox accord-ing to classical rules but which, though novel, are seldom displeasing and always refreshing to ears on which certain combinations of sounds have fallen so long that they are unconsciously anticipated."[153]

The clash between local melodic modes and common practice harmony was also the result of the widespread adoption of imported chordal instruments. As early as 1935, the song collector Rodney Gallop noted the way the adoption of the guitar had shaped the music of the fado. "The vocal line of the *Fado* is clearly conditioned by the harmonic accompaniment, chords of the tonic and dominant repeated in strictly symmetrical rotation, from which it is never divorced and without which indeed it would be difficult or even impossible to sing." This guitar-influenced vocal style was, he suggested, the outcome of the tension between traditional modes and tonal harmony: "For cen-turies the Portuguese guitar which ... was 'well-tempered' long before the days of Bach, has been used to accompany peasant song. Its har-monic system is based not on the famous Andaluzian 'Phrygian' scale of Southern Spain, but on the modern major and minor." Thus "the instrumentalist ... a semi-professional" had a "natural tendency to modernise old tunes, to tidy up what to him appear loose ends of rhythm and tonality to harmonise them according to modern ideas."[154]

In many cases this produced what musicologist Peter Manuel has called a "vernacular tonality,"[155] distinct from common practice harmony and modal practice alike. Ethnomusicologists have analyzed non-Western modal systems, Manuel writes, but they have neglected "the syncretic musical systems that have arisen ... as products of the confluence of modal traditions with Western chordal harmony." Each of these vernacular tonalities took shape when chordal instruments were adopted to accompany the vocal phrases of modal melodies; the chords—major and minor triads—were used not for their traditional functions in common practice harmony, but for "color ... sonority, or ... simple oscillation."[156]

Manuel developed this hypothesis through his exploration of a "Mediterranean tonality," in which local variants of the Arabic *Hijaz* mode or maqam, with its characteristic augmented second interval, were harmonized with European triads in urban musics from Seville and Cádiz to Istanbul, Athens, and Smyrna. In these musics, he argues, "chordal accompaniments consist either of static non-directional oscillations between a tonic and a secondary chord, or else they function as enhancements of a melody which remains predominantly modal." For example, in the Phrygian tonality of the gypsy-derived *cantes* of flamenco, "the guitar accompaniment, where present, invariably consists of an ornamented oscillation between two chords—usually, the tonic and the flat supertonic—with occasional forays in the minor fourth chord, thence descending to the tonic via the familiar iv-III-II-I pattern [the "Andalusian cadence" of, for example, Am-G-F-E]." This Mediterranean tonality was often circulated by musical diasporas, including Jewish *klezmorim*, professional secular musicians who transmitted "stylistic features and musical genres … across international borders," and Gypsy musicians who "in Eastern Europe as in Andalusia … tended to preserve and perpetuate older … musical practices, synthesizing them with modern, generally more Western styles, and thereby playing important roles in the evolution of a system of modal harmony which, in many respects, is common to the entire region."[157]

In a series of essays, Manuel extended this analysis of the "Mediterranean tonality" to other forms of "vernacular tonality," syncretic regional harmonic practices that are "qualitatively distinct" from common practice harmony, including what he calls "dual tonicity" in Latin American musics like the *guajira*, the country-style Cuban music of the early twentieth century (well known through the song "Guantanamera"), and the urban son, one of the fundamental musics of the recording boom of the late 1920s.[158] Though "most of the harmonies of *son*," Manuel writes, "… are fairly straightforward, based on I-IV-V pillars," many son tracks recorded during the first half of the twentieth century "illustrate what would seem to be a curious indifference to finality, concluding, for example, on the subdominant, or … on what might otherwise be heard as the dominant." This yields a "distinctive tonicity … even more resistant to Western musicological analysis than is the Andalusian tonality of flamenco." Though Manuel acknowledges that these harmonic progressions can be (and have been) analyzed in common practice terms, he argues that these "simple and familiar-looking chordal vocabularies operate in a form of tonality quite distinct from common practice, with its relatively unambiguous sense of tonicity." They are better understood as "a set of vernacular, guitar-derived conventions, consisting of simple chordal ostinatos, that emerged in the formative period of tonality and subsequently followed relatively independent trajectories," enjoying "a prolonged life in various Latin American folk genres" as well as becoming "a harmonic feature of mid-twentieth-century Cuban popular music." Manuel's hypothesis of modal harmonies in the "vernacular margins of the Western mainstream" is a powerful way of understanding analogous harmonic practices in the recorded vernacular musics of the Polynesian Pacific and the black Atlantic.[159]

In Hawaii, a syncretic harmony was enabled by the central chordal instrument, the 'ukulele, a Hawaiian adaptation of the *machete* brought by contract laborers from the colonial Atlantic island archipelago of Madeira in 1879. "The ukulele is now the common companion of every group of Hawaiian youths," Helen Roberts commented in 1925, "who generally achieve with it only the necessary chords with which to accompany their songs, and these, like the vocal harmonies, are not always orthodox but often delightfully unexpected."[160] In West Africa, such a syncretic harmony developed in highlife: "highlife's tonal types juggle the pressures of a closed I-V-I progression with various open modal structures."[161] Local modal sound fields and traditional playing techniques also changed the way chordal instruments were played: for example, in palm-wine guitar music, the two-note accompaniments of the traditional *seprewa* harp lute fused with the chordal forms of the guitar. Despite the differences between the two instruments, musicologist Kwadwo Adum-Attah writes, "the rural musician did not find it difficult … to play the old melodies on the guitar." "The tunes of the traditional Asante 'blues' known as *Odonson* were transferred from the *seprewa* to the guitar." However, "as a result of being exposed to Western hymn singing and its four-part chordal structure, the rural musician started to add more chords based on Western harmonic practices to his guitar accompaniment."[162]

These modal harmonies or vernacular tonalities may have emerged as the result of colonial music industries and colonial musical training, involving the spread of commercial sheet music, the training in part-singing by missionaries, the travels of semi-professional dance musicians, and the circulation of mass-produced chordal instruments. However, the musical consequence was a soundscape defined by these

weird if rudimentary harmonic rhythms, chord ostinatos, and oscillations, that, far from impoverishing the music, gave rise to a fourth
aspect regularly noted of the recorded vernacular musics: their new
forms of virtuosic improvisation.

Recorded Improvisations

One of the remarkable paradoxes of the vernacular phonograph
musics was that the unprecedented inscription of these un-notated
musics in shellac led to a new concentration on—indeed a revaluation
of—the place of musical improvisation. The elements of music that
had seemed most fleeting and unrepeatable—extemporized variations
and ornaments—were now fixed on disc and subject to mechanical
repetition. The recorded improvisation was a new form of reification,
as a momentary relation between people became a material object;
but it also initiated a new dialectic between recording and musicking,
as improvisations were learned and copied from records, inspiring a
spiral of improvisations on improvisations.

Improvisation in music had of course long existed, but, in nineteenth-
century Europe and the European settler societies of the Americas, it
lost recognition and value as printed composition came to dominate
both art music and popular song.[163] Improvisation was often dismissed
as inessential, at best a virtuoso ornamentation, at worst a traducing
of the composer's intentions.[164] Moreover, as improvisation declined
in prestige, it became increasingly associated with subaltern castes of
musical performers: "Extemporisation or improvisation," the 1927
edition of the authoritative *Grove's Dictionary of Music and Musicians*
stated, is "the primitive act of music-making, existing from the moment
that the untutored individual obeys the impulse to relieve his feelings
by bursting into song. Accordingly, therefore, amongst all primitive
peoples musical composition consists of extemporization subsequently
memorized."[165] Gypsy musicians were particularly associated with
improvisation in the late nineteenth and early twentieth centuries.[166]
Gypsy music, Liszt had argued, "more than any other belongs to the
domain of improvisation, without which it does not exist." The gypsy
master "most to be admired is he who enriches his theme with such a
profusion of traits (appoggiaturas, tremolos, scales, arpeggios, and diatonic or chromatic passages) that under this luxuriant embroidery the
primitive thought appears no more prominently than the fabric of his

garment appears upon his sleeve."[167] A half-century later, the improvising violinist of the tzigane orchestra was described as follows by an Irish observer: "In Hungary, the gipsy 'Primás' develops his rhapsody in the following way: first of all the slow, sad *lassu* in which the solo violin improvises arabesques and embroiders the Magyar tune possessing so many memories for his audience; meanwhile the accompanying fiddles and the cymbalum support his improvisation and when his inspiration wearies and sinks they enable him to soar again."[168]

By the 1920s, this association of improvisation with the tzigane orchestras of eastern Europe made them a point of comparison with the new jazz bands. "A semblance of this lost, and rediscovered, art [of improvisation] is contained in the music of the Russian and Hungarian gypsies," the musicologist Carl Engel noted in 1922. "Just as that music is a riotous improvisation, throbbing with a communicative beat, so is jazz. Just as the gypsy players are held together by an identical, inexplicable rhythmic spell, following the leader's fiddle in its harmonic meanderings, each instrument walking in a bypath of its own, so is the ideal jazz band constituted—that is, the jazz band made up of serious jazz artists."[169] When the French composer Darius Milhaud first heard African-American jazz musicians in New York in 1922, his account was an uncanny echo of Liszt's encounter with gypsy musicians a half century earlier:

> In the jazz of the whites everything has been worked out to perfection and studied in the most thorough way. Among the Negroes there is far more improvisation. But what tremendous musical gifts and what power of performance are necessary to bring improvisation to such a pitch of perfection! In their technique they possess great freedom and facility. Each instrument follows its natural melodic line and improvises even while it adheres to the harmonic framework which underlies and supports the piece as a whole. We find this music perpetually employing a rich and confusing interweaving of elements. It uses major and minor chords together with quarter tones, which are produced by a combination of glissando and vibrato techniques—an exaggeration of the trombone tones, as well as vigorous vibration of the trumpet pistons and strange uses of the fingers on the violin strings.[170]

Throughout this discourse, improvisation was understood primarily as a performance practice, a supplement to an original song or dance. Despite Liszt's praise, gypsy musicians were more often reproached for "tasteless 'ornamentation.'"[171] Bartók's 1931 argument that "even the much vaunted performance of the gypsies is lacking in uniform character … [and] authenticity" is echoed in Adorno's 1933 argument that "even the much-invoked improvisations [of jazz], the *hot* passages and *breaks*, are merely ornamental in their significance, and never part of the overall construction or determinant of the form."[172] Though there is, as we will see, a material circumstance underlying this perception, it must be insisted that the improvisations of the vernacular phonograph musics such as tzigane and jazz, like those of other cultures of musical improvisation, were *not* fundamentally a matter of performance practice, of idiosyncratic ornamentations and elaborations. Rather, they were forms of what Derek Bailey called "idiomatic improvisation," rooted in a sense of belonging to a musical speech community.[173]

The ability to speak freely in a musical vernacular is based on a knowledge of the musical idiom, its figures, its gestures, and its grooves. "Improvisation occurs always within a set of rules, or rather, conventions," the pioneering musicologist Christopher Small has argued, and it depends "on the existence of a commonly agreed language."[174] The musical idioms of the colonial ports were such commonly agreed languages, embedded by ear in lips and hips, fingers and vocal cords. Their rules and conventions, vocabularies and rhetorics, were learned by playing in the small ensembles—the trios and sextets—that proliferated in the ports' streets and parks, in the back corners of taverns and the bandstands of dance halls. Some idioms accented vocal improvisation, others dance improvisation, still others instrumental improvisation. A 1909 account of the improvised Hawaiian mele claimed that many Hawaiians "possessed the gift of improvisation in a remarkable degree."[175] The improvised music of Cairo's ṭarab was based on the melodic designs embodied in the various modes, the *maqamat*. As a result, ṭarab improvisations were, as Ali Racy writes, "devoid of verse-like repetitions; solo-oriented; and nonmetric, or 'rhythmically free.'"[176]

At the other end of the Mediterranean, the flamenco guitarists of Seville and Cádiz were known for their improvisations. "Take a characteristic gipsy guitarist in a tavern," the critic and folklorist Walter Starkie wrote in 1935, "and you will find that he divides his accompaniment into three parts. First of all we have the *rasgueado* or general improvised prelude leading into the second part which is called the *paseo* or promenade. Then comes the theme which leads to the third part called *falsetas* or variations."[177] Across the black Atlantic, the emerging dance musics were characterized by forms of improvisation: in Johannesburg, marabi was, in the words of the *Drum* journalist Todd Matshikiza, "largely the illiterate improvisations of the musicians of the day";[178] in Buenos Aires and Montevideo, the early tango and milonga were "played by ear and the music was largely improvised."[179] In Rio de Janeiro, choro was an improvised music played by groups known as "*pau e corda*" (wood and strings): "The flute played the ornamented melodies, while the guitar and cavaquinho provided the improvised harmonic and rhythmic accompaniment as well as the melodic counterpoint."[180] In Havana, son "was the first [music] to prominently feature musical and vocal improvisation"; its *montuno* section, musicologist Peter Manuel writes, "usually commences with the trumpet player improvising two-bar phrases in alternation with the choral refrains (*coros*); typically, after four of these exchanges, the lead singer improvises his own *soneos* in alternation with the *coro*, which may continue indefinitely, perhaps interrupted by a solo on the bongo, or, less often, the *tres*."[181] "The swing idea of free improvisation by the players was," Louis Armstrong said in 1936, "at the core of jazz when it started back there in New Orleans."[182]

Out of these ensembles came two distinct forms of improvisation, determined by who set the "time." In some cases, the time was established by a rhythm section, and solo voices conversed in the framework of a cyclic pattern, whether a periodic harmonic rhythm (a repeated "chord progression") or a timeline stated by clave or bell. In other cases, the time was established by the call of a lead voice—expanding and contracting the time—to which other voices and instrumentalists responded: one hears this in the ṭarab recordings of Umm Kulthūm as well as in the flamenco recordings of Pastora Pavón.

Paradoxically, the word improvisation was often avoided by improvising musicians. "Idiomatic improvisers," Derek Bailey points out, "in describing what they do, use the name of the idiom. They 'play flamenco' or 'play jazz'; some refer to what they do as just 'playing.'" "In most of the world's musical traditions," Christopher Small concludes, "the word 'improvisation' has little significance, since what we have been calling improvisation is just the normal way of musicking; they call it, quite simply, playing, and the idiom in which they work as, equally simply, 'the way we play.'"[183]

If most vernacular musicking is, in this sense, improvisation, the real question posed by the moment of the vernacular phonograph musics is not "why were they improvised?" but "why did the idea of improvisation become so prominent?" Why did many of these musics develop a rhetoric, even ideology, of improvisation? I would suggest that the improvisations that flourished in the vernacular phonograph musics were not simply the appearance on record of long-standing practices of musicking. Rather, these "recorded improvisations" mark the emergence of a new, specifically modern, culture of musical improvisation that depended on a feedback loop between three elements: urban vernacular idioms that prized competitive virtuosity, embodied in public contests; an industry of printed sheet music that inspired the practice of "faking"; and the emergence of electrically recorded discs that captured and circulated the improvisations of star musicians.

The first element in this feedback loop was a product of the urban musical economy. In the local venues of live entertainment that exploded in the late nineteenth and early twentieth centuries—from vaudeville theaters and dance halls to sports stadiums—forms of virtuosic performance and athleticism flourished, creating stars and becoming a kind of entertainment currency. In the vernacular musics, improvisation became not just the normal practice of variation and extemporization within the conventions of an oral tradition, but part of a culture of improvisatory display in a continual round of contests among musicians. Some were informal, like the *rodas* of Rio's choro or the "jam sessions" of jazz (the phrase emerges in the late 1920s).[184]

But many were public competitions and contests—*concursos* in Spanish—sponsored by dance halls, radio stations, and record companies. In Batavia, there were regular kroncong competitions—*concours kroncong*—from 1915 into the 1920s; some matched kroncong groups against one another, others were song duels between lead singers.[185] The 1922 Concurso de Cante Jondo in Granada not only marked the resurgence of traditional flamenco but led to Odeon recordings of the guest artist, Manuel Torre, and the prizewinner, El Tenazas.[186] The first son *concurso* in Havana in 1926 was won by the Sexteto Habanero for their performance of "Tres Lindas Cubanas"; they recorded it for Victor a few months later.[187] From 1924 to 1930, the record label Discos Nacional sponsored tango contests in Buenos Aires: "the finest composers and poets presented their work, which was then judged by the members of the audience. The prize-winning compositions were made into records and the entire contest proceedings were broadcast" on radio.[188] In Atlanta, the Georgia Old-Time Fiddlers' Convention took place annually from 1913 to 1935, and success in the fiddling contest often led to recording contracts for local fiddlers like Fiddlin' John Carson and string bands like Gid Tanner and his Skillet Lickers.[189]

And in Trinidad, the world of calypso depended on regular competitions during carnival season. "Competitions were a major source of income," the historian Gordon Rohlehr writes: the calypsonian "had to be where the competitions were ... in Princes Town or Sangre Grande, Port of Spain, Tunapuna or San Fernando."[190] These formal and informal contests put a new emphasis on improvisatory prowess; as Thomas Brothers notes of early New Orleans jazz, "quickness, extended-range playing, speed of execution, fresh ideas, harmonic experimentation—all were sources of reward and prestige in the manly musical world of New Orleans ... The twin pressures of commercial reward and the climb toward urban sophistication helped stimulate improvisation."[191]

The second element of this feedback loop was the place of notated music in these vernacular idioms. The notion of these musics as "improvised" depended on their relation to the commercial hegemony of the popular song, circulated as sheet music. In the face of popular printed music, modern "improvising" emerged in tension with "reading," as can be seen in the curious appearance of the notion of "faking" music. In the US in the 1910s, the terms "fake," "improvise," and "interpolate" were used interchangeably; by 1924, a critic in the music trade paper, the *Musical Courier*, joked that "improvise" was "the polite word for 'fake.'"[192] The two contrary, if complementary, senses of faking captured the clash between "ear" cultures and "reading" cultures that ran through many of the musics of the colonial ports. On the one hand, vernacular musicians who played by ear and did not read European notation were confronted not only with the ubiquitous sheet music of popular song, but with the "charts" of commercial dance bands, "stock arrangements" of popular hits,[193] and the "method books" of instrumental instruction. Flamenco method books dated from Rafael Marín's *Método de Guitarra pro Música y Cifra* in 1902,[194] while the *Kamiki Hawaiian Guitar Method Book*, which appeared in a number of editions from 1916, was only the best known of many Hawaiian steel guitar manuals. By the mid-1920s, reams of such printed materials accompanied the recording boom: for example in Batavia, the Odeon record dealer Tio Tek Hong, who issued kroncong disks, also published a series of kroncong songbooks for violin and mandolin from 1924 on.[195]

In the face of this print music culture, "faking" was the ability—at once respected and disrespected—to improvise a song (or a part in an arrangement) without reading the notation. On the other hand, those vernacular musicians who could "read"—having received formal training on their instruments through religious schools, military bands, or traditional musical apprenticeships—often found that this training did not prepare them for the practices of the urban dance musics. The figures and gestures of the music rarely appeared in the notated sheet music. So, for reading musicians, "faking" was the ability to improvise beyond the bare bones of the sheet music (bootlegged collections of lead sheets came to be known as "fake books"[196]). By the mid-1920s, publications appeared that instructed reading musicians in the art of faking and improvising. Reading musicians could pick up riffs from a new genre of sheet music that printed solos, like *Kaai's Method and Solos for Ukulele or Tiple* (1926; Ernest Kaai was the leading Hawaiian 'ukulele player of the era) and Louis Armstrong's *125 Jazz Breaks for Cornet* (1927, notated two-bar turnarounds in a variety of keys) and *50 Hot Choruses for Cornet* (1927, more than a quarter of which were improvisations on tunes by Jelly Roll Morton).[197] When the composer Milhaud visited the US in 1924, he found the method books of the Winn School of Popular Music "extraordinarily valuable ... as regards improvisation," showing how "such devices as arpeggios, trills, runs, broken chords, omissions, dissonances, embellishments, ornaments, variations, and cadenzas ... are introduced ad libitum at the end of the parts of the various instruments, but in such a way that the rhythmic regularity of the whole does not suffer."[198]

The third element in this feedback loop was the emergence of recorded improvisations, a trend that accelerated with electrical recording. The earliest acoustic recordings of these vernacular musics tended to ignore improvisation, in large part because the early recording industry borrowed its commercial model from the sheet music industry: it was selling songs rather than performances. Moreover, the technical difficulties of acoustic recording meant that there was little room for spontaneity in early recording; relatively anonymous studio musicians trained to play for acoustic horns were usually more successful at recording than were musicians known for their live performances.

The microphone of electrical recording changed this dramatically: it not only created new kinds of "location" or "field" recording, but also what one might call a new "moment" recording. The spontaneous performance in the studio became more important than the carefully rehearsed rendition of a song. At first, these improvisations remained restricted to relatively short passages: "hot riffs" within the three-minute limits of the 78 disc and the standardized structure of the commercial popular song. But as performances rather than songs became the currency of the recording industry, virtuosic improvisers became celebrities, and their records circulated widely. For example, in Rio de Janeiro, the recordings of the flutist Alfredo da Rocha Viana, Jr., better known as Pixinguinha, marked a distinct shift; he was "one of the first choro musicians to improvise over more than a few bars, a practice which soon became characteristic of the genre."[199] In Cairo, Umm Kulthūm was celebrated for performances and recordings in which she could "spontaneously produce multiple versions of a single line." Using "familiar and well-loved modes: *rast, bayati, nahawand,* and *huzam* … Kulthūm's varied repetitions were," Virginia Danielson writes, "… intended to bring the listener closer to the mood of the line with each successive iteration. The tools she brought to bear were tone color, rhythm, and articulation rather than melodic excursions that might obscure the words."[200] In the US, electrical recording triggered an explosion of jazz improvisation: Victor's electrical recordings of Jelly Roll Morton's Red Hot Peppers in the fall of 1926 and the spring of 1927 were followed by OKeh's first electric session with Louis Armstrong's expanded Hot Seven in May 1927, the session that produced the famous stop-time trumpet solo on "Potato Head Blues,"* a landmark in "playing the changes."[201] In Cuba, Armstrong's equivalent for the son was Félix Chappottín, the trumpeter who first recorded with the Septeto Habanero in 1928, inaugurating, on tracks like "Coralia,"* the distinctive improvisational style that was to make him "the most important trumpet player in Afro-Cuban music history."[202]

The new prominence of improvisation was also evident as instrumental recordings appeared in idioms that had been dominated by singers, like Hawaiian hula and Andalusian flamenco. In hula ku'i, steel guitarists adopted a handful of standard tunes for displays of instrumental virtuosity. "Hilo March,"* composed in the late nineteenth century by Joseph Kapaeau Ae'a for a wind band, became, in the 1920s, a popular vehicle for a generation of young Hawaiian steel guitarists, including Sol Ho'opi'i, Mike Hanapi of Kalama's Quartet, and M. K. Moke of Johnny Noble's band.[203] They also recorded a number of instrumentals featuring the popular "chimes" effect—using the guitar's string harmonics—like Ho'opi'i's "Chimes" (a version of the popular "Maui NoKa 'Oi," often known as "Maui Chimes") and Moke's "Moana Chimes." In flamenco, two guitarists who had accompanied singers on dozens of discs in the 1920s, playing brief improvised *falsetas*—the *gitano* veteran Ramón Montoya, a regular at Gramófono sessions, and the younger virtuoso from Seville, Niño Ricardo, Montoya's equivalent at Regal—made the first recordings of solo flamenco guitar in 1928.[204] Montoya—"whose virtuosity is quite astonishing," a record reviewer wrote in 1930—went on to pioneer concerts of flamenco guitar, with a celebrated 1936 appearance in Paris that was linked to the release of an album of instrumentals, *Arte clásico flamenco*.[205] The younger Ricardo also became well known for improvising lengthy *falsetas*, and his recorded improvisations later became flamenco standards.[206]

Paradoxically, it was the repetitive nature of phonograph culture—record listeners playing the same improvised performance over and over again—that produced a distinctly modern conception of musical improvisation. As a self-conscious ideology, the notion of "improvisation" was most elaborated in North American jazz, and many of those who pioneered forms of recorded improvisation—including Sol Ho'opi'i, Pixinguinha, and Django Reinhardt—were often characterized as "jazz" players. The absence of this ideology of improvisation has been noted in some idioms: "there was little free or 'jazz' solo improvisation in *marabi*," David Coplan writes, and Eric Prieto argues that "the art of improvisation was simply not a priority of the biguine style popularized by Stellio and his contemporaries ... nowhere do we find a hot chorus of the kind that a New Orleans musician like Louis Armstrong or Sidney Bechet would have used to put his mark on a tune."[207] Nonetheless, marabi and beguine were cultures of idiomatic improvisation, not of notation. Moreover, the combination of urban musical contests, printed method books, and phonograph discs that produced modern improvisation was found across the archipelago of colonial ports, and so modern improvisation is better understood as the reverberations of a variety of musical idioms and practices.[208] The recordings of the flute solos of Pixinguinha, the trumpet solos of Armstrong and Chappottín, and the guitar solos of Ho'opi'i and Montoya pulled their respective musical idioms away from the time and space of local dancers and singers and into the time and space of circulating phonograph records. Tempos became faster, harmonies denser, and instrumental prowess ever more evident, as many of these idioms developed increasingly elaborate modes of improvisation.

These new forms of improvised virtuosity—together with the timbral fusions of local percussion with industrial instruments in an explosion of rhythm sections creating a host of distinct, and sometimes mutually incomprehensible, rhythmic dialects and vernacular tonalities—were thus not so much a new sound—"jazz"—nor a new "world music," as they were a profound revolution in musical practices, a remaking of the musical ear across each of the musical arcs of the colonial archipelago: the black Atlantic, the gypsy Mediterranean, and the Polynesian Pacific. Embedded in the grooves of shellac discs, this noise uprising was not only circulated and amplified at the time; it also set the stage for a series of remasterings, as the sonic legacy of this brief recording boom shaped the century that followed.

7

Remastering the 78s: Reverberations of a Musical Revolution

The vernacular music recording boom ended as abruptly as it began. As the worldwide depression took hold in 1930, record sales plummeted and the electrical recording industry collapsed. "The story of the phonograph, as a self-contained, independent industry, was done," the *American Mercury* concluded in September 1932.[1] "In 1932 and 1933," *Fortune* magazine wrote, "phonograph records had the worst years in recent history," which led to "the strong suspicion, if not conviction, among record men that the year of 1932 or 1933 would be the industry's last. They seemed to be experiencing not a slump but a final collapse, brought on by depression and their own neglect."[2] After a decade of start-ups, takeovers, and mergers, the record companies that had prospered in the recording boom found themselves on the brink of bankruptcy, ripe for takeover by large conglomerates based in radio manufacturing and broadcasting: "anybody with one eye could see that records were done for, that radio was the thing."[3]

In 1929, the Radio Corporation of America (RCA)—which, *Fortune* wrote, "knew little about records and cared less"[4]—bought out the Victor Talking Machine Company, "the great Camden plant being remodelled for radio production."[5] Two years later, in 1931, Electric & Musical Industries Ltd. (EMI) swallowed up the Gramophone Company as well as British Columbia, which had earlier acquired the Lindström labels and Pathé. Finally, in Germany, the electrical corporation Telefunken GmbH took over much of the recording business in the early 1930s, acquiring Deutsche Grammophon in 1937.[6]

"By 1938," historian Peter Tschmuck writes, "all of the traditional companies (Victor, Columbia, HMV, Lindström, etc.) were merely subdivisions of larger corporations."[7]

The recording of vernacular music was cut back drastically, as export sales collapsed (see Figure 1, p. 75). Recording sessions dried up even for successful musicians, and there were fewer location trips to find new artists. Columbia had released fifty-five Hawaiian discs in 1928; in 1930 they released only six.[8] Recording seems to have ceased in coastal West Africa after 1931, not resuming until 1936. By 1932 in the US, Columbia had "delete[d] almost everything in its 'foreign' catalogues" and Victor had also cut back.[9] There were no new blues or gospel recordings during the last quarter of 1932.[10] In Germany, the recording of vernacular music faced not only the economic downturn but the Nazi campaign against what they called "degenerate music," especially "Nigger-Jew jazz," which led to the ban on the sale of records by Jewish artists and to a series of radio bans on jazz.[11] The radio ban provoked Adorno into writing his essay, "Farewell to Jazz," in which he argued that "jazz no more has anything to do with authentic Negro music" but has "long been in the process of dissolution, in retreat into military marches and folklore."[12] The "Aryanization" of record catalogs from 1934 resulted in the destruction of recordings by Jewish, black, Roma, and Arab musicians in Germany.[13] The repression echoed throughout the archipelago of colonial ports: in Havana, "Cuban critics used the fact that jazz had been banned on German radio in 1933 to justify their own campaigns against Afro-Cuban genres."[14]

In 1937, Béla Bartók decried the vandalism of this moment:

> It is well known that [the gramophone] companies are ... busy recording the folk music of exotic countries; those records are bought by the natives, hence the expected profit is there. However, as soon as sales diminish for whatever reasons, the companies withdraw the records from circulation and the matrices are most likely melted down ... If matrices of this kind actually are destroyed, it represents vandalism of such nature that the different countries ought to enact laws to prevent it, just as there are laws in certain countries prohibiting destruction or marring of historic monuments.[15]

In the place of the explosion of vernacular musics in the late 1920s, national radio broadcasting networks, whether state-run or commercial, pioneered programs of musical uplift as the European repertoire of philharmonic music reached new heights in commercial culture, figured by star conductors like Arturo Toscanini in the US and Wilhelm Furtwängler in Germany.[16] By the mid-1930s, the phonograph boom and the vernacular music revolution it embodied looked like a minor episode, a series of musical "crazes" for novelties that would be forgotten. When Adorno drafted his critique of radio music in the late 1930s, he wrote of "the phonograph era" as a time gone by. The reverberations of the musical revolution seemed to have subsided completely.[17]

However, fifty years later these musics had become revered and valued, collected, studied, and celebrated around the world. "It is paradoxical," Peter Manuel wrote in his pioneering 1988 survey of *Popular Musics of the Non-Western World*, "that these marginal misfits in their milieu of bars and brothels should be so crucial in the development of new musical forms, especially since the genres they create are often destined later to become celebrated as national expressions."[18] Hermano Vianna called this reversal the "mystery of samba": "Samba's unexplained leap from infamous outcast to (virtually official) national emblem ... is the great mystery of its history."[19] But it is also the mystery of hula, rebetika, and son, among others. "Maligned in the early territorial period, by the 1930s hula had become essential to the growth of tourism and Hawai'i's economic development," Adria Imada points out.[20] "Some decades ago, [rebetika] was scorned by puritans, nationalists, official state ideologues, and dogmatic Leftists, all of whom regarded it as an undesirable Anatolian residue of the Ottoman Empire and an immoral product of the urban underworld," sociologist Yiannis Zaimakis notes. By the time of 2004 Olympic Games in Athens, it was featured in "the opening ceremony ... as a symbol of the rich cultural heritage of the nation."[21] Or, as Robin Moore posed the question in his pioneering study of son: "how [had] the music of a 'despised' minority—African descendants in the Americas—... become so central to national identity in various countries that continue to discriminate against them."[22]

This transformation of these musics depended on the literal and figurative remastering of the 78s, their rediscovery, repackaging, reissue, and reinterpretation by collectors and folklorists, art music composers and amateur folk revivalists, independent labels and national archives, bootleggers and, occasionally, the multinational corporations of the entertainment industry. Through these remasterings, the musics of this sonic revolution were not only preserved and transmitted but were also claimed as the fundamental and inescapable "roots" of a host of musics around the world.

It is not that the musics recorded in the late 1920s and early 1930s *are* necessarily the quintessential "roots" music. Rather, it was the very constitution of them as such a taproot that was at the heart of the efforts to remaster the 78s. Each remastering had its own forms and ideologies, and generated controversies and debates from which we inherit contested musical canons and counter-canons, what Raymond Williams once called the "selective tradition."[23] The history of those remasterings could make up another book; in this concluding chapter, I will briefly survey two of the most influential remasterings: the remastering of them as national "folk musics" in the middle decades of the twentieth century, and the remastering of them as "world musics" in the decades at the turn of the twenty-first century. Both of these remasterings were caught in the antinomies of mass culture, the dialectic of "reification and utopia," as Fredric Jameson put it, in which "works of mass culture cannot be ideological without at one and the same time being implicitly or explicitly Utopian as well." For if the remastering of these records as folk music was a form of state institutionalization, it was also part of the cultural politics of a variety of emancipatory social movements; and if the remastering of them as world music is a form of commercial enclosure, it has also figured the cultural recognition and sonic enfranchisement of a planet of slums.[24]

Antinomies of Folk Revivals

The first remastering of the vernacular phonograph musics was the remarkable and paradoxical process summed up in Vianna's "mystery of samba": the remaking of musics that had been largely despised and disrespected into emblems of national identity. "In the 1930s and 1940s," the Brazilian cultural critic António Cândido wrote in 1980, "samba and marcha, practically confined to the favelas and poor peripheral neighborhoods in previous years, won over the whole country, becoming the daily bread of cultural consumption for all social classes. During the 1920s, a master sambista like Sinhô performed in restricted settings, but after 1930 sambistas … gained national recognition."[25] "The dances of the rabble," Cuban musicologist Fernando Ortiz noted in 1950, had been "accepted by aristocrats in their palaces."[26]

This nationalization of vernacular musics was a complex and contradictory struggle, as both oppositional social movements and political regimes attempted to define the nation and its people through music. If the nation was embodied in its plebeian masses, those masses were defined by their music, and those musics were reimagined as "folk" musics. This musical version of what Antonio Gramsci dubbed the "national-popular"—the articulation of common-sense notions and ideological themes to constitute a nation and its people—was achieved through a series of "folk revivals," often pioneered by social movements and radical intellectuals, and later ratified by populist governments.

The paradox of these revivals was that the commercial vernacular musics of the 1920s had, as I have noted, been discounted by earlier folklorists. They were were now reimagined through rhetorics of folk authenticity, as a new generation of aficionados, collectors, and cultural critics began to assemble discographies, publish histories, and insist on the significance of the commercial recordings. "Some day," the African-American critic Alain Locke (who a decade earlier had dismissed jazz) wrote in 1936, "when Negro folk music is being scientifically studied, the old cheap discarded OKeh and Columbian records of ... the early 'Blues-singers'—Bessie, Clara, and Mamie Smith and Ma Rainey, will be priceless material in showing how jazz was created."[27] In 1939, when the Cuban composer Emilo Grenet edited a "guide" to the "rhythms and melodies which have awakened universal interest in the last decade," he highlighted the popular son recordings of such "intuitive" musicians as Miguel Matamoros and Ignacio Piñeiro, whose works "contain the purest expression of the people."[28] At the same time, the folklorist Alan Lomax surveyed the discs record companies were scrapping; he not only appreciated their value, but challenged the assumptions of an earlier generation of folklorists. "My opinion," he wrote to the Library of Congress music director in 1939, "is that the commercial recording companies have done a broader and more interesting job of recording American folk music than the folklorists and that every single item of recorded American rural, race, and popular music that they have in their current lists and plan to release in the future should be in our files." In addition, Lomax came away

from this listening experience with the certainty that American music, while certain folklore specialists have been mourning its decline, has been growing in new directions to compete with "thick" commercial music, and that it is today in its most "distorted" form in a healthier condition, roving across the radio stations and recording studios, than it has ever been or ever will be in the notebooks of collectors.[29]

In several places, art music composers were significant figures in this reevaluation of vernacular musics. This created a kind of "folk revival" within philharmonic music, as classically trained nationalist and populist composers sought to elevate and dignify the vernacular musics by incorporating them into European symphonic forms, moving their performance from the dance hall or vaudeville theater to the concert hall. In the wake of the Mexican Revolution of 1910–20, not only did the muralists draw inspiration from Mexican vernacular musics—in 1928 Diego Rivera illustrated two corridos about the revolution in his Ministry of Education murals[30]—but a host of young art music composers like Carlos Chávez and Blas Galindo began to explore popular genres; Galindo traveled to Jalisco for his 1940 composition "Sones de Mariachi."[31] In Spain, the composer Manuel de Falla was not only central to the revival of traditional flamenco, *cante jondo*, but had incorporated its sound into his music. Flamenco may be "an acquired taste," a record reviewer wrote, "but it is of intense interest as a genuine example of the raw material used to such effect by Albeniz, Granados, Falla, and Turina."[32] In 1940, the Brazilian art composer Heitor Villa-Lobos recruited a number of Brazilian vernacular musicians, including the sambista Cartola, for a recording session on a ship moored in Rio Harbor organized by the conductor Leopold Stokowski and issued as a boxed set of 78 rpm discs entitled *Native Brazilian Music*.[33]

In the decade after World War II, as the long-playing record emerged in phonograph culture, there were a host of revivals of the musics of the recording boom. In Brazil, the sense that Brazilian music was endangered led to a remarkable rediscovery of the early choro and samba pioneers, particularly Pixinguinha, as the *Velha Guarda* or Old Guard, with a radio program (beginning in 1947), long-playing records, and festivals (in 1954–55).[34] The United States witnessed an analogous revival of early New Orleans jazz in the 1940s and early 1950s, as figures like Bunk Johnson and Kid Ory were brought out of retirement for radio programs and the early 78s were reissued by specialist record labels.[35] In the late 1940s and early 1950s, black South African writers like Henry Nxumalo and Todd Matshikiza, associated with *Drum* magazine, the voice of the "Sophiatown renaissance," revived the culture of marabi in a series of essays;[36] in 1952, the eccentric

Beat writer Harry Smith issued the influential Folkways LP collection, *Anthology of American Folk Music*; and the middle 1950s marked a "turnabout in flamenco's fortunes," with new festivals—the 1956 *Concurso Nacional* in Córdoba—and the canon-making *Anthologie du Cante Flamenco*, produced in 1954 by guitarist Perico el de Lunar (and first released in France), "the first attempt made by anyone to record for posterity the traditional elements of *cante*."[37]

In the late 1950s and early 1960s, young aficionados begin to track down musicians who had not returned to a recording studio after the end of boom of the late 1920s. In the late 1950s, the Gypsy singer Aurelio de Cádiz (Aurelio Sellés), who had recorded two dozen cantes in 1929 for Polydor, was rediscovered, interviewed and recorded by flamenco fans.[38] In the United States, Memphis bluesman Furry Lewis, who had recorded a dozen blues in the late 1920s (one of which had been included on the Folkways *Anthology of American Folk Music*), was working as a street sweeper when he was found and recorded by Samuel Charters in 1959.[39] Within a few years, a "blues revival" emerged as other "lost" recording artists of the 1920s like Mississippi John Hurt, Son House, and Skip James were rediscovered and introduced to the civil rights generation, often through the mediation of the newly established Newport Folk Festival.[40]

In Brazil, several early Afro-Brazilian sambistas were rediscovered: in 1955, the new Brazilian label Sinter released the first LP by the veteran samba composer Ismael Silva, titled *O samba na voz do sambista*, "samba in the voice of a sambista," in an implicit critique of the decades-old practice of sambas in the voice of white crooners. A year later, another veteran sambista, Cartola, was discovered working in a carwash; he returned to performing and eventually recorded an influential album, complete with *cuíca*, the friction drum—a sound so foreign to recording that the producer thought it was a dog barking.[41] Cartola also opened his legendary restaurant, Zicartola, a center for the samba revival that, along with the emergence of bossa nova, was part of the cultural ferment of the new developmentalist and modernizing Brazil, figured by the radical *Centro Popular de Cultura*.[42] In Hawaii, Herb Ono's newly established Sounds of Hawaii Studio brought Lena Machado, a singer who had first recorded in the 1928 Honolulu Brunswick sessions, back to the studio in 1962; the revitalization of "slack key" and steel guitar music in the midst of a new movement for sovereignty helped spur the "Hawaiian Renaissance" of the 1960s and 1970s. By the mid-1980s, an aging Tau Moe, who had toured across Asia and the Pacific in the 1920s and 1930s, contacted the young steel guitarist and collector Bob Brozman, leading to a 1989 recording session that recreated the music of the 1929 sessions.[43]

These "folk revivals" of the middle decades of the twentieth century often served as the movement cultures of radical political campaigns and organizations. Many of the collectors and composers were affiliated with the Popular Front communisms, which tapped popular nationalism for the struggles of industrial workers; with the nationalisms of the anti-fascist resistance; with the civil rights movements combatting racist states and social orders; with the various "New Lefts" that took shape in the early 1960s; and with anticolonial struggles in regions where political independence had not been achieved. In Trinidad, the calypsonian Atilla the Hun—by then a member of the Legislative Council—hailed the lifting of calypso regulations in 1951: "belated though it was, it marked the culmination of long and bitter years of incessant struggle by kaisonians supported by the more far-seeing apostles of West Indian culture ... Politically, it heralded the growth of nationalist consciousness."[44]

However, the folk revivals had contradictory political valences as nationalist and populist regimes also mobilized subaltern sounds to anchor their cultural policies. Several post-revolutionary regimes used folk revivals as part of radical attempts to reform musical practice and create a new music. The new secular Turkish republic of Ataturk suppressed Ottoman classical music, encouraged European musics, and sent out musicologists to collect and foster Turkish folk musics.[45] In China, the victory of the Communist movement in 1949 marked a striking divide in the reappropriation of the urban vernacular music of prewar Shanghai, *huangse yinyue*, "yellow music." On the one hand, most of the music of the Shanghai dance halls was seen as part of the colonial culture, commercial, decadent, and Western, and was rejected in the cultural revolutions that transformed China. The Shanghai record industry fled the mainland to the British colony of Hong Kong, as did most of its great singing stars of the 1930s.[46] The new state emphasized the stylization of rural folk traditions by political composers, like Wang Luobin. On the other hand, since a number of the most important musicians and composers in Shanghai's music industry were affiliated with the Communist movement—like Nie Er—some aspects of "yellow music" were adopted by the new regime, most notably in the use of Nie Er's film song as the Chinese national anthem.[47]

Across the Americas, a variety of populist governments encouraged and appropriated vernacular musics. As early as 1916, the Radical Party of Hipólito Irigoyen used tangos to mobilize the urban poor in Argentina,[48] and by the 1940s, tango was a key part of the cultural program of Peronism.[49] In Mexico, in 1934, the Mariachi Coculense de Cirilo Marmolejo was the official mariachi of Cárdenas's presidential campaign.[50] In Brazil, samba was quickly incorporated into Vargas's *Estado Novo*, becoming a mainstay of state-run radio, and Carnival parades became a "festival of civic instruction." In the United States, the folk revival had its roots in the New Deal support by Franklin and Eleanor Roosevelt for the folk music initiatives of Alan Lomax at the Library of Congress and Charles Seeger in the Resettlement Administration.[51]

This state mobilization of popular music was a contradictory process, as one can see in the relations between fado, flamenco, and rebetika and the southern European fascist regimes. In Portugal, fado was at first condemned and censored by the fascist regime; by the 1960s, however, it was increasingly incorporated into fascist nationalism: the regime depended on the popularity of fado, football, and Fatima.[52] There was a similar trajectory in Spain, where flamenco was ultimately incorporated into Franco's nationalism. In contrast, in Greece, rebetika was rejected by the dictatorship of Metaxas in the 1930s; censorship and "Metaxas's concerted efforts to stop the further recording of *café amán* songs" led to "the virtual disappearance of *smyrnéïka* by 1937."[53] Regarded as a legacy of the Ottoman Empire, the music became the subject of debate on the Greek left during the 1940s.[54] In 1949, "toward the end of the bitter civil conflict between the royalist government and communist guerrillas that followed the Second World War, the famous 'high art' Greek composer Manos Hadzidakis used *rebetika* to rally the nation, claiming that it was a true music of the people, beloved of all Greeks regardless of class or region."[55] The first mythology of rebetika, Elias Petropoulos's *Rebetika Traghoudhia*, which linked the music to the Greek underworld, was published in 1968 and immediately banned by the junta; a rebetika revival emerged in the mid-1970s, after the fall of the junta.[56]

In the moment of political decolonization—the three decades after the end of World War II when more than one hundred new states joined the United Nations—the recognition of vernacular music was often a fundamental part of a new nationalist consciousness. If, in

India, raga-based music was reframed as "simultaneously classical and national,"[57] in Indonesia, popular kroncong became an emblem of nationalism. Though the Japanese occupation during World War II encouraged kroncong (having banned most Western popular music), the very popularity of the genre led to the emergence of *kroncong revolusi* that served as "fighting songs for the masses."[58] After independence, the new postcolonial government attempted to establish kroncong as a national music, a process later criticized by novelist Pramoedya Toer: "kroncong still had a power before independence, it still contained a vitality—the vitality of a nation that was not yet free. As the Revolution erupted and as it passed, kroncong remained just a kind of narcissism, a bouquet of empty words, a culture of masturbation. Equal to the culture of great speeches, and of puppet shadow theater."[59]

Across postcolonial Africa, the vernacular gramophone musics became the soundtrack of independence, and entwined in a complex audiopolitics that involved the creation of new national recording industries, the postcolonial state's mobilization of folklore, and the emergence of global Afro-diasporic musics from soul and reggae to Afrobeat in Nigeria (associated with the figure of Fela), rumba and soukous in the Congos, and taarab in Tanzania.[60] In Tanzania, for example, the postcolonial "nationalization of taarab" involved the revival of the early taarab recording artist Siti binti Saad, first as a nationalist figure, and later as a feminist figure.[61]

The elaboration of these musics as national musics often required the reinterpretation, and even remaking, of them. These were not simple or uncontested processes, and the "folk revivals" were sites of constant struggle over music and ideology. Indeed the key contradictions of these folk revivals lay at the crossroads of race, music, and the nation. Who were the nation's people? What was their music?

In many cases, there was a process of folklorization, as hybrid and syncretic urban musics were reinterpreted as authentic traditional musics, untouched by modernity. In other cases, the music of a particular region was adopted as the music of the nation: one thinks of the successful postwar effort by musicians, critics and collectors to establish Rio's *samba de morro* as the mythic heart of Brazilian culture, or the way that "mariachi, out of all the regional musical traditions in Mexico, achieve[d] the status of national ensemble."[62] In yet other cases, a line was drawn between respectable and disreputable aspects of the musics: in Brazil, for example, Vargas's regime sought to prescribe sambas that glorified the nation, while proscribing the popular genre of *malandro*—outlaw, bad man—sambas.[63]

In many cases, these newly respectable musics became part of the emerging tourist industry. In Cuba, after the 1933 revolution against Machado, the ban on the carnival *comparsas* was lifted in 1937, with the active support of the National Tourist Commission.[64] In South Africa, *ingoma* dancing was transformed, between 1929 and 1939, "from a militant, oppositional, and suppressed form of popular culture to a tourist attraction."[65] And in Trinidad, when the regulations on calypso were amended in 1951, Atilla noted that "economically, the new status accorded the kaiso stemmed from the realisation of its tremendous potential, especially as a tourist attraction."[66]

Moreover, the folk revivals often used these reclaimed "folk" musics against newer forms of commercial popular music. For the revivals combined a powerful new respect and recognition for the vernacular musics of the 1920s and 1930s with a sometimes stultifying purism and cult of authenticity. The first national samba congress convened in 1962, and issued a "Carta do samba" to preserve the traditional characteristics of samba.[67] "The crystallization of a set musical formula for samba ... based principally on what is known as samba de morro, or favela samba, became," Hermano Vianna notes, "a model to be preserved at all costs by musical nationalists. When bossa nova emerged to violate that formula in the late 1950s, many defenders of 'true Brazilian-ness' attacked the new music as if it were high treason."[68] Similarly, in Spain, the new "flamencology" associated with the Gypsy vocalist and scholar Antonio Mairena not only documented and codified the classic repertoire but insisted on the recognition of the Gypsy role in creating flamenco; however, as Peter Manuel notes, "his purist insistence that the repertoire was thenceforth fixed and inviolate promoted a kind of ossification."[69]

Nevertheless, it would be a mistake to read these musical revivals as essentially conservative. In spite of their preservationist rhetoric and traditionalist ideologies, these "folk" revivals often proved to be prophetic. The "traditional" musics revivalists sought to collect and preserve proved, ironically, to be close cousins of the new urban plebeian musics they rejected, musics that accompanied the massive displacements and migrations that created a planet of urban slums and shantytowns. Looking backward for an authentic musical past, the folk revivals often heralded the latest urban sounds brought by the most recent migrants.

Antinomies of World Music

Beginning in the 1980s, the recorded vernacular musics that had been revived over the previous half-century as "folk musics" began to be systematically marketed under a new rubric: "world music," a term invented by the recording industry to designate a specific sector of the music market, and an early symptom of the more general "globalization" of the culture in the neoliberal era.[70] In retrospect, the early decades of vernacular music recording now look like a period of national cultural enclosure, when national recording industries and states used popular vernacular music as a kind of "import-substitution industrialization," not only commodifying musics that had largely been in the public domain, but also protecting the autonomy and profitability of a national music industry from the foreign competition of imported musics.

The emergence of a specific "world music" market sector that specialized in the transnational trafficking of "ethnic" musics was a by-product of the collapse of this import-substitution model in the 1970s and 1980s, as the enforcement of "free trade" imperatives led to a consolidation of the global recording industry, based on the production of a handful of global stars sold in markets around the world—albeit with a huge shadow trade in pirated discs and tapes. If the moment of "folk music" brought regional vernacular musics to national audiences as the nation's music, the moment of "world music" brought those same vernacular musics to global audiences as the world's beat.

Two elements of the world music era stand out. First, whereas earlier companies, whether foreign or domestic, had aimed primarily at the internal national market, the US and European independent labels that pioneered "world music"—like Virgin and Island—targeted external markets, attempting to sell distinct vernacular musics to a transnational audience. For the recording industry, it marked the shift from the moment of import substitution—when local music was the basis of a national industry, a "national champion"—to a moment of export processing, when the work of local musicians would be exported around the globe. This promotion of "world" musicians—like the iconic Bob Marley—to a transnational audience took a variety of forms: introducing musics to North Atlantic audiences through collections curated by rock musicians, as in David Byrne's successful series of Luaka Bop anthologies of Brazilian music; mimicking earlier transnational crossovers, as when Island Records attempted to replicate

Marley's success by backing Nigerian highlife bandleader Sunny Ade; and mixing different versions of the same tracks for different markets in order to resolve the tension between local demands for cutting-edge, hi-tech musical production and the "world music" demand for "rootsy," "authentic" sounds and production values.[71] Perhaps the most successful—and controversial—strategy brought rock musicians together with "world music" artists in the studio, as in Paul Simon's collaboration with the South African isicathamiya group, Ladysmith Black Mambazo, on *Graceland*, and the US slide guitarist Ry Cooder's series of collaborations with Ali Farka Toure, V. M. Bhatt, and the Cuban musicians who became known as the Buena Vista Social Club. In the wake of this "export-processing," national recording industries that had emerged and flourished in the postcolonial decades declined sharply, as they found themselves under pressure not only from new technologies of music "piracy" (ever since the 1970s boom in street-vended cassettes), but also from the movement of musicians to the global cities of transnational music production and promotion: Paris, London, New York, Hong Kong.[72]

The second element of the moment of "world music" was the globalization of copyright battles over vernacular music, figured by a series of cases that centered on songs that had been recorded in the late 1920s and early 1930s. In part, this was due to the general neoliberal turn: by the 1980s, international financial institutions like the IMF and the World Bank were strong-arming postcolonial states to adopt neoliberal trade and property regimes, one of which was a stricter delineation and protection of what were coming to be called "intellectual property rights," notably copyright. At the same time as the World Intellectual Property Organization was promoting copyright standards, the postcolonial struggle to combat the expropriation of national resources by foreign corporations was being extended to cultural resources—forms of indigenous knowledge and arts—as part of the campaign, taking shape in the late 1970s out of the Brandt Report on North–South inequalities, to create a "new world information order." These converging if somewhat antagonistic tendencies condensed into a series of fascinating and contradictory disputes over the ownership of early recorded vernacular music: the decades-long struggle over "Guantanamera," the Cuban *guajira-son* made popular by Joseíto Fernández on his 1930s radio broadcasts;[73] the 1990 lawsuit over the ownership of "The Lion Sleeps Tonight," which was actually "Mbube," orginally recorded by the South African isicathamiya singing group of Solomon Linda and the Evening Birds in 1939;[74] and the 1990s battle over the Ghanaian highlife standard, "Yaa Amponsah."[75]

In each case, the very dynamic that had made the moment of recorded vernacular music a musical revolution and renaissance—the dialectic between informal popular musicking by street and café musicians that was only loosely connected to the world of copyrighted sheet music, and the formal objectification, even reification, of particular performances by distinctive musical personalities, vocal and instrumental, on shellac discs—became the bone of contention. Who was the creator, the owner of "Yaa Amponsah"? There had been copyright controversies from the beginning of recorded music, but these tended to be relatively minor skirmishes on the ever-advancing front where the recording industry was steadily and inexorably enclosing the musical commons, copyrighting arrangements of unclaimed "folk songs" in the public domain.

The "Yaa Amponsah" affair in Ghana was triggered by a Paul Simon "world music" project. On *The Rhythm of the Saints*, a 1990 recording featuring Brazilian and African musicians, Simon recorded "Spirit Voices," based on "Yaa Amponsah." When he approached the Ghanaian copyright authorities to pay royalties on the song, it triggered an investigation into the song's origins. The initial finding was that it was created by Kwame Asare, the guitarist of the Kumasi Trio who had first recorded it for Zonophone in 1928; subsequent research led to the decision that the song was folklore, and thus owned by the Ghanaian government, which used Simon's royalties to establish a National Folklore Board in 1991. This led to a decade-long debate in Ghana over the nature of this national ownership of folklore: though there was little objection to collecting royalties from foreign users, like Simon, when it was extended to Ghanaian citizens it appeared to be, in John Collins's words, a "folklore tax." Moreover, it raised the question of the national state's right to a claim on a "folklore" that was associated with particular regions and communities (did not the local ethnic or language community have a claim to their "folklore"?) as well as with neighboring countries ("folklore" rarely respected national boundaries, and, as Collins notes, the distinctive guitar pattern of "Yaa Amponsah" was brought to Ghana by Kru seamen).[76]

If "world music" was in one sense a form of transnational marketing and the global enclosure of the cultural commons, it might also be understood as a cultural recognition and sonic enfranchisement of the urban syncretic musics that circulated across a planet of slums. In the

1980s and 1990s, ethnomusicologists who had hitherto focused on non-Western learned traditions or rural folk musics, began studying urban popular musics. Bronia Kornhauser's landmark essay of 1978, "In Defence of Kroncong," began with a critique of ethnomusicologists' dismissal of syncretic musics like kroncong as "degenerate hybrids"; and it was followed by such pioneering works of urban ethnomusicology as David Coplan's 1985 study of South African township musics, Chris Waterman's 1990 study of Nigerian *jùjú*, Hermano Vianna's 1995 study of Brazilian samba, and Virginia Danielson's 1997 study of Cairo's Umm Kulthūm.

These accounts of urban musics in the era of world music often challenged the reified notions of folk purity and authenticity that had prevailed over the previous half-century. An important part of this critique of folk authenticity was the reevaluation of female vaudeville and theater singers, as in Hazel Carby's influential essay on blues women, taking apart the marked tendency in folk revivals to celebrate traditions of male instrumentalists while disparaging female vocalists.[77] Established canons and apparently natural national musics were revealed to be products of an invention of tradition, and there were parallel critiques of the nationalist appropriations of tango in Argentina, rebetika in Greece, and samba in Brazil.[78]

By the final decade of the century, alongside the highly visible "world music" projects of Paul Simon, Ry Cooder, and David Byrne, collectors of 78s began to reissue the early vernacular recordings on the new media of digital compact discs: Revivendo Musicas in Brazil (from 1987), Kalan Müzik in Turkey (from 1991), Hano Ola Records in Hawaii, Sonifolk in Spain, among others. Even China's "yellow music" of the 1930s began to be reclaimed during the "culture fever" of globalizing 1980s, beginning with cassette releases of the Shanghai songs of Zhou Xuan in 1985 and 1993. The rehabilitation of Shanghai's commercial culture was amplified when EMI found hundreds of Chinese Pathé masters in Mumbai, and began releasing them as "The Legendary Chinese Hits of Pathé."[79]

If Paul Vernon's carefully annotated collections for Heritage and Harlequin, his pioneering discography of *Ethnic and Vernacular Music, 1898–1960*, and his essays in *Folk Roots* were examples of the kind of systematic study that Sam Charters had brought to the country blues in the 1950s, then Pat Conte was the Harry Smith of this "world music" on 78s: his five-CD collection, *The Secret Museum of Mankind* (1995–98), echoed the brilliance, obsessiveness, and idiosyncrasy of Harry Smith's *Anthology of American Folk Music* a half-century earlier.[80]

In many ways, it was this very work that made the present book possible. It has allowed us to hear the vernacular phonograph music revolution not simply as "Musics of All Nations"—the title of the pioneering Parlophone series in the 1930s—but as a fundamental remaking of the world of music. The Marxist musicologist Günter Mayer once argued that two revolutions in music occurred between 1200 and 2000—the visualization of music (through notation) in the eleventh and twelfth centuries and the electrification of music in the twentieth century. "Just as in the eleventh and twelfth centuries secular music (folk music) ... penetrated into the sacred realm," he argued, "in the twentieth century, everyday music (popular music)—now a global phenomenon—is invading the quasi-sacred realm of 'art' music. With these developments, the distinction between 'serious' and 'entertaining' music is at first sharpened, but then, with the electrification of the latter, increasingly effaced."[81]

If we take this long view of music history, we see that the age of sheet music, of notated, composed music—which coincided with the age of the public concert—was itself the first wave of musical mass culture. It was not only the earliest form of the mechanical storage of music, but was tied to the emergence of an entire musical industry, with publishers of piano-extract sheet music, instrument manufacturers, and concert impresarios. Moreover, the peculiarity of the European trajectory stands out in greater relief: for it was in Europe that the print interregnum—the brief centrality of printed music in the long historical shift from the aural transmission of both courtly and popular (refined and vulgar) musics to the electrical storage and transmission of music—was longest and most developed.

This second musical revolution—triggered by the noise uprising of the late 1920s—demands a revision of our sense of the audiopolitics of recorded music. Adorno's aesthetic, which placed the highest value on intense modes of musical contemplation, underestimated the emancipatory powers of the distracted musics of everyday life, even under the sway of the commodity form. One might well agree with his argument that "the social alienation of music ... cannot be corrected within music, but only within society: through the change of society." But his claim that "it is the prerequisite of every historical-materialistic method ... that under no conditions is music to be understood as a 'spiritual' phenomenon ... which can anticipate through its imagery any desire for social change independently from the empirical realization thereof" is less persuasive.[82]

Moreover, the schizophonia of recorded sound—the rupture of the spatial and temporal union of musical performer and audience, long regarded with suspicion by social and cultural theorists—is the very condition of our musical world. There is no question that recording, organized as a multinational industry, leads to the expropriation and exploitation of musical labors, as well as the isolated, repetitive, and fetishized consumption of its commodities. But it also makes possible new and unexpected reverberations, new forms of affiliation and solidarity across space and time.

If the vernacular phonograph musics were not just a technical revolution but also a cultural revolution; if their very noise promised a music beyond the racial orders of colonialism and settler colonialism, a music beyond the commodity forms and labor processes of capitalism: this remains an unfulfilled promise and an unfinished revolution. Ernst Bloch once wrote that "*no one has yet heard Mozart, Beethoven, Bach as they truly call, name, teach*; this will happen only much later, in the fullest after-ripening of these and of all great works."[83] Nor has anyone yet heard the full reverberations of the vernacular shellac discs of hula and samba, kroncong and tzigane, jazz and marabi.

Acknowledgments

This book began as part of a collective project of the Yale Working Group on Globalization and Culture, *Audiopolitics: Measures of Global Soundscapes*, during 2006–2007. My thanks to the Audiopolitics group—Amanda Ciafone, Rossen Djagalov, Daniel Gilbert, Naomi Paik, Van Truong, Charlie Samuya Veric, and Kirsten Weld—for inspiring *Noise Uprising*, as well as to the members of the Working Group before and since. The Working Group has been a "liberation cultural studies orchestra" where this and other compositions have begun.

Two remarkable conferences gave me the opportunity to present this work as keynote addresses: my thanks to Carol Oja and Anne Schreffler, organizers of *Crosscurrents: American and European Music in Interaction, 1900–2000*, at Harvard University in 2008, and to Ron Radano and Teju Olaniyan, organizers of *Music-Race-Empire* at the University of Wisconsin, Madison, in 2011. Early versions appeared in the conference volumes: *Crosscurrents: American and European Music in Interaction, 1900–2000*, edited by Felix Meyer, Carol J. Oja, Wolfgang Rathert, and Anne C. Shreffler (The Boydell Press, 2014); and *Audible Empire: Music, Global Politics, Critique*, edited by Ronald Radano and Tejumola Olaniyan (Duke University Press, 2015). My thanks also to David Shumway and Kathy Newman at Carnegie-Mellon, Sumanth Gopinath at the University of Minnesota, Cecilia Tichi and Rachel Clare Donaldson at Vanderbilt, Jairo Moreno at New York University, and my colleagues in American Studies, English, and music at Yale for organizing conversations about this work.

The archivists at EMI Archive Trust in Hayes were very helpful; I also must acknowledge two people I have not met but who blazed trails I followed: Paul Vernon, whose liner notes, discographies, and articles first drew my attention to these records; and Jonathan Ward, whose Excavated Shellac blog was a constant source of sounds and knowledge.

This book also derives from decades of thinking about vernacular music: my first extended essay was a high school independent study on "The American Folk Music Tradition," accompanied by a dubbed cassette tape. When I arrived at Dartmouth in the 1970s, Lou Renza was teaching one of the early courses on Bob Dylan, and our conversations have continued for years, not least at the 2006 Dartmouth conference on Dylan that Lou organized.

By the time I hazarded a few chapters on music in *The Cultural Front*, I was inspired by the example of my students: Eric Lott writing on minstrelsy, Rachel Rubin on country music, David Stowe on everything from big band jazz to Amazing Grace, Benjamin Filene on folk revivals, Suzanne Smith on Motown, Carlo Rotella on Buddy Guy, Scott Saul on free jazz and Caetano Veloso, Tina Klein on musicals, Sally Bick on Popular Front film music, Michelle Stephens on Bob Marley, Adria Imada on Hawaiian hula, Imani Perry and Simon Rodberg on hip-hop, Ben Looker on the jazz of the Black Arts Group, Shana Redmond on social movement anthems, Josh Jelly-Schapiro on musics of the Caribbean, Dalton Anthony Jones on Louis Armstrong, Ryan Brasseaux on Cajun music, Rossen Djagalov on Russian guitar poets, Drew Hannon on the music of the counterculture, and Sumanth Gopinath on Steve Reich, ringtones, and mobile music. Many other friends and colleagues have given useful recordings, advice, criticisms, and guidance, including Celso Castro Alves, Paul Gilroy, Jesse Ramirez, Eli Jelly-Schapiro, Paul Joseph, Jorge Cuéllar, Sigma Colón, Brent Edwards, Andrew Friedman, Yenisey Rodriguez, Andrew Jones, Mandi Isaacs Jackson, Tao Leigh Goffe, Andrew Seal, Andrew Ross, Ed King, and the members of the Recording Vernacular Musics seminars.

At Verso, I thank Sebastian Budgen and Mark Martin, who supported the project from the beginning and saw it through to the end.

Three readers of the manuscript made this a better book. Hazel Carby, who lived with the sound of these musics; Sumanth Gopinath, a vital interlocutor since the project was first conceived and a generous, if rigorous, reader; and Nicholas Carby Denning, whose last-minute reading led me to recast it.

Notes

Introduction

1. The oft-cited translation by A. D. Lindsay in *The Republic of Plato*, J. M. Dent & Co., 1908, p. 124; "changes in styles of music are always politically revolutionary," in the recent translation by Tom Griffith: G. R. Ferrari, ed., *Plato: The Republic*, Cambridge University Press, 2000, p. 117.
2. Early accounts distinguished between Edison's phonograph, which used cylinders, and Berliner's gramophone, which used discs. However, by the 1920s, *gramophone* was the common term for all talking machines in the United Kingdom and *phonograph* served a similar role in the United States. To accent the transnational nature of talking machine culture, I will use them interchangeably.
3. William Maas, "Jazz Poetry," *Daily Chronicle*, 1920, quoted in "From Education to Jazz," *The Living Age*, October 16, 1920, pp. 158–9.
4. Theodor W. Adorno, "Farewell to Jazz," in his *Essays on Music*, Richard Leppert, ed., University of California Press, 2002, p. 497.
5. Adorno, "The Curves of the Needle," in *Essays on Music*, p. 273.
6. Theodor W. Adorno, *Current of Music: Elements of a Radio Theory*, Polity, 2009, p. 114.
7. Jacques Attali, *Noise: The Political Economy of Music*, University of Minnesota Press, 1985, p. 103.
8. Karl Marx, "Economic and Philosophic Manuscripts of 1844," in *Karl Marx Frederick Engels Collected Works*, vol. 3, International Publishers, 1975, pp. 301–2.
9. Ranajit Guha, *Elementary Aspects of Peasant Insurgency in Colonial India*, Duke University Press, 1999, p. 39.
10. Mark Slobin, "Ensembles—Banding versus Bonding," in his *Subcultural Sounds: Micromusics of the West*, Wesleyan University Press, 2000; Josh Kun, *Audiotopia: Music, Race, and America*, University of California Press, 2005.
11. Adorno, *Current of Music*, p. 65; Adorno, "On the Social Situation of Music," in *Essays on Music*, p. 392.
12. Ernst Bloch, *The Principle of Hope*, MIT Press, 1986, p. 1103.
13. Attali, *Noise*, pp. 19, 27.

14. Ibid., pp. 35, 5.
15. Ibid., pp. 6, 143, 5.
16. Karl Marx and Frederick Engels, *The Holy Family*, in *Karl Marx Frederick Engels Collected Works*, vol. 4, International Publishers, 1975, pp. 67–8. For "polkamania," see Charles Henry Knox, *The Spirit of the Polka*, John Olliveir, 1845, p. 11; and Charles Keil, Angeliki V. Keil, and Dick Blau, *Polka Happiness*, Temple University Press, 1992, p. 13.
17. Bloch, *Principle of Hope*, p. 394.
18. Attali, *Noise*, pp. 117, 19.

1. Turnarounds

1. Michael Iván Avalos, liner notes to *Sextetos Cubanos*, Arhoolie CD 7003, 1992, p. 3.
2. Sexteto Habanero, "Maldita timidez," Victor 78510, 1926, re-released on *Sexteto y Septeto Habanero: Grabaciones Completas 1925–1931*, Tumbao CD 300, 1998; Alejo Carpentier, *Music in Cuba*, University of Minnesota Press, 2001, p. 231.
3. *Sextetos Cubanos Sones Vol. II*, Arhoolie CD 7006, 1995; *Sexteto Nacional 1927–1928 "Cubaneo" Primeras Grabaciones*, Tumbao TCD 097, 1999.
4. Carpentier, *Music in Cuba*, p. 228.
5. Ibid., p. 232.
6. Louis Armstrong, "Heebie Jeebies," OKeh 8300-A, 1926, re-released on *Louis Armstrong: The Complete Hot Five and Hot Seven Recordings*, Columbia/Legacy C4K 63527, 2000.
7. "How the 'Heebie Jeebies' Reached Apex of Popularity and Developed a New Dance," *Talking Machine World* 22.11 (1926), p. 128.
8. Danny Barker, *A Life in Jazz*, Alyn Shipton, ed., Macmillan Press, 1986, p. 42.
9. Dave Peyton, "The Musical Bunch: Things in General," *Chicago Defender*, July 2, 1927, p. 6.
10. See Hazel V. Carby, "Women, Migration, and the Formation of a Blues Culture," in her *Cultures in Babylon: Black Britain and African America*, Verso, 1999.
11. Rosita Quiroga, "La Musa Mistonga," Victor 79632, 1926; Donald S. Castro, *The Argentine Tango as Social History, 1880–1955: The Soul of the People*, Mellen Research University Press, 1990, pp. 189–91; Néstor Pinsón, "Rosita Quiroga," *Todo Tango*, todotango.com; Matthew B. Karush, *Culture of Class: Radio and Cinema in the Making of a Divided Argentina, 1920–1946*, Duke University Press, 2012, p. 101. On Flores, see Robert Farris Thompson, *Tango: The Art History of Love*, Pantheon Books, 2005, pp. 31–4.
12. Roberto Firpo, "La Cumparsita," Odeon 483, 1916, re-released on *Roberto Firpo—De la guardia vieja*, EMI 83757723, 2002; Carlos Gardel, "Mi noche triste," Odeon 18010-B, 1917, re-released on *The Magic of Carlos Gardel*, Harlequin HQ CD 145, 1999.
13. Castro, *The Argentine Tango as Social History*, p. 137.
14. Simon Collier, *The Life, Music and Times of Carlos Gardel*, University of Pittsburgh Press, 1986, p. 93.
15. Simon Collier, "The Tango Is Born: 1880s–1920s," in Simon Collier et al., *Tango! The Dance, the Song, the Story*, Thames and Hudson, 1995, p. 62.

16. Quoted in Adriana J. Bergero, *Intersecting Tango: Cultural Geographies of Buenos Aires, 1900–1930*, University of Pittsburgh Press, 2008, p. 90.

17. Paul Vernon, "Odeon Records: Their 'Ethnic' Output," *Musical Traditions* 3 (1997), mustrad.org.uk.

18. Virginia Danielson, *The Voice of Egypt: Umm Kulthūm, Arabic Song, and Egyptian Society in the Twentieth Century*, University of Chicago Press, 1997, pp. 54, 56, 58; Umm Kulthūm, "Akhadt Sootak min Ruuhi," His Master's Voice 72–2, 1926, re-released on *Omme Kolsoum: La Diva 2*, EMI CD 0964310953-2, 1996.

19. Quoted in Ali Jihad Racy, *Musical Change and Commercial Recording in Egypt, 1904–1932*, dissertation, University of Illinois at Urbana-Champaign, 1977, p. 172.

20. Danielson, *The Voice of Egypt*, pp. 28–34.

21. Ibid., pp. 73, 85–7; Umm Kulthūm, "In Kunt Asaamih," His Master's Voice 72–12, 1928.

22. Gokhan Ara, liner notes to *To Scratch Your Heart: Early Recordings from Istanbul*, Honest Jon's Records HJRCD 48, 2010, p. 2.

23. Hafiz Sadettin Kaynak, "Nâr-i Hicrane Düşüp," Columbia 12554, c.1926–7; Hafiz Burhan Bey, "Nitschun Guerdum," Columbia 12289, 1927; Martin Stokes, *The Republic of Love: Cultural Intimacy in Turkish Popular Music*, University of Chicago Press, 2010, p. 21 n. 53.

24. Harold G. Hagopian, liner notes to *Women of Istanbul*, Traditional Crossroads CD 4280, 1998, pp. 3, 17.

25. J. M. O'Connell, "Song Cycle: The Life and Death of the Turkish Gazel: A Review Essay," *Ethnomusicology* 47.3 (2003), pp. 404–6.

26. Harold G. Hagopian, liner notes to *Istanbul 1925*, Traditional Crossroads CD 4266, 1994, pp. 2–3.

27. Dalgás, "Melemenio," His Master's Voice HMV AO166, 1926; Lisbet Torp, *Salonikiós, "The Best Violin in the Balkans,"* Muscum Tusculanum Press, 1993, p. 25 n. 34, n. 36.

28. Edmund Michael Innes, "Report on Visit to Greece April–May 1930," ed. Hugo Strötbaum, 2010, recordingpioneers.com, p. 64.

29. Ibid., p. 69.

30. Márkos Vamvakáris, "Karadouzéni," Parlophon B21654, 1932, re-released on *Márkos Vamvakáris Bouzouki Pioneer 1932–1940*, Rounder CD 1139, 1998.

31. Quoted in Charles Howard, liner notes to *Márkos Vamvakáris Bouzouki Pioneer 1932–1940*. See also Gail Holst, *Road to Rembetika: Music of a Greek Sub-Culture. Songs of Love, Sorrow and Hashish*, Denise Harvey Publisher, 2006, pp. 44–7.

32. Fritna Darmon, "Aroubi Rasd Eddil, Pt. 1 & 2," Pathé 59167/68, 1926, re-released on *Secret Museum of Mankind: Music of North Africa*, Yazoo 7011, 1997; Ahmed and Mohamed Elhabib Hachlaf, *Anthologie de la musique arabe: 1906–1960*, Publisud, 1993, pp. 163–73.

33. On Cheikh El-Afrit, see Jonathan Ward, liner notes to *Opika Pende: Africa at 78rpm*, Dust-to-Digital DTD-22, 2011, p. 14.

34. Paul Vernon, *Ethnic and Vernacular Music, 1898–1960: A Resource and Guide to Recordings*, Greenwood Press, 1995, p. 281. See also Hachlaf, *Anthologie*, pp. 302, 306; Hadj Miliani, "Le Cheikh et le phonographe: notes de recherche pour un corpus des phonogrammes et des vidéogrammes des musiques et des chansons Algériennes," *Turath* 4 (2004), p. 43–67.

35. Ward, liner notes to *Opika Pende*, p. 30.

36. Cheikh Hamada, "Adjouadi hadi ouadjba," Gramophone K 4216, 1930, on

Gallica, gallica.bnf.fr. Hachlaf, p. 302. See also Angelica Maria DeAngelis, "Moi Aussi, Je Suis Musulman: Rai, Islam, and Masculinity in Maghrebi Transnational Identity," *Alif: Journal of Comparative Poetics* 23 (2003), pp. 284–5; Susana Asensio Llamas, "The Politics of Hybridization in Rai Music," in Gerhard Steingress, ed., *Songs of the Minotaur: Hybridity and Popular Music in the Era of Globalization*, LIT Verlag, 2002, pp. 55–6.

37. Paul Vernon, *A History of the Portuguese Fado*, Ashgate, 1998, pp. 65, 23–5.

38. Adelina Fernandes, "Fado Penim," HMV EQ220, 1928.

39. Rui Vieira Nery, quoted in Simon Broughton, "Secret History," *New Statesman*, October 15, 2007, p. 43; Rodney Gallop, "Some Records of the Portuguese Fado," *The Gramophone* (October 1931) p. 173.

40. Vernon, *History of the Portuguese Fado*, p. 48.

41. Nery, quoted in Broughton, "Secret History," p. 43.

42. V. S. Pritchett, "Spring in Lisbon," *Fortnightly Review* (June 1932), p. 711-2.

43. Hirabai Barodekar, "(Jilha) shantvaho manasa/(Durga) ananda mani gudha mani (Marathi drama–Patwardhan),"HMV Black Label P-8754, 1926; Suresh Chandvankar, "Records of Smt. Heerabai Barodekar," *Record News* (2005), p. 53–79.

44. Janaki Bakhle, *Two Men and Music: Nationalism and the Making of an Indian Classical Tradition*, Oxford University Press, 2005, pp. 216–17.

45. Sushanta Kumar Chatterjee, "The Uncrowned King of the Legendary Bengali Songs: Mr. Krishna Chandra Dey," *Record News* 25–26 (1997), p. 5–70; Jyoti Prakash Guha, "Life and Records of Indubala," *Record News* (2008), p. 35–50.

46. Stephen Hughes, "The 'Music Boom' in Tamil South India: Gramophone, Radio and the Making of Mass Culture," *Historical Journal of Film, Radio and Television* 22.4 (2002), p. 445–73.

47. Mariachi Coculense Rodríguez, "El Toro"* (The Bull)/"El Gavilancillo" (The Young Hawk), Victor 79173, 1927.

48. Chris Strachwitz, "A History of Commercial Recordings of Corridos," liner booklet for *The Mexican Revolution: Corridos about the Heroes and Events 1910–1920 and Beyond*, Arhoolie Folkloric CD 7041-7044, 1996, 13. For a discussion of Los Hermanos Bañuelos, see Alicia Schmidt Camacho, *Migrant Imaginaries: Latino Cultural Politics in the U.S.-Mexico Borderlands*, New York University Press, 2008, pp. 30–2.

49. Guty Cárdenas, "Flor"/"Rayito de Sol," Columbia 3118-X, ca.1928. See also *Guty Cárdenas: El Trovador Yucateco*, Discos Corasón NM 15 892 CD, 2006. See Marco Velázquez and Mary Kay Vaughan, "*Mestizaje* and Musical Nationalism in Mexico," in Rick A. Lopez, Desmond Rochfort, Mary Kay Vaughan, and Stephen Lewis, eds, *The Eagle and the Virgin: Nation and Cultural Revolution in Mexico, 1920–1940*, Duke University Press, 2006, pp. 106–7; Mark Pedelty, "The Bolero: the Birth, Life, and Decline of Mexican Modernity," *Latin American Music Review* 20.1 (1999), p. 36–40.

50. Rodney Gallop, "Mexique Ho!," *The Gramophone* (June 1937), p. 41.

51. Miss Riboet, "Krongtjong Moeritskoe," Beka B 15104, 1926, transcribed and discussed in Philip Yampolsky, "Kroncong Revisited: New Evidence from Old Sources," *Archipel* 79 (2010), pp. 37–9. The same recording session also produced Miss Riboet, "Dji Hong,"* Beka B 15107, 1926, re-released on *Longing for the Past: The 78rpm Era in Southeast Asia*, Dust-to-Digital DTD 28, 2013 (with accompanying book, p. 216).

52. Matthew Isaac Cohen, *The Komedie Stamboel: Popular Theater in Colonial Indonesia, 1891–1903*, Ohio University Press, 2006, p. 338.

53. Miss Riboet with Orkes Dengen Di Njanjiken Oleh, "Krontjong Dardanella," Beka B15662-II, 1928, re-released on *Kroncong: Early Indonesian Pop Music, Vol. 1*, Rice ISR 3006, 2006.

54. E. V. Solomons, "The Krontjong—Java's Ukelele," *The Lloyd Mail*, October 1933, p. 238.

55. Liem Liang Hoo's *My Dream House* is quoted in James T. Siegel, *Fetish, Recognition, Revolution*, Princeton University Press, 1997, p. 120.

56. D. J. H. Nyèssen, *The Races of Java*, G. Kolff & Co., 1929, p. 58.

57. Takonai Susumu, "Soeara NIROM and Musical Culture in Colonial Indonesia," trans. Ishibashi Makoto, *Kyoto Review of Southeast Asia* 8–9 (2007), kyotoreviewsea.org.

58. Margaret Kartomi, "The Pan-East/Southeast Asian and National Indonesian Song Bengawan Solo and Its Javanese Composer," *Yearbook for Traditional Music* 30 (1998), p. 85.

59. Wilmoth Houdini, "Caroline," Victor 80078, 1927; Donald R. Hill, *Calypso Calaloo: Early Carnival Music in Trinidad*, University Press of Florida, 1993, pp. 125–6; The Classic Calypso Collective, *West Indian Rhythm: Trinidad Calypsos on World and Local Events, Featuring the Censored Recordings 1938–1940*, Bear Family Records BCD 16623 JM, 2006, p. 22. See also John Cowley, "West Indies Blues: An Historical Overview, 1920s–1950s: Blues and Music from the English-speaking West Indies," in Robert Springer, ed., *Nobody Knows Where the Blues Come From: Lyrics and History*, University Press of Mississippi, 2006.

60. John Cowley, liner notes to *Wilmoth Houdini: "Poor but Ambitious,"* Arhoolie Folkloric CD 7010, 1993, p. 2.

61. *West Indian Rhythm*, p. 22.

62. John Cowley, *Music and Migration: Aspects of Black Music in the British Caribbean, the United States, and Britain, Before the Independence of Jamaica and Trinidad & Tobago*, dissertation, University of Warwick, 1992, p. 444.

63. Patrick Huber, *Linthead Stomp: The Creation of Country Music in the Piedmont South*, University of North Carolina Press, 2008, pp. 19–20.

64. Charles K. Wolfe and Ted Olson, eds, *The Bristol Sessions: Writings about the Big Bang of Country Music*, McFarland & Company, 2005.

65. The Carter Family, "Single Girl, Married Girl," Victor 20937, 1927. Mark Zwonitzer, *Will You Miss Me When I'm Gone? The Carter Family and Their Legacy in American Music*, Simon & Schuster, 2002.

66. Nolan Porterfield, *Jimmie Rodgers: The Life and Times of America's Blue Yodeler*, University Press of Mississippi, 2007, pp. 46–63.

67. Jimmie Rodgers, "Blue Yodel," Victor 21142, 1928; Abbe Niles, "Ballads, Songs and Snatches," *The Bookman: A Review of Books and Life* 67 (July 1928), p. 566; ibid., 68 (September 1928), p. 77.

68. Richard A. Peterson, *Creating Country Music: Fabricating Authenticity*, University of Chicago Press, 1997; Barry Mazor, *Meeting Jimmie Rodgers*, Oxford University Press, 2009, pp. 85–108.

69. The 1927 Regal recordings have been re-released on *Niña de los Peines: Registros Sonoros*, Fonotrón D.L., 2004, CD 9. Cristina Cruces Roldán, *La Niña de los Peines: El mundo flamenco de Pastora Pavón*, Almuzara, 2009, pp. 286–7.

70. Pedro Vaquero and Christopher Maurer, liner notes to *El Concurso de Cante Jondo, Colección Manuel de Falla, Granada, Corpus de 1922/Colección Federico García Lorca: Discografía flamenca utilizada por el poeta*, Sonifolk CD 20106, 1997. See also James Woodall, *In Search of the Firedance: Spain through Flamenco*, Sinclair-Stevenson, 1992, pp. 182, 217–19.

71. Irving Brown, *Deep Song: Adventures with Gypsy Songs and Singers in Andalusia and other Lands, with Original Translations*, Harper & Brothers, 1929, p. 25; Ian Nagoski, liner notes to *Black Mirror: Reflections in Global Musics*, Dust-to-Digital DTD 10, 2008, track 18.

72. Langston Hughes, *I Wonder as I Wander: An Autobiographical Journey*, Reinhart, 1956, pp. 332–3. See also Brent Hayes Edwards, "Langston Hughes and the Futures of Diaspora," *American Literary History* 19.3 (Fall 2007), p. 689–711; and Nathaniel Mackey, "Cante Moro," in Anne Waldman and Andrew Schelling, eds, *Disembodied Poetics: Annals of the Jack Kerouac School*, University of New Mexico Press, 1994.

73. Rodney Gallop, "Spanish Folk-Music Records," *The Gramophone* (November 1930), p. 266.

74. Dào Nha, "Tả cảnh cô đầu thua bạc," Victor 40027, 1928, re-released on *Longing for the Past*, p. 77.

75. Van Thanh Ban, "Khổng Minh—Mẫu Tầm Tử," Beka 20137, ca.1929, re-released on *Longing for the Past*, pp. 45, 88–9.

76. Erich deWald, "Taking to the Waves: Vietnamese Society around the Radio in the 1930s," *Modern Asian Studies* 46.1 (2012), p. 155.

77. Jason Gibbs, "Spoken Theater, La Scène Tonkinoise, and the First Modern Vietnamese Songs," *Asian Music* 31.2 (2000), p. 6. Quoted in Jason Gibbs, "The West's Songs, Our Songs: The Introduction and Adaptation of Western Popular Song in Vietnam Before 1940," *Asian Music* 35.1 (2003/2004), p. 61.

78. Kalama's Quartet, "Medley of Hulas"/"Inikiniki Malie," OKeh 40957, 1928, and "He Manao Healoha," OKeh 41023, 1928; T. Malcolm Rockwell, *Hawaiian and Hawaiian Guitar Records 1891–1960*, Mahina Piha Press, 2007, p. 575.

79. Niles, "Ballads, Songs, and Snatches," *The Bookman* 67 (July 1928), p. 567. A month later he added a second notice: "A particularly lovely Hawaiian record for summer nights is 'Ua Like No A Like', by Kalama's Quartet)," Niles, "Ballads, Songs, and Snatches," *The Bookman*, 67 (August 1928), p. 688.

80. Sol Ho'opi'i, "Sweet Lei Lehua,"* Columbia 1250-D, 1927. In 1927 and 1928, Victor recorded Kane's Hawaiians in San Francisco; Columbia recorded the South Sea Islanders in New York; Gennett recorded Francis Lei in Indiana; and Sam Ku West recorded for Gennett, Banner, Vocalion, and Victor. For the biography of Hanapi, see George S. Kanahele, ed., (revised and updated by John Berger), *Hawaiian Music and Musicians: An Encyclopedic History*, Mutual Publishing, 2012, pp. 242–4.

81. "Brunswick Sends Men to Honolulu to Make New Hawaiian Records," *Honolulu Advertiser*, quoted in Ross Laird, *Brunswick Records: A Discography of Recordings, 1916–1931*, Greenwood Press, 2001, p. 22.

82. Kanahele, *Hawaiian Music and Musicians*, pp. 479, 679; Rockwell, *Hawaiian Records*, p. xiii; Gurre Ploner Noble, *Hula Blues: The Story of Johnny Noble, Hawaii, Its Music and Musicians*, Tongg Publishing, 1948, pp. 75–7.

83. Amy Ku'uleialoha Stillman, "Published Hawaiian Songbooks," *Notes* 44.2 (1987), p. 231.

84. Kanahele, *Hawaiian Music and Musicians*, pp. 352–3.

85. Rockwell, *Hawaiian Records*, pp. 988–9.

86. Steva Nikolič, "Arnautka," Victor V-3049-B, 1928, available on Jonathan Ward, *Excavated Shellac*, excavatedshellac.com.

87. Sofka Nikolić, "Ali Pašina pesma," HMV AM1073, ca. 1928; Sofka Nikolić, "Tri put ti čuknal," HMV AM 1068, ca. 1928, both available digitally on Europeana, europeana.eu. See also Sofka Nikolić, "Čuješ Seko,"* Victor V-3097,

available on *Tamburitza and more … Tamburitza and Folk Music from America and Europe*, tamburitza78s.blogspot.com. Her first recordings were apparently made for Edison Bell Penkala, a Zagreb company, about the same time: see Ventsislav Dimov, "Roma Music: Anthropological Interpretations, Roma Contribution to Media and Recorded Music," *Население* 3–4 (2012), p. 190.

88. Rodney Gallop, "Some Records of Serbian Folk Music," *The Gramophone* (May 1931), p. 601.

89. Shay Loya, "Beyond 'Gypsy' Stereotypes: Harmony and Structure in the Verbunkos Idiom," *Journal of Musicological Research* 27.3 (2008), p. 254 n. 1.

90. See *Tziganes: Paris/Berlin/Budapest/1910–1935*, Frémeaux FA006, 1993; Michael Dregni, *Django: The Life and Music of a Gypsy Legend*, Oxford University Press, 2004, p. 63; Bálint Sárosi, *Gypsy Music*, Corvina Press, 1978, p. 208.

91. "Gypsy Music: Fiddling in Hungary," *The Times*, April 15, 1933, p. 13.

92. Dregni, *Django*, pp. 31, 40, 87–95.

93. "EC's gramophone notes," *West Africa* (June 15, 1929), quoted in Paul Vernon, liner notes to *Early Guitar Music from West Africa 1927–1929*, Heritage HT CD 33, 2003.

94. John Cowley, "*uBungca* (Oxford Bags): Recordings in London of African and West Indian Music in the 1920s and 1930s," *Musical Traditions* 12 (1994), p. 13–26, available at mustrad.org.uk.

95. *West Africa* (July 21, 1928), quoted in Paul Vernon, liner notes to *Kumasi Trio 1928*, Heritage HT CD 22, 1993.

96. John Collins, "One Hundred Years of Censorship in Ghanaian Popular Music Performance," in Michael Drewett and Martin Cloonan, eds, *Popular Music Censorship in Africa*, Ashgate, 2006, p. 176.

97. Asare reported in David Coplan, "Go To My Town, Cape Coast! The Social History of Ghanaian Highlife," in Bruno Nettl, ed., *Eight Urban Musical Cultures: Tradition and Change*, University of Illinois Press, 1978, p. 102.

98. Kumasi Trio, "Amponsah, Part One"/"Amponsah, Part Two," Zonophone 1001, 1928.

99. W. E. Ward, "Music in the Gold Coast," *The Gold Coast Review* 3.2 (1927), p. 205.

100. "Ephraim Amu and the Story of Yaa Amponsah," *Copyright News* [Ghana] (March 1990), p. 5.

101. Collins, "One Hundred Years of Censorship," in Drewett and Cloonan, eds., *Popular Music Censorship in Africa*, p. 177.

102. Harry E. Quashie, "Anadwofa,"* Zonophone, ca. 1929, re-released on *Living Is Hard: West African Music in Britain, 1927–1929*, Honest Jon's Records HJRCD33, 2008.

103. Jolly Orchestra, "Abonsa," Parlophone PO.531, ca. 1936, re-released on cassette tape accompanying Christopher Alan Waterman, *Jùjú: A Social History and Ethnography of an African Popular Music*, University of Chicago Press, 1990.

104. Maud Cuney-Hare, *Negro Musicians and Their Music*, Da Capo Press, 1974 [c. 1936], p. 259.

105. Waterman, *Jùjú*, pp. 47–8.

106. See "Ephraim Amu and the Story of Yaa Amponsah"; A. O. Amegatcher, "Protection of Folklore by Copyright: A Contradiction in Terms," *Copyright Bulletin* 36.2 (2002), pp. 33–42; John Collins, "The 'Folkloric Copyright Tax' Problem in Ghana," *Media Development* 50.1 (2003), pp. 10–14.

107. Janet Topp Fargion, liner notes to *Poetry and Languid Charm: Swahili Music from Tanzania and Kenya from the 1920s to the 1950s*, Topic TSCD 936, 2007, p. 2.
108. Werner Graebner, "Between Mainland and Sea: The *Taarab* Music of Zanzibar," in Kevin Dawe, ed., *Island Musics*, Berg, 2004, pp. 173–4.
109. Quoted in Vernon, "Odeon Records."
110. Graebner, "Between Mainland and Sea," p. 174.
111. Laura Fair, *Pastimes and Politics: Culture, Community, and Identity in Post-Abolition Urban Zanzibar, 1890–1945*, Ohio University Press, 2001, p. 1.
112. Ibid., p. 3.
113. Ibid., p. 179.
114. Ibid. pp. 179–82. See also Gerry Farrell, "The Early Days of the Gramophone Industry in India: Historical, Social and Musical Perspectives," *British Journal of Ethnomusicology* 2 (1993), p. 38.
115. Siti binti Saad, "Wewe Paka," Columbia WE 46, ca. 1930; the lyrics in Swahili and English are in Fair, *Pastimes and Politics*, pp. 207–9.
116. Kelly M. Askew, *Performing the Nation: Swahili Music and Cultural Politics in Tanzania*, University of Chicago Press, 2002, pp. 109–12.
117. Francisco Alves, "Me Faz Carinhos," Odeon 10100-B, 1928, and "A Malandragem," Odeon 10113-B, 1928, re-released on Humberto M. Franceschi, *A Casa Edison e Seu Tempo*, Sarapuí, 2002; Carlos Sandroni, *Feitiço decente: transformações do samba no Rio de Janeiro, 1917–1933*, Editora UFRJ, 2001, p. 186.
118. Carlos Sandroni, "Transformations of the Carioca Samba in the Twentieth Century," available at dc.itamaraty.gov.br, pp. 80–1.
119. Hermano Vianna, *The Mystery of Samba: Popular Music and National Identity in Brazil*, University of North Carolina Press, 1999, p. 87.
120. Almirante com O Bando de Tangaras, "Na Pavuna," Parlophon 13.089-A, 1930; Carlos Sandroni, "Dois Sambas de 1930 ea Constituição do Gênero: 'Na Pavuna' e 'Vou te Abandonar,'" *Cadernos do Colóquio* 1.4 (2001), pp. 8–21.
121. Ismael Silva, "Samba raiado"/"Louca," Odeon 10835, 1931; and Ismael Silva, "Me Diga o Teu Nome"/"Me Deixa Sossegado," Odeon 10858, 1931, available at O Instituto Moreira Salles, acervo.ims.com.br. The other recording of a samba school figure at the time was Brunswick's 1930 recording of Paulo da Portela: Grupo Prazeres, "Vou te Abandonar," Brunswick 10037-B, 1930, discussed by Sandroni, "Dois Sambas."
122. Halpin Trio, "Rogha-An-Fhile"/"Over the Moor to Maggie," Parlophone E3627, 1929. "Over the Moor to Maggie" is available at Irish Traditional Music Archive, itma.ie. See also Irish Traditional Music Archive, "Parlophone Irish 78s, 1929," and Irish Traditional Music Archive, "Parlophone Irish 78s, 1930," both at itma.ie.
123. Gearóid Ó hAllmhuráin, *O'Brien Pocket History of Irish Traditional Music*, The O'Brien Press, 1998, p. 121.
124. Reg Hall, liner notes to *Irish Dance Music*, Topic TSCD 602, 1995; Reg Hall, liner notes to *Past Masters of Irish Dance Music*, Topic TSCD 604, 2000; Reg Hall, liner notes to *Past Masters of Irish Fiddle Music*, Topic TSCD 605, 2001.
125. Harry Bradshaw, liner notes to *Michael Coleman 1891–1945*, Gael Linn/Viva Voce CEFCD 161, 1992.
126. Li Minghui, "Maomao yu," Pathé 34278, 1929. Andrew F. Jones, *Yellow Music: Media Culture and Colonial Modernity in the Chinese Jazz Age*, Duke University Press, 2001, pp. 83–4, 90–1, 93, 113, 131, 134. Szu-Wei Chen, "The Rise

and Generic Features of Shanghai Popular Songs in the 1930s and 1940s," *Popular Music* 24.1 (2005), p. 108. Wong Kee Chee, *The Age of Shanghainese Pops: 1930–1970*, Joint Publishing, 2001, pp. 12–15.

127. Chen, "Shanghai Popular Songs," p. 123 n. 2.

128. Though "yellow" is a literal translation, "'blue music' would be more suggestive of the associations the term *huangse yinyue* brings." Jonathan Stock, "Reconsidering the Past: Zhou Xuan and the Rehabilitation of Early Twentieth-Century Popular Music," *Asian Music* 26.2 (1995), p. 32 n. 4.

129. Andrew Field, *Shanghai's Dancing World: Cabaret Culture and Urban Politics, 1919–1954*, Chinese University Press, 2010, p. 63.

130. Jones, *Yellow Music*, p. 113.

131. Wang Renmei, quoted in ibid., p. 91.

132. On Zhou Xuan, see Stock, "Reconsidering the Past"; Jones, *Yellow Music*; Field, *Shanghai's Dancing World*, p. 183.

133. L'Orchestre Antillais, "Sêpent Maigre," Odeon Ki 2655, 1929. See the discussion of "Sêpent Maigre" in Eric Prieto, "Alexandre Stellio and the Beginnings of the Biguine," *Nottingham French Studies* 43.1 (2004), p. 36. See also Richard Spottswood, liner notes to *Au Bal Antillais: Creole Biguines from Martinique*, Arhoolie CD 7013, 1992; Jean-Pierre Meunier, "La Biguine à Paris: migration et mutation d'une musique métisse de la Caraïbe," 2005, lameca.org.

134. Andrée Nardal, "Notes on the Biguine Créole," *La Revue Du Monde Noir* 2 (1931), p. 51.

135. "In Europe with J. A. Rogers," *New York Amsterdam News*, September 2, 1931, p. 10.

136. Gisèle Dubouillé, "New Records of Negro Music," *La Revue Du Monde Noir* 3 (1932), p. 56.

137. Nardal, "Notes on the Biguine Créole," p. 52.

138. Waterman, *Jùjú*, p. 47. They were re-released on *Domingo Justus: Roots of Juju 1928*, Heritage HT CD 18, 1993.

139. Ibid., p. 27.

140. Abibu Oluwa, "Orin Herbert Macaulay," Odeon A248505; see Waterman, *Jùjú*, pp. 36, 234 n. 6, 235 n. 13, 40.

141. Waterman, *Jùjú*, p. 55; Jolly Orchestra, "Abonsa," Parlophone PO.531, ca. 1936, re-released on cassette tape accompanying Waterman, *Jùjú*; "African Test Pressing, Number 4," *Excavated Shellac*, excavatedshellac.com.

142. Irewolede Denge, "Orin Asape Eko," HMV JZ3. For an analysis of the song, see Waterman, *Jùjú*, pp. 50–2.

143. Richard K. Spottswood, *Ethnic Music on Records: A Discography of Ethnic Recordings Produced in the United States, 1893 to 1942*, University of Illinois Press, 1990, vol. 4, p. 2417. Laird, *Brunswick Records*, vol. 3, pp. 1366–72. On Ballecer, see E. San Juan, Jr., *Introduction to Modern Pilipino Literature*, Twayne Publishers, 1974, p. 17.

144. Urbano A. Zafra, "Danza Filipina," Columbia 3910-X, 1929.

145. Tim Couzens, *The New African: A Study of the Life and Work of H. I. E. Dhlomo*, Ravan Press, 1985, p. 68. Zonophone had released a few earlier recordings of Zulu traditional songs, by James Stuart in 1927 and by Simon Sibiya and John Matthews Ngwane in 1929: Veit Erlmann, *African Stars: Studies in Black South African Performance*, University of Chicago Press, 1991, pp. 74, 188 n. 30.

146. Caluza's Double Quartet, "uBangca"/"Ingoduso," Zonophone 4276, 1930. See Erlmann, *African Stars*, p. 143; Couzens, *The New African*, p. 69.

147. Couzens, *The New African*, pp. 67–8.
148. Griffiths Motsieloa, "Aubuti Nkikho," Singer GE 1, 1930, re-released on CD accompanying Christopher Ballantine, *Marabi Nights: Jazz, "Race" and Society in Early Apartheid South Africa*, University of KwaZulu-Natal Press, 2012. See Ballantine, pp. 207–8.
149. Couzens, *The New African*, p. 68; Griffiths Motsieloa, "Ndhiya eBhai," Singer GE4, 1930, available on South African Music Archive Project, disa.ukzn.ac.za.
150. Griffiths Motsieloa, "Nkosi Sikelel' iAfrika," Singer GE13, re-released on *Opika Pende: Africa at 78rpm*, Dust-to-Digital, DTD 22, 2011.
151. Hugh Masekela and D. Michael Cheers, *Still Grazing: The Musical Journey of Hugh Masekela*, Crown Publishers, 2004, p. 15; Ballantine, *Marabi Nights*, pp. 68–9.
152. Amanzimtoti Players, "Sbhinono," HMV GU 130, 1932, and Bantu Glee Singers, "Ndunduma," HMV GU 94, 1932, both re-released on CD accompanying Ballantine, *Marabi Nights*. See also Erlmann, *African Stars*, pp. 92, 66. Ballantine notes that "as the quintessential music of the slumyards, marabi in its classic original form was—tragically—never recorded. What were recorded, however, were a number of performances which refracted the early music of the slumyards: in particular, these include marabi in imitations, rec-reations and arrangements—all of them typically performed by elite groups" (*Marabi Nights*, p. 209).
153. Caluza's Double Quartet, "uTebetjana Ufana Ne'mfene," HMV 4284. Griffiths Motsieloa and Company, "Sponono naMarabi," Singer GE 67, 1931, re-released on CD accompanying Ballantine, *Marabi Nights*. David Coplan, *In Township Tonight!: South Africa's Black City Music and Theatre*, Ravan Press, 1985, p. 105. Coplan says Tebetjane composed the song, and that it made "his name … synonymous with the marabi genre" (p. 97); Ballantine says it was written in "mocking tribute (*Marabi Nights*, pp. 203–4)" Quoted in Brett Pyper, "Sounds Like: [Todd] John Matshikiza's Jazz Writing for *Drum* Magazine, 1951–1957," *Glendora Review: African Quarterly on the Arts* 3.3–4 (2004), p. 19.
154. Pyper, "Sounds Like," p. 19.

2.   The Polyphony of Colonial Ports

1. Beatriz Sarlo, *Una modernidad periférica: Buenos Aires 1920 y 1930*, Ediciones Nueva Visión, 1988.
2. David Montgomery, *The Fall of the House of Labor: The Workplace, the State, and American Labor Activism, 1865–1925*, Cambridge University Press, 1987, pp. 70–1.
3. Josef W. Konvitz, "The Crisis of Atlantic Port Cities, 1880 to 1920," *Comparative Studies in Society and History* 36.2 (1994), pp. 297, 293.
4. Ibid., pp. 299–300.
5. Frank Thistlethwaite, "Migration from Europe Overseas in the Nineteenth and Twentieth Centuries," in International Congress of Historical Sciences, *Rapports V: Historie Contemporaine*, Almquist and Wiksell, 1960.
6. Konvitz, "Crisis of Atlantic Port Cities," p. 318.
7. Urban population figures for the first half of the twentieth century are inexact; for a sense of the general magnitudes, these figures are drawn from the

preeminent port directory of the period: Evan Rowland Jones, ed., *The "Shipping World" Year Book 1910*, "Shipping World" Offices, 1910; and Sir Archibald Hurd, ed., *The "Shipping World" Year Book 1930*, "Shipping World" Offices, 1930.

8. Christopher Alan: *A Social History and Ethnography of an African Popular Music*, University of Chicago Press, 1990, Waterman, *Jùjú*, pp. 35, 31.

9. Davianna Pomaika'i McGregor, *Kupa'a I Ka 'Aina: Persistence on the Land*, dissertation, University of Hawaii, 1989, pp. 164–5.

10. B. S. Hoyle, "Maritime Perspective on Ports and Port Systems: The Case of East Africa," in Frank Broeze, ed., *Brides of the Sea: Port Cities of Asia from the 16th–20th Centuries*, University of Hawaii Press, 1989, p. 196.

11. Donald Cohen, ed., *Tango Voices: Songs from the Soul of Buenos Aires and Beyond*, Wise Publications, 2007, p. 7.

12. Robin Moore, *Nationalizing Blackness: Afrocubanismo and Artistic Revolution in Havana, 1920–1940*, University of Pittsburgh Press, 1997, p. 64.

13. Rodney Gallop, "The Fado (The Portuguese Song of Fate)," *Musical Quarterly* 19.2 (1933), p. 204.

14. Tan Tai Yong, "Singapore's Story: A Port City in Search of Hinterlands," in Arndt Graf and Chua Beng Huat, eds, *Port Cities in Asia and Europe*, Routledge, 2009, pp. 211–12.

15. Faruk Tabak, "Imperial Rivalry and Port-Cities: a View From Above," *Mediterranean Historical Review* 24.2 (2009), pp. 79–94. See also Henk Driessen, "Mediterranean Port Cities: Cosmopolitanism Reconsidered," *History and Anthropology* 16.1 (2005), pp. 129–41.

16. Thomas Brothers, *Louis Armstrong's New Orleans*, W. W. Norton, 2006, p. 14; Donald R. Hill, *Calypso Calaloo: Early Carnival Music in Trinidad*, University Press of Florida, 1993, pp. 52–5; Virginia Danielson, *The Voice of Egypt: Umm Kulthūm, Arabic Song, and Egyptian Society in the 20th Century*, University of Chicago Press, 1998, pp. 30, 40; Gregory T. Cushman, "¿De Qué Color Es el Oro? Race, Environment, and the History of Cuban National Music, 1898–1958," *Latin American Music Review* 26.2 (2005), p. 170; Moore, *Nationalizing Blackness*, pp. 29–30.

17. Perry Anderson, "Modernity and Revolution," *New Left Review* 144 (1984), p. 104.

18. Brothers, *Louis Armstrong's New Orleans*, pp. 136–7.

19. Quoted in Ballantine, *Marabi Nights*, p. 37.

20. Dhlomo quoted in ibid., p. 36.

21. Canaro quoted in Simon Collier, "The Tango Is Born: 1880s–1920s," in Simon Collier et al., *Tango! The Dance, the Song, the Story*, Thames and Hudson, 1995, p. 58.

22. Gurre Ploner Noble, *Hula Blues: The Story of Johnny Noble, Hawaii, Its Music and Musicians*, Tongg Publishing, 1948, p. 44. Jack London, *In Hawaii with Jack London*, Routledge, 2011, p. 82.

23. John Collins, "The Early History of West African Highlife Music," *Popular Music* 8.3 (1989), p. 222.

24. Andrew Field, *Shanghai's Dancing World: Cabaret Culture and Urban Politics, 1919–1954*, Chinese University Press, 2010, pp. 43 (quoting Smith), 36.

25. Isabelle Leymarie, *Cuban Fire: The Saga of Salsa and Latin Jazz*, Continuum, 2002, p. 46.

26. Matthew B. Karush, *Culture of Class: Radio and Cinema in the Making of a Divided Argentina, 1920–1946*, Duke University Press, 2012, p. 50.

27. Noble, *Hula Blues*, p. 52.
28. Moore, *Nationalizing Blackness*, pp. 98–9.
29. Tan Sooi Beng, "The 78rpm Record Industry in Malaya Prior to World War II," *Asian Music* 28.1 (1996), p. 17.
30. Rafael José de Menezes Bastos, "Brazil in France, 1922: An Anthropological Study of the Congenital International Nexus of Popular Music," *Latin American Music Review* 29.1 (2008), p. 20.
31. Moore, *Nationalizing Blackness*, p. 38.
32. Gallop, "The Fado," p. 199.
33. Afolabi Alaja-Browne, *Juju Music: A Study of Its Social History and Style*, dissertation, University of Pittsburgh, 1985, p. 43.
34. Moore, *Nationalizing Blackness*, pp. 38–9.
35. Langston Hughes, *I Wonder as I Wander: An Autobiographical Journey*, Reinhart, 1956, p. 8.
36. Field, *Shanghai's Dancing World*, pp. 19–82.
37. Moore, *Nationalizing Blackness*, pp. 38–9.
38. William Howland Kenney, *Chicago Jazz: A Cultural History, 1904–1930*, Oxford University Press, 1993, pp. 16–24.
39. Matthew Isaac Cohen, *The Komedie Stamboel: Popular Theater in Colonial Indonesia, 1891–1903*, Ohio University Press, 2006, p. 338.
40. Khalid Amine and Marvin Carlson, *The Theatres of Morocco, Algeria and Tunisia: Performance Traditions of the Maghreb*, Palgrave Macmillan, 2012, p. 92.
41. Stephen Hughes, "The 'Music Boom' in Tamil South India: Gramophone, Radio and the Making of Mass Culture," *Historial Journal of Film, Radio and Television* 22.4 (2002), p. 460.
42. Cushman, "¿De Qué Color Es el Oro?," p. 174. Ned Sublette, *Cuba and Its Music: From the First Drums to the Mambo*, Chicago Press Review, 2004, pp. 383–7.
43. Claude McKay, *Banjo: A Story without a Plot*, Harcourt, Brace, Jovanovich, 1970, p. 67.
44. Ibid., pp. 257, 71, 243, 298.
45. Ibid., pp. 105, 166, 197.
46. Ibid., pp. 4, 47, 11–12, 3.
47. Ibid., pp. 19, 4–9, 14, 48, 54, 56.
48. Ibid., p. 89.
49. Ibid., p. 97.
50. Ibid., p. 109.
51. Paul Vernon, "Special Agents," *Vintage Jazz Mart* 96 (1994).
52. T. Malcolm Rockwell, "Sol Hoopii: The Early Years," liner notes to *Sol Hoopii in Hollywood: His First Recordings, 1925*, Grass Skirt Records, GSR 1002, 2007, p. 7.
53. Simon Collier, liner notes to *Se Va La Vida: Tango Ladies 1923–1954*, Harlequin HQ CD 52, 1995. Donald S. Castro, *The Argentine Tango as Social History, 1880–1955: The Soul of the People*, Mellen Research University Press, 1990, p. 189.
54. Collins, "Early History of West African Highlife Music," p. 223.
55. Helio Orovio, *Cuban Music from A to Z*, Duke University Press, 2004, p. 165.
56. Ibid., p. 165. Holst, *Road to Rembetika*, p. 42. Harry Owens, *Sweet Leilani: The Story behind the Song: An Autobiography*, Hula House, 1970, p. 39.
57. Mark Ainley, liner notes to *Living Is Hard: West African Music in Britain, 1927–1929*, Honest Jon's Records HJRCD33, 2008.

58. Hill, *Calypso Calaloo*, pp. 9, 100.
59. Gail Holst, *Road to Rembetika: Music of a Greek Subculture. Songs of Love, Sorrow and Hashish*, Denise Harvey Publisher, 2006, p. 43; Orovio, *Cuban Music from A to Z*, p. 165; quoted in Stephen Collier, *The Life, Music and Times of Carlos Gardel*, University of Pittsburgh Press, 1986, p. 11.
60. Patrick Huber, *Linthead Stomp: The Creation of Country Music in the Piedmont South*, University of North Carolina Press, 2008, p. 22.
61. Waterman, *Jùjú*, p. 9.
62. Danielson, *The Voice of Egypt*, pp. 23–4.
63. Martin Stokes, *The Republic of Love: Cultural Intimacy in Turkish Popular Music*, University of Chicago Press, 2010, p. 21 n. 53.
64. Veit Arlt, "The Union Trade Company and Its Recordings: An Unintentional Documentation of West African Popular Music, 1931–1957," *History in Africa* 31 (2004), pp. 401–2.
65. George S. Kanahele, ed. *Hawaiian Music and Musicians: An Encyclopedic History*, Mutual Publishing, 2012, p. 303; Amy Kuʻuleialoha Stillman, "Prelude to a Comparative Investigation of Protestant Hymnody in Polynesia," *Yearbook for Traditional Music* 25 (1993), p. 94.
66. Kanahele, *Hawaiian Music and Musicians*, pp. 55, 239–40.
67. Nate Plageman, *Highlife Saturday Night: Popular Music and Social Change in Urban Ghana*, Indiana University Press, 2013, pp. 48–9.
68. Philip Yampolsky, "Kroncong Revisited: New Evidence from Old Sources," *Archipel* 79 (2010), p. 28.
69. David Coplan, *In Township Tonight!: South Africa's Black City Music and Theatre*, Raven Press, 1985, p. 102; Ballantine, *Marabi Nights*, pp. 30–3.
70. Nate Plageman, *Highlife Saturday Night: Popular Music and Social Change in Urban Ghana*, Indiana University Press, 2012, p. 47.
71. Waterman, *Jùjú*, p. 43.
72. Moore, *Nationalizing Blackness*, p. 92.
73. George Bilainkin, *Hail Penang: Being the Narrative of Comedies and Tragedies in a Tropical Outpost, Among Europeans, Chinese, Malays, and Indians*, Areca Books, 2010, p. 195.
74. Isaac O. Delano, *The Soul of Nigeria*, T. W. Laurie, Ltd., 1937, pp. 155, 153–4, 157.
75. Waterman, *Jùjú*, p. 39.
76. Veit Erlmann, "'Horses in the Race Course': The Domestication of *Ingoma* Dance, 1929–1939," in his *African Stars: Studies in Black South African Performance*, University of Chicago Press, 1991.
77. Moore, *Nationalizing Blackness*, pp. 64, 67.
78. Quoted in Hill, *Calypso Calaloo*, p. 70.
79. Carlos Sandroni, "Transformations of the Carioca Samba in the Twentieth Century," available at dc.itamaraty.gov.br, p. 80.
80. Bryan McCann, *Hello, Hello Brazil: Popular Music in the Making of Modern Brazil*, Duke University Press, 2004, pp. 47–8.
81. Sandroni, "Transformations of the Carioca Samba," 81–2.
82. Erlmann, *African Stars*, p. 102.
83. Raymond Quevedo (Atilla the Hun), *Atilla's Kaiso: A Short History of Trinidad Calypso*, University of the West Indies, 1983, p. 35.
84. Moore, *Nationalizing Blackness*, p. 75.
85. John Cowley, *Carnival, Canboulay and Calypso: Traditions in the Making*, Cambridge University Press, 1996, pp. 84, 100, 135, 140.

86. Moore, *Nationalizing Blackness*, p. 69.
87. Ibid., pp. 71, 72.
88. Erlmann, *African Stars*, p. 96.
89. Quevedo, *Atilla's Kaiso*, pp. 36, 38–9, 43.
90. Angèle David-Guillou, "Early Musicians' Unions in Britain, France, and the United States: On the Possibilities and Impossibilities of Transnational Militant Transfers in an International Industry," *Labour History Review* 74.3 (2009); James P. Kraft, *Stage to Studio: Musicians and the Sound Revolution, 1890–1950*, Johns Hopkins University Press, 1996.
91. J. H. Nketia, "The Gramophone and Contemporary African Music in the Gold Coast," *Proceedings of the Fourth Annual Conference of the West African Institute of Social and Economic Research*, 1956, p. 193.
92. Quoted in Danielson, *The Voice of Egypt*, p. 54.
93. John Collins, *Musicmakers of West Africa*, Three Continents Press, 1985, p. 15.
94. Lisbet Torp, *Salonikiós, "The Best Vision in the Balkans,"* Museum Tusculanum Press, 1993, p. 14.
95. Burnet Hershey, "Jazz Latitude," *New York Times*, June 25, 1922, p. SM5. See also Lee Watkins, "Minstrelsy and Mimesis in the South China Sea: Filipino Migrant Musicians, Chinese Hosts, and the Disciplining of Relations in Hong Kong," *Asian Music* 40.2 (2009), pp. 72–99. E. Taylor Atkins, *Blue Nippon: Authenticating Jazz in Japan*, Duke University Press, 2001, pp. 58–60, 289 n. 48. Peter Keppy, "Southeast Asia in the Age of Jazz: Locating Popular Culture in the Colonial Philippines and Indonesia," *Journal of Southeast Asian Studies* 44.3 (2013), p. 457.
96. Ruth Glasser, *My Music Is My Flag: Puerto Rican Musicians and their New York Communities, 1917–1940*, University of California Press, 1995, pp. 85–6; Kanahele, *Hawaiian Music and Musicians*, pp. 172–7.
97. Brothers, *Louis Armstrong's New Orleans*, pp. 174, 181.
98. Moore, *Nationalizing Blackness*, pp. 5–6.
99. Hill, *Calypso Calaloo*, chapters 3 and 4.
100. Coplan, *In Township Tonight!*, Chapter 2.
101. Waterman, *Jùjú*, p. 81.
102. Collins, "Early History of West African Highlife Music," pp. 222, 225.
103. See Derek B. Scott, *Sounds of the Metropolis: The Nineteenth-Century Popular Music Revolution in London, New York, Paris, and Vienna*, Oxford University Press, 2008; and Peter Van der Merwe, *Origins of the Popular Style: The Antecedents of Twentieth-Century Popular Music*, Clarendon Press, 1989.
104. Hermano Vianna, *The Mystery of Samba: Popular Music and National Identity in Brazil*, University of North Carolina Press, 1999, pp. 1–2.
105. McCann, *Hello, Hello Brazil*, pp. 7, 60–2. See also Micol Seigel, *Uneven Encounters: Making Race and Nation in Brazil and the United States*, Duke University Press, 2009.
106. Paul Morand, *East India and Company*, A. & C. Boni, 1927, p. 28.
107. Brothers asks, "Why did a unique way of playing ragtime develop in New Orleans?" (*Louis Armstrong's New Orleans*, p. 133). See also Charles Hersch, *Subversive Sounds: Race and the Birth of Jazz in New Orleans*, University of Chicago Press, 2007.

3. Phonographing the Vernacular

1. Paul Vernon, "Cairo Practice," *Folk Roots* 141 (1995), pp. 26–7. Vernon was one of the first scholars to recognize this "worldwide explosion of recording activity with the mass market as its target."
2. Pekka Gronow, "The Record Industry: The Growth of a Mass Medium," *Popular Music* 3 (1983), p. 62.
3. The difficulty with the term "world music"—which emerged in the early 1980s to designate a specific sector of the music market, specializing in the transnational trafficking of "ethnic" musics—lies in the implicit suggestion that, on the one hand, there is a relatively clear divide between the "music" of the West, whether "classical" or "popular," and the "world music" of the rest, and, on the other hand, that "world music" is a single global music, a "world beat."
4. "We can … speak of a music industry from the moment that music production and consumption severed ties with the context of the feudal court and church … The foundation of … the music industry only resulted from the interplay between a blossoming music publishing business and an emerging public music concert culture in the 18th century." Peter Tschmuck, *Creativity and Innovation in the Music Industry*, Springer, 2006, p. 1.
5. David Suisman, *Selling Sounds: The Commercial Revolution in American Music*, Harvard University Press, 2009, p. 101.
6. Steve J. Wurtzler, *Electric Sounds: Technological Change and the Rise of the Corporate Mass Media*, Columbia University Press, 2007, p. 3.
7. Albin J. Zak III, *The Poetics of Rock: Cutting Tracks, Making Records*, University of California Press, 2001.
8. Greg Milner, *Perfecting Sound Forever: An Aural History of Recorded Music*, Faber and Faber, 2009, p. 301.
9. Michael E. Veal, *Dub: Soundscapes and Shattered Songs in Jamaican Reggae*, Wesleyan University Press, 2007; Mark Katz, *Groove Music: The Art and Culture of the Hip-Hop DJ*, Oxford University Press, 2012.
10. Peter Doyle, *Echo and Reverb: Fabricating Space in Popular Music, 1900–1960*, Wesleyan University Press, 2005, p. 55.
11. Doyle, *Echo and Reverb*, p. 57; Theodor W. Adorno, "The Curves of the Needle," in *Essays on Music*, Richard Leppert, ed., University of California Press, 2002, p. 271.
12. Quoted in Milner, *Perfecting Sound*, p. 59.
13. "Louis Sterling, Columbia Head, Gives Interesting Views on Gramophone's Future," *Talking Machine World* 22.8 (August 1926): 140.
14. James P. Kraft, *Stage to Studio: Musicians and the Sound Revolution, 1890–1950*, Johns Hopkins University Press, 1996.
15. Pekka Gronow and Björn Englund, "Inventing Recorded Music: The Recorded Repertoire in Scandinavia 1899–1925," *Popular Music* 26.2 (2007), p. 282.
16. Suisman, *Selling Sounds*, p. 231.
17. Ali Jihad Racy, *Musical Change and Commercial Recording in Egypt, 1904–1932*, dissertation, University of Illinois at Urbana-Champaign, 1977, p. 111.
18. Robin Moore, *Nationalizing Blackness: Afrocubanismo and Artistic Revolution in Havana, 1920–1940*, University of Pittsburgh Press, 1997, p. 257 n. 22.
19. Rian Malan, *In the Jungle*, Cold Type Modern Classics, 2003, coldtype.net, p. 7–8.
20. See Paul Vernon, "Odeon Records: Their 'Ethnic' Output," *Musical Traditions* 3 (1997), mustrad.org.uk.

21. Stephen Hughes, "The 'Music Boom' in Tamil South India: Gramophone, Radio and the Making of Mass Culture," *Historical Journal of Film, Radio and Television* 22.4 (2002), p. 464

22. Quoted by Nicholas G. Pappas, "Concepts of Greekness: The Recorded Music of Anatolian Greeks after 1922," *Journal of Modern Greek Studies* 17.2 (1999), p. 355.

23. UK figures from Statistical Office of the Customs and Excise Department, *Annual Statement of the Trade of the United Kingdom with Foreign Countries and British Possessions* [*Countries*, from 1925], vol. 3 (from 1923 to 1933); German figures from Statistischen Reichsamt, *Monatliche Nachweise über den auswärtigen Handel Deutschlands* (from December 1925 to December 1933); US figures from US Department of Commerce, Bureau of Foreign and Domestic Commerce, *Foreign Commerce and Navigation of the United States* (from 1922 to 1933). The French figures are my estimate based on the reported weight of exports in République Française, Direction Général des Douanes, *Tableau Général du Commerce et de la Navigation*, vol. 1 (from 1923 to 1927); and République Française, Direction Général des Douanes, *Tableau Général du Commerce* (from 1928 to 1933). Before 1929, the weight of exported discs was not distinguished from that of exported phonograph machines; I extrapolated the proportion between discs and machines over 1929–33 to get an estimate of the weight of discs from 1923 to 1928. I then used Gronow's estimate of 4.5 discs per kilogram to get an estimate of discs (Pekka Gronow, *The Recording Industry: An Ethnomusicological Approach*, University of Tampere, 1996, p. 112).

24. Statistical Office of the Customs and Excise Department, *Annual Statement of the Trade of the United Kingdom with Foreign Countries and British Countries 1929 Compared with the Years 1925–1928*, His Majesty's Stationery Office, 1930, vol. 3, pp. 340–1. Though it is not clear what his source is, John Collins has written that "the sales of these vernacular guitar songs from Ghana and elsewhere in West Africa were so profitable that the record company HMV/Zonophone sold 181,484 of them in 1930, whilst this British company and German Odeon sold eight hundred thousand of them before the Second World War." Collins, "One Hundred Years of Censorship," in Drewett and Cloonan, eds, *Popular Music Censorship in Africa*, Ashgate, 2006, p. 174.

25. Statistischen Reichsamt, *Monatliche Nachweise über den auswärtigen Handel Deutschlands*, December 1925, p. 159; ibid., December 1929, p. 177.

26. US Department of Commerce, Bureau of Foreign and Domestic Commerce, *Foreign Commerce and Navigation of the United States for the Calendar Year 1929*, Government Printing Office, 1930, vol. 1, pp. 202–3.

27. Moore, *Nationalizing Blackness*, pp. 3–4.

28. Indeed, the picture Andrew Jones gives in *Yellow Music* of the Shanghai recording industry in the 1920s has uncanny parallels to labor historian Elizabeth Perry's description of the Shanghai tobacco and silk industries in the same period. Elizabeth J. Perry, *Shanghai on Strike: The Politics of Chinese Labor*, Stanford University Press, 1993.

29. Dane Yorke, "The Rise and Fall of the Phonograph," *American Mercury* 27.105 (1932), p. 9.

30. Geoffrey Jones, "The Gramophone Company: An Anglo-American Multinational, 1898–1931," *Business History Review* 59.1 (1985), pp. 81–96. Gramophone's profits had quadrupled from 1925 (£296,385) to 1928 (£1,232,553).

31. *Talking Machine World* (March 1928), p. 20–1. Victor's sales had more than doubled from 1925 (about $21 million) to 1927 (about $47 million). Victor's

disc sales had grown from 25 million discs in 1925 to almost 38 million discs in 1927 and 1928 (though they did not match 1921's high of nearly 55 million discs sold, when Victor had little US competition). See "Victor Record Sales Statistics (1901–1941)," Mainspring Press, mainspringpress.com, 2009.

32. Pekka Gronow, "The Record Industry Comes to the Orient," *Ethnomusicology* 25.2 (May 1981); Tschmuck, *Creativity and Innovation*, p. 27; Allan Sutton, *Recording the 'Twenties: The Evolution of the American Recording Industry, 1920–29*, Mainspring Press, 2008, p. 257.

33. Herfrid Kier, "The Lindström AG between the world economic crisis and the merger with EMI Electrola," in Pekka Gronow and Christiane Hofer, eds, *The Lindström Project: Contributions to the History of the Record Industry, Volume 1*, Gesellschaft für Historische Tonträger, 2009, p. 27.

34. Tschmuck, *Creativity and Innovation*, p. 50. For a good account of the boom in the UK, see Peter Martland, *Recording History: The British Record Industry, 1888–1931*, Scarecrow Press, 2013, pp. 241–4.

35. "Phonograph Records," *Fortune* (September 1939), pp. 92, 94. In a 1943 court case, Victor later reported figures that indicated an even greater drop, with a 1929 figure of almost 35 million discs. See "Victor Record Sales Statistics (1901–1941)," Mainspring Press, mainspringpress.com, 2009.

36. Martland, *Recording History*, p. 243.

37. Kier, "The Lindström AG," in Gronow and Hofer, eds, *The Lindström Project*, p. 27.

38. Gronow, "The Record Industry: The Growth of a Mass Medium," p. 63. Working from the dollar value of record sales in the US, Gronow shows a comparable drop from $75 million to $11 million; Jones shows that Gramophone's world profits dropped from 1.2 million pounds in 1928 to .3 million pounds in 1930 ("The Gramophone Company," p. 96).

39. On the complex history of Telefunken and Deutsche Grammophon, see Tschmuck, *Creativity and Innovation*, pp. 63–9.

40. Harry O. Sooy, "Memoirs of My Career at Victor Talking Machine Company 1898–1925," n.d., The David Sarnoff Library, davidsarnoff.org.

41. Ross Laird and Brian Rust, *Discography of OKeh Records, 1918–1934*, Praeger, 2004, pp. 8–14. See also Paul Oliver, *Barrelhouse Blues: Location Recording and the Early Traditions of the Blues*, Basic Books, 2009.

42. Niles, "Ballads, Songs, and Snatches," *The Bookman* (July 1928), p. 565.

43. Patrick Huber, *Linthead Stomp: The Creation of Country Music in the Piedmont South*, University of North Carolina Press, 2008, pp. 26–7.

44. John Lilienthal, "Selling Latin-American Field Successfully," *Talking Machine World* 24:5 (1928), pp. 16, 19. See also "Will Represent Columbia Co. in Central America," *Talking Machine World* 23.6 (1927), p. 98.

45. "Brunswick Export Manager Makes Extensive Visit to Latin America," *Talking Machine World* 24.6 (1928), p. 86.

46. "Brunswick Sends Men to Honolulu to Make New Hawaiian Records," *Honolulu Advertiser*, quoted in Ross Laird, *Brunswick Records: A Discography of Recordings, 1916–1931*, Greenwood Press, 2001, pp. 21–2. See also "Elmer Avery," *Recording Pioneers*, recordingpioneers.com.

47. Fowler quoted in Vernon, "Cairo Practice," pp. 26–7.

48. Paul Vernon, "A Look at the Engineers Who Made History Travelling the World Recording Its Music," *Vintage Jazz Mart* 94 (1994). Vernon tracks the recording sessions of many of the Gramophone engineers in his *Ethnic and*

Vernacular Music, 1898–1960: A Resource and Guide to Recordings, Greenwood Press, 1995.

49. Topp Fargion, liner notes to *Poetry and Languid Charm,* p. 2.

50. T. Malcolm Rockwell, *Hawaiian and Hawaiian Guitar Records 1891–1960,* Mahina Piha Press, 2007, p. xiii.

51. Ross Laird, *Brunswick Records: A Discography of Recordings, 1916–1931,* Greenwood Press, 2001, p. 24

52. Vernon, "Odeon Records." Paul Vernon, "Ancient Greeks," *Folk Roots* 133 (1994), pp. 32–3. Chris Waterman, liner notes to *Jùjú Roots 1930s–1950s,* Rounder CD5017, 1993.

53. Paul Vernon, "The Tango Trip," *Folk Roots* 136 (1994), pp. 33–4.

54. Franceschi, *A Casa Edison e Seu Tempo,* Sarapui, 2002; Wander Nunes Frota, "The Enactment of the Field of Cultural and Artistic Production of Popular Music in Brazil: A Case Study of the 'Noel Rosa Generation' in the 1930s," *Popular Music* 25.1 (2006), pp. 117–25.

55. Tschmuck, *Creativity and Innovation,* p. 24.

56. Suresh Chandvankar, "Odeon Label Discs in India," *The Record News* (2010), p. 16.

57. Philip Yampolsky, "Kroncong Revisited: New Evidence from Old Sources," *Archipel* 79 (2010), p. 13.

58. Sooy, "Memoir."

59. Du Jun Min, "The Development of Chinese Records to 1911," *Antique Phonograph News* (January–February 2008), capsnews.org.

60. Racy, *Musical Change and Commercial Recording in Egypt,* p. 97.

61. On pocketbook companies, see Andrew F. Jones, *Yellow Music: Media Culture and Colonial Modernity in the Chinese Jazz Age,* Duke University Press, 2001, p. 63.

62. For example, "Due to his position and responsibilities as recording director and as a result of his good ear and knowledge of music, Sémsis often transcribed the music of other composers and musicians who did not know how to write music themselves." Lisbet Torp, *Salonikiós,* "The Best Violin in the Balkans," Museum Tusculanum Press, 1993, p. 34.

63. Frota, "Enactment of the Field of Cultural and Artistic Production," p. 118.

64. Ibid., pp. 118–19.

65. Karush, *Culture of Class,* p. 48.

66. Pappas, "Concepts of Greekness," p. 358.

67. Quoted in Torp, *Salonikiós,* pp. 30 n. 52, 30 n. 51.

68. Harold G. Hagopian, liner notes to *Istanbul 1925,* Traditional Crossroads CD 4266, 1994, p. 3.

69. Mark Ainley, liner notes to *Living Is Hard: West African Music in Britain, 1927–1929,* Honest Jon's Records HJRCD33, 2008.

70. Paul Vernon, liner notes to *Early Guitar Music from West Africa 1927–1929,* Heritage HT CD 33, 2003.

71. David Coplan, *In Township Tonight!: South Africa's Black City Music and Theatre,* Ravan Press, 1985, p. 137.

72. Ahmed and Mohamed Elhabib Hachlaf, *Anthologie de la musique arabe: 1906–1960,* Publisud, 1993 , pp. 182–4.

73. Miliani, "Le Cheikh et le phonographe," p. 48 n. 17; Jonathan Ward, liner notes to *Opika Pende: Africa at 78rpm,* Dust-to-Digital DTD-22, 2011, p. 27.

74. William Howland Kenney, *Chicago Jazz: A Cultural History, 1904–1930,* Oxford University Press, 1993, p. 48; Stephen Calt, "The Anatomy of a 'Race'

Music Label: Mayo Williams and Paramount Records," in Norman Kelley, ed., *Rhythm & Business: The Political Economy of Black Music*, Akashic Books, 2002.

75. Anne Key Simpson, "Those Everlasting Blues: The Best of Clarence Williams," *Louisiana History* 40.2 (1999), p. 184; Lynn Abbott, "'Brown Skin, Who You For?' Another Look at Clarence Williams's Early Career," *The Jazz Archivist* 8.1–2 (1993), pp. 1–20; Tom Lord, *Clarence Williams*, Storyville Publications, 1976.

76. Quoted in Nat Shapiro and Nat Hentoff, eds, *Hear Me Talkin' to Ya: The Story of Jazz by the Men who Made It*, Penguin, 1962, p. 180.

77. Quoted in Laird, *Brunswick Records*, p. 22.

78. Pascale Casanova, *The World Republic of Letters*, Harvard University Press, 2004, pp. 88, 83, 13.

79. "In musical contexts," the *Grove Music Dictionary* notes, "the word 'guild'— like the German words *Zunft*, *Gilde*, and *Bruderschaft*, the French *confrérie*, the Spanish *corporación*, the Italian *arte* or the Czechoslovakian *cech*—denotes the gathering of individual musicians into a professional society." Heinrich W. Schwab, "Guilds," *Grove Music Online*, oxfordmusiconline.com.

80. Matthew Gelbart, *The Invention of "Folk Music" and "Art Music": Emerging Categories from Ossian to Wagner*, Cambridge University Press, 2007; Peter Van der Merwe, *Roots of the Classical: The Popular Origins of Western Music*, Oxford University Press, 2004, pp. 273–6.

81. Donald Sassoon, *The Culture of the Europeans: From 1800 to the Present*, HarperPress, 2006; David Gramit, *Cultivating Music: The Aspirations, Interests, and Limits of German Musical Culture, 1770–1848*, University of California Press, 2002; Scott, *Sounds of the Metropolis*.

82. Gerry Farrell, "The Early Days of the Gramophone Industry in India: Historical, Social and Musical Perspectives," *British Journal of Ethnomusicology* 2 (1993); pp. 31–9.

83. Frederick W. Gaisberg, *The Music Goes Round*, Macmillan Co., 1942, p. 34.

84. Min, "The Development of Chinese Records."

85. Vernon, "Cairo Practice."

86. Vernon, "Empire State"; Gokhan Ara, liner notes to *To Scratch Your Heart: Early Recordings from Istanbul*, Honest Jon's Records HJRCD 48, 2010.

87. Michael Kinnear, *The Gramophone Company's First Indian Recordings 1899–1908*, Popular Prakashan, 1994.

88. Stephen Hughes, "The 'Music Boom' in Tamil South India: Gramo phone, Radio and the Making of Mass Culture," *Historical Journal of Film, Radio and Television* 22.4 (2002), p. 449.

89. See Erika Brady, *A Spiral Way: How the Phonograph Changed Ethnography*, University Press of Mississippi, 1999.

90. Ernest Ansermet, "Sur un Orchestre Nègre," *Revue Romande* (October 1919), translated in Robert Walser, ed., *Keeping Time: Readings in Jazz History*, Oxford University Press, 1999; Darius Milhaud, "The Jazz Band and Negro Music," *Living Age* 323.4189 (1924), pp. 169–73.

91. There is an excellent literature on the mainstream reception of jazz in the 1920s, from Neil Leonard, *Jazz and the White Americans: The Acceptance of a New Form*, University of Chicago Press, 1962, and Kathy J. Ogren, *The Jazz Revolution: Twenties America and the Meaning of Jazz*, Oxford University Press, 1989, to Matthew F. Jordan, *Le Jazz: Jazz and French Cultural Identity*, University of Illinois Press, 2010.

92. "African Music: Where Is It?," *Ilanga Lase Natal*, February 10, 1933, quoted in Tim Couzens, *The New African: A Study of the Life and Work of H. I. E. Dhlomo*, Ravan Press, 1985, p. 54.

93. Isaac O. Delano, *The Soul of Nigeria*, T. W. Laurie, Ltd., 1937, pp. 153, 157.

94. This is a tendency of some excellent recent scholarship, including a fine collection of essays: E. Taylor Atkins, ed., *Jazz Planet*, University Press of Mississippi, 2003.

95. Tamara Elena Livingston-Isenhour and Thomas George Caracas Garcia, *Choro: A Social History of a Brazilian Popular Music*, Indiana University Press, 2005, p. 94. See also Rafael José de Menezes Bastos, "Brazil in France, 1922: An Anthropological Study of the Congenital International Nexus of Popular Music," *Latin American Music Review* 29:1 (2008), and Micol Seigel, *Uneven Encounters: Making Race and Nation in Brazil and the United States*, Duke University Press, 2009.

96. Noble, quoted in Elizabeth Tatar, *Strains of Change: The Impact of Tourism on Hawaiian Music*, Bishop Museum Press, 1987, p. 13.

97. Quoted in George S. Kanahele, ed., (revised and updated by John Berger), *Hawaiian Music and Musicians: An Encyclopedic History*, Mutual Publishing, 2012, p. 475.

98. Emilio Grenet, *Popular Cuban Music: 80 Revised and Corrected Compositions, Together with an Essay on the Evolution of Music in Cuba*, Carasa & Co., 1939, p. xxxiii.

99. Theodor W. Adorno, "On Jazz," and "Farewell to Jazz," in his *Essays on Music*, ed. Richard Leppert, University of California Press, 2002, pp. 470, 497, 472, 479, 483.

100. Burnet Hershey, "Jazz Latitude," *New York Times*, June 25, 1922.

101. J. A. Rogers, "Jazz at Home," in Alain Locke, ed., *The New Negro*, Simon & Schuster, 1997, p. 217.

102. Jeffrey H. Jackson, *Making Jazz French: Music and Modern Life in Interwar Paris*, Duke University Press, 2003, p. 23.

103. Michael Dregni, *Django: The Life and Music of a Gypsy Legend*, Oxford University Press, 2004, p. 96.

104. Jackson, *Making Jazz French*, p. 107. Jackson does note the fluidity of the term "jazz," pointing out that the title of the first French jazz periodical, *Jazz-Tango*, emphasized "that what united these two styles of dance music was more important than what distinguished them" (p. 42).

105. Dregni, *Django*, pp. 99–103.

106. Waterman, *Jùjú*, p. 8.

107. Jorge Luis Borges, "Genealogy of the Tango," in Borges, *On Argentina*, ed. Alfred Mac Adam, Penguin, 2010, p. 68.

108. Simon Collier, "The Tango Is Born: 1880s–1920s," in Simon Collier et al., *Tango! The Dance, the Song, the Story*, Thames and Hudson, 1995, pp. 41–2; Cohen, ed., *Tango Voices: Songs from the Soul of Buenos Aires and Beyond*, Wise Publications, 2007, p. 9.

109. Robert Farris Thompson, *Tango: The Art History of Love*, Pantheon Books, 2005, p. 82.

110. Peter Fryer, *Rhythms of Resistance: African Musical Heritage in Brazil*, Wesleyan University Press, 2000, p. 103.

111. Janet Sarbanes, "Musicking and Communitas: The Aesthetic Mode of Sociality in Rebetika Subculture," *Popular Music and Society* 29.1 (2006), p. 22; Stathis Gauntlett, "Mammon and the Greek Oriental Muse: Rebetika as a

Marketing Construct," in Elizabeth Close, Michael Tsianikas, and George Frazis, eds, *Greek Research in Australia: Proceedings of the Biennial International Conference of Greek Studies*, Flinders University, 2005, p. 183. See also Risto Pekka Pennanen, "The Development of Chordal Harmony in Greek Rebetika and Laika Music, 1930s to 1960s," *Ethnomusicology Forum* 6.1 (1997), p. 65 n. 1.

112. Wong Kee Chee, *The Age of Shanghainese Pops: 1930–1970*, Joint Publishing, 2001; Jonathan Stock, "Reconsidering the Past: Zhou Xuan and the Rehabilitation of Early Twentieth Century Popular Music," *Asian Music* 26.2 (1995), p. 32 n. 4.

113. Waterman, *Jùjú*, pp. 62–3, 75. See also Afolabi Alaja-Browne, *Juju Music: A Study of Its Social History and Style*, dissertation, University of Pittsburgh, 1985, p. 25.

114. Yampolsky, "Kroncong Revisited," p. 8.

115. Coplan, *In Township Tonight!*, pp. 94–5.

116. Moore, *Nationalizing Blackness*, p. 180.

117. Grenet, *Popular Cuban Music*, p. xlvii.

118. Quevedo, *Atilla's Kaiso*, pp. 3–4: "In my own experience of over a half-century's association with kaiso, carnival, and kaiso tents, the first word which I heard used to describe this song and dance form was 'kaiso.'" John Cowley, in *Carnival, Canboulay and Calypso*, pp. 138, 98, finds "calipso" first appearing in Trinidad's newspapers about 1900, though the earliest use is an 1882 account of the "abominable dance called Calypso."

119. Lawrence Gushee, *Pioneers of Jazz: The Story of the Creole Band*, Oxford University Press, 2005.

120. Brothers, *Louis Armstrong's New Orleans*, p. 133.

121. Ali Jihad Racy, *Making Music in the Arab World: The Culture and Artistry of Tarab*, Cambridge University Press, 2003, pp. 195–208.

122. Quevedo, *Atilla's Kaiso*, p. 4.

123. Quoted in Shapiro and Hentoff, eds, *Hear Me Talkin' to Ya*, p. 68. Brothers makes a similar argument about ragtime, distinguishing between ragtime as a "*genre*" and ragtime as "a set of *performance practices*" (*Louis Armstrong's New Orleans*, pp. 155–6).

124. E. V. Solomons, "The Krontjong—Java's Ukelele," *The Lloyd Mail*, October 1933, p. 238.

125. G. T., "Dancing," *Encyclopedia Britannica*, 12th edition, 1922, vol. 30, p. 796.

126. Hershey, "Jazz Latitude."

127. Dregni, *Django*, p. 40.

128. Jackson, *Making Jazz French*, p. 31.

129. E. Taylor Atkins, *Blue Nippon: Authenticating Jazz in Japan*, Duke University Press, 2001, pp. 108–9.

130. Quoted in Ballantine, *Marabi Nights*, p. 112.

131. Attali, *Noise*, p. 19.

132. Quoted in Jackson, *Making Jazz French*, p. 31.

133. Quoted in Moore, *Nationalizing Blackness*, p. 33.

134. Marta E. Savigliano, *Tango and the Political Economy of Passion*, Westview Press, 1995, p. 159.

135. Flavia Camargo Toni, ed., *A música popular brasileira na vitrola de Mário de Andrade*, SENAC, 2004.

136. *La Revue Du Monde Noir* 2 (1931).

137. *Musicalia* (January–February 1929).

138. *Revista de la Habana,* May 1930.
139. Alain Locke, "The Negro in American Culture," in V. F. Calverton, ed., *Anthology of American Negro Literature,* The Modern Library, 1929; Sterling Brown, "The Blues as Folk Poetry," *Folk-Say, A Regional Miscellany* 2 (1930).
140. Federico García Lorca, "Deep Song," in *In Search of Duende,* New Directions, 2010; Blas Infante, *Orígenes de lo Flamenco y Secreto del Cante Jondo (1929–1933),* Consejería de Cultura de la Junta de Andalucía, 1980. Both García Lorca and Infante would be killed by Franco's forces in the Spanish Civil War a few years later.
141. Ali Jihad Racy, "Historical Worldviews of Early Ethnomusicologists: An East-West Encounter in Cairo, 1932," in Stephen Blum, Philip V. Bohlman, and Daniel M. Neuman, eds, *Ethnomusicology and Modern Music History,* University of Illinois Press, 1991; Danielson, *The Voice of Egypt,* pp. 77, 81.
142. Lakshmi Subramanian, *From the Tanjore Court to the Madras Music Academy: A Social History of Music in South India,* Oxford University Press, 2011; Amanda J. Weidman, *Singing the Classical, Voicing the Modern: The Postcolonial Politics of Music in South India,* Duke University Press, 2006.
143. Jones, *Yellow Music,* pp. 35–52.
144. Mary Kawena Pukui, "Ancient Hulas of Kauai," *The Garden Island,* February–March 1936, and Mary Kawena Pukui, "The Hula, Hawaii's Own Dance," *Thrum's Hawaiian Almanac and Annual* (1942), both reprinted in Dorothy B. Barrère, Mary Kawena Pukui, and Marion Kelly, *Hula: Historical Perspectives,* Bishop Museum, 1980; Mary Kawena Pukui, "Songs (Meles) of Old Ka'u, Hawaii," *Journal of American Folklore* 62 (1949), pp. 247–58.
145. Gelbart, *The Invention of "Folk Music" and "Art Music."*
146. Rodney Gallop, "The Fado (The Portuguese Song of Fate)," *Musical Quarterly* 19.2 (1933), p. 211.
147. Quoted in Moore, *Nationalizing Blackness,* p. 106.
148. Stephen Erdely, "Bartók and folk music," in Amanda Bayley, ed., *The Cambridge Companion to Bartók,* Cambridge University Press, 2001.
149. Helen H. Roberts, *Ancient Hawaiian Music,* Bishop Museum, 1926.
150. Coplan, *In Township Tonight!,* p. 136.
151. Martin Stokes, *The Republic of Love: Cultural Intimacy in Turkish Popular Music,* University of Chicago Press, 2010, p. 17.
152. James Clifford, *The Predicament of Culture: Twentieth-Century Ethnography, Literature, and Art,* Harvard University Press, 1988.
153. John Szwed, *Alan Lomax: The Man Who Recorded the World,* Viking Penguin, 2010.
154. Sean Stroud, *The Defence of Tradition in Brazilian Popular Music: Politics, Culture and the Creation of Música Popular Brasileira,* Ashgate, 2008, p. 131–58.
155. Aaron Copland, "The World of the Phonograph," *American Scholar* 6.1 (1937), p. 33.
156. *Voice of Victor,* April 1923, quoted in Paul Vernon, "The World at 80 RPM," *Folk Roots* 119 (1993).
157. Béla Bartók, "At the Congress for Arab Music—Cairo, 1932 [1933]," in Benjamin Suchoff, *Béla Bartók Essays,* Faber & Faber, 1976, p. 38.
158. Jaap Kunst, "Musicological Exploration in the Indian Archipelago," *Asiatic Review* 32.112 (1936), p. 814.
159. "Musicus," *Umteteli wa Bantu,* November 11, 1933, quoted in Coplan, *In Township Tonight!,* p. 109.

160. *Umteteli wa Bantu*, January 9, 1932, quoted in Veit Erlmann, *African Stars: Studies in Black South African Performance*, University of Chicago Press, 1991, p. 145.
161. *Umteteli wa Bantu*, July 9, 1932, quoted in Ballantine, *Marabi Nights*, p. 31.
162. Quoted in Stroud, *Defence of Tradition in Brazilian Popular Music*, p. 13.
163. McCann, *Hello, Hello Brazil*, p. 16.
164. Quoted in Mark Pedelty, "The Bolero: the Birth, Life, and Decline of Mexican Modernity," *Latin American Music Review* 20.1 (Spring–Summer 1999), p. 40.
165. Newman I. White, *American Negro Folk-songs*, Harvard University Press, 1928, pp. 389–90.
166. Locke, "The Negro in American Culture," pp. 248–9.
167. José Maciel Ribeiro Fortes, quoted in Gallop, "The Fado," p. 201.
168. Jorge Luis Borges, "A History of the Tango," in Borges, *On Argentina*, ed. Alfred Mac Adam, Penguin, 2010, p. 102.
169. Pedelty, "The Bolero," p. 36.
170. "Jazzmania," *Umteteli wa Bantu*, February 11, 1933, quoted in Couzens, *The New African*, pp. 56–7.
171. Mary Kawena Pukui, "Games of My Hawaiian Childhood," *California Folklore Quarterly* 2.3 (1943), p. 220.
172. Andrée Nardal, "Notes on the Biguine Créole," *La Revue Du Monde Noir* 2 (1931), p. 51.
173. Amy Ku'uleialoha Stillman, "Textualizing Hawaiian Music," *American Music* 23.1 (2005), p. 76; Aiko Yamashiro, "Ethics in Song: Becoming Kama 'Āina in Hapa-Haole Music," *Cultural Analysis* 8 (2009), p. 17.
174. Quoted in Cushman, "¿De Qué Color Es el Oro?," p. 173.
175. Borges, "Genealogy of the Tango," p. 72.
176. Borges, "A History of the Tango," p. 108.
177. E. M. von Hornbostel, "African Negro Music," *Africa* 1.1 (1928), pp. 60 n. 2, 61.
178. Christopher A. Waterman, "The Uneven Development of Africanist Ethnomusicology: Three Issues and a Critique," in Bruno Nettl and Philip V. Bohlman, eds, *Comparative Musicology and Anthropology of Music: Essays on the History of Ethnomusicology*, University of Chicago Press, 1990, p. 175.
179. Quoted in Coplan, *In Township Tonight!*, p. 136.
180. Bálint Sárosi, *Gypsy Music*, Corvina Press, 1978, p. 60.
181. Van der Merwe, *Roots of the Classical*, pp. 108–9. Franz Liszt, *The Gipsy in Music: The Result of the Author's Life-Long Experiences and Investigations of the Gipsies and Their Music*, W. Reeves, 1926 (originally published in French in 1859). See Sárosi's excellent account of the Liszt controversy, *Gypsy Music*, pp. 141–50.
182. Béla Bartók, "Gypsy Music or Hungarian Music?," *Musical Quarterly* 33.2 (1947), pp. 240–1, 251. See also Julie Brown, "Bartók, the Gypsies and Hybridity in Music," in Georgina Born and David Hesmondhalgh, eds, *Western Music and Its Others: Difference, Representation, and Appropriation in Music*, University of California Press, 2000; and Katie Trumpener, "Béla Bartók and the Rise of Comparative Ethnomusicology: Nationalism, Race Purity, and the Legacy of the Austro-Hungarian Empire," in Ronald Radano and Philip V. Bohlman, eds, *Music and the Racial Imagination*, University of Chicago Press, 2000.
183. Ibid., p. 252.

184. For a fine history of the relation between the gypsy band and the popular sheet music, see Sárosi, *Gypsy Music*, Chapter 8.

185. Bartók, "Gypsy Music or Hungarian Music?," p. 242.

186. George Pullen Jackson, "The Genesis of the Negro Spiritual," *The American Mercury* 26.102 (1932), pp. 243–55.

187. Lee Watkins, "Minstrelsy and Mimesis in the South China Sea: Filipino Migrant Musicians, Chinese Hosts, and the Disciplining of Relations in Hong Kong," *Asian Music* 40.2 (2009), p. 89.

188. Hugh Tracey, "The State of Folk Music in Bantu Africa: A Brief Survey Delivered to the International Folk Music Council, on Behalf of the African Music Society," *African Music* 1.1 (1954), p. 11.

189. Van der Merwe, *Roots of the Classical*, pp. 461–2.

190. See, for example, "Light Music, Past and Present," *The Musical Standard* 18.469 (1902), p. 403. Derek B. Scott, "Other Mainstreams: Light Music and Easy Listening, 1920–70," in Nicholas Cook and Anthony Pople, eds, *The Cambridge History of Twentieth-Century Music*, Cambridge University Press, 2004; David Lelyveld, "Upon the Subdominant: Administering Music on All-India Radio," *Social Text* 39 (1994), pp. 120–1.

191. Bartók, "Gypsy Music or Hungarian Music?," pp. 241–2.

192. Quoted in Thomas Y. Levin and Michael von der Linn, "Elements of a Radio Theory: Adorno and the Princeton Radio Research Project," *Musical Quarterly* 78.2 (1994), p. 317.

193. Adorno, "On the Social Situation of Music," in *Essays on Music*, p. 425.

194. Rafael José de Menezes Bastos, "The 'Origin of Samba' as the Invention of Brazil (Why Do Songs Have Music?)," *Ethnomusicology Forum* 8.1 (1999), pp. 69–71. He argues that the first "musical universal of the West" was Gregorian chant, the motor of the Christianization of Europe, and the second was "Western music of the seventeenth to the nineteenth centuries, which defined Europe as a 'concert of nations' within the context of the relations between modern nation-states and the colonial world." Another powerful account sees the popular style as a musical universal but argues that it is not new: Peter Van der Merwe, in *Origins of the Popular Style*, argues that the musical language that dominates twentieth-century popular music—the blues ("the worldwide influence of the blues in the twentieth century is comparable in influence with the influence of the Italian popular style in the seventeenth and eighteenth centuries," p. 117)—was fully formed by 1900: "with the publication of the first blues the materials of the twentieth-century popular composer were complete … [Popular music] has come up with nothing that, fundamentally, cannot be traced back to 1900 or earlier" (p. 286).

195. There are a handful of early uses of the phrase in English in writings on folk musics: they range from an 1847 review of books of nursery rhymes that speaks of "what may be termed our vernacular music" ("Nursery Rhymes," *The Literary Gazette and Journal of the Belles Lettres* [February 6, 1847], p. 106) to an 1881 discussion of song and dance as "the vernacular music of the human race" ("State of Music Before the Rise of the Opera," *Monthly Musical Record* 11 [October 1, 1881], p. 185).

196. However, H. Evans's 1931 internal EMI report, "Review of the Present Vernacular Record Trade," still seems to refer to records made in the vernacular languages of Africa.

197. Charles Seeger, "Folk Music as a Source of Social History," in Caroline Ware, ed., *The Cultural Approach to History*, Columbia University Press, 1940,

p. 320. For a discussion of the early uses of vernacular as well as the Popular Front development of the concept, see Archie Green, "Vernacular Music: A Naming Compass," *Musical Quarterly* 77.1 (1993), p. 35. The term entered musicology in the 1970s and 1980s with influential uses in H. Wiley Hitchcock, *Music in the United States: A Historical Introduction*, Prentice-Hall, 1969; and Christopher Small, *Music of the Common Tongue: Survival and Celebration in Afro-American Music*, Riverrun Press, 1987.

198. It thus draws on a long and contested tradition of thinking of music as a language, discussed in, for example, Kathleen Marie Higgins, *The Music Between Us: Is Music a Universal Language?*, University of Chicago Press, 2012.

4.   Phonograph Culture

1. Theodor W. Adorno, "The Curves of the Needle," in his *Essays on Music*, Richard Leppert, ed., University of California Press, 2002, p. 273.

2. Theodor W. Adorno, *Current of Music: Elements of a Radio Theory*, Polity, 2009, p. 76.

3. This separation in time and place between making a sound and listening to it was dubbed "schizophonia" by the pioneering theorist of the soundscape R. Murray Schafer, *The Soundscape: Our Sonic Environment and the Tuning of the World*, Destiny Books, 1994, pp. 88, 90.

4. Adorno, *Current of Music*, pp. 90, 65, 118.

5. Pekka Gronow, "The Record Industry: The Growth of a Mass Medium," *Popular Music* 3 (1983), pp. 62–4.

6. "Louis S. Sterling, Chairman of Board of Columbia Co., Discusses World Trade," *Talking Machine World* 23.3 (1927), p. 1.

7. Tan Sooi Beng, "The 78rpm Record Industry in Malaya Prior to World War II," *Asian Music* 28.1 (1996), pp. 8–9.

8. S. Theodore Baskaran, *The Message Bearers: The Nationalist Politics and the Entertainment Media in South India, 1880–1945*, Cre-A, 1981, p. 56.

9. Stephen Hughes, "The 'Music Boom' in Tamil South India: Gramophone, Radio and the Making of Mass Culture," *Historical Journal of Film, Radio and Television* 22.4 (2002), p. 452.

10. *Rūz al-Yūsuf*, September 29, 1926, quoted in Virginia Danielson, *The Voice of Egypt: Umm Kulthūm, Arabic Song, and Egyptian Society in the Twentieth Century*, University of Chicago Press, 1997, p. 210 n. 32.

11. Quoted in Paul Vernon, "Empire State," *Folk Roots* 167 (1997), pp. 28–9.

12. Quoted in Rebecca P. Scales, "Subversive Sound: Transnational Radio, Arabic Recordings, and the Dangers of Listening in French Colonial Algeria, 1934–1939," *Comparative Studies in Society and History* 52.2 (2010), p. 399.

13. Quoted in Paul Vernon, "Feast of East," *Folk Roots* 145 (July 1995), pp. 26–7.

14. Christopher Ballantine, *Marabi Nights: Jazz, "Race" and Society in Early Apartheid South Africa*, University of KwaZulu-Natal Press, 2012, p. 24.

15. *Ilanga Lase Natal*, February 8, 1929, quoted in Tim Couzens, *The New African: A Study of the Life and Work of H. I. E. Dhlomo*, Ravan Press, 1985, p. 67.

16. Chris Waterman, liner notes to *Jùjú Roots 1930s–1950s*, Rounder CD5017, 1993.

17. John Collins, "One Hundred Years of Censorship in Ghanaian Popular Music Performance," in Michael Drewett and Martin Cloonan, eds, *Popular*

Music Censorship in Africa, Ashgate, 2006, p. 174. J. H. Nketia writes that "with increasing economic wealth offered by cocoa, many farmers in rural areas have been turning more and more to the products of industry and the gramophone is finding its way into many homes ... Stories are told in Kumasi of farmers who come down from the rich cocoa area of Ahafo to buy gramophones for their wives" ("The Gramophone and Contemporary African Music in the Gold Coast," Proceedings of the Fourth Annual Conference of the West African Institute of Social and Economic Research, 1956, p. 196.).

18. "Nation-wide Survey of Phonographs and Radios in Homes," *Talking Machine World* 23.4 (1927), pp. 10–11. Overall, phonographs were found in 46.2 percent of homes, ranging from 60.3 percent in cities larger than 100,000 to 29.0 percent in towns under 1,000. Radios, on the other hand, were found in only about a quarter of households.

19. Sebok quoted in *Talking Machine World* 23.2 (1927), p. 18.

20. Robert S. Lynd and Helen Merrell Lynd, *Middletown: A Study in Modern American Culture*, Harcourt Brace Jovanovich, 1956 [1929], p. 244 n. 35.

21. Quoted in Patrick Huber, *Linthead Stomp: The Creation of Country Music in the Piedmont South*, University of North Carolina Press, 2008, p. 15. A 1927 survey found that almost 40 percent of families in Gaston County, North Carolina owned phonographs, radios, or musical instruments; a 1935 survey of North Carolina mill families found that a third of them owned phonographs (Huber, p. 36).

22. Marybeth Hamilton, *In Search of the Blues*, Basic Books, 2008, p. 14.

23. Charles Hiroshi Garrett, *Struggling to Define a Nation: American Music and the Twentieth Century*, University of California Press, 2008, p. 91.

24. Ruth Glasser, *My Music Is My Flag: Puerto Rican Musicians and their New York Communities, 1917–1940*, University of California Press, 1995, p. 129.

25. Manuel Gamio, *Mexican Immigration to the United States: A Study of Human Migration and Adjustment*, University of Chicago Press, 1930, pp. 146–7, 70, 226.

26. Donald S. Castro, *The Argentine Tango as Social History, 1880–1955: The Soul of the People*, Mellen Research University Press, 1990, p. 137.

27. Oscar Chamosa, "Indigenous or Criollo: The Myth of White Argentina in Tucuman's Calchaqui Valley," *Hispanic American Historical Review* 88.1 (2008), p. 90.

28. Quoted in Gokhan Ara, liner notes to *To Scratch Your Heart: Early Recordings from Istanbul*, Honest Jon's Records HJRCD48 2010, p. 1.

29. Mark Ainley and Yeheskel Kojaman, liner notes, *Give Me Love: Songs of the Brokenhearted—Baghdad, 1925–1929*, Honest Jon's Records HJRCD35, 2008.

30. Glasser, *My Music Is My Flag*, p. 30.

31. Ali Jihad Racy, *Musical Change and Commercial Recording in Egypt, 1904–1932*, dissertation, University of Illinois at Urbana-Champaign, 1977, p. 169.

32. Nicholas G. Pappas, "Concepts of Greekness: The Recorded Music of Anatolian Greeks after 1922," *Journal of Modern Greek Studies* 17.2 (1999), p. 368 n. 13.

33. Jonathan Stock, "Reconsidering the Past: Zhou Xuan and the Rehabilitation of Early Twentieth Century Popular Music," *Asian Music* 26.2 (1995), p. 123.

34. Yokomitsu Riichi, *Shanghai*, University of Michigan Press, 2001, p. 7.

35. Beng, "The 78rpm Record Industry in Malaya," p. 14.

36. Waterman, liner notes to *Jùjú Roots 1930s-1950s*.

37. Nketia, "The Gramophone and Contemporary African Music," p. 196.
38. Ibid., p. 200.
39. Quoted in Danielson, *The Voice of Egypt*, p. 54.
40. Andrée Nardal, "Notes on the Biguine Créole," *La Revue Du Monde Noir* 2 (1931), p. 53.
41. Harold G. Hagopian, liner notes to *Women of Istanbul*, Traditional Crossroads CD 4280, 1998, p. 4.
42. *Straits Times*, quoted in Beng, "The 78rpm Record Industry in Malaya," p. 15.
43. Evans quoted in Janet Topp Fargion, liner notes to *Poetry and Languid Charm: Swahili Music from Tanzania and Kenya from the 1920s to the 1950s*, Topic TSCD 936, 2007, p. 3.
44. Paul Bowles, *Paul Bowles on Music*, eds Timothy Mangan and Irene Herrmann, University of California Press, 2003, pp. 75–6, orginally published in 1943.
45. Quoted in Rodney Gallop, "Some Records of the Portuguese Fado," *The Gramophone* (October 1931), p. 173.
46. Bryan McCann, *Hello, Hello Brazil: Popular Music in the Making of Modern Brazil*, Duke University Press, 2004, p. 26.
47. Robin Moore, *Nationalizing Blackness: Afrocubanismo and Artistic Revolution in Havana, 1920–1940*, University of Pittsburgh Press, 1997, p. 168.
48. Couzens, *The New African*, p. 67.
49. See McCann, *Hello, Hello Brazil*, pp. 12, 57, 87, for details on Afro-Brazilians and the music industry.
50. Paul Gilroy, *The Black Atlantic: Modernity and Double Consciousness*, Harvard University Press, 1993, p. 4.
51. Sunil Amrith, "Tamil Diasporas across the Bay of Bengal," *American Historical Review* 114.3 (2009), pp. 561–3; Stephen Hughes, "The Sound of RMRL," *Maatruveli Aayvitazh* 4 (2010), pp. 77–8; Peter Manuel, *East Indian Music in the West Indies: Tān-Singing, Chutney, and the Making of Indo-Caribbean Culture*, Temple University Press, 2000, p. 46.
52. Maud Cuney-Hare, *Negro Musicians and Their Music*, Da Capo Press, 1974, [ca. 1936], pp. 29, 259.
53. Vernon, liner notes to *West African Instrumental Quintet 1929*, Heritage HT CD 16, 1992.
54. *Parlophon: Discos Publicados, Junho 1928–Junho 1929*, p. 33.
55. Ballantine, *Marabi Nights*, p. 23.
56. Waterman, *Jùjú*, pp. 46–7; Bob W. White, *Rumba Rules: The Politics of Dance Music in Mobutu's Zaire*, Duke University Press, 2008, p. 39; Veit Erlmann, *African Stars: Studies in Black South African Performance*, University of Chicago Press, 1991, p. 94.
57. Hugh Tracey, "Recording Tour, May to November 1950 East Africa," *Newsletter, African Music Society*, 1951, p 41.
58. Rita Montaner, "El Manisero," Columbia 2965x, 1928; Trio Matamoros, "El Manicero," Victor 46401, 1929; Havana Casino Orchestra, "The Peanut Vendor," Victor 224830, 1930. For the recording history, see Discography of American Historical Recordings, adp.library.ucsb.
59. Takonai Susumu, "Soeara NIROM and Musical Culture in Colonial Indonesia," trans. Ishibashi Makoto, *Kyoto Review of Southeast Asia* 8–9 (2007), kyotoreviewsea.org.
60. The Don Apiazu version was GV1 and the Trio Matamoros version was GV3; see *Out of Cuba: Latin American Music Takes Africa By Storm*, Topic Records TSCD 927, 2004. See also John Cowley, "uBungca (Oxford Bags): Recordings

in London of African and West Indian Music in the 1920s and 1930s," *Musical Traditions* 12 (1994), mustrad.org.uk.

61. Richard M. Shain, "Roots in Reverse: Cubanismo in Twentieth-Century Senegalese Music," *International Journal of African Historical Studies* 35.1 (2002), p. 87.

62. Waterman, *Jùjú*, p. 47.

63. Quoted in Gary Stewart, *Rumba on the River: A History of the Popular Music of the Two Congos*, Verso, 2004, p. 13.

64. Bob W. White, *Rumba Rules: The Politics of Dance Music in Mobutu's Zaire*, Duke University Press, 2008, p. 40.

65. See Adria L. Imada, *Aloha America: Hula Circuits Through the U.S. Empire*, Duke University Press, 2012; Cyril LeFebvre, "Hawaiian Music in France," and John D. Marsden, "Hawaiian Music in Great Britain," in George S. Kanahele, ed., (revised and updated by John Berger), *Hawaiian Music and Musicians: An Encyclopedic History*, Mutual Publishing, 2012, pp. 156–82, 222–35; Shuhei Hosokawa, "East of Honolulu: Hawaiian Music in Japan from the 1920s to the 1940s," *Perfect Beat* 2.1 (1994), pp. 51–67.

66. Kanahele, *Hawaiian Music and Musicians*, pp. 352–5. Jim Tranquada and John King, *The 'Ukulele: A History*, University of Hawaii Press, 2012, pp. 130–1.

67. Bob Brozman, "The Tau Moe Family," bobbrozman.com. See also The Tau Moe Family with Bob Brozman, *Ho'Omana'o I Na Mele O Ka Wa U'i (Remembering the Songs of Our Youth)*, Rounder CD 6028, 2002.

68. Kanahele, *Hawaiian Music and Musicians*, pp. 348–51. Martin Clayton, "The Many Lives of the Indian Guitar," in Andy Bennett and Kevin Dawe, eds, *Guitar Cultures*, Berg, 2001, pp. 187–8.

69. Kanahele, *Hawaiian Music and Musicians*, pp. 352–5. Philip Yampolsky, *Music and Media in the Dutch East Indies: Gramophone Records and Radio in the Late Colonial Era, 1903–1942*, dissertation, University of Washington, 2013, p. 38.

70. Miss Ninja, "Terang Beolan"/"Gitaar Berboenji," Columbia DB30192, 1937, the first track re-released on *Rhythm of the Islands: Music of Hawaii 1913–1952*, Harlequin HQ CD 92, 1996, and the second on *Steeling Around the World Hawaiian Style*, Harlequin HQ CD 182, 2003. See Rockwell, *Hawaiian Records*, pp. 872–3; Beng, "The 78rpm Record Industry in Malaya," 15.

71. *Parlophon*, p. 33.

72. Rockwell, *Hawaiian Records*, pp. 50–2.

73. Waterman, *Jùjú*, p. 47.

74. Motsieloa, "Aubuti Nkikho," 1930, re-released on CD accompanying Ballantine, *Marabi Nights*; see Ballantine, pp. 207–8.

75. Clayton, "The Many Lives of the Indian Guitar," in Bennett and Dawe, eds, *Guitar Cultures*, p. 206 n. 19.

76. E. V. Solomons, "The Krontjong—Java's Ukelele," *The Lloyd Mail*, October 1933, p. 236.

77. "The term 'rumba' was used more loosely in the Congos—nearly anything with a clave-type rhythm was labeled a rumba." Jonathan Ward, liner notes to *Opika Pende: Africa at 78rpm*, Dust-to-Digital DTD 22, 2011, p. 64.

78. Danielson, *The Voice of Egypt*, pp. 27–8; Racy, *Musical Change and Commercial Recording in Egypt*, p. 169.

79. Brothers, *Louis Armstrong's New Orleans*, p. 246.

80. Danny Barker, *A Life in Jazz*, Alyn Shipton, ed., Macmillan Press, 1986, p. 42.; Rex Stewart, *Boy Meets Horn*, Claire P. Gordon, ed., University of Michigan Press, 1991, p. 72.

81. Gerald Howson, *The Flamencos of Cádiz Bay*, Bold Strummer, 1994, p. 13. The story has its origin in Fernando el de Triana, *Arte y Artistas Flamencos*, Madrid, 1935, pp. 216–20.
82. Nketia, "The Gramophone and Contemporary African Music," p. 201.
83. Shain, "Roots in Reverse," pp. 87–8.
84. Michael Dregni, *Django: The Life and Music of a Gypsy Legend*, Oxford University Press, 2004, p. 53.
85. Kanahele, *Hawaiian Music and Musicians*, p. 560.
86. Ibid., pp. 321–4, 746–8.
87. Kumasi Trio, "Asin Asin Part Two," Zonophone EZ, re-released on *Living Is Hard: West African Music in Britain, 1927–1929*, Honest Jon's Records HJRCD33, 2008.
88. Lyrics translated from Fante in liner notes to *Living Is Hard*.
89. Solomons, "The Krontjong," p. 238.
90. Quoted in Vernon, "Feast of East," 26–7.
91. Quoted in Vernon, "Odeon Records."
92. Waterman, *Jùjú*, p. 77.
93. Moore, *Nationalizing Blackness*, p. 108.
94. G. N. Joshi, "A Concise History of the Phonograph Industry in India," *Popular Music* 7.2 (1988), pp. 151–2.
95. Nat Shapiro and Nat Hentoff, eds, *Hear Me Talkin' to Ya: The Story of Jazz by the Men who Made It*, Penguin, 1962, p. 240. Dorsey quoted in Sandra Lieb, *Mother of the Blues: A Study of Ma Rainey*, University of Massachusetts Press, 1983, p. 29.
96. Niles, "Ballads, Songs, and Snatches" (February 1928), p. 652.
97. Niles, "Ballads, Songs, and Snatches" (January 1929), p. 570.
98. The best account of Niles is Elliott S. Hurwitt, "Abbe Niles, Blues Advocate," in David Evans, ed., *Ramblin' on My Mind: New Perspectives on the Blues*, University of Illinois Press, 2008.
99. Rodney Gallop, "Basque Songs," *The Gramophone* (June 1928), p. 44.
100. Rodney Gallop, "The New H.M.V. Greek Records," *The Gramophone* (June 1928), p. 27. The best account of Gallop is Paul Vernon, "Strange Music: Rodney Gallop," *fRoots* 305 (2008), pp. 51–3.
101. Gallop, "Spanish Folk-Music Records," p. 266.
102. Niles, "Ballads, Songs, and Snatches" (June 1928), p. 423.
103. Gallop, "Some Records of the Portuguese Fado," p. 173.
104. Gallop, "The New H.M.V. Greek Records," p. 27.
105. Niles, "Ballads, Songs, and Snatches" (June 1928), p. 422.
106. Niles, "Ballads, Songs, and Snatches" (July 1928), p. 565.
107. Niles, "Ballads, Songs, and Snatches" (September 1928), p. 76.
108. Rodney Gallop, "The Parlophone Music of All Nations Series," *The Gramophone* (March 1935), p. 405.
109. Rodney Gallop, "In Praise of the Gramophone," *The Gramophone* (July 1934), p. 47.
110. As the *Oxford English Dictionary* puts it, "a piece or collection of music issued on record, cassette, CD, etc.," citing an early instance in 1919.
111. The use of the standard phrase "78 rpm" obscured much variation in actual recording and playing speeds, an issue that has engaged subsequent recording engineers and music transcribers as they analyze and remaster the recordings, often uncertain about the original key of a work.
112. Howson, *The Flamencos of Cádiz Bay*, p. 185. Occasionally, a single song

was divided into two parts, one on each side of the disc (the Kumasi Trio's "Yaa Amponsah" and Charley Patton's "High Water Everywhere" are examples). Radio and film tempered this tendency: for example, in Egypt, Umm Kulthūm's radio broadcasts from 1934 allowed her to perform longer works than did the 78 rpm disc, and became much more central to the electrical circulation of her music.

113. Walter Benjamin, "The Work of Art in the Age of Its Technical Reproducibility: Third Version," in *Walter Benjamin: Selected Writings, Volume 4, 1938–1940*, eds. Howard Eiland and Michael W. Jennings, Harvard University Press, 2003, pp. 266–9. It was this character that was a fundamental basis of Adorno's critique of gramophone music: "They show, instead, a tendency to mingle in his everyday life because they can appear at practically every moment, and because he can accompany brushing his teeth with the Allegretto of the Seventh" (Adorno, *Current of Music*, p. 91).

114. Michael E. Veal, *Fela: The Life and Times of an African Musical Icon*, Temple University Press, 2000, p. 35.

115. Simon Collier, "The Tango Is Born: 1880s–1920s," in Simon Collier et al., *Tango! The Dance, the Song, the Story, Thames and Hudson*, 1995, pp. 62–4.

116. Gallop, "The Fado," p. 211; Virgil Thomson, "The Cult of Jazz," *Vanity Fair* (June 1925).

117. Robert Sprigge, "The Ghanaian Highlife: Notation and Sources," *Music in Ghana* 2 (1961), pp. 89–94.

118. Solomons, "The Krontjong," p. 236.

119. Kenneth Burke, "Literature as Equipment for Living," in his *The Philosophy of Literary Form*, University of California Press, 1974.

120. W. C. Handy, ed., *Blues: An Anthology*, Albert & Charles Boni, 1926; *Johnny Noble's Collection of Ancient and Modern Hulas*, Miller Music, 1935; see Amy Kuʻuleialoha Stillman, "'Aloha Aina': New Perspectives on 'Kaulana Nā Pua'," *Hawaiian Journal of History* 33 (1999), pp. 91–2.

121. Quoted in Alison Raphael, *Samba and Social Control: Popular Culture and Racial Democracy in Rio de Janeiro*, dissertation, Columbia University, 1980, pp. 80–1. Instances of popular crooners buying samba songs from vernacular musicians was such a common occurrence that the story became part of samba's folklore; a film depiction of such a scene from the early 1930s is included in the documentary film *Cartola*, directed by Lírio Ferreira and Hilton Lacerda, Europa Filmes, 2007.

122. For the US case, see Karl Hagstrom Miller, *Segregating Sound: Inventing Folk and Pop Music in the Age of Jim Crow*, Duke University Press, 2010, pp. 235–7.

123. Béla Bartók, "Gypsy Music or Hungarian Music?," *Musical Quarterly* 33.2 (1947): 240–1, p. 252.

124. Curt Sachs, *World History of the Dance*, W. W. Norton, 1937, pp. 444–5.

125. Quoted in Timothy Brennan, "Introduction" to Alejo Carpentier, *Music in Cuba*, University of Minnesota Press, 2001, p. 50.

126. Nathaniel Bright Emerson, *Unwritten Literature of Hawaii: The Sacred Songs of the Hula*, Bureau of American Ethnology, Bulletin 38, 1909, pp. 250–1.

127. Elijah Wald, "What the Records Missed," in his *Escaping the Delta: Robert Johnson and the Invention of the Blues*, Amistad, 2004, pp. 43–69; Miller, *Segregating Sound*, pp. 216–17.

128. Waterman, *Jùjú*, p. 235 n. 6.

129. Gisèle Dubouillé, "New Records of Negro Music," *La Revue Du Monde Noir* 3 (1932): p. 57.

130. William Washabaugh, *Flamenco: Passion, Politics, and Popular Culture*, Berg Publishers, 1996, pp. 63–4.

131. Peter Doyle, *Echo and Reverb: Fabricating Space in Popular Music, 1900–1960*, Wesleyan University Press, 2005, pp. 8, 36, 68–70.

5. Decolonizing the Ear

1. Vijay Prashad, *The Darker Nations: A People's History of the Third World*, The New Press, 2007, pp. 16–30; Ricardo Melgar Bao, "The Anti-Imperialist League of the Americas Between the East and Latin America," *Latin American Perspectives* 35.2 (March 2008), pp. 9–24; Cemil Aydin, *The Politics of Anti-Westernism in Asia: Visions of World Order in Pan-Islamic and Pan-Asian Thought*, Columbia University Press, 2007, p. 156.

2. Martin Shipway, *Decolonization and Its Impact: A Comparative Approach to the End of the Colonial Empires*, Blackwell Publishing, 2008, p. 2.

3. Frederick Cooper, *Colonialism in Question: Theory, Knowledge, History*, University of California Press, 2005, pp. 200, 24.

4. Shipway, *Decolonization and Its Impact*, p. 11.

5. Brent Hayes Edwards, *The Practice of Diaspora: Literature, Translation, and the Rise of Black Internationalism*, Harvard University Press, 2003, p. 243.

6. For the idea of the Third World as a political project, see Prashad, *The Darker Nations*.

7. Kofi Agawu, "How Europe Underdeveloped Africa Tonally," in Tejumola Olaniyan and Ronald Radano, eds, *Audible Empire: Music, Global Politics, Critique*, Duke University Press, forthcoming.

8. On Caluza, see Veit Erlmann, *African Stars: Studies in Black South African Performance*, University of Chicago Press, 1991; on Amu, see Kofi Agawu, "The Amu Legacy," *Africa* 66.2 (1996): 274–9.

9. E. M. von Hornbostel, "African Negro Music," *Africa* 1.1 (1928), p. 62.

10. Rob Boonzajer Fleas, *Brass Unbound: Secret Children of the Colonial Brass Band*, Royal Tropical Institute, 2000. Andrew Jones argues that, in China, "by the 1860s, choral singing and brass bands, introduced by foreign military advisors, had become a standard means of drill instruction and morale-building in the Qing army. These practices were later adopted by warlord armies, nationalist military units, and Communist guerillas in the 1920s and 1930s" (*Yellow Music: Media Culture and Colonial Modernity in the Chinese Jazz Age*, Duke University Press, 2001, p. 25).

11. Trevor Herbert and Margaret Sarkissian, "Victorian Bands and Their Dissemination in the Colonies," *Popular Music* 16.2 (1997), p. 172.

12. For Egypt, see Virginia Danielson, *The Voice of Egypt: Umm Kulthūm, Arabic Song, and Egyptian Society in the Twentieth Century*, University of Chicago Press, 1997, p. 27; for Cuba, see Robin Moore, *Nationalizing Blackness: Afrocubanismo and Artistic Revolution in Havana, 1920–1940*, University of Pittsburgh Press, 1997, p. 19; for East Africa, see Stephen H. Martin, "Brass Bands and the Beni Phenomenon in Urban East Africa," *African Music* 7.1 (1991), pp. 72–81; for Vietnam, see Jason Gibbs, "Spoken Theater, La Scène Tonkinoise, and the First Modern Vietnamese Songs," *Asian Music* 31.2 (2000), pp. 1–33.

13. Askari Wa K.A.R. Ya Sita (6th K.A.R.), "Kofia Nyekundu," Columbia WE

10, 1930, re-released on *Echoes of Africa: Early Recordings*, Wergo SM 1624 2, 2002.

14. Agawu, "How Europe Underdeveloped Africa Tonally," in Olaniyan and Radano, eds, *Audible Empire*.

15. Mohandas K. Gandhi, *An Autobiography: The Story of My Experiments with Truth*, Beacon Press, 1993, pp. 50–1, 172–3.

16. David Lelyveld, "Upon the Subdominant: Administering Music on All-India Radio," *Social Text* 39 (Summer 1994), p. 113.

17. Theodor W. Adorno, "On Jazz," in his *Essays on Music*, Richard Leppert, ed., University of California Press, 2002, pp. 477–8.

18. Quoted in Joshua H. Howard, "The Making of a National Icon: Commemorating Nie Er, 1935–1949," *Twentieth-Century China* 37.1 (2012), pp. 8–9.

19. Claude McKay, *Banjo: A Story without a Plot*, Harcourt, Brace, Jovanovich, 1970, pp. 311, 315–16.

20. Ibid., p. 316.

21. David Macey, *Frantz Fanon: A Biography*, Picador, 2000, pp. 123–4.

22. Frantz Fanon, *Toward the African Revolution*, Grove Press, 1967, p. 19.

23. Frantz Fanon, *A Dying Colonialism*, Grove Press, 1967, p. 74.

24. Macey, *Frantz Fanon*, p. 124.

25. Frantz Fanon, *Black Skin, White Masks*, Grove Press, 2008, pp. 183–4, 200–1.

26. Fanon, *Toward the African Revolution*, p. 37.

27. Frantz Fanon, *The Wretched of the Earth*, Grove, 2005, pp. 175–6.

28. Édouard Glissant, *Caribbean Discourse: Selected Essays*, University Press of Virginia, 1989, pp.110–12.

29. Moore, *Nationalizing Blackness*, pp. 166–7.

30. Marta E. Savigliano, *Tango and the Political Economy of Passion*, Westview Press, 1995, pp. 1–2.

31. Edwards, *The Practice of Diaspora*, p. 146. In Edwards's account of beguine in the music halls of Paris, he distinguishes between dance venues, noting that the second Bal Nègre "became a means for the Antillean community to evade the throngs of European spectators who were overwhelming the first Bal Nègre."

32. Haunani-Kay Trask, "'Lovely Hula Hands': Corporate Tourism and the Prostitution of Hawaiian Culture," in her *From a Native Daughter: Colonialism and Sovereignty in Hawai'i*, University of Hawaii Press, 1999, pp.144–5.

33. Fanon, *The Wretched of the Earth*, p. 176.

34. Danielson, *The Voice of Egypt*, pp. 47, 49, 213, 83; see also Amira Mitchell, liner notes to *Women of Egypt, 1924–1931*, Topic TSCD931, 2006, 9–10.

35. Quoted in Jones, *Yellow Music*, p. 91.

36. S. Theodore Baskaran, *The Message Bearers: The Nationalist Politics and the Entertainment Media in South India, 1880–1945*, Cre-A, 1981, p. 57.

37. Ibid., pp. 38, 57; see also the documentary film *K. B. Sundarambal: The Legend*, Central Institute of Indian Languages.

38. Christopher Ballantine, *Marabi Nights: Jazz, "Race" and Society in Early Apartheid South Africa*, University of KwaZulu-Natal Press, 2012, pp. 68–70; David Coplan, *In Township Tonight!: South Africa's Black City Music and Theatre*, Ravan Press, 1985, pp. 134–5, 142 n. 84; Erlmann, *African Stars*, p. 171.

39. Ballantine, *Marabi Nights*, pp. 71–2.

40. Moore, *Nationalizing Blackness*, p. 78.

41. Ibid., p. 97.

42. Ned Sublette, *Cuba and Its Music: From the First Drums to the Mambo*, Chicago Press Review, 2004, pp. 408, 455, 495, 508, 492.

43. Savigliano, *Tango and the Political Economy of Passion*, p. 159.
44. Quoted in Savigliano, *Tango and the Political Economy of Passion*, p. 143.
45. Robert Farris Thompson, *Tango: The Art History of Love*, Pantheon Books, 2005, pp. 199–204; María Susana Azzi, "The Tango, Peronism, and Astor Piazzolla during the 1940s and '50s," in Walter Aaron Clark, ed., *From Tejano to Tango: Latin American Popular Music*, Routledge, 2002, p. 29.
46. Matthew B. Karush, *Culture of Class: Radio and Cinema in the Making of a Divided Argentina, 1920–1946*, Duke University Press, 2012, pp. 152–6, 188, 199–200.
47. Waterman, *Jùjú*, pp. 80, 75.
48. Ballantine, *Marabi Nights*, p. 68; see also Erlmann, *African Stars*, pp. 87–91.
49. Quoted in Stephen Hughes, "The 'Music Boom' in Tamil South India: Gramophone, Radio and the Making of Mass Culture," *Historical Journal of Film, Radio and Television* 22.4 (2002), p. 468. See S. Theodore Baskaran, "Satyamurthi: the Link That Snapped," *Economic and Political Weekly* 29.38 (September 17, 1994), pp. 2482–5; and S. Theodore Baskaran, "Music for the Masses: Film Songs of Tamil Nadu," *Economic and Political Weekly* 26.11/12 (March 1991), pp. 755–8.
50. Jonathan Derrick, *Africa's "Agitators": Militant Anticolonialism in Africa and the West, 1918–1939*, Columbia University Press, 2008, p. 277.
51. Quoted in ibid., p. 229.
52. Mark Ainley, liner notes to *Living Is Hard: West African Music in Britain, 1927–1929*, Honest Jon's Records HJRCD33, 2008.
53. John Cowley, "Cultural 'Fusions': Aspects of British West Indian Music in the USA and Britain 1918–51," *Popular Music* 5 (1985), pp. 81–96.
54. Raymond Quevedo (Atilla the Hun), *Atilla's Kaiso: A Short History of Trinidad Calypso*, University of the West Indies, 1983, pp. 37–8. The date is not stated, but seems to coincide with the visit of Calthorpe's cricket team to Trinidad, January 21–23, 1926. Gordon Rohlehr, however, dates it at 1920 (*Calypso and Society in Pre-Independence Trinidad*, G. Rohlehr, 1990, pp. 105, 546 n. 45).
55. Baskaran, *The Message Bearers*, p. 54.
56. *The Mexican Revolution: Corridos about the Heroes and Events 1910–1920 and Beyond*, Arhoolie Folkloric CD7041-7044, 1996.
57. Lawrence P. Frank, "Ideological Competition in Nigeria: Urban Populism Versus Elite Nationalism," *Journal of Modern African Studies* 17.3 (1979), p. 442.
58. Oluwa, "Orin Herbert Macaulay,"* Parlophone PO. 508, 1936 Tunde King and His Group, "Aronke Macaulay,"* Waterman, *Jùjú*, p. 234 n. 6, 56–7.
59. Caluza's Double Quartet, "Vul'indhlela mnta ka Dube,"* Zonophone 4280, 1930. Tim Couzens writes of the published version of Caluza's "directly political songs such as 'Vulindlela Mtaka Dube' and 'Bashuka Ndabazine,'" in which "he exhorted his listeners to unite behind [ANC leader John] Dube and the other representatives of the 1914 delegation to England because 'We are taxed heavily—we have to pay poll-tax, carry passes for which we must pay, we have to pay dipping fees and even dog tax—we have no parliamentary representative—we want Africans to represent us'" (*The New African: A Study of the Life and Work of H. I. E. Dhlomo*, Ravan Press, 1985, p. 56). See also Erlmann, *African Stars*, p. 120.
60. Jolly Orchestra, "Wallace Johnson," Parlophone PO.570, 1936, re-released on cassette accompanying Waterman, *Jùjú*; see Waterman, p. 50. On Wallace Johnson, see Derrick, *Africa's "Agitators,"* pp. 202–5, 294.
61. For a detailed account, see Dick Spottswood, "Who Was Butler?" in The Classic

Calypso Collective, *West Indian Rhythm*, p. 53. See also Donald R. Hill, *Calypso Calaloo: Early Carnival Music in Trinidad*, University Press of Florida, 1993, pp. 197–203; and Rohlehr, *Calypso and Society in Pre-Independence Trinidad*, pp. 200–12.

62. Atilla the Hun, "The Commission's Report," Decca De 17350, 1938, re-released on *Calypsos from Trinidad: Politics, Intrigue & Violence in the 1930s*, Arhoolie CD 7004, 1991, and on *West Indian Rhythm*.

63. Quevedo, *Atilla's Kaiso*, pp. 58–9.

64. Atilla the Hun, "Mr Nankivell's Speech," Decca De 17394, 1938; Atilla the Hun, "The Governor's Resignation," Decca De 17363, 1938, both re-released on *Calypsos from Trinidad* and on *West Indian Rhythm*.

65. Atilla the Hun, "The Strike," Decca De 17371, 1938, and Atilla the Hun, "Where Was Butler?" Decca De 17385, 1938, both re-released on *Calypsos from Trinidad* and on *West Indian Rhythm*.

66. Sexteto Nacional, "Incitadora Región," Brunswick 41092, 1930; Moore, *Nationalizing Blackness*, p. 123.

67. Jones, *Yellow Music*, pp. 69, 111.

68. Gibbs, "The West's Songs, Our Songs," pp. 62–3. Gibbs, "Spoken Theater, La Scène Tonkinoise, and the First Modern Vietnamese Songs," p. 28 n. 27.

69. Umm Kulthūm, "Ljmay Ya Misr!" Odeon FA 224 639, 1936.

70. Couzens, *The New African*, p. 56. See also Coplan, *In Township Tonight!*, p. 75.

71. Akropong Singing Band, "Yen Ara Asase Ni," Parlophone UTC89, 1931. Arlt, "The Union Trade Company and Its Recordings," 401 n. 17. See also Agawu, "The Amu Legacy," pp. 274–5.

72. Gibbs, "The West's Songs, Our Songs," p. 63; The West African Instrumental Quintet, "Bea Tsin No. 2," Zonophone EZ 494, 1929, re-released on *West African Instrumental Quintet 1929*, Heritage HT CD 16.

73. Ranajit Guha, *Elementary Aspects of Peasant Insurgency in Colonial India*, Duke University Press, 1999, p. 39.

74. Bronia Kornhauser, "In Defence of Kroncong," in Margaret Kartomi, ed., *Studies in Indonesian Music*, Center of Southeast Asian Studies, Monash University, 1978, pp. 104–83.

75. Quoted in Rudolf Mrázek, *Engineers of a Happy Land: Technology and Nationalism in a Colony*, Princeton University Press, 2002, p. 196.

76. Tan Sooi Beng, "The 78rpm Record Industry in Malaya Prior to World War II," *Asian Music* 28.1 (1996), pp. 14–15.

77. Quevedo, *Atilla's Kaiso*, p. 55.

78. Collins, "One Hundred Years of Censorship," in Drewett and Cloonan, eds, *Popular Music Censorship in Africa*, pp. 172, 173.

79. Noenoe K. Silva, "He Kānāwai E Ho'opau I Na Hula Kuolo Hawai'i: The Political Economy of Banning the Hula," *Hawaiian Journal of History* 34 (2000), p. 46.

80. Quevedo, *Atilla's Kaiso*, p. 55.

81. Moore, *Nationalizing Blackness*, p. 96.

82. Ibid., pp. 31, 170.

83. Isabelle Leymarie, *Cuban Fire: The Saga of Salsa and Latin Jazz*, Continuum, 2002, pp. 54–6, 44–5.

84. Marc A. Hertzman, *Making Samba: A New History of Race and Music in Brazil*, Duke University Press, 2013, pp. 31–65.

85. Ballantine, *Marabi Nights*, p. 88.

86. Thomas Brothers, *Louis Armstrong's New Orleans*, W. W. Norton, 2006, p. 14; Gregory T. Cushman, "¿De Qué Color Es el Oro? Race, Environment, and the History of Cuban National Music, 1898–1958," *Latin American Music Review* 26.2 (2005), p. 170; Moore, *Nationalizing Blackness*, pp. 29–30.

87. Gisèle Dubouillé, "New Records of Negro Music," *La Revue Du Monde Noir*, 3, 1932, 55.

88. Jorge Luis Borges, "Genealogy of the Tango," in Borges, *On Argentina*, edited by Albert Mac Adam, Penguin, 2010, p. 68. See also Matthew Karush, "Blackness in Argentina: Jazz, Tango and Race before Perón," *Past and Present* 216 (2012), pp. 215–45.

89. Sánchez de Fuentes quoted in Moore, *Nationalizing Blackness*, p. 25; Carpentier, *Music in Cuba*, pp. 256, 266–7. See also Gema R. Guevara, "Narratives of Racial Authority in Cuban Popular Music," *Journal of Popular Music Studies* 17.3 (2005), pp. 255–74.

90. Frederick W. Gaisberg, "The Gramophone Goes East," in his *The Music Goes Round*, Macmillan Co., 1942.

91. Jones, *Yellow Music*, pp. 11–12.

92. Nketia, "The Gramophone and Contemporary African Music," p. 200.

93. Baskaran, *The Message Bearers*, pp. 57, 60.

94. Rebecca P. Scales, "Subversive Sound: Transnational Radio, Arabic Recordings, and the Dangers of Listening in French Colonial Algeria, 1934–1939," *Comparative Studies in Society and History* 52.2 (2010), pp. 402, 403–4.

95. Quevedo, *Atilla's Kaiso*, pp. 57–8.

96. Scales, "Subversive Sound," p. 400.

97. Susumu, "Soeara NIROM and Musical Culture in Colonial Indonesia," kyotoreviewsea.org.

98. Margaret Kartomi, "The Pan-East/Southeast Asian and National Indonesian Song Bengawan Solo and Its Javanese Composer," *Yearbook for Traditional Music* 30 (1998), pp. 90, 86.

99. See Patrick Huber, *Linthead Stomp: The Creation of Country Music in the Piedmont South*, University of North Carolina Press, 2008, p. 245, for a discussion of the steel guitar in "hillbilly music" by Jimmie Tarlton.

100. The major exceptions are the essays of Amy Ku'uleialoha Stillman, and Adria L. Imada, *Aloha America: Hula Circuits Through the U.S. Empire*, Duke University Press, 2012, which have deeply influenced my argument.

101. Quoted in Albertine Loomis, *For Whom Are the Stars?*, University Press of Hawaii, 1976, p. 86.

102. Eleanor C. Nordyke and Martha H. Noyes, "Kaulana Nā Pua: A Voice for Sovereignty," *Hawaiian Journal of History* 27 (1993), p. 29. For the history of the song see also Amy Ku'uleialoha Stillman, "'Aloha Aina': New Perspectives on 'Kaulana Nā Pua'," *Hawaiian Journal of History* 33 (1999), pp. 83–99. Stillman discovered that Johnny Noble registered an arrangement of the song as "Na Pua O Hawaii" in 1934, but it was not included in his 1935 collection of hulas.

103. Samuel H. Elbert and Noelani Mahoe, eds, *Nā Mele o Hawai'i Nei: 101 Hawaiian Songs*, University of Hawaii Press, 1970, p. 5.

104. Mary Kawena Pukui, "Songs (Meles) of Old Ka'u, Hawaii," *Journal of American Folklore* 62 (1949), p. 162.

105. Waikiki Hawaiian Trio, "The Four Islands," Sunset 1053, 1925; Kalama's Quartet, "Na Moku Eha," OKeh 41048, 1928; William Ewaliko, "Na Moku Eha," Columbia 1510-D, 1928.

106. Lyrics and translation in liner notes to *Nā Leo Hawai'i Kahiko: The Master Chanters of Hawai'i/Songs of Old Hawai'i*, Mountain Apple MACD 2043, 1997.
107. Lyrics and translation in Elbert and Mahoe, eds, *Nā Mele o Hawai'i Nei*, pp. 63–4.
108. Amy Ku'uleialoha Stillman, "Of the People Who Love the Land: Vernacular History in the Poetry of Modern Hawaiian Hula," *Amerasia Journal* 28.3 (2002), p. 96. See also Noenoe K. Silva, *Aloha Betrayed: Native Hawaiian Resistance to American Colonialism*, Duke University Press, 2004.
109. Adria L. Imada, *Aloha America: Hula Circuits Through the U.S. Empire*, Duke University Press, 2012, pp. 63–4, 123.
110. Walter Benjamin, "The Work of Art in the Age of Its Technical Reproducibility: Third Version," in *Walter Benjamin: Selected Writings, Volume 4, 1938–1940*, eds. Howard Eiland and Michael W. Jennings, Harvard University Press, 2003, p. 262.
111. Quoted in Danielson, *The Voice of Egypt*, p. 4.
112. Quoted in Leymarie, *Cuban Fire*, p. 33.
113. Quevedo, *Atilla's Kaiso*, p. 28.
114. Nardal, "Notes on the Biguine Créole," p. 53.
115. Borges, "A History of the Tango," pp. 108, 106. Citing a classic debate over the politics of tango, Marta Savigliano argued that tango lyrics were not songs of protest, they were about the "miseries of everyday life" (*Tango and the Political Economy of Passion*, p. 13).
116. Caluza's Double Quartet, "Ixegwana Ricksha Song," Zonophone 4280, 1930; Veit Erlmann, liner notes to *Caluza's Double Quartet 1930*.
117. Carlos Gardel, "Organito de la Tarde," Disco National 18128A, 1925.
118. Zhou Xuan, "Tianya Genü," 1937. See Jones, *Yellow Music*, pp. 134–6; and *Antique Shanghai Pop Music 1930–1949*, Podcast 2: "Gold and Silver," antiquepopmusic.com.
119. Bessie Smith, "Mean Old Bed Bug Blues,"* Columbia 14250-D, 1928. Niles, "Ballads, Songs, and Snatches" (February 1928), p. 653.
120. Trio Matamoros, "Mamá, Son de la Loma," Victor V81378, 1928. See Sublette, *Cuba and Its Music*, p. 368.
121. Caluza's Double Quartet, "Ingoduso," Zonophone 4276, 1930.
122. George Williams Aingo, "Akuko Nu Bonto," Zonophone, ca. 1928; lyrics translated in liner notes to *Living Is Hard*.
123. Rosita Quiroga, "La Musa Mistonga," Victor 79632, 1926. Eduardo Romano, ed., *Las Letras del Tango: Antología Cronológica 1900–1980*, Editorial Fundación Ross, 1990, pp. 97–8. Lyrics translated in Thompson, *Tango*, p. 34. Flores quoted in Castro, *The Argentine Tango as Social History*, p. 190. See also Carlos Gardel, "Mi Buenos Aires Querido," 1934; Carlos Gardel, "Arrabalero," 1927, both re-released on *The Magic of Carlos Gardel*, Harlequin HQ CD 145, 1999.
124. Borges, "The Language of the Argentines," in Borges, *On Argentina*, p. 80.
125. Ibid., p. 82.
126. Carlos Sandroni, "Dois Sambas de 1930 ea Constituição do Gênero: 'Na Pavuna' e 'Vou te Abandonar,'" *Cadernos do Colóquio* 1.4 (2001).
127. "The Peanut Vendor," Edward B. Marks Music, 1930, Wolfsonian FIU, wolfsonian.org. See also Sublette, *Cuba and Its Music*, pp. 385–6, 395–9.
128. Lyrics translated in Leymarie, *Cuban Fire*, p. 89.
129. Rodney Gallop, "The Folk Music of Portugal: II," *Music and Letters* 14.4 (1933), p. 343.

130. Andrew Field, *Shanghai's Dancing World: Cabaret Culture and Urban Politics, 1919–1954*, Chinese University Press, 2010, p. 164.
131. Leymarie, *Cuban Fire*, p. 4.
132. Carmen Miranda, "A Preta do Aracajé," Odeon M710, 1939. McCann, *Hello, Hello Brazil*, p. 110.
133. Ronald Radano, *Lying Up a Nation: Race and Black Music*, University of Chicago Press, 2003, p. 11.
134. Albin J. Zak III, *The Poetics of Rock: Cutting Tracks, Making Records*, University of California Press, 2001, p. 76.
135. Philip Yampolsky, *Music and Media in the Dutch East Indies: Gramophone Records and Radio in the Late Colonial Era, 1903–1942*, dissertation, University of Washington, 2013, pp. 305–313.

6. "A Noisy Heaven and a Syncopated Earth"

1. Karl Marx, "Economic and Philosophic Manuscripts of 1844," in *Karl Marx Frederick Engels Collected Works*, International Publishers, 1975, volume 3, pp. 301–2.
2. For this conception of cultural revolution, I am indebted to the work of Fredric Jameson, including, but by no means limited to, "Cultural Revolution," in his *Valences of the Dialectic*, Verso, 2009.
3. Fredric Jameson, "Beyond the Cave: Demystifying the Ideology of Modernism," *Bulletin of the Midwest Modern Language Association* 8.1 (1975), pp. 4–7.
4. Theodor W. Adorno, "On Jazz," in his *Essays on Music*, Richard Leppert, ed., University of California Press, 2002, p. 491.
5. Adorno, "On the Fetish Character in Music and the Regression of Listening," in Adorno, *Essays on Music*, p. 307.
6. Adorno, "On Jazz," p. 485.
7. The *Oxford English Dictionary* cites a first use in *Melody Maker* in 1927. The n-gram for "dance band" shows the phrase skyrocketing from nothing in 1920 to a peak in 1940; see also G. T., "Dancing," *Encyclopedia Britannica*, 12th Edition, 1922, vol. 30, p. 796: "The music of the modern ballroom is almost entirely supplied by the United States. The music used in the American dances is no longer a string band and piano, but consists of various combinations, the most common of which perhaps is: piano, violin, alto or tenor saxophone, banjo, and jazz-drum … There is as much variety in the method of playing dance music today as in the dances themselves. Dance bands therefore vary considerably in skill, as might be expected, and the best known command very high salaries. The skill of a modern dance band lies in two essentials: first good rhythm; and secondly cleverness in extemporising on the tune by the different executors."
8. William Maas, "Jazz Poetry," *Daily Chronicle*, 1920, quoted in "From Education to Jazz," *The Living Age*, October 16, 1920.
9. Ronald Radano, *Lying Up a Nation: Race and Black Music*, University of Chicago Press, 2003, p. 187; Albin J. Zak III, *The Poetics of Rock: Cutting Tracks, Making Records*, University of California Press, 2001, p. 127.
10. Ali Jihad Racy, *Making Music in the Arab World: The Culture and Artistry of Tarab*, Cambridge University Press, 2003, pp. 76–7.
11. J. Bradford Robinson, "V. Jazz Bands," in "Band," *Grove Music Online*.

12. Virgil Thomson, "Jazz," *American Mercury* 2.8 (1924), p. 466.
13. Jim Tranquada and John King, *The 'Ukulele: A History*, University of Hawaii Press, 2012, p. 76.
14. Jason Gibbs, "The West's Songs, Our Songs: The Introduction and Adaptation of Western Popular Song in Vietnam Before 1940," *Asian Music* 35.1 (2003/2004), p. 58.
15. John Collins, "The Early History of West African Highlife Music," *Popular Music* 8.3 (1989), p. 222.
16. J. H. Nketia, "The Gramophone and Contemporary African Music in the Gold Coast," Proceedings of the Fourth Annual Conference of the West African Institute of Social and Economic Research, 1956, p. 193.
17. Keith Chandler, liner notes to *Echoes of Africa: Early Recordings*, Wergo SM1624 2, 2002, 21.
18. Andrew F. Jones, *Yellow Music: Media Culture and Colonial Modernity in the Chinese Jazz Age*, Duke University Press, 2001, p. 41.
19. George S. Kanahele, ed., (revised and updated by John Berger), *Hawaiian Music and Musicians: An Encyclopedic History*, Mutual Publishing, 2012, pp. 787–801; Lorene Ruymar, ed., *The Hawaiian Steel Guitar and Its Great Hawaiian Musicians*, Centerstream Publishing, 1996. For a selection of such recordings around the world, see *Steeling Round the World Hawaiian Style*, Harlequin HQCD 182, 2003.
20. William Washabaugh, *Flamenco: Passion, Politics, and Popular Culture*, Berg Publishers, 1996, pp. 63–4.
21. Kofi Agawu, *Representing African Music: Postcolonial Notes, Queries, Positions*, Routledge, 2003, p. 148.
22. Christopher Alan Waterman, *Jùjú: A Social History and Ethnography of an African Popular Music*, University of Chicago Press, 1990, p. 45.
23. Hugh Tracey, "The State of Folk Music in Bantu Africa: A Brief Survey Delivered to the International Folk Music Council, on Behalf of the African Music Society," *African Music* 1.1 (1954), p. 11.
24. Quoted in Collins, "Kwaa Mensah," in *Musicmakers of West Africa*, p. 15.
25. Michael E. Veal, *Fela: The Life and Times of an African Musical Icon*, Temple University Press, 2000, pp. 92–3.
26. Asare reported in David Coplan, "Go To My Town, Cape Coast! The Social History of Ghanaian highlife," in Bruno Nettl, ed., *Eight Urban Musical Cultures: Tradition and Change*, University of Illinois Press, 1978, p. 102.
27. Waterman, *Jùjú*, p. 47.
28. Christoph Wagner, liner notes to *Global Accordion: Early Recordings*, Wergo SM 1623 2, 2001.
29. Ibid., p. 13.
30. Stuart Eydmann, "As Common as Blackberries: The First Hundred Years of the Accordion in Scotland, 1830–1930," *Folk Music Journal* 7.5 (1999), p. 598.
31. María Susana Azzi, "The Golden Age and After: 1920s to 1990s," in Simon Collier et al., *Tango! The Dance, the Song, the Story*, Thames and Hudson, 1995, p. 138.
32. Wagner, liner notes to *Global Accordion*, pp. 13, 16.
33. Chandler, liner notes to *Echoes of Africa*, p. 22.
34. George Williams Aingo, "Tarkwa Na Abosu,"* Zonophone EZ 4, 1927.
35. Matt Rahaim, "That Ban(e) of Indian Music: Hearing Politics in the Harmonium," *Journal of Asian Studies* 70.3 (2011), p. 662.
36. Azzi, "The Golden Age and After," p. 138.

37. Rahaim, "That Ban(e)," p. 662.
38. Ibid., pp. 658, 664 n. 5.
39. David Coplan, *In Township Tonight!: South Africa's Black City Music and Theatre*, Ravan Press, 1985, pp. 23–4.
40. Wagner, liner notes to *Global Accordion*, 15.
41. Theodor W. Adorno, *Current of Music: Elements of a Radio Theory*, Polity, 2009, p. 97.
42. Quoted in Michael Dregni, *Django: The Life and Music of a Gypsy Legend*, Oxford University Press, 2004, p. 21.
43. Rahaim, "That Ban(e)," 658.
44. Dregni, *Django*, p. 29.
45. Emilio Grenet, *Popular Cuban Music: 80 Revised and Corrected Compositions, Together with an Essay on the Evolution of Music in Cuba*, Carasa & Co., 1939, p. xxxiii.
46. Adorno "On Jazz," p. 471.
47. Micol Seigel, *Uneven Encounters: Making Race and Nation in Brazil and the United States*, Duke University Press, 2009, p. 106; Sol Ho'opi'i, "Hano Hano Hawaii,"* Columbia 1370-D, 1928, Ramón Montoya, "Flor de Petenera,"* Gramófono AE 4148, 1933.
48. Roland Barthes, "The Grain of the Voice," in Barthes, *Image-Music-Text*, Hill and Wang, 1977.
49. E. M. von Hornbostel, "African Negro Music," *Africa* 1.1 (1928), p. 32.
50. Rodney Gallop, "Some Records of the Portuguese Fado," *The Gramophone* (October 1931), p. 173.
51. Allan Sutton, *Recording the 'Twenties: The Evolution of the American Recording Industry, 1920–29*, Mainspring Press, 2008, pp. 228–30.
52. Abbe Niles, "Ballads, Songs and Snatches," *The Bookman: A Review of Books and Life* 67 (July 1928), p. 566; ibid., 68 (September 1928), p. 77; ibid., 66 (February 1928), p. 653.
53. Brent Hayes Edwards, "Louis Armstrong and the Syntax of Scat," *Critical Inquiry* 28.3 (2002), pp. 618–49; Kanahele, *Hawaiian Music and Musicians*, pp. 134–45.
54. Helen Roberts, "Hawaiian Music," in Thos. G. Thrum, ed., *The Hawaiian Annual for 1926*, Thos. G. Thrum, 1925, p. 76.
55. Hornbostel, "African Negro Music," p. 32.
56. Solomons, "The Krontjong," p. 238.
57. Niles, "Ballads, Songs, and Snatches," *Bookman* (January 1929), p. 572; ibid, (September 1928), p. 77.
58. Danielson, *The Voice of Egypt*, pp. 92–6, 138.
59. Ling Tai Kor, "2. Gold and Silver," *Antique Shanghai Pop Music, 1930–1949*, antiquepopmusic.com.
60. Mantle Hood, "Musical Ornamentation as History: The Hawaiian Steel Guitar," *Yearbook for Traditional Music* 15 (1983), pp. 141–2.
61. Lakshmi Subramanian, "A Language for Music: Revisiting the Tamil Isai Iyakkam," *Indian Economic and Social History Review* 44.1 (2007), pp. 36–7.
62. Gallop, "The Fado," p. 200.
63. "Jass and Jassism," *New Orleans Times-Picayune*, reprinted in Robert Walser, ed., *Keeping Time: Readings in Jazz History*, Oxford University Press, 1999, p. 8.
64. Adorno, "Farewell to Jazz," in *Essays on Music*, p. 498.
65. Agawu, *Representing African Music*, p. 56. See also John Blacking, "Some Notes

on a Theory of African Rhythm Advanced by Erich von Hornbostel," *African Music* 1.2 (1955), pp. 12–20; and Christopher A. Waterman, "The Uneven Development of Africanist Ethnomusicology: Three Issues and a Critique," in Bruno Nettl and Philip V. Bohlman, eds, *Comparative Musicology and Anthropology of Music: Essays on the History of Ethnomusicology*, University of Chicago Press, 1990.

66. Hornbostel, "African Negro Music," p. 61.
67. W. E. Ward, "Music in the Gold Coast," *The Gold Coast Review* 3.2 (1927), pp. 223, 222.
68. Radano, *Lying Up a Nation*, pp. 246, 247, 234.
69. Rogers, "Jazz at Home," in Locke, ed., *The New Negro*, p. 220.
70. Franz Liszt, *The Gipsy in Music: The Result of the Author's Life-Long Experiences and Investigations of the Gipsies and Their Music*, W. Reeves, 1926 (originally published in French in 1859), p. 304.
71. Nathaniel Bright Emerson, *Unwritten Literature of Hawaii: The Sacred Songs of the Hula*, Bureau of American Ethnology, Bulletin 38, 1909, p. 171.
72. Roberts, "Hawaiian Music," in Thrum, ed., *Hawaiian Annual for 1926*, p. 74.
73. Orme Johnson, "Musical Instruments of Ancient Hawaii," *Musical Quarterly* 25.4 (1939), p. 503.
74. Sigmund Spaeth, "Hawaii Likes Music," *Harper's Monthly Magazine* (March 1938), p. 423; "Paradise," *Time* (July 8, 1929), p. 13.
75. Ward, "Music in the Gold Coast," pp. 216, 215. Hornbostel argues that "The plantation songs and spirituals, and also the blues and rag-times which have launched or helped to launch our modern dance-music are the only remarkable kinds of music brought forth in America by immigrants" (African Negro Music," p. 60).
76. "Syncopation," in H. C. Colles, ed., *Grove's Dictionary of Music and Musicians*, 3rd ed., The Macmillan Company, 1928, vol. 5, p. 243.
77. Andrée Nardal, "Notes on the Biguine Créole," *La Revue Du Monde Noir* 2 (1931), p. 52.
78. Nathaniel Bright Emerson, *Unwritten Literature of Hawaii: The Sacred Songs of the Hula, Bureau of American Ethnology*, Bulletin 38, 1909, p. 171.
79. Anne Shaw Faulkner, "Does Jazz Put the Sin in Syncopation?," *Ladies Home Journal* (1921), reprinted in Robert Walser, ed., *Keeping Time: Readings in Jazz History*, Oxford University Press, 1999, p. 34.
80. "Musicus" [Mark Radebe], "Jazzmania," quoted by Couzens, *The New African*, pp. 56–7.
81. Shaw Faulkner, "Does Jazz Put the Sin in Syncopation?," p. 34.
82. Adorno, "Farewell to Jazz," p. 498.
83. Carlos Sandroni, *Feitiço decente: transformações do samba no Rio de Janeiro, 1917–1933*, Editora UFRJ, 2001, pp. 20, 21, 27.
84. The earliest use of "rhythm section" that I have found is in Paul Specht, "American Popular Music and Its Progress," *Melody: A Magazine for Lovers of Popular Music* (July 1924), reprinted in Karl Koenig, *Jazz in Print (1856–1929): An Anthology of Selected Early Readings in Jazz History*, Pendragon Press, 2002, p. 326. Specht wrote that "when making up a modern jazz orchestra, particular care must be exercised in combining the rhythm section, so that all tempos and the complex, alternating syncopated beats shall be uniform and precise." The *Oxford English Dictionary* cites the first use in 1926.
85. Su Zheng, *Claiming Diaspora: Music, Transnationalism, and Cultural Politics in Asian/Chinese America*, Oxford University Press, 2010, p. 122.

86. Carlos Sandroni writes that "This word—and not the much more recent 'percussionists'—was used to refer to the popular musicians coming from the samba schools, specialists in surdos, cuícas, tamborins, and pandeiros" (Carlos Sandroni, "Transformations of the Carioca Samba in the Twentieth Century," dc.itamaraty.gov.br, pp. 80–1).

87. Alejo Carpentier, *Music in Cuba*, University of Minnesota Press, 2001, p. 228.

88. Moore, *Nationalizing Blackness*, p. 89.

89. Leymarie, *Cuban Fire*, pp. 44–5.

90. Carpentier, *Music in Cuba*, p. 228.

91. Moore, *Nationalizing Blackness*, p. 78.

92. Sandroni, "Transformations of the Carioca Samba," p. 81. Sandroni notes that he is "not aware of any recordings including the cuíca at the time: the instrument was considered too bizarre, exotic, strange, as numerous accounts confirm." See also Sandroni, "Dois Sambas de 1930," pp. 8–21.

93. Kalama's Quartet, "Heeia (Ancient Hula),"* OKeh 41414, 1930; Kalama's Quartet, "Kawika/Liliu E," OKeh 41455, 1930, re-released on Kalama's Quartet, *Early Hawaiian Classics*; Kalama's Quartet, "Pehea Hoi Au?" OKeh 41456, 1930, re-released on *It's Hotter in Hawaii*. Malcolm Rockwell identifies this as the "earliest commercially recorded example of the 'ancient chant' style" (T. Malcolm Rockwell, *Hawaiian and Hawaiian Guitar Records 1891–1960*, Mahina Piha Press, 2007, p. 579). There are at least two other lesser-known early commercial recordings of Hawaiian percussion: the remarkable track from Columbia's May 1928 Honolulu sessions with ipu, pahu, and uliʻuli, released as The Honolulu Players, "Leilehua," Columbia 1666-D, 1928, re-released on *Hawaiian Steel Guitar Classics 1927–1938*, Arhoolie Folkloric CD 7027, 1993, and the uliʻuli on Rose Tribe's "Pu Ana Kamakani," Brunswick 55038, 1929. The kalaʻau (Hawaiian rhythm sticks) do not seem to have been used in commercial recording in this period.

94. Royal Hartigan, "The Heritage of the Drumset," *African American Review* 29.2 (1995), p. 234. In his account of early New Orleans jazz, Lawrence Gushee notes that "only after 1905 did the drum set gradually become a normal if not indispensable member of a dance band" (*Pioneers of Jazz: The Story of the Creole Band*, Oxford University Press, 2005, p. 17).

95. James Blades, *Percussion Instruments and Their History*, Bold Strummer, 1992, p. 458.

96. G. T., "Dancing," *Encyclopedia Britannica*, p. 796.

97. Dregni, *Django*, p. 23.

98. Burnet Hershey, "Jazz Latitude," *New York Times*, June 25, 1922, p. SM5.

99. Hartigan, "Heritage of the Drumset," p. 234.

100. Blades, *Percussion Instruments*, pp. 170–1.

101. Hershey, "Jazz Latitude."

102. Blades, *Percussion Instruments*, p. 458.

103. Karush, *Culture of Class*, p. 9.

104. Sublette, *Cuba and Its Music*, pp. 442, 124.

105. Sandroni, "Transformations of the Carioca Samba," p. 81.

106. Carpentier, *Music in Cuba*, pp. 229–30.

107. Peter Manuel, "Improvisation in Latin American Dance Music: History and Style," in Bruno Nettl and Melinda Russell, eds, *In the Course of Performance: Studies in the World of Musical Improvisation*, University of Chicago Press, 1998, p. 133.

108. Tony Lombardozzi, personal communication. See Christiane Gerischer, "O

Suingue Baiano: Rhythmic Feeling and Microrhythmic Phenomena in Brazilian Percussion," *Ethnomusicology* 50.1 (2006), p. 99, which opens with a discussion of "different rhythmic dialects."

109. Brothers, *Louis Armstrong's New Orleans*, p. 145.
110. Sandroni, *Feitiço decente*, p. 25.
111. Brothers, *Louis Armstrong's New Orleans*, p. 145.
112. Agawu, *Representing African Music*, p. 85, see also pp. 78–9.
113. Jeff Pressing, "Black Atlantic Rhythm: Its Computational and Transcultural Foundations," *Music Perception* 19.3 (2002), pp. 288, 290.
114. Louise Meintjes, *Sound of Africa! Making Music Zulu in a South African Studio*, Duke University Press, 2003, p. 149.
115. Adorno, "Farewell to Jazz," p. 498.
116. Ibid.
117. Here I am particularly indebted to David Schiff's illuminating discussion of the clave and the continuo: David Schiff, *The Ellington Century*, University of California Press, 2012, pp. 59–62.
118. The term was first used by Kwabena Nketia in 1963: Kofi Agawu, "Structural Analysis or Cultural Analysis? Competing Perspectives on the 'Standard Pattern' of West African Rhythm," *Journal of the American Musicological Society* 59.1 (2006), pp. 3.
119. Ibid., p. 1.
120. The "standard" timeline is a bell pattern of southern Ewe music often notated as 2+2+1+2+2+2+1; the *kpanlogo* is a pattern associated with a Ga dance notated as 3+3+4+2+4; and the *Gahu* is played on the gankogui bell in a Southern Ewe dance and notated as 3+3+4+4+2. Agawu, *Representing African Music*, pp. 73–9; Royal Hartigan, *West African Rhythms for Drumset*, Manhattan Music, 1995, p. 63–4.
121. See Godfried T. Toussaint, *The Geometry of Musical Rhythm: What Makes a "Good" Rhythm Good?*, CRC Press, 2013, p. 16; Schiff, *The Ellington Century*, p. 60; Martin Clayton, *Time in Indian Music: Rhythm, Metre, and Form in North Indian Rāg Performance*, Oxford University Press, 2000, p. 40, discusses the tala and the timeline. The *tresillo* is usually notated as 3+3+2, the *cinquillo* as 2+1+2+1+2, the *son clave* as 3+3+2+(2)+2+2+(2), the *habanera* or tango rhythm as 3+1+2+2, and the bossa nova as 3+3+2+(2)+3+3. Manuel, "Improvisation in Latin American Dance Music," pp. 128–9; Sandroni, *Feitiço decente*, pp. 28–32.
122. Agawu, *Representing African Music*, p. 73.
123. Toussaint, *Geometry of Musical Rhythm*, p. 13.
124. Agawu, *Representing African Music*, p. 131.
125. Ballantine, *Marabi Nights*, pp. 33–5; Coplan, *In Township Tonight!*, pp. 106, 258–63.
126. Eric Prieto, "Alexandre Stellio and the Beginnings of the Biguine," *Nottingham French Studies* 43.1 (2004), p. 35.
127. Peter Manuel, "Flamenco in Focus: An Analysis of a Performance of Soleares," in Michael Tenzer, ed., *Analytical Studies in World Music*, Oxford University Press, 2006, pp. 97, 104–5.
128. Pennanen, "Development of Chordal Harmony in Greek Rebetika and Laika Music," pp. 65–116.
129. Amy Ku'uleialoha Stillman, "Not All Hula Songs Are Created Equal: Reading the Historical Nature of Repertoire in Polynesia," *Yearbook for Traditional Music* 27 (1995), pp. 6–7.

130. Yampolsky, "Kroncong Revisited," pp. 11, 15.
131. Curiously, one of the roots of these chord cycles was an earlier appropriation of New World dances by Europeans. In the late 1500s and early 1600s, forms of improvised chordal accompaniment to melodies—*basso continuo*—emerged when Spanish dance ensembles adopted the disreputable and "licentious" dances from the Americas, particularly the *zarabanda*. As played on the Spanish five-string guitar, in *rasgueado* manner, the *zarabanda* denoted not only a dance rhythm but a particular chord cycle, what one musicologist has called a "chord row." Richard Hudson, "The 'Zarabanda' and 'Zarabanda Francese' in Italian Guitar Music of the Early 17th Century," *Musica Disciplina* 24 (1970), pp. 125–49. See also Craig H. Russell, "Radical Innovations, Social Revolution, and the Baroque Guitar," in Victor Anand Coelho, ed., *The Cambridge Companion to the Guitar*, Cambridge University Press, 2003.
132. Grenet, *Popular Cuban Music*, p. xvii.
133. Blues scholars like Paul Oliver and Gerhard Kubik have used the absence of timelines to suggest connections between the blues and the musics of the African savannah of the West and Central Sudanic belt. Paul Oliver, "Savannah Syncopators: African Retentions in the Blues," in Paul Oliver et al., *Yonder Come the Blues: The Evolution of a Genre*, Cambridge University Press, 2001; Gerhard Kubik, *Africa and the Blues*, University Press of Mississippi, 2008, pp. 51–62.
134. Christopher Washburne, "The Clave of Jazz: A Caribbean Contribution to the Rhythmic Foundation of an African-American Music," *Black Music Research Journal* 17.1 (1997), pp. 59–80.
135. Schiff, *The Ellington Century*, p. 62.
136. Agawu, "Structural Analysis," 28.
137. Robert Sprigge, "The Ghanaian Highlife: Notation and Sources," *Music in Ghana* 2 (1961), pp. 89–94.
138. Abbe Niles, "Introduction" in W. C. Handy, ed., *Blues: An Anthology*, Albert & Charles Boni, 1926, p. 14.
139. Agawu, *Representing African Music*, p. 145.
140. Liszt, *The Gipsy in Music*, pp. 299, 301, 300–3. Shay Loya, *Liszt's Transcultural Modernism and the Hungarian-Gypsy Tradition*, University of Rochester Press, 2011, pp. 9–10, 51–2.
141. Van der Merwe, *Roots of the Classical*, p. 278.
142. Rahaim, "That Ban(e)," p. 667. Similarly, Risto Pekka Pennanen argues that "ever since the nineteenth century, folk music researchers in the Balkans have concentrated on intervals, tetrachords, pentachords, and scales" ("Lost in Scales: Balkan Folk Music Research and the Ottoman Legacy," *Muzikologija* 8.8 [2008], p. 130).
143. "'Honey Boy' Minstrels Please Large Audience at Atlanta," *Atlanta Constitution*, March 12, 1915, p. 12.
144. *Dramatic Mirror*, February 8, 1919; W. C. Handy, *Father of the Blues: An Autobiography*, Da Capo Press, 1985, ca. 1941, p. 74. There is a long debate over the meaning and existence of blue notes: see Hans Weisethaunet, "Is There Such a Thing as the 'Blue Note'?" *Popular Music* 20.1 (2001), pp. 99–116; Kubik, *Africa and the Blues*, pp. 118–45.
145. Bálint Sárosi, *Gypsy Music*, Corvina Press, 1978, p. 27; Shay Loya, "Beyond 'Gypsy' Stereotypes: Harmony and Structure in the Verbunkos Idiom," *Journal of Musicological Research* 27.3 (2008), p. 258.

146. Sárosi, *Gypsy Music*, p. 142.
147. Niles, "Introduction" in Handy, *Blues: An Anthology*, p. 14.
148. Kofi Agawu, "How Europe Underdeveloped Africa Tonally," in Olaniyan and Radano, eds, *Audible Empire*.
149. Brothers, *Louis Armstrong's New Orleans*, pp. 67, 294.
150. Ibid., pp. 299, 300, 302.
151. Agawu, "How Europe Underdeveloped Africa Tonally."
152. Agawu, *Representing African Music*, p. 131.
153. Roberts, "Hawaiian Music," in Thrum, ed., *Hawaiian Annual for 1926*, p. 76.
154. Rodney Gallop, "The Development of Folk-Song in Portugal and the Basque Country," *Proceedings of the Musical Association* 61 (1934-5), p. 70.
155. Peter Manuel, "From Scarlatti to 'Guantanamera': Dual Tonicity in Spanish and Latin American Musics," *Journal of the American Musicological Society* 55.2 (2002), p. 314.
156. Peter Manuel, "Modal Harmony in Andalusian, Eastern European, and Turkish Syncretic Musics," *Yearbook for Traditional Music* 21 (1989), pp. 70, 71.
157. Manuel, "Modal Harmony," pp. 90, 74, 76–7.
158. Manuel, "From Scarlatti to 'Guantanamera,'" p. 314; Manuel, "Modal Harmony," p. 70. See also Peter Manuel and Orlando Fiol, "Mode, Melody, and Harmony in Traditional Afro-Cuban Music: From Africa to Cuba," *Black Music Research Journal* 27 (2007), pp. 62–8; Peter Manuel, "Flamenco in Focus: An Analysis of a Performance of Soleares," in Michael Tenzer, ed., *Analytical Studies in World Music*, Oxford University Press, 2006; and Peter Manuel, "Flamenco Guitar: History, Style, Status," in Victor Anand Coelho, ed., *The Cambridge Companion to the Guitar*, Cambridge University Press, 2003.
159. Manuel, "From Scarlatti to 'Guantanamera,'" pp. 329, 330, 331–2, 333–4. The most detailed development of Manuel's framework is Pennanen, "The Development of Chordal Harmony in Greek Rebetika and Laika Music," pp. 65–116.
160. Roberts, "Hawaiian Music," in Thrum, ed., *Hawaiian Annual for 1926*, p. 78.
161. Agawu, *Representing African Music*, p. 131.
162. Kwadwo Adum-Attah, *Nana Ampadu: Master of Highlife Music*, thesis, University of Cape Coast, 1997, pp. 13–14.
163. Robin Moore, "The Decline of Improvisation in Western Art Music: An Interpretation of Change," *International Review of the Aesthetics and Sociology of Music* 23.1 (1992), pp. 61–84; Christopher Small, "On Improvisation," in his *Music of the Common Tongue: Survival and Celebration in Afro-American Music*, Riverrun Press, 1987.
164. Anna G. Piotrowska, "Expressing the Inexpressible: The Issue of Improvisation and the European Fascination with Gypsy Music in the 19th Century," *International Review of the Aesthetics and Sociology of Music* 43.2 (2012), pp. 326–7.
165. "Extemporisation," in Colles, ed., *Grove's Dictionary of Music and Musicians*, 3rd Edition, vol. 2, p. 184.
166. See David Malvinni, *The Gypsy Caravan: From Real Roma to Imaginary Gypsies in Western Music and Film*, Routledge, 2004, pp. 43–62.
167. Liszt, *The Gipsy in Music*, pp. 319, 307–8.
168. Walter Starkie, "The Gipsy in Andalusian Folk-Lore and Folk-Music," *Proceedings of the Musical Association* 62 (1935–1936), p. 8.

169. Carl Engel, "Jazz: A Musical Discussion," *Atlantic Monthly* (August 1922), p. 187.
170. Darius Milhaud, "The Jazz Band and Negro Music," *Living Age* 323 (October 18, 1924), p. 172.
171. Sárosi, *Gypsy Music*, p. 106. See also Malvinni, *The Gypsy Caravan*, p. 91.
172. Bartók, "Gypsy Music or Hungarian Music?," p. 252. Adorno, "On Jazz," in *Essays on Music*, p. 477.
173. Derek Bailey, *Improvisation: Its Nature and Practice in Music*, Da Capo Press, 1993, p. xi.
174. Small, *Music of the Common Tongue*, p. 290.
175. Emerson, *Unwritten Literature of Hawaii*, p. 254.
176. Racy, *Making Music in the Arab World*, p. 93.
177. Starkie, "The Gipsy in Andalusian Folk-Lore," pp. 10–11.
178. Quoted in Ballantine, *Marabi Nights*, p. 30.
179. Cohen, ed., *Tango Voices*, p. 10.
180. Tadeu Coelho and Julie Koidin, "The Brazilian Choro: Historical Perspectives and Performance Practices," *The Flutist Quarterly* (Fall 2005), p. 17.
181. Moore, *Nationalizing Blackness*, p. 89. Manuel, "Improvisation in Latin American Dance Music," in Nettl with Russell, eds, *In the Course of Performance*, p. 130. Manuel notes that "the improvisational styles of the early *son* ... are fairly well documented in recordings of the 1920s and 1930s."
182. Louis Armstrong, *Swing That Music*, Da Capo Press, 1993, pp. 104–5.
183. Bailey, *Improvisation*, p. xii. Small, *Music of the Common Tongue*, p. 309.
184. Tamara Elena Livingston-Isenhour and Thomas George Caracas Garcia, *Choro: A Social History of a Brazilian Popular Music*, Indiana University Press, 2005, pp. 43–7. Gushee suggests that "jam session" emerged between 1925 and 1935: Lawrence Gushee, "Improvisation and Related Terms in Middle-Period Jazz," in Gabriel Solis and Bruno Nettl, eds, *Musical Improvisation: Art, Education, and Society*, University of Illinois Press, 2009, pp. 276–7.
185. Yampolsky, "Kroncong Revisited," pp. 23–7.
186. James Woodall, *In Search of the Firedance: Spain through Flamenco*, Sinclair-Stevenson, 1992, pp. 179–85.
187. James Robbins, "The Cuban 'Son' as Form, Genre, and Symbol," *Latin American Music Review* 11.2 (1990), p. 186.
188. Azzi, "The Golden Age and After," in Collier et al., *Tango!*, p. 120.
189. Wayne W. Daniel, *Pickin' on Peachtree: A History of Country Music in Atlanta, Georgia*, University of Illinois Press, 1990, pp. 15–44; Gavin James Campbell, "The Georgia Old-Time Fiddling Contest," in his *Music and the Making of a New South*, University of North Carolina Press, 2004.
190. Rohlehr, *Calypso and Society*, p. 118.
191. Brothers, *Louis Armstrong's New Orleans*, pp. 207–9.
192. H. O. Osgood, "First He Played the Viola—And Now He's Paul Whiteman," *Musical Courier* (May 22, 1924), reprinted in Koenig, *Jazz in Print*, p. 307.
193. John L. Clark, Jr., "Archie Bleyer and the Lost Influence of Stock Arrangements in Jazz," *American Music* 27.2 (Summer 2009), pp. 138–79.
194. Manuel, "Flamenco Guitar," in Coelho, ed., *The Cambridge Companion to the Guitar*, p. 16.
195. Yampolsky, "Kroncong Revisited," p. 26.
196. See Barry Kernfeld, *The Story of Fake Books: Bootlegging Songs to Musicians*, Scarecrow Press, 2006; and, for a more comprehensive account, Barry

Kernfeld, *Pop Song Piracy: Disobedient Music Distribution since 1929*, University of Chicago Press, 2011.

197. "Louis has penned in book form some of his eccentric styles of playing," wrote Dave Peyton in the *Chicago Defender* ("The Musical Bunch," April 16, 1927, p. 6); actually, Armstrong had made special recordings of the breaks and choruses that were then transcribed by the publisher's arranger. Lawrence Gushee, "The Improvisation of Louis Armstrong," in Nettl and Russell, eds, *In the Course of Performance*, pp. 270–2; Harker, *Louis Armstrong's Hot Five and Hot Seven Recordings*, p. 76; Gene H. Anderson, *The Original Hot Five Recordings of Louis Armstrong*, Pendragon Press, 2007, p. 135.

198. Milhaud, "The Jazz Band and Negro Music," pp. 171–2.

199. McCann, *Hello, Hello Brazil*, p. 164; see also Livingston-Isenhour and Garcia, *Choro: A Social History*, pp. 87–98.

200. Danielson, *The Voice of Egypt*, pp. 146, 145, 149.

201. Louis Armstrong, "Potato Head Blues," OKeh 8503, 1927. See Harker, *Louis Armstrong's Hot Five and Hot Seven Recordings*, chapter 3; Gushee, "Improvisation and Related Terms," in Solis and Nettl, eds, *Musical Improvisation*, pp. 305–7.

202. Rick Davies, *Trompeta: Chappottín, Chocolate, and the Afro-Cuban Trumpet Style*, Scarecrow Press, 2003, p. 205, see also pp. 35–48; Septeto Habanero, "Coralia," Victor 81751, 1928.

203. Sol Hoʻopiʻi, "Hilo March," Sunset 1086, 1925; Kalama's Quartet, "Hilo March," OKeh 41082, 1928; Johnny Noble's Hawaiians featuring M. K. Moke, "Hilo March," Brunswick 55011, 1928, re-released on *History of Hawaiian Steel Guitar*, Hana Ola Records HOCD 34000, 1999.

204. The early solo guitar discs include Ramón Montoya, "Soleares en Mi"*/"La Caña," Gramófono AE2153, 1928; and Niño Ricardo, "Alegrías"*/"Variaciones por Granadina," Regal RS-732, 1928.

205. Rodney Gallop, "Spanish Folk-Music Records," *The Gramophone* (November 1930), p. 266.

206. Julia Banzi, *Flamenco Guitar Innovation and the Circumscription of Tradition*, dissertation, University of California, Santa Barbara, 2007, p. 234.

207. Coplan, *In Township Tonight!*, p. 106. Prieto, "Alexandre Stellio and the Beginnings of the Biguine," p. 35.

208. For example, Peter Manuel notes that "Latin improvisation has evolved as a form parallel to jazz rather than derivative from it; indeed since the beginnings of jazz history, the influences between the two genres have been mutual rather than unidirectional" ("Improvisation in Latin American Dance Music," in Nettl and Russell, eds, *In the Course of Performance*, p. 128).

7.   Remastering the 78s

1. Dane Yorke, "The Rise and Fall of the Phonograph," *American Mercury* 27 (September 1932), p. 12.

2. "Phonograph Records," *Fortune* (September 1939), p. 72.

3. Ibid., p. 94.

4. Ibid.

5. Yorke, "Rise and Fall of the Phonograph," p. 12.

6. Tschmuck, *Creativity and Innovation*, pp. 48, 50, 66; "Phonograph Records," 94.

7. Peter Tschmuck, *Creativity and Innovation in the Music Industry*, Springer, 2006, p. 68.
8. George S. Kanahele, ed., (revised and updated by John Berger), *Hawaiian Music and Musicians: An Encyclopedic History*, Mutual Publishing, 2012, p. 679.
9. Paul Vernon, "A Quick Cantor: The Early Days of Recording Jewish Music," *Folk Roots* 127–8 (1994), p. 19.
10. Robert M. W. Dixon, John Godrich, and Howard Rye, *Blues and Gospel Records 1890–1943*, Clarendon Press, 1997, p. xxiii.
11. Michael H. Kater, "Forbidden Fruit? Jazz in the Third Reich," *American Historical Review* 94.1 (1989), pp. 14–15.
12. Theodor W. Adorno, "Farewell to Jazz," in his *Essays on Music*, Richard Leppert, ed., University of California Press, 2002, p. 496.
13. Paul Vernon, "Odeon Records: Their 'Ethnic' Output," Musical Traditions 3 (1997), mustrad.org.uk; Tschmuck, *Creativity and Innovation*, pp. 71–4; Pekka Gronow and Christiane Hofer, eds, *The Lindström Project: Contributions to the History of the Record Industry, Volume 1*, Gesellschaft für Historische Tonträger, 2009, pp. 19, 28–9.
14. Robin Moore, *Nationalizing Blackness: Afrocubanismo and Artistic Revolution in Havana, 1920–1940*, University of Pittsburgh Press, 1997, p. 170.
15. Béla Bartók, "Mechanical Music [1937]," in Benjamin Suchoff, *Béla Bartók Essays*, Faber & Faber, 1976, pp. 294–5.
16. Joseph Horowitz, *Understanding Toscanini: How He Became an American Culture-god and Helped Create a New Audience for Old Music*, Knopf, 1987.
17. Theodor W. Adorno, *Current of Music: Elements of a Radio Theory*, Polity, 2009, p. 103.
18. Peter Manuel, *Popular Musics of the Non-Western World: An Introductory Survey*, Oxford University Press, 1988, p. 18.
19. Hermano Vianna, *The Mystery of Samba: Popular Music and National Identity in Brazil*, University of North Carolina Press, 1999, p. 10.
20. Adria L. Imada, *Aloha America: Hula Circuits Through the U.S. Empire*, Duke University Press, 2012, p. 153.
21. Yiannis Zaimakis, "'Forbidden Fruits' and the Communist Paradise: Marxist Thinking on Greekness and Class in Rebetika," *Music & Politics* 4.1 (2010), p. 2.
22. Moore, *Nationalizing Blackness*, p. ix.
23. Raymond Williams, "Base and Superstructure in Marxist Cultural Theory," *Problems in Materialism and Culture*, Verso, 1980, p. 39.
24. Fredric Jameson, "Reification and Utopia in Mass Culture," *Social Text* 1 (1979), p. 144.
25. Quoted in Vianna, *The Mystery of Samba*, p. 11.
26. Quoted in Moore, *Nationalizing Blackness*, p. 5.
27. Alain Locke, *The Negro and His Music*, Ayer Co. Publishing, 1969, p. 80.
28. Emilio Grenet, *Popular Cuban Music: 80 Revised and Corrected Compositions, Together with an Essay on the Evolution of Music in Cuba*, Carasa & Co., 1939, pp. ix, xxxvii.
29. Quoted in John Szwed, *Alan Lomax: The Man Who Recorded the World*, Viking Penguin, 2010, pp. 143, 146.
30. Desmond Rochfort, *Mexican Muralists: Orozco, Rivera, Siqueiros*, Chronicle Books, 1998, pp. 63–7.
31. Marco Velázquez and Mary Kay Vaughan, "Mestizaje and Musical National-ism in Mexico," in Rick A. Lopez, Desmond Rochfort, Mary Kay Vaughan,

and Stephen Lewis, eds, *The Eagle and the Virgin: Nation and Cultural Revolution in Mexico, 1920–1940*, Duke University Press, 2006, p. 104, p. 266.

32. Rodney Gallop, "Spanish Folk-Music Records,"The Gramophone (November 1930), p. 266.

33. *Native Brazilian Music*, Columbia C 83-C 84/36503-36510, 1942; Bryan McCann, *Hello, Hello Brazil: Popular Music in the Making of Modern Brazil*, Duke University Press, 2004, p. 152; Daniella Thompson, "Stalking Stokowski," *Brazzil* (February 2000), reprinted on *Musica Brasiliensis*, daniellathompson. com.

34. Bryan McCann, "Inventing the Old Guard of Brazilian Popular Music," in his *Hello, Hello Brazil*, pp. 160–80.

35. Bruce Boyd Raeburn, *New Orleans Style and the Writing of American Jazz History*, University of Michigan Press, 2009, pp. 111–41.

36. Henry Nxumalo ("Mr. DRUM") unearthed the history of the 1930 London recordings of Caluza and Motsieloa recordings in a 1949 article: Tim Couzens, *The New African: A Study of the Life and Work of H. I. E. Dhlomo*, Ravan Press, 1985, p. 68; on Matshikiza's essays in *Drum*, see Brett Pyper, "Sounds Like: [Todd] John Matshikiza's Jazz Writing for Drum Magazine, 1951–1957," Glendora Review: African Quarterly on the Arts 3.3-4 (2004), pp. 13–22.

37. James Woodall, *In Search of the Firedance: Spain through Flamenco*, Sinclair-Stevenson, 1992, pp. 225, 248; *Anthologie du Cante Flamenco*, Ducretet-Thomson LA 1051-1052-1053, 3 LP set, 1954, re-released as *Antología del Cante Flamenco*, Hispavox CD 7-91456-2, 1988.

38. Gerald Howson, *The Flamencos of Cádiz Bay*, Bold Strummer, 1994, pp. 50, 247–8. See "Flamenco Singer Aurelio Sellés (Aurelio de Cádiz) speaks—1962 interview by Anselmo González Climent," at Brook Zern, The Flamenco Experience, flamencoexperience.com.

39. Liner notes to *Furry Lewis, Recorded in Memphis Tennessee, October 3, 1959, by Samuel B. Charters*, Folkways Records FS 3823, 1959.

40. Barry Pearson, "I Once Was Lost, But Now I'm Found: The Blues Revival of the 1960s," in Lawrence Cohn et al., *Nothing But the Blues: The Music and the Musicians*, Abbeville Press, 1993; Jeff Todd Titon, "Reconstructing the Blues: Reflections on the 1960s Blues Revival," in Neil V. Rosenberg, ed., *Transforming Tradition*, University of Illinois Press, 1993, pp. 220–40.

41. *Cartola*, directed by Lírio Ferreira and Hilton Lacerda, Europa Filmes, 2007. See also Sean Stroud, "Marcus Pereira's *Música Popular Do Brasil*: Beyond Folklore?," *Popular Music* 25.2 (2006), pp. 310, 316 n. 16.

42. Ruy Castro, *Bossa Nova: The Story of the Brazilian Music that Seduced the World*, A Cappella, 2000, pp. 265–7; Roberto Schwarz, *Misplaced Ideas: Essays on Brazilian Culture*, Verso, 1992.

43. Liner notes to *Hawaiian Song Bird: Lena Machado*, Hana-Ola Records HOCD 29000, 2007; The Tau Moe Family with Bob Brozman, *Ho'Omana'o I Na Mele O Ka Wa U'i (Remembering the Songs of Our Youth)*, Rounder CD 6028, 2002. On the Hawaiian Renaissance, see George H. Lewis, "Da Kine Sounds: The Function of Music as Social Protest in the New Hawaiian Renaissance," *American Music* 2.2 (1984), pp. 38–52; and Amy Ku'uleialoha Stillman, "Hawaiian Hula Competitions: Event, Repertoire, Performance, Tradition," *Journal of American Folklore* 109 (1996), p. 360.

44. Raymond Quevedo (Atilla the Hun), *Atilla's Kaiso: A Short History of Trinidad Calypso*, University of the West Indies, 1983, p. 63.

45. Koray Değirmenci, "On the Pursuit of a Nation: The Construction of Folk and

Folk Music in the Founding Decades of the Turkish Republic," *International Review of the Aesthetics and Sociology of Music* 37.1 (2006), pp. 47–65.

46. Wong Kee Chee, *The Age of Shanghainese Pops: 1930–1970*, Joint Publishing, 2001, pp. 76–97.

47. Rachel Harris, "Wang Luobin: Folk Song King of the Northwest or Song Thief? Copyright, Representation, and Chinese Folk Songs," *Modern China* 31.3 (2005), pp. 381–408; Joshua H. Howard, "The Making of a National Icon: Commemorating Nie Er, 1935–1949," *Twentieth-Century China* 37.1 (2012).

48. Donald S. Castro, *The Argentine Tango as Social History, 1880–1955: The Soul of the People*, Mellen Research University Press, 1990, p. 115.

49. Matthew B. Karush, *Culture of Class: Radio and Cinema in the Making of a Divided Argentina, 1920–1946*, Duke University Press, 2012, pp. 196–201.

50. Donald Andrew Henriques, *Performing Nationalism: Mariachi, Media and Transformation of a Tradition (1920–1942)*, dissertation, University of Texas at Austin, 2006, p. 7 n. 10.

51. McCann, *Hello, Hello Brazil*, p. 67. Michael Denning, *The Cultural Front: The Laboring of American Culture in the Twentieth Century*, Verso, 1997.

52. Simon Broughton, "Secret History," *New Statesman* (October 15, 2007), p. 43.

53. Nicholas G. Pappas, "Concepts of Greekness: The Recorded Music of Anatolian Greeks after 1922," *Journal of Modern Greek Studies* 17.2 (1999), p. 360. He adds that "Dalgás did record again briefly in 1938 for Gramophone and in 1939 for Odeon, although Metaxas's censorship laws had by then diluted much of the potency of Smyrneïc composition and performance" (p. 370 n. 42).

54. Gail Holst, *Road to Rembetika: Music of a Greek Sub-Culture. Songs of Love, Sorrow and Hashish*, Denise Harvey Publisher, 2006, p. 10; Yiannis Zaimakis, "'Bawdy Songs and Virtuous Politics': Ambivalence and Controversy in the Discourse of the Greek Left on Rebetiko," *History and Anthropology* 20.1 (2009), pp. 15–36; Zaimakis, "'Forbidden Fruits' and the Communist Paradise."

55. Janet Sarbanes, "Musicking and Communitas: The Aesthetic Mode of Sociality in Rebetika Subculture," *Popular Music and Society* 29.1 (2006), pp. 30–1.

56. Holst, *Road to Rembetika*, pp. 11, 22. See also Elias Petropoulos, *Songs of the Greek Underworld: The Rebetika Tradition*, Saqi Books, 2000.

57. Janaki Bakhle, *Two Men and Music: Nationalism and the Making of an Indian Classical Tradition*, Oxford University Press, 2005, p. 3. See also Amanda J. Weidman, *Singing the Classical, Voicing the Modern: The Postcolonial Politics of Music in South India*, Duke University Press, 2006.

58. Bronia Kornhauser, "In Defence of Kroncong," in Margaret Kartomi, ed., *Studies in Indonesian Music*, Center of Southeast Asian Studies, Monash University, 1978, p. 129.

59. Quoted in Rudolf Mrázek, *Engineers of a Happy Land: Technology and Nationalism in a Colony*, Princeton University Press, 2002, p. 196.

60. See *Africa: 50 Years of Music*, Discograph, 2010. John Collins, "Ghana and the World Music Boom," in Tuulikki Pietilä, ed., *World Music: Roots and Routes*, Helsinki Collegium for Advanced Studies, vol. 6, 2009, p. 69; Michael E. Veal, *Fela: The Life and Times of an African Musical Icon*, Temple University Press, 2000; Bob W. White, *Rumba Rules: The Politics of Dance Music in Mobutu's Zaire*, Duke University Press, 2008.

61. Kelly M. Askew, *Performing the Nation: Swahili Music and Cultural Politics in Tanzania*, University of Chicago Press, 2002, p. 263; Laura Fair, *Pastimes and*

Politics: Culture, Community, and Identity in Post Abolition Urban Zanzibar, 1890–1945, Ohio University Press, 2001, pp. 95–6, 297 n. 88; Leila Sheikh-Hashim's "Siti's Magnetic Voice" appeared in the first issue of the women's journal *Sauti ya Siti* in 1988.

62. Henriques, *Performing Nationalism*, p. 1.
63. McCann, *Hello, Hello Brazil*, pp. 65–7.
64. Moore, *Nationalizing Blackness*, pp. 80–4.
65. Erlmann, *African Stars*, p. 96.
66. Quevedo, *Atilla's Kaiso*, p. 63.
67. Sandroni, *Feitiço decente*, p. 19.
68. Vianna, *The Mystery of Samba*, p. 95.
69. Peter Manuel, "Composition, Authorship, and Ownership in Flamenco, Past and Present," *Ethnomusicology* 54.1 (2010), p. 113.
70. On the naming of world music, see Collins, "Ghana and the World Music Boom," in Pietilä, ed., *World Music*, pp. 62–3; and Timothy D. Taylor, *Global Pop: World Music, World Markets*, Routledge, 1997, pp. 1–37.
71. Collins, "Ghana and the World Music Boom," in Pietilä, ed., *World Music*, pp. 62, 64–5.
72. For Marley, see Paul Gilroy, "Could You Be Loved? Bob Marley, Anti-politics and Universal Sufferation," *Critical Quarterly* 47.1–2 (2005), pp. 226–45; and Michelle A. Stephens, "Babylon's 'Natural Mystic': The North American Music Industry, the Legend of Bob Marley, and the Incorporation of Transnationalism," *Cultural Studies* 12.2 (1998), pp. 139–67. For excellent case studies of this process, see Veal, *Fela*, and Meintjes, *Sound of Africa!*.
73. Peter Manuel, "The Saga of a Song: Authorship and Ownership in the Case of 'Guantanamera,'" *Latin American Music Review* 27.2 (2006), pp. 121–47.
74. Rian Malan, *In the Jungle*, Cold Type Modern Classics, 2003, coldtype.net, pp. 1–40.
75. See the essays written by two members of Ghana's National Folklore Board: John Collins, "The 'Folkloric Copyright Tax' Problem in Ghana," *Media Development* 50:1 (2003), pp. 10–14.; John Collins, "Copyright, Folklore and Music Piracy in Ghana," *Critical Arts* 20.1 (2006): 158–70; and A. O. Amegatcher, "Protection of Folklore by Copyright: A Contradiction in Terms," *Copyright Bulletin* 36.2 (2002), pp. 33–42.
76. Collins, "The 'Folkloric Copyright Tax' Problem in Ghana," pp. 10–14.
77. Hazel V. Carby, "It Jus Be's Dat Way Sometime: The Sexual Politics of Women's Blues," *Radical America* 20.4 (1986), pp. 9–24.
78. Morgan James Luker, "Tango Renovación: On the Uses of Music History in Post-Crisis Argentina," *Latin American Music Review* 28:1 (2007), pp. 68–93; Risto Pekka Pennanen, "The Nationalization of Ottoman Popular Music in Greece," *Ethnomusicology* 48.1 (2004), pp. 1–25; Vianna, *The Mystery of Samba*; Sandroni, *Feitiço decente*.
79. Jonathan Stock, "Reconsidering the Past: Zhou Xuan and the Rehabilitation of Early Twentieth Century Popular Music," *Asian Music* 26.2 (1995), p. 123; Szu-Wei Chen, "The Rise and Generic Features of Shanghai Popular Songs in the 1930s and 1940s," *Popular Music* 24.1 (2005): 108; Claudia Cornwall, "The Triumphant Return of the Shanghai Lounge Divas," *The Tyee*, March 25, 2005, thetyee.ca.
80. *The Secret Museum of Mankind: Ethnic Music Classics, 1925–48, Volumes 1–5*, Yazoo CDs 7004, 1995; 7005, 1995; 7006, 1996; 7010, 1997; 7014, 1998.
81. Günter Mayer, "On the Relationship of the Political and Musical Avant-garde

(1989)," in Jost Hermand and Michael Gilbert, eds, *German Essays on Music*, Continuum, 1994, pp. 266, 268.

82. Adorno, "On the Social Situation of Music," in *Essays on Music*, pp. 392, 393.
83. Ernest Bloch, *The Principle of Hope*, MIT Press, 1986, p. 1069.

Appendix: Playlist

This playlist follows the order of the tracks marked with an asterisk in the text. It includes the earliest commercial release (if known) and the most significant CD or web re-release, emphasizing those re-releases with significant historical and discographical notes. Those tracks available through Spotify will be on a "Noise Uprising" playlist at Spotify; as vehicles of online music change, check versobooks.com for further details.

Sexteto Habanero, "Maldita timidez," Victor 78510, 1926, re-released on *Sexteto y Septeto Habanero: Grabaciones Completas 1925–1931*, Tumbao CD 300, 1998.

Louis Armstrong, "Heebie Jeebies," OKeh 8300-A, 1926, re-released on *Louis Armstrong: The Complete Hot Five and Hot Seven Recordings*, Columbia/Legacy C4K 63527, 2000.

Rosita Quiroga, "La Musa Mistonga," Victor 79632, 1926, re-released on *Tango Collection—Rosita Quiroga*, RGS Music 1649.

Umm Kulthūm, "In Kunt Asaamih," His Master's Voice 72-12, 1928, re-released on *Omme Kolsoum: La Diva 3*, EMI CD 0964310957-2, 1997.

Hafiz Sadettin Kaynak, "Nâr-i Hicrane Düşüp," Columbia 12554, ca.1926–7, re-released on *Hafiz Sadettin Kaynak*, Kalan CD 129, 1999.

Hafiz Burhan Bey, "Nitschun Guerdum," Columbia 12289, 1927, re-released on *Great Voices of Constantinople 1927–1933*, Rounder CD 1113, 1997.

Dalgás, "Melemenio," His Master's Voice HMV AO166, 1926, re-released on *Rembetika: Greek Music from the Underground: The Ottoman Legacy 1925–1927*, JSP Records JSP7776A, 2006.

Márkos Vamvakáris, "Karadouzéni," Parlophon B21654, 1932, re-released on *Márkos Vamvakáris Bouzouki Pioneer 1932–1940*, Rounder CD 1139, 1998.

Fritna Darmon, "Aroubi Rasd Eddil, Pt. 1," Pathé 59167, 1926, re-released on *Secret Museum of Mankind: Music of North Africa*, Yazoo 7011, 1997.

Cheikh Hamada, "Adjouadi hadi ouadjba," Gramophone K 4216, 1930, available on Gallica, gallica.bnf.fr.

Adelina Fernandes, "Fado Penim," HMV EQ220, 1928, re-released on *Fado's Archives, Volume Three: Lisbon Women (1928–1931)*, Heritage HT CD 24, 1994.

Hirabai Barodekar, "Sakhi Mori Rumjhum (Durga)," HMV Black Label P-6209, ca. 1926, re-released on Hirabai Barodekar, *Golden Milestones*, Saregama CDNF 150556, 1998.

Mariachi Coculense Rodríguez, "El Toro," Victor 79173, 1927, re-released on *Mexico's Pioneer Mariachis, Vol. 1: Mariachi Coculense De Cirilo Marmolejo, 1926–1936*, Arhoolie Folkloric CD 7011, 1993.

Guty Cárdenas, "Rayito de Sol," Columbia 3118-X, ca. 1928, re-released on Alvaro Vega and Enrique Martin, eds, *Guty Cárdenas: Cancionero*, Instituto de Cultura de Yucatán, 2006.

Miss Riboet, "Dji Hong," Beka B 15107, 1926, re-released on *Longing for the Past: The 78 rpm Era in Southeast Asia*, Dust-to-Digital DTD 28, 2013.

Wilmoth Houdini, "Caroline," Victor 80078, 1927, re-released on *Calypso Pioneers 1912–1937*, Rounder CD 1039, 1989.

The Carter Family, "Single Girl, Married Girl," Victor 20937, 1927, re-released on *The Bristol Sessions 1927–1928: The Big Bang of Country Music*, Bear Family BCD 16094 EK, 2011.

Jimmie Rodgers, "Blue Yodel," Victor 21142, 1928, re-released on *Jimmie Rodgers: The Singing Brakeman*, Bear Family BCD 15 540, 1992.

La Niña de los Peines, "Había preguntado en una ocasión," Regal RS 550, 1927, re-released on *Niña de los Peines: Registros Sonoros*, Fonotrón D.L., 2004, CD 9.

Dào Nha, "Tả cảnh cô đầu thua bạc," Victor 40027, 1928, re-released on *Longing for the Past: The 78 rpm Era in Southeast Asia*, Dust-to-Digital DTD 28, 2013.

Van Thanh Ban, "Không Minh—Mẫu Tâm Tử," Beka 20137, ca. 1929, re-released on *Longing for the Past: The 78 rpm Era in Southeast Asia*, Dust-to-Digital DTD 28, 2013.

Kalama's Quartet, "He Manao Healoha," OKeh 41023, 1928, re-released on *Kalama's Quartet: Early Hawaiian Classics 1927–1932*, Arhoolie Folkloric CD 7028, 1993.

Sol Ho'opi'i, "Sweet Lei Lehua," Columbia 1250-D, 1927, re-released on *Sol Hoopii: Master of the Hawaiian Guitar, Volume 1*, Rounder CD 1024, 1991.

Steva Nikolić, "Arnautka," Victor V-3049 B, 1928, available on Jonathan Ward, *Excavated Shellac*, 2008, excavatedshellac.com.

Sofka Nikolić, "Čuješ Seko," Victor V-3097, ca. late 1920s, available on *Tamburitza and More … Tamburitza and Folk Music from America and Europe*, tamburitza78s.blogspot.com.

Django Reinhardt, "Dinah," Ultraphone P 77161, 1934, re-released on *Django Reinhardt: The Classic Early Recordings in Chronological Order: Volume One*, JSP CD 341, 1992.

Kumasi Trio, "Amponsah, Part One"/"Amponsah, Part Two," Zonophone 1001, 1928, re-released on *Kumasi Trio 1928*, Heritage HT CD 22, 1993.

Harry E. Quashie, "Anadwofa," Zonophone, ca. 1929, re-released on *Living Is Hard: West African Music in Britain, 1927–1929*, Honest Jon's Records HJRCD33, 2008.

Siti binti Saad, "Wewe Paka," Columbia WE 46, ca. 1930, re-released on *Poetry and Languid Charm: Swahili Music from Tanzania and Kenya from the 1920s to the 1950s*, Topic TSCD 936, 2007.

Francisco Alves, "Me Faz Carinhos," Odeon 10100-B, 1928, re-released on Humberto M. Franceschi, *A Casa Edison e Seu Tempo*, Sarapuí, 2002.

Ismael Silva, "Me Diga o Teu Nome," Odeon 10858, 1931, available at O Instituto Moreira Salles, acervo.ims.com.br.

Halpin Trio, "Rogha-An-Fhile," Parlophone E3627, 1929, re-released on *Past Masters of Irish Fiddle Music*, Topic TSCD 605, 2001.

Li Minghui, "Maomao yu," Pathé 34278, 1929, re-released on *EMI Pathé Classics 101, Volume 1*, Universal, 2014.

L'Orchestre Antillais, "Sêpent Maigre," Odeon Ki 2655, 1929, re-released on *Biguine: Biguine, Valse et Mazurka Créoles (1929–1940)*, Frémeaux FA007, 1993.

Abibu Oluwa, "Orin Herbert Macaulay," Parlophon B861351, re-

released on *Àwon Ojísé Olorun: Popular Music in Yorubaland 1931–1952*, Savannaphone CD AF 010, 2006.

Irewolede Denge, "Orin Asape Eko," HMV JZ3, re-released on *Jùjú Roots 1930s–1950s*, Rounder CD5017, 1993.

Urbano A. Zafra, "Danza Filipina," Columbia 3910-X, 1929, available on Jonathan Ward, *Excavated Shellac*, 2007, excavated shellac.com.

Caluza's Double Quartet, "uBangca," Zonophone 4276, 1930, re-released on *Caluza's Double Quartet 1930*, Heritage HT CD 19, 1992.

Griffiths Motsieloa, "Aubuti Nkikho," Singer GE 1, 1930, re-released on CD accompanying Christopher Ballantine, *Marabi Nights: Jazz, "Race" and Society in Early Apartheid South Africa*, University of KwaZulu-Natal Press, 2012.

Amanzimtoti Players, "Sbhinono," HMV GU 130, 1932, re-released on CD accompanying Ballantine.

Sara Martin, "Yes Sir, That's My Baby," OKeh 8262, 1925, re-released on *Sara Martin in Chronological Order: Volume 4 (1925–1928)*, Document DOCD 5398, 1996.

Papa Charlie Jackson, "Shake That Thing," Paramount 12281, 1925, re-released on *Papa Charlie Jackson: Complete Recorded Works in Chronological Order, Volume 1*, Document DOCD 5087, 1991.

Freetown's Leading Sextet, "Stay, Carolina, Stay," re-released on *Sierra Leone Music: West African Gramophone Records Recorded at Freetown in the 50s and Early 60s*, Zensor ZS 41, 1988, available on African Music on 78RPM, african78s.wordpress.com.

Les Loups, "La Cumparsita," Victor 80936, 1928, re-released on *Oscar Aleman: Buenos Aires–Paris 1928–1943*, Frémeaux FA 020, 1994.

Rita Montaner, "El Manisero," Columbia 2965x, 1928, re-released on *Rita Montaner: Rita de Cuba*, Tumbao TCD 46, 1994.

Trio Matamoros, "El Manicero," Victor 46401, 1929, re-released on *The Legendary Trio Matamoros*, Tumbao TCD 16, 1992.

Havana Casino Orchestra, "The Peanut Vendor," Victor 224830, 1930, re-released on *Antonio Machin—El Manisero: Early Recordings 1929–1930*, Tumbao TCD 26, 1993.

Kumasi Trio, "Asin Asin Part Two," Zonophone EZ, re-released on *Living Is Hard: West African Music in Britain, 1927–1929*, Honest Jon's Records HJRCD33, 2008.

Blind Willie Johnson, "It's Nobody's Fault But Mine," Columbia

14303-D, 1928, re-released on *The Complete Blind Willie Johnson*, Columbia C2K 52835, 1992.

Rabbit Brown, "Sinking of the Titanic," Victor 35840, 1927, re-released on *Never Let the Same Bee Sting You Twice: Blues, Ballads, Rags and Gospel in the Songster Tradition*, Document DOCD 5678, 2005.

K. B. Sundarambal, "Gandhi London," Columbia, 1931, re-released on Archive of Indian Music, archiveofindianmusic.org.

Tunde King and His Group, "Aronke Macaulay," Parlophone PO.508, 1936, re-released on *Musique Populaire Africaine: Archives 1926–1952*, Buda, 2008.

Caluza's Double Quartet, "Vul'indhlela mnta ka Dube," Zonophone 4280, 1930, re-released on *Caluza's Double Quartet 1930*.

Atilla the Hun, "The Commission's Report," Decca De 17350, 1938, re-released on *The Classic Calypso Collective, West Indian Rhythm: Trinidad Calypso on World and Local Events, Featuring the Censored Recordings 1938–1940*, Bear Family Records BCD 16623JM, 2006.

Atilla the Hun, "The Strike," Decca De 17371, 1938, re-released on *West Indian Rhythm*.

Sexteto Nacional, "Incitadora Región," Brunswick 41092, 1930, re-released on *Sextetos Cubanos: Sones 1930*, Arhoolie Folkloric CD 7003, 1992.

Umm Kulthūm, "Ljmay Ya Misr!," Odeon FA 224 639, 1936, re-released on *Oum Kalthoum, El Sett (La Dame/The Lady)*, Buda Musique 82244-2, 2002.

Griffiths Motsieloa, "Nkosi Sikelel'iAfrika," Singer GE13, re-released on *Opika Pende: Africa at 78 RPM*, Dust-to-Digital, DTD 22, 2011.

Caluza's Double Quartet, "Umteto we Land Act," Zonophone 4298, re-released on *Caluza's Double Quartet 1930*.

Waikiki Hawaiian Trio, "The Four Islands," Sunset 1053, 1925, re-released on *Sol Hoopii in Hollywood: His First Recordings 1925*, Grass Skirt Records GSK 1002, 2007.

Kalama's Quartet, "Na Moku Eha," OKeh 41048, 1928, re-released on *Kalama's Quartet: Early Hawaiian Classics 1927–1932*, Arhoolie Folkloric CD 7028, 1993.

William Ewaliko, "Na Moku Eha," Columbia 1510-D, 1928, re-released on *Nā Leo Hawai'i Kahiko: The Master Chanters of Hawai'i/Songs of Old Hawai'i*, Mountain Apple MACD 2043, 1997.

Caluza's Double Quartet, "Ixegwana Ricksha Song," Zonophone 4280, 1930, re-released on *Caluza's Double Quartet 1930*, Heritage HT CD 19, 1992.

Carlos Gardel, "Organito de la Tarde," Disco Nacional 18128A, 1925, re-released on *The Magic of Carlos Gardel*, Harlequin HQ CD 145, 1999.

Zhou Xuan, "Tianya Genü," 1937, re-released on *Shanghai Lounge Divas: The Original Recordings*, EMI 7243 4 73052 21, 2004.

Bessie Smith, "Mean Old Bed Bug Blues," Columbia 14250-D, 1928, re-released on *Bessie Smith: The Complete Columbia Recordings*, Sony Legacy, 2012.

Trio Matamoros, "Mamá, Son de la Loma," Victor V81378, 1928, re-released on *Trio Matamoros: "La China en la Rumba,"* Tumbao TCD 39, 1994.

Caluza's Double Quartet, "Ingoduso," Zonophone 4276, 1930, re-released on *Caluza's Double Quartet 1930*, Heritage HT CD 19, 1992.

George Williams Aingo, "Akuko Nu Bonto," Zonophone, ca. 1928, re-released on *Living Is Hard: West African Music in Britain, 1927–1929*, Honest Jons Records HJRCD 33, 2008.

Carmen Miranda and Dorival Caymmi, "A Preta do Aracajé," Odeon 11710, 1939, re-released on *Bresil: Choro, Samba, Frevo, 1914–1945*, Frémeaux FA 77, 1998.

George Williams Aingo, "Tarkwa Na Abosu," Zonophone EZ 4, 1927, re-released on *Global Accordion: Early Recordings*, Wergo SM 1623 2, 2001.

Sol Ho'opi'i, "Hano Hano Hawai'i," Columbia 1370-D, 1928, re-released on *Sol Hoopii: Master of the Hawaiian Guitar, Volume Two*, Rounder CD 1025, 1991.

Ramón Montoya, "Flor de Petenera," Gramófono AE 4148, 1933, re-released on *Ramón Montoya: El Genio de la Guitarra Flamenca–Grabaciones Históricas 1923–1936*, Sonifolk 20130, 1999.

Kalama's Quartet, "Heeia (Ancient Hula)," OKeh 41414, 1930, re-released on *Nā Leo Hawai'i Kahiko: The Master Chanters of Hawai'i/Songs of Old Hawai'i*, Mountain Apple MACD 2043, 1997.

Louis Armstrong, "Potato Head Blues," OKeh 8503, 1927, re-released on *Louis Armstrong: The Complete Hot Five and Hot Seven Recordings*, Columbia/Legacy C4K 63527, 2000.

Septeto Habanero, "Coralia," Victor 81751, 1928, re-released on

Sexteto y Septeto Habanero: Grabaciones Completas, 1925–1931,
Tumbao CD 300, 1998.

Orquestra Tipica Pixinguinha-Donga, "Carinhoso," Parlophon 12.
877-B, 1928, re-released on *O Jovem Pixinguinha: Gravações de
1919 a 1920,* EMI 5936362, 2007.

Sol Ho'opi'i, "Hilo March," Sunset 1086, 1925, re-released on *Sol
Hoopii in Hollywood: His First Recordings 1925,* Grass Skirt
Records GSK 1002, 2007.

Kalama's Quartet, "Hilo March," OKeh 41082, 1928, re-released on
Kalama's Quartet, *Early Hawaiian Classics,* Arhoolie Folkloric
CD 7028, 1993.

Johnny Noble's Hawaiians featuring M. K. Moke, "Hilo March,"
Brunswick 55011, 1928, re-released on *History of Hawaiian Steel
Guitar,* Hana Ola Records HOCD 34000, 1999.

Ramón Montoya, "Soleares en Mi," Gramófono AE2153, 1928, re-
released on *Ramón Montoya, El genio de la guitarra flamenca:
Grabaciones Históricas 1923–1936,* Sonifolk 20130, 1999.

Niño Ricardo, "Alegrías," Regal RS-732, 1928, re-released on *1°
Centenario del nacimiento de Niño Ricardo,* Fonotrón, 2004.

Index